Reflexive Labour Law in the World Society

Reflexive Labour Law in the World Society

Ralf Rogowski

Professor of Law, University of Warwick, UK

Cheltenham, UK • Northampton, MA, USA

Published by
Edward Elgar Publishing Limited
The Lypiatts
15 Lansdown Road
Cheltenham
Glos GL50 2JA
UK

Edward Elgar Publishing, Inc.
William Pratt House
9 Dewey Court
Northampton
Massachusetts 01060
USA

Paperback edition 2015

A catalogue record for this book
is available from the British Library

Library of Congress Control Number: 2013942207

This book is available electronically in the **Elgar**online
Law Subject Collection
DOI 10.4337/9780857936592

ISBN 978 0 85793 658 5 (cased)
ISBN 978 1 78536 543 0 (paperback)

Typeset by Servis Filmsetting Ltd, Stockport, Cheshire
Printed and bound in Great Britain by the CPI Group (UK Ltd)

Contents

Preface

Labour law is under attack. The powerful critique of conservative neo-liberal labour economics claims that it is both possible and desirable to abolish labour law and return to a market order exclusively regulated by private law norms. Labour law is viewed as interference with the market mechanism and produces, according to Friedrich August von Hayek, 'injustice in the form of new privileges, obstacles to mobility and frustration of efforts' (Hayek 1976, pp. 139–40).

Astonishingly labour law is under a similar attack from left libertarian positions. Their critique alleges that labour and employment laws privilege employees and employers in standard employment relationships and contends that large parts of the working population are excluded from being protected. The alleged 'dualism' of the employment relationship is viewed as outmoded in the world of 'work after globalization': 'Labour law must be phased out, not further refined; it should become part of common law, covered by contract and tort law' (Standing 2009, pp. 268–9). It is ironic, if not paradoxical, however, that this position demands at the same time a new regime of 'work rights' for all social activity. For such a new system of rights to be effective, in particular when protecting those workers that constitute a new 'precariat' (Standing 2011, pp. 160–64), a reformed labour law seems essential.

This book claims to offer an alternative to abolitionist theories by advocating a reform of labour law that pays particular attention to the global context. The book will try to show that the political reforms of labour law based on neoliberal economic beliefs led in effect to contradictory results. It will be argued that the proper way ahead in reforming labour law is making it reflexive. In a reflexive labour law perspective neoliberal deregulation has to be understood not only as a particular form of regulation but as necessarily accompanied by new regulation or re-regulation.

Reflexive labour law claims to be a new type of labour law that understands the limits and exclusionary effects of traditional labour law while at the same time facilitating strategies of re-regulation that overcome these problems through reflexive second-order or meta-governance of the field. Reflexive labour law can be understood as part of the tradition that views labour and employment law as public regulation (Deakin and Wilkinson

2005; Collins 2010). However, it adds to these debates a thorough rethinking of labour law as a regulatory regime within the legal system of the world society.

The book is divided into three parts. Part I contains three chapters outlining the theoretical approach. Chapter 1 discusses the global context of modern labour law with the help of Niklas Luhmann's concept of the world society (Chapter 1). This is followed in Chapter 2 by an overview of main features of reflexive labour law. Chapter 3 provides a theoretical account of industrial relations from a social systems theory perspective.

Part II contains four chapters that apply the reflexive labour law approach in analysing current trends in modern labour law. Readers who are interested in substantive analyses from a reflexive law perspective are advised to go directly to these chapters. The chapters include assessments from a reflexive labour law perspective of employment protection (Chapter 4), regulation and deregulation of labour market policies and labour law (Chapters 5 and 6) and labour and employment conflict resolution (Chapter 7).

Part III consists of three chapters on European and international labour law. These include discussions of reflexive coordination of European social and employment policies (Chapter 8) and reflexive implementation of European employment law – a case study of the EU's Working Time Directive (Chapter 9). The final chapter is devoted to an analysis of reflexive trends in global labour law (Chapter 10).

A number of chapters are based on earlier publications, although in each case they have been substantially revised. Copyright permissions are hereby acknowledged. Chapter 2 is in parts based on my chapter 'The Concept of Reflexive Labour Law – Its Theoretical Background and Possible Applications', published in David Nelken and Jiri Priban (eds), *Law's New Boundaries – The Consequences of Legal Autopoiesis*. Aldershot: Ashgate 2001, pp. 179–96. Chapter 3 is a revised version of my article 'Industrial Relations as a Social System', published in *Industrielle Beziehungen*, The German Journal of Industrial Relations, Vol. 7 (1), 2000, pp. 97–126. Chapter 5 is in parts based on the chapter (jointly written with Ton Wilthagen) entitled 'The Legal Regulation of Transitional Labour Markets' that was published in Günther Schmid and Bernard Gazier (eds), *The Dynamics of Full Employment. Social Integration through Transitional Labour Markets*. Cheltenham, UK and Brookfield, USA: Edward Elgar 2002, pp. 233–73. Chapter 6 is in parts based on a translation of a German publication (jointly written with Günther Schmid), 'Reflexive Deregulierung – Ein Ansatz zur Dynamisierung des Arbeitsmarktes', published in Berndt Keller and Hartmut Seifert (eds), *Deregulierung am Arbeitsmarkt*. Hamburg: VSA 1998, pp. 215–53.

Chapter 7 is a revised version of my chapter 'Reflexive Regulation of Labour and Employment Conflict Resolution', published in Gralf-Peter Calliess, Andreas Fischer-Lescano, Dan Wielsch and Peer Zumbansen (eds), *Soziologische Jurisprudenz. Festschrift für Gunther Teubner*. Berlin: De Gruyter Recht 2009, pp. 573–86. And finally, Chapter 8 is in parts based on the book chapter 'Flexicurity and Reflexive Coordination of European Social and Employment Policies', published in Henning Jørgensen and Per K. Madsen (eds), *Flexicurity and Beyond. Finding a new agenda for the European Social Model*. Copenhagen: DJØF Publishing 2007, pp. 131–53.

Figure and tables

FIGURE

TABLES

Abbreviations

ACAS	Advisory, Conciliation and Arbitration Service
ACP	African, Caribbean and Pacific countries
AFL	American Federation of Labor
BAG	Bundesarbeitsgericht
BIAC	Business and Industry Advisory Committee of the OECD
CAS	Court of Arbitration for Sports
CEEP	European Centre of Employers and Enterprises providing Public services
CSR	Corporate Social Responsibility
DWP	Decent Work Programme
ECJ	European Court of Justice
EEA	European Economic Area
EEC	European Economic Community
EEOC	Equal Employment Opportunities Commission
EES	European Employment Strategy
EPL	Employment Protection Legislation
EMU	European Economic and Monetary Union
EPZ	Export Processing Zones
ESM	European Social Model
ETUC	European Trade Union Congress
EU	European Union
GATT	General Agreement on Tariffs and Trade
GSP	Generalised System of Preferences
ICANN	Internet Corporation for Assigned Names and Numbers
IFAs	International Framework Agreements
ILO	International Labour Organization
IMF	International Monetary Fund
ISO	International Organization of Standardization
MNEs	Multinational Enterprises
NAALC	North American Agreement on Labor Co-operation
NAPs	National Action Plans
NCP	National Contact Points
NGOs	Non-governmental Organisations
NLRA	National Labor Relations Act

NLRB	National Labor Relations Board
OMC	Open Method of Coordination
OECD	Organisation of Economic Cooperation and Development
OSHA	Occupational Safety and Health Administration
PIGs	Private Interest Groups
SEA	Single European Act
SER	Standard Employment Relationship
TFEU	Treaty on the Functioning of the EU
TLM	Transitional Labour Markets
TUAC	Trade Union Advisory Council
UEAPME	Union Européenne de l'Artisanat et des Petites et Moyennes Entreprises
UN	United Nations
WTD	Working Time Directive
WTO	World Trade Organisation
WTR	Working Time Regulations

Table of cases

PART I

Theory

1. The world society context: the globalisation of labour law

An assessment of modern labour law that does not take the impact of global processes seriously can nowadays no longer claim to have an adequate understanding of the field. The thesis developed in this chapter will be that the sociological theory of the world society espoused by Niklas Luhmann and the accompanying theory of global law, of which Gunther Teubner is a leading protagonist, provide useful concepts for the interpretation of developments in modern labour law.

The chapter consists of five sections. The first section provides a brief overview of the development of Luhmann's thinking about law and politics as social systems, followed in the second section by an outline of his theory of world society. The third section contains observations on specific problems of law and politics in the world society. The fourth section is devoted to an introduction of Luhmann's concept of world law and Gunther Teubner's ideas on global law, and finally, building on Luhmann's and Teubner's concepts, the fifth section gives a first assessment of globalisation of labour law.

1.1 THE THEORETICAL BACKGROUND: NIKLAS LUHMANN'S THEORY OF LAW AND POLITICS AS SOCIAL SYSTEMS

Modern society is, according to Niklas Luhmann, a system of communication. It is characterised by a specific mode of integration called functional differentiation which implies that modern society is no longer hierarchically ordered but differentiated into a number of function systems. Functional differentiation has replaced segmentation and stratification as the dominant modes of integration and as a consequence modern society has become plural in nature. It has no centre that controls its development as a whole or is capable of directing its function systems. Each function system in modern society follows its own trajectory.

Law and politics are two main societal function systems and they have been prominent in Luhmann's sociological approach. Since the beginning of developing his theory of modern society in the 1960s, Luhmann conceived law and politics as social systems that fulfil specific functions in modern society and engage in performances for each other and other function systems. However, Luhmann analysed different aspects of law and politics in his early work, his writings of the middle period and his late work.[1]

The majority of Luhmann's early writings of the 1960s and 1970s dealt with aspects of law and administration and borrowed from his work experiences as a trained jurist and civil servant. Probably the most ambitious theoretical account of law in this period was put forward in his *Rechtssoziologie* (Sociology of Law) (Luhmann 1972).[2] The traditional behaviourist approach of sociolegal studies was replaced in this work with a surprising new starting point in studying law in society. This new view took a fresh look at how law emerges in society by claiming that stabilisation of expectations in society is the main function of law. The autonomy of the function system of law is viewed as the result of a cunning combination of cognitive and normative attitudes in dealing with disappointments of expectations. This approach represents a brilliant attempt in analysing the emergence and development of law and the creation of a legal system by using concepts borrowed from cybernetics and evolution theory.

In accordance with modern legal theory and classical sociology of law, in particular Max Weber, Emile Durkheim and Eugen Ehrlich, the main focus is on explaining conditions that make positive law possible. However, Luhmann switches the focus from themes central in debates on legal positivism, i.e. validity or legitimation of law in society, to an analysis of norms, institutions and legal doctrine as mechanisms that enable law to control its own development by upholding normative expectations. The crucial aspect in Luhmann's sociological account of positive law is that law now has the means to change itself. Furthermore, modern law is capable of dealing with and adopting cognitive expectations. Normative structures can no longer claim to have eternal value. Modern legal norms are adaptable and can always be changed, although not on the spot and only through the use of procedures. The fundamental character of modern positive law is that it is contingent and open towards the future.

Luhmann refined his system theory approach in the second phase which was marked by the adoption of the theory of autopoiesis in conceptualising

---

[1]   Distinguishing stages in Luhmann's analyses of law and politics does not imply that the different concepts of law and politics that are dominant in each period contradict each other. In fact, they complement each other.

[2]   The English title of this book, *A Sociological Theory of Law* (Luhmann 1985a), captures its content more accurately.

social systems (Luhmann 1995a; first published in German in 1984). This phase culminated, insofar as law is concerned, in the publication of *Recht der Gesellschaft* (Luhmann 1993, translated into English as *Law as a Social System* in 2005) and in relation to politics in the posthumous *Politik der Gesellschaft* (Luhmann 2000a). Law and politics are no longer conceived as just autonomous but as autopoietic in nature. Law and politics are systems of communication that are operationally closed and reproduce themselves. Specific political and legal communications, and not political or legal actions or institutions, enable these function systems to engage in sophisticated processes of self-reproduction.

By adopting the concept of autopoiesis, Luhmann radicalised the notion of autonomy of social systems. Systems are not only capable of reproducing themselves, but any perception of society and the world at large becomes system-specific and happens inside a social system. This radical internalisation in sociological thinking and the almost exclusive focus on self-reference of systems led to the critique of Jürgen Habermas that Luhmann endows social system with attributes characteristic of the subject in the tradition of idealist philosophy (Habermas 1987, pp. 368–85).

The last phase in Luhmann's work was devoted to an elaboration of the fundamental characteristics of modern society. The book *Gesellschaft der Gesellschaft* (Luhmann 1997a), written a year before Luhmann's death, is in many respects the *opus magnum* of this phase. Law and politics are consistently analysed from the perspective of a functionally differentiated world society. In his last phase Luhmann became particularly interested in the emergence of global structures and the problems that function systems create for each other in the world society. The economy, science and technology are viewed as fully globalised due to their cognitive orientations. Other function systems such as law and politics, although also globalising, lag behind because they still operate to a large degree with territorial boundaries (see Stichweh 1995, 2000a, 2000b, and on world law see in particular Lieckweg 2003, and also Rogowski 2000b and Schulte and Stichweh 2009).

1.2 THEORY OF THE WORLD SOCIETY

The concept of the world society that dominates Luhmann's late work was already conceptually developed in his early work. In the article *Die Weltgesellschaft*, published in 1971 (Luhmann 1975 [1971]), the emergence of the world society is described as a necessary consequence of functional differentiation. Function systems that have a high degree of autonomy 'detonate' societal boundaries. Most advanced in this respect are the economy, technology and science. In particular science is said to have adopted universal intersubjectivity as its own structuring principle and criterion of performance. In contrast law and politics remain backward in this respect by clinging on to territorial boundaries.

In his 1982 article 'The World Society as a Social System' (Luhmann 1990a [1982]) Luhmann outlines how the main features of his theory of society can be used for a study of society at the world level. The concept of the world society 'provides one world for one system; and it integrates all world horizons as horizons of one communicative system' (Luhmann 1990a [1982], p. 178). Luhmann adopts the radical solution of not distinguishing between the society and world society. On a number of occasions he stated in this period of his writings that 'there exists today only one society on earth: the world society' (Luhmann 1976, p. 526) and that it therefore does not make sense to talk about national societies in the plural.

What is remarkable is the overlap of the main sections of the World Society article with the chapters of his final book on the theory of society, *Gesellschaft der Gesellschaft*, published 15 years later in 1997 (English translation of Vol. 1 in Luhmann 2012). In the 1982 article we already find a brief general outline of how system theoretical features can be used to conceptualise world society, including remarks on evolution, differentiation and self-description of society. This theoretical design reveals resilience in Luhmann's unique approach in developing a sociology of modern society, including the world society. Luhmann is realistic in that system theory is unlikely to contribute much in solving society's problems but, as he states at the end of the World Society article, it promises at least 'arriving at a higher level of intelligibility' (Luhmann 1990a [1982], p. 187).

An important reason for the globalisation of function systems rests in the fact that at the operational level they consist of self-reproducing communications. Since it is difficult to prevent communications from flowing across territorial boundaries, it makes it almost impossible to isolate function systems from world processes. All function systems are exposed to the pressure of globalisation that results from worldwide communications.

Luhmann's theory of the world society is neither a new theory of international relations nor a new version of globalisation theory. It is a theory about the structures of society at world level that possess genuine properties. It thus does not predict a diminishing of territorial borders; it only emphasises the increasing necessity to redefine national borders as a result of the evolving world society (see Stichweh 1995, 2000a, 2000b, 2005). There are remarkable differences between Luhmann and Parsons in defining world society. The 'international system' was genuinely political for Parsons and nation states and territorial boundaries mattered. For

Luhmann world society consists of only one global system in which at least conceptually countries do not matter (Stichweh 2005).

In his posthumously published political sociology Luhmann analysed the paradoxical impact of globalisation on national political and legal systems. National law and politics are at the same time weakened and strengthened. The conditions of the new political order require that a minimum degree of statehood is guaranteed. States become recognised as full members by the international community if they fulfil international legal criteria of statehood (Albert 2005). It is this external recognition that constitutes the core of sovereignty of states in the world society.

> Regions cannot participate in politics without adopting the form of a 'sovereign' state (and there are no regions that can avoid this). That this does no longer guarantee stability becomes increasingly the main problem in the new international order (as it is called optimistically). However, a state must be more than simply an address for international communications. Political effectiveness and internal authority are indispensable conditions. It cannot be excluded that the system of world politics will increasingly be driven to act as guarantor of statehood without intermingling in regional politics. However, suitable forms of intervention that match this task do not yet exist and will have to be developed (Luhmann 2000a, pp. 225–6, translation R.R.).

In his article 'Globalization or World Society: How to Conceive of Modern Society?' (Luhmann 1997b), Luhmann went a step further. The world society does not only impose new conditions on politics and law but is itself the cause for manifold regional, economic, cultural, climatic and ecological differences. In the case of the global political system he demonstrated that the global demand for a functioning 'political state' can lead to new nationalisms and even more importantly that the lack of recognition, assistance and powers of intervention at the global level can constitute 'global neglect', which stimulates negative reactions at national level.

> . . . a sociological theory that wants to explain these differences, should not introduce them as givens, that is, as independent variables; it should rather start with the assumption of a world society and then investigate, how and why this society tends to maintain or even increase regional inequalities. It is not very helpful to say that the Serbs are Serbs and, therefore, they make war. The relevant question is rather, whether or not the form of the political state forced upon all regions on earth fits to all local and ethnic conditions, or, whether or not the general condition, not of exploitation or suppression but of global neglect stimulates the search for personal and social, ethnic or religious identities (Luhmann 1997b, p. 73).

Luhmann criticises standard sociological accounts of globalisation and contemporary moral and philosophical theories of distributive justice of misunderstanding the real reasons for the new miseries at the world level. The real reasons are related in Luhmann's account to the fundamental shift from stratification to functional differentiation in modern society and concepts such as 'exploitation' and 'suppression', prominent in international relations theory, overlook for him the fact that the world society has no hierarchical order.

> If we look at the huge masses of starving people, deprived of all necessities for a decent human life, without access to any of the function systems, or if we consider all the human bodies, struggling to survive the next day, neither 'exploitation' nor 'suppression' – terms that refer again to stratification – are adequate descriptions. It is only by habit and by ideological distortion that we use these terms. But there is nothing to exploit in the *favelas*; nor are there, at the higher levels of society, actors or dominant groups that use their power to suppress these people. (There are of course individuals, families or groups which, like everyone else, use their networks to their own advantage.) 'Exploitation' and 'suppression' are outdated mythologies, negative utopias suggesting an easy way out of this situation, e.g. by 'revolution'. The predominant relation is no longer a hierarchical one, but one of inclusion and exclusion; and this relates not to stratification but to functional differentiation (Luhmann 1997b, p. 70).

The problem of exclusion is likely to reach dangerous proportions in the world society according to Luhmann. In fact he went so far as to predict that inclusion and exclusion will become the new metacode in the world society. In describing the consequences of exclusion he paints a real dystopia that comes close to the analysis of bare life in Giorgio Agamben's *Homo Sacer* (Agamben 1998):

> The worst imaginable scenario might be that the society of the next century will have to accept the metacode of inclusion/exclusion. And this would mean that some human beings will be persons and others only individuals; that some are included into function systems for (successful or unsuccessful) careers and others are excluded from these systems, remaining bodies that try to survive the next day; that some are emancipated as persons and others are emancipated as bodies; that concern and neglect become differentiated along this boundary; that tight coupling of exclusions and loose couplings of inclusions differentiate fate and fortune: and that two forms of integration will compete: the negative integration of exclusions and the positive integration of inclusions (Luhmann 1997b, p. 76).

Luhmann's world society concept overcomes many of the weaknesses of international relations theory. In the major strands of international relations theory, be it realist, liberal or constructivist approaches (Armstrong et al. 2012), the process of internationalisation is usually simply conceptualised as a gradual process of expanding international trade, of intensified interdependence of nation states or an increase in functions and powers of intergovernmental organisations. Such a view of internationalisation is criticised by the world society concept for insufficiently assessing the fundamental transformations that are happening in the process of internationalisation.

In sociological and political discussions an alternative paradigm that tries to grasp the new quality of these processes has emerged which is commonly referred to as the concept of globalisation. Theories of globalisation can be divided into approaches which reserve the concept of society to the nation state and those which opt for an encompassing concept of a world society (see also Anderson 2005). The first type is still the most common approach. In his account of the global system Leslie Sklair, for example, focuses on practices of transnational corporations (Sklair 1995, 2002). Anthony Giddens prefers a low-key approach to globalisation by simply mapping institutional dimensions centred on notions of increased time and space distanciation and of disembedding of social relations from local contexts (Giddens 1990, pp. 63–78). Malcolm Waters emphasises symbolic cultural exchanges, liberated from spatial referents, as key factors of globalisation (Waters 2000). Roland Robertson promotes the idea of the global field with culture as the core instance and institutionalisation of local particularisms as core processes of globalisation (Robertson 1992). And finally Martin Albrow puts forward a grandiose phenomenological account of fundamental historical transformations which give birth to a new epoch of mankind, called the global age (Albrow 1996). He criticises postmodern analyses, in particular the thesis of the end of meta-narratives (Lyotard 1984 [1979]) as end-of-epoch accounts which Albrow replaces with his beginning-of-epoch idea of the global age.

These accounts of globalisation processes are quite perceptive in describing the many forms in which the globe serves as focus for human activities (see the overview in Scholte 2005). However, they are unable to understand how the heterogeneous processes are used by the social system at world level in creating its own structure. Theories which study the global social system as such argue that non-synchronical levels of development should be understood as structural effects of the world social system. Three main approaches can be distinguished in this respect: John W. Meyers' concept of the world society, Immanuel Wallerstein's world-systems theory and Niklas Luhmann's theory of the world society.

John W. Meyers' approach constitutes an ambitious attempt of a phenomenology of the world society based on rigid empirical studies of major function systems operating at the global level. His optimistic idea of a world society is particularly interested in alternative trajectories of 'world histories' and 'world futures'. Meyer's actor-centred institutionalist approach is overtly normative. His optimism rests on a belief in the transformative capacity of institutions and professions in creating the world society as a 'culturally imagined community' (Meyers 2010, p. 58).

The world-systems analysis of Immanuel Wallerstein is essentially an analysis of the history of capitalism. It assumes a 'single social system' at world level which consists of 'boundaries, structures, member groups, rules of legitimation and coherence' (Wallerstein 1974–1984, Vol. I, p. 347). These structures are analysed historically and statistically. There exist varieties of world-systems which include world-empires (political systems) and world-economies. Wallerstein analyses political blocks at the world level (the triadic scenario: US, Japan and Europe) and assumes that the world economy is following historical cycles (*à la* Kondratieff).

Aspects of labour and industrial relations are discussed under the rubric of 'world welfare' in Wallerstein's system. The world labour force is hierarchically structured. This structure is a prerequisite for the uneven distribution of wealth in the world-system. Labour is discussed as migrant labour, part-time female labour, wage impact on households, and rural labour (Tabak 1996; see also Shannon 1989, ch. 6 and 7). However, a reductionist economic bias hinders Wallerstein and his followers from adequately grasping the heterogeneous nature of global processes, including the independent and dynamic nature of law and industrial relations. The economic bias prevents this theory ultimately from becoming sociological and analysing the world system as world society. In defining society, Wallerstein adheres to an old-fashioned semantic concept of society as the entangled opposite of the state (see Wallerstein 1991, pp. 244–8).

There are few concepts that conceptualise the world society as a complex, encompassing system. An early concept was John Burton's *World Society* (Burton 1972). He proposed to study networks of social relations at the global level in which global 'systems' and 'states' interact. Since his intervention there has been a lively debate among international relations scholars, mainly refuting Burton's ideas as either too abstract or not going far enough. The dispute seems to have settled on a debate over an international versus a world society (Buzan 2004; on new systems theories of world society and world politics see Albert et al. 2010), whereby the concept of international society is clearly favoured by international relations scholars who feel more comfortable viewing the society at the global level as composed of and created by states (see Brown 2004 and the discussion in Bellamy 2004). Defenders of the world society concept among international relations theorists tend to emphasise the need to understand normative integration at the global level. They see the function of the world society concept in analysing the normative principles on which the international society rests (Clark 2007). Sociologists emphasise instead the inadequacy of applying the notion of national to the concept of society (Shaw 1994).

Luhmann's notion of the world society aims at a sociological analysis of modern society and is not intended to make a contribution to international relations theory. At best his theory can be used to observe this discipline (Albert and Hilkermeier 2004). However, in many respects his concept overcomes the weaknesses of world-systems theory and international relations theories by assuming functional differentiation of social systems at the world level. Luhmann's theory is an inclusive concept of world society which explains developments of the world society as a result of its internal operations (Stichweh 1995, p. 34).

Among Luhmann scholars, his theory of the world society has led to a lively discussion (see for example Albert et al. 2010). Helmuth Willke argues that it is still too early to speak of a world society. He only sees a few function systems that display true tendencies of globalisation. Globalisation has so far not led to a world society that is able to steer itself. He suggests that the global order should be called, somewhat artificially, a lateral world system (Willke 2001, in particular pp. 131–44). Willke's analysis focuses on the legal and political aspects of governance of the world society. This, however, is problematic because his analysis is ultimately based on the model of a society constituted by a nation state in which law and politics dominate the evolution of society as a whole.

Rudolf Stichweh emphasises that Luhmann himself has not carried out his programme of analysing all function systems consistently from the perspective of the world society, including law and politics (Stichweh 2002, p. 289). This is also true of his final work on the theory of society, *Gesellschaft der Gesellschaft* (Luhmann 1997a, 2012). However, from the fact that Luhmann himself did not analyse extensively international organisations, respectively, globally active non-governmental organisations or global legal processes beyond traditional international law it cannot be concluded that he rejected the notions of world politics or world law. In fact, he has emphasised on numerous occasions that the world society possesses emergent properties and that this is true for world law and world politics as well.

Luhmann's theory of society is superior to most debates on globalisation because it not only avoids conceptual ambiguities but overcomes the helpless attitude when it comes to define the context in which globalisation happens. Methodologically it is a 'purely analytical' concept that rejects the notion of globalisation as a mere processualist narrative. In particular it refutes ethical claims and challenges views that associate world society with a global village or global polis (Schütz 1997).

Luhmann's concept of the world society transcends in a crucial aspect existing theories of globalisation. It ascribes to the world society emergent properties and demands from sociology to contextualise globalisation. It might be useful to distinguish conceptually between internationalisation, globalisation and world society. Internationalisation can be defined as intensification of relations between nations, respectively states in the form of strengthening of existing as well as the creation of new international organisations and entering new agreements. Globalisation tries to describe the new quality and dynamic that comes with the change in temporal and spatial distances as a result of new communication technologies. The concept of the world society, finally, describes the context in which these globalisation processes occur.

1.3   LAW AND POLITICS IN THE WORLD SOCIETY

If the analysis of the world society is orientated consistently at worldwide processes of communication, there should be no doubt that structures of world law and world politics emerge. Luhmann's theory of politics is able to 'grasp the world in its radical contingency' (Christodoulidis 1998, p. 281). Furthermore, what Luhmann emphasises is that each function system shows high degrees of complexity that require not only sophisticated ways of reducing these complexities but that function systems create problems for each other due to the lack of any proper coordination at the global level.

> ... there is no longer a quasi cosmological guarantee that structural developments within function systems remain compatible with each other. Science does not add knowledge to power but uncertainty and risk to decisions. Physics made it possible to produce the atomic bomb, the economy finds it profitable to use high risk technologies – both with enormous impacts on the political system. The free press changes politics into a turmoil of scandals and enforces and reveals hypocrisy as the typical style of political talk, and this leads to a widespread critique of the 'political class' and to a decline of political trust. The highly efficient modern medicine has demographic consequences. The new centrality of international financial markets, the corresponding marginalization of production, labour and trade, and the transfer of economic security from real assets and first rate debtors to speculation itself, leads to a loss of jobs and seduces politicians to 'promise' jobs (without markets?). The welfare state produces completely new problems for the legal supervision of politics and leads to deformations of legal doctrine that undermine the predictability of legal decisions. On the other hand, the corresponding judicial 'legislation' of constitutional courts affects politics in a way that can hardly be called 'democratic' (the degree of centralization of the emerging European Union will not be decided by the governments in London, Paris or Berlin but by the European Court in Luxembourg) (Luhmann 1997b, p. 76).

Luhmann outlines here the particular challenges that the legal system faces in the world society. Its performances for other social systems change, in the first place due to the changing role of the political system that is no longer organised by a state at the global level. For Luhmann the role of law and politics as risk-bearers of societal evolution decreases in the world society. However, this does not mean that law is withering away but that we can expect a change of the legal form. Luhmann emphasised early on that the growing importance of the economy, science and technology in the world society is the result of an increase in cognitive expectations in a world society oriented towards the future rather than the past (Luhmann 1975 [1971], pp. 55–8, 1985a, pp. 262–3). I view this early thesis of Luhmann, despite Rudolf Stichweh's objections (Stichweh 2002, p. 287), as still being valid. In the world society the relevance of law and politics (although not necessarily their amount) for the society as a whole decreases. At the same time we can expect an increase in cognitive mechanisms within the normative structure of world law.

In describing the backwardness of law and in particular politics in the world society, Luhmann uses the interesting comparison with the diminishing role of families in the formation of complex societies.

> A rapid increase in worldwide coherence is perceptible in all ... areas. The same is true for political power to the extent, that all, at least great, powers can no longer afford to ignore the shifts in power relations amongst the small powers somewhere on the globe. In contrast to this, political decision-making, and hence political rationality within more narrow boundaries, seems to lag behind – just like the family used to in the construction of larger and highly cultivated societal systems (Luhmann 1985a, p. 256).

Like other function systems, the political system is governed by a binary code. Luhmann identified this code as government and opposition. Some critics have accused him of adhering to a model of politics predating the Enlightenment period in which democracy is substituted by administration (King and Thornhill 2003, p. 181). This criticism is not only unfair but misleading, since Luhmann is particularly aware of the problems of politics in a late stage of modernity in which world politics become increasingly dominant. However, questions can be asked at a different level about Luhmann's code; it creates problems in relation to the system of world politics since there is no single government representing the system. Mathias Albert has made the interesting point that in the development of the world political system, for a while at least, the East-West divide during the period of the Cold War acted as functional equivalent to the binary code of government and opposition (Albert 2004b, pp. 27–8; see also Albert 2004a).

Law and politics are the function systems that have the most difficulties in accepting their links with and dependence on the world society as central to their self-understanding. Territorial boundaries and national and regional identities play a larger role in comparison with other function systems. In addition, law and politics reinforce each other in their insistence on national and regional self-identity.

The specific concept Luhmann adopted in order to theorise links between function systems is structural coupling. Zones of structural coupling are areas in which the systems have the potential to irritate each other. The constitution is Luhmann's main example of structural coupling of the legal and the political system; property and contract are the main mechanism of structural coupling of the economic and the legal system (see Luhmann 2004, ch. 10).

The concept of structural coupling rests on three assumptions. First, the systems involved are conceived as autopoietic in nature and thus, despite any relationship, ultimately guided by their necessity to self-reproduce. Second, structural coupling means a specific, non-causal form of influencing; through mechanisms of structural coupling systems irritate each other by becoming aware of different operations and interpretations of the other system that can become the cause for internal structural adjustments.[3] Third, over the long run structural coupling is a condition that enables co-evolution of the coupled systems.

The last aspect refers to a specific relationship that is assessed with concepts borrowed from the general theory of evolution and contingency theory. Luhmann discards any deterministic theory of society and thus rejects explicitly viewing the relationship of societal and legal, respectively, political development as being causally linked. Law and politics are seen as genuinely autonomous areas and their study requires non-linear thinking. His insistence on difference as the starting point in theorising the social world, his system-relative worldview and the prominence his theory puts on non-causal relationships bears resemblances to postmodern thinking. The closeness of Luhmann's system theory to postmodern thinking about law has been commented upon in the writings of Teubner, Ladeur, Clam and a few others (see Teubner 2001, 2006b; Ladeur 1995; Clam 2000; see also Goodrich 1999). We find indeed a number of affirmative remarks on Derrida's *différance* concept in Luhmann's late work (for example Luhmann 1993, 1995b), although, one should be fair, these

---

[3]   Teubner has suggested using the term 'interference' for the description of simultaneous effects of communication events in several function systems. See Teubner 1993a, pp. 86–90.

constitute only side remarks and show no real engagement with postmodern theorising.

Luhmann is sceptical whether the concept of structural coupling of law and politics via constitutions can be transposed to the world society. Even before he adopted the concept of structural coupling he argued in the early article on *Weltgesellschaft*: 'It might be possible that the peculiar relationship of law and politics is an aberrant specialisation that, for the time being, cannot be transferred on to the system of the world society' (Luhmann 1975 [1971], p. 57, translation R.R.). A similarly radically negative attitude is taken at the end of *Law as a Social System* regarding the future role of law in the world society:

> ... it may well be that the current prominence of the legal system and the dependence of society itself and of most function systems on a functioning legal code are nothing but a European anomaly, which might well level off with the evolution of the world society (Luhmann 2004, p. 490, translation adjusted by R.R.).

However, despite Luhmann's pessimism there might be new relationships between law and politics developing at the global level. Structural coupling might be replaced by new links between law and politics. An interesting concept is pursued by Poul Kjaer, who suggests that world politics provides new forms of legitimacy for world law (Kjaer 2012). National political structures like the public sphere and representation are replaced in world politics by new structures of communication based on general principles of accountability and transparency (Kjaer 2011). It might well be that a major function of world law in the form of global administrative law is vice versa to provide support for the building of political structures on the basis of these principles (on global administrative law see Kingsbury et al. 2005).

Nevertheless, it is worthwhile remembering that Luhmann was particularly sceptical about the capacity of law to address and regulate the problems that world society creates for itself. He identified these problems as related to tendencies of exclusion and failed inclusion of large parts of the global population into function systems. The emergence of the metacode of exclusion and inclusion in the world society has consequences for the application of the legal code of legal and illegal.

> The difference between legal and illegal certainly exists and there are legislative programmes (statutes) that regulate how the values of legal and illegal are attributed to facts. But this question is of little importance to the excluded groups of the population compared with what is imposed on them by this exclusion. They are treated legally or illegally and accordingly conduct themselves legally or illegally (Luhmann 2004, p. 489).

He then continues in a typical Luhmannian twist that a similar observation can be made about inclusion.

> The same applies to those who are included and, in particular, to the politicians and the staff of bureaucracies (Ibid.).

The most severe problems in the world society result from negative functional differentiation. World politics and world law lose their role as main sources for the creation of structures in the world society. Due to high internal complexity, function systems develop along their own trajectories at different speeds and there are no instances in the world society prepared to deal with collisions of function systems. The global financial crisis might well have revealed this dark side of functional differentiation of the world society (Kjaer et al. 2011).

Luhmann's bleak view of future dangers of the world society bears remarkable similarities with Max Weber's pessimism about the development of modern society. Weber's view of an ever more efficient rational bureaucratised society becoming an uninhabitable iron cage for mankind finds an echo in Luhmann's warning of increasing burdens that function systems create for each other. Weber's scepticism towards rationality in general re-emerges at the end in Luhmann's negative appraisal of chances for system rationality in the world society in coping with its self-inflicted problems.

1.4   NIKLAS LUHMANN'S WORLD LAW AND GUNTHER TEUBNER'S GLOBAL LAW

The theory of world law tries to understand the emergence of a separate order of norms at the global level. Traditionally world law is identified with international law, which comprises public international law, including fundamental and human rights. Public international law is created through agreements between states and the states are 'primary subjects' of international law. There is an on-going discussion in international law in which way it is capable of becoming autonomous and develops, despite fragmentation, its own structures and dynamisms beyond the control of nation states (Cassese 2005, Part II; Koskenniemi 2007).

In *Law as a Social System* Luhmann argues that the world society 'has a legal order, even if it does not have central legislation and decision-making' (Luhmann 2004, p. 481). This world law is based on a number of commonalities among the different regional or national legal orders: the universal existence of legal concepts such as property, contract and rules of private international law as well as legislation as source of law. However, unlike science or the economy, the legal system in the world society is characterised by enormous differences among regional and national legal orders. These are to a significant degree the result of 'segmentation' of the political system into states at the global level. This 'secondary differentiation' has negative consequences for the establishment of a system of world law.

Human rights constitute a special case. At the international level the cornerstone of human rights legislation has been the Universal Declaration of Human Rights of 1948. This document not only contains a wide range of individual rights, including liberty and security, equality before the law, freedom of expression and religion and prohibitions on torture, but also political, social and economic rights such as asylum, right of assembly, right to work and equal pay, right to social security and right to education.

In assessing the role of human rights within world law it might be helpful to compare them with Luhmann's assessment of world religions. He describes the emergence of world religions in *A Systems Theory of Religion* (Luhmann 2013) as a prime example of anticipation of the world society. They are the most important contribution to the differentiation of religion as a social system in the world society. What prepares some religions more than others to become world religions is their universal nature and that they offer their religious contents to all human beings. World religions do not operate with ethnic, racial or territorial limitations nor are they supported, like Japanese Shintoism or Judaism, by these factors. Gods are de-regionalised and the only criterion that matters is belief. World religions are radically individualistic and have to find justification in themselves (Luhmann 2013, pp. 199–200).

I suggest viewing human rights as a parallel case to world religions within the legal system. Human rights grant rights to all human beings on the globe. They are individualistic and inclusive and play an important role in the establishment of a world legal system.

Furthermore, Gert Verschraegen has rightly emphasised that Luhmann's theory of human rights grants them a double meaning in modern society: human rights not only protect individuals but also society from de-differentiation (Verschraegen 2002, 2006). Human and fundamental rights play an important role in preventing the political system from resorting to drastic solutions. Fundamental rights are 'institutions' that protect modern society from regression (see Luhmann 1965).

Luhmann notes in the last part of *Law as a Social System* (Luhmann 2004, pp. 479–90) the difficulties legal theory has in justifying human rights. Natural law and social contract theories are exhausted and all attempts to recognise human rights as positive law in constitutional law are riddled with paradoxes. Why is something supposedly above positive law in need to become positive? Furthermore, Luhmann diagnoses under-mining tendencies that derive from an inflationary use of human rights as a symbolic medium, a warning resembling Hannah Arendt's "perplexi-ties of the rights of man" (Arendt 1973, pp. 290–304), which, insofar as economic and social rights are concerned, has never been very convincing from a labour law perspective.

Nevertheless, Luhmann acknowledges that human rights play an invaluable part in the emerging law of the world society and are one of 'the most important indicators of a global legal system' (Luhmann 2004, p. 482). In Luhmann's sociolegal analysis the reasons for the human rights discourse to flourish are external. Outcries about severe violations keep the discourse on human rights alive. Thus, neither increasing efforts to legalise human rights through codes and attempts to clarify them in precise legal texts nor the expansion of human rights from protective to supportive rights are the main reasons for the growth of human rights. Instead, external factors such as public demands for reactions to massive incursions of human rights and crass cases of violation of human dignity are the guarantors that human rights continue to be taken seriously (Luhmann 2004, pp. 483–7).

Luhmann's theory of world law is not a normative theory and differs in this respect from current political and legal theory. Unlike John Rawls' *The Law of Peoples* (Rawls 1999), Luhmann does not offer a normative programme of how to create a 'just' international order on the basis of 'just' institutions.[4] Luhmann's world society concept also differs from the Kantian programme of establishing a utopian world order that guarantees eternal peace for cosmopolitan citizens. This Kantian project has recently been reformulated by Jürgen Habermas in his 'Political Constitution for the Pluralist World Society' (Habermas 2008; see also Habermas 2006, 2009). Habermas proposes a new form of world organisation that replaces the UN and derives its legitimation partly from a well-informed global public sphere.

> The goal of a democratic constitution of world society calls for the creation of a community of *world citizens* . . . a *constitution-building cooperation of citizens and states* . . . a *cosmopolitan* community. The latter would not constitute itself as a world republic . . . but as a supranational association of citizens and peoples (Habermas 2012, p. 58, emphasis in text).

Habermas's theorising of world law privileges political and constitutional aspects and largely overlooks other processes that typify modern law. This

---

[4]   And Luhmann is certainly not interested, like Rawls, in justifying 'just' wars against so-called illiberal and indecent people.

narrow view has characterised his understanding of law since he embarked on rethinking the relationship between law and democracy in *Between Facts and Norms* (Habermas 1996a). Luhmann criticises Habermas's normative approach for too much 'faith in the legal process' and 'a very traditional emphasis on legislation' (Luhmann 1996a, pp. 891, 892). Furthermore, Habermas's concern with legitimation as the most pressing problem of modern law and politics itself lacks legitimation (Luhmann 1996a and reply by Habermas 1996b; see also the debate over the question of legitimation in Habermas and Luhmann 1971).

For Luhmann world law is more than public international law. Although he has not analysed world law in detail, there was no doubt for him that a legal system exists in the world society which has 'a structure of legal norms, independent of regional traditions and the political interests of regional states' (Luhmann 2004, p. 487). However, since this global legal system is not regulated by central legislation and decision-making, public international law and, for example, an international court do not occupy the centre of Luhmann's understanding of world law.

Gunther Teubner has further developed Luhmann's rudimentary thoughts about law in the world society in his studies on global law without the state. The legal system of the world society has no centre from which it can expect to be governed in order to preserve its unity (Teubner 1997). Teubner looks beyond (public) international law, which, in his view, gets too much attention in comparison with the law of conflicts or 'collisions' between legal orders, which is traditionally seen as the sphere of private international law (Fischer-Lescano and Teubner 2004). A theory of global or world law has to focus in Teubner's view on the genuine properties of the legal system that emerges at the world level.

Teubner has convincingly applied the theory of legal pluralism in studying world law (Teubner 1997). In his account, global law is plural in nature and consists of a variety of legal orders that globalise gradually and at different speeds. In theorising global law Teubner makes creative use of Eugen Ehrlich (Ehrlich 2002 [1936]) and his study of customary law in modern society. For Teubner, global law, like customary law, derives from a multiplicity of legal sources and, by viewing global law as similar to customary law he started a third wave of studies in legal pluralism, following the first wave of legal pluralism studies of colonial legal orders and a second wave of successfully applying the theory of legal pluralism in studies of multicultural Western law and its semi-autonomous ethnic, cultural and religious legal orders (Teubner 1997). In creatively using Ehrlich's original ideas, Teubner argues that world law emerges from social peripheries and not from political centres occupied by nation states or international organisations. He emphasises that main sources for the

emerging world law are international trade agreements and their interpretation through international commercial arbitration and other quasi-
judicial bodies.

Three examples of genuine world law can illustrate Teubner's claim of a
global law beyond the state. Probably the best example is *lex mercatoria*.
This legal practice, which dates back to medieval times, has developed into
an established, separate legal order of international trade law. According
to Ursula Stein, indicators for the existence of a separate legal order are
high standards of transparency, observance of principles of international
law, use of precedents for establishing principles used in decision-making
and an efficient practice of commercial arbitration that is able to enforce
its decisions (see Stein 1995, pp. 241–3 and ch. 7 III on *lex mercatoria* as a
legal order). The legal order of *lex mercatoria* has emerged as a subsystem
within the world legal system through self-referential, reflexive operations.
It is an indication that law is undergoing a structural transformation in
the world society. Its traditionally close relations with politics are loosen-
ing and are exchanged in the case of *lex mercatoria* with closer links with
transnational economics (Albert 2002, pp. 262–3; Lieckweg 2003).

A further example of the emergence of a specific type of world law
independent of international, respectively, interstate law is the area of
professional sports. The globalisation of sports has led to an increase in
activities of athletes, clubs, federations, sponsors or event organisers at
regional or global levels. These sport-related, including economic, activities are governed by specific rules that require specialist knowledge from
judicial bodies dealing with disputes arising from these activities. Like *lex
mercatoria*, international sports law has developed into a highly complex
legal order adhering to high standards. Ken Foster has made an interesting distinction between international and global sports law:

> International sports law (consists of) general principles of law that are auto-
> matically applicable to sport. Basic protections, such as due process and the
> right to a fair hearing, are by this route incorporated into sport and represent a
> 'rule of law' in sport. Global sports law . . . describes the principles that emerge
> from the rules and regulations of international sporting federations as a private
> contractual order. They are distinctive and unique (Foster 2003, p. 4).

Crucial for the development of global sports law has been the Court of
Arbitration for Sport (CAS), which, since the early 1980s, resolves sports
disputes of the international sporting community. CAS is a separate judiciary that has its seat in Switzerland. It is an independent institution under
the administrative and financial authority of the International Council
of Arbitration for Sport that provides the settlement of sports-related
disputes through arbitration or mediation by means of procedural rules

adapted to the specific needs of the sports world. CAS has had a decisive function in establishing internationally recognised principles on which sports law developed into a separate global legal order.

A third example is *lex digitalis*, or the law of the Internet. Gralf-Peter Calliess has called this legal order genuine transnational law, which he defines as follows: 'a third-level autonomous legal system beyond municipal and public international law, created and developed by the law-making forces of an emerging global civil society, founded on general principles of law as well as societal usages, administered by private dispute resolution service providers, and codified (if at all) by private norm for-mulating agencies' (Calliess 2002, p. 188). His example is the system of dispute resolution of the Internet Corporation for Assigned Names and Numbers (ICANN), which has been in operation since 1999 and shows all the attributes mentioned in his definition. Calliess emphasises that the transparency and the fact of full publication of all ICANN decisions have been decisive for the emergence of a separate legal order resulting from self-referential decision-making, a case based on precedent. Teubner goes a step further and sees in this decision-making signs of an emergent digital constitution (Teubner 2004a).[5]

The new quality of global law lies for Teubner in mirroring functional differentiation of the world society and so-called polycentric globalisation in the sources of law. To a large extent world law originates in self-regula-tion processes in function systems. These processes lead to complex legal orders within function systems that develop their own strategies of reduc-tion of complexities. This gives world law the character of polycentric law (Teubner 2012).

In recent studies of these global legal orders, Teubner has gone a step further. What is most characteristic for him about legal globalisation is the emergence of societal constitutions in these legal orders (Teubner 2002, 2004a, 2004b, 2010a, 2010b, 2011a, 2011b, 2011c). Societal consti-tutionalisation accompanies constitutionalisation in the public sphere, in international politics and in international organisations, epitomised in the development of human rights applied worldwide (on constitutionalisation beyond the state in public international law see Pernice et al. 2012). For Teubner this constitutionalisation of international politics represents only a:

---

[5] Six further examples of emerging legal orders in the world society are discussed in Fischer-Lescano and Teubner (2004). These include transnational copyright law, medical patent protection, transnational construction law (*lex constructionis*), transnational criminal law (law of the disappeared), international financial regulations (*lex financiaria*) and transnational cybercrime law.

sub-constitution of world society among others, which can no longer use any *pars pro toto* claim. ... The ongoing constitutionalisation of international politics has no monopoly over constitutionalising world society. A kind of constitutional competition is set into motion by the autonomisation of global sub-constitutions (Teubner 2004b, p. 15).

Teubner is not alone. We witness an increasing interest in global legal structures that have led to a multitude of normative and empirical studies. In philosophical perspectives global legal structures are assessed as normative orders, predominantly focusing on questions of distributive justice (Rawls 1972; Pogge 1989, 2007a, 2007b). Newer philosophical accounts transcend the narrow justice discourse and focus on broader legitimacy questions. In this view the problem of the global order is not justice but justification and world law is assessed whether it guarantees a so-called right to justification (Forst 2011). The analytical interest shifts to studying the emergence of the global normative order from a particular normative perspective that asks whether global law is a site for the creation of concrete moral and legal norms guaranteeing the possibility and chances for resistance of this order (Forst and Günther 2011).

However, such views on world law are limited. More promising is sociological theory and in particular legal sociology. World society theorists argue that international law is only possible because of the existence of a normative structure of expectations at the world level (Stichweh 2000a, p. 55). These expectations develop in different function systems and lead not only to separate systems of norms but to a whole range of institutions dealing with upholding expectations. An overarching unifying view based on moral principles is no longer providing integration of world law or steering these institutions. Questions of legitimacy no longer play a central role and the global legal orders engage at best in 'reflexive legitimacy' through procedural rationalisation and professionalisation of self-regulation (Banakar 1998; Dezalay and Garth 1998).

Sociolegal research has begun to analyse the diverse global legal processes and institutions and the orders in which they are embedded. Law plays a specific role in multi-level governance of global trade (Picciotto 2011) and in areas such as global environmental law (Perez 2004). In transnational commercial disputes, in particular in the case of cross-border debt, a privatisation of debt collection and the emergence of a private law order have been observed (Budak 1998). And there is the fascinating case of globalisation of law firms and legal practice (see Dezalay and Garth 2012; Günther 2004; Flood 2008).

Studies report a number of ways in which global legal orders strengthen themselves through self-regulation. Empirical studies of self-governance in transnational economic transactions emphasise the public function of so-called private forms of self-regulation (Glinski 2008 and other studies in Dilling et al. 2008; see also Teubner 1994, 2010a). Volkmar Gessner (1998) identified legal rules, professions, so-called third cultures (scientific communities, the mafia, the London reinsurance market or the diamond industry) and state and non-governmental support structures as factors that produce 'legal certainty' in global law.

1.5 FROM THE IDEA OF LABOUR LAW TO A THEORY OF LABOUR LAW IN THE WORLD SOCIETY

What do these theoretical and empirical findings about an emerging world law mean for labour law and how can we assess its role in the world society? This has to be a central question for a theory of reflexive labour law. There is currently much uncertainty about the future of labour law. Guy Davidov, Brian Langille and their colleagues evaluate the status of labour law by re-assessing the normative and intellectual foundations of what they call the *Idea of Labour Law* (Davidov and Langille 2011). However, such internal reconstruction of the logic of labour law development and its challenges provides limited answers. For a proper understanding of modern labour law it is necessary to move beyond retrospective analyses or using memory as means of regaining a lost world of pluralist labour regulations (Arthurs 1998). What is needed is an assessment of labour law's changing role in the world society.

For this an analysis is required that looks at internal transformations of labour law as well as its co-evolution with the economic and political system but also industrial relations. These systems have themselves encountered transformations in large part due to globalisation. Industrial relations operate as a separate social system in the world society (see Chapter 3). The creation of labour law as a separate field of regulation and discipline is originally a response to the emerging industrial relations system within the legal system. The relationship of labour law as a subfield of the legal system to the industrial relations system is of central concern for a system theoretical account of labour law.

Furthermore, labour law is linked to politics, in particular in the context of economic policy-making. It is regularly exposed to attempts of the political system that try to regulate labour law in the hope of achieving economic goals. For an understanding of the development of modern labour law we have to look at different levels of governance. As far as the global level is concerned, I would like to suggest that global labour law, at least in the form of international labour law, is located in a specific zone of structural coupling between world law and world politics. Mathias Albert emphasises in his studies on world politics a specific mechanism of structural coupling of law and politics in the world society which he calls international regimes (Albert 2002, pp. 291–8, 2004a). These regimes transcend international organisations, which themselves become dependent on processes resulting from transnational regimes. In using this analysis, global labour law can be understood as having evolved into a legal regime in the world society (further discussed in Chapter 10).

However, globalisation of labour law does not only happen at the global level. Tania Lieckweg (2003, pp. 133–4) has rightly emphasised that globalisation of law differs among areas of law, in particular in relation to relevance of sources of law other than legislation. Labour law has a long tradition of dealing with norms created in non-statist settings and might indeed be a case of spontaneous creation of law in peripheries. Important sources of norm creation in labour law are collective bargaining and company negotiations resulting in collective bargaining agreements and company agreements. These are acknowledged as sources of law and play an important role in shaping economic processes. From a reflexive law perspective they constitute mechanisms of self-regulation that pose challenges for public labour law regulations (a topic that will be further discussed in Chapter 2).

What should be clear from these remarks is that labour law operates in a particular context and this is created by the social system of industrial relations. Industrial relations are also undergoing transformations due to globalisation in the world society. A few remarks should suffice to illustrate these globalisation processes, which will be further discussed in subsequent chapters.

In the global age strikes of a certain size are reported worldwide as important economic news. Wage struggles and negotiations over working conditions are perceived as events which have an impact beyond national markets. The costs of transnational companies with production sites in several countries are directly affected by strikes in a particular country. Thus, collective bargaining and strike threats in German industries are important beyond Germany. Furthermore, strikes of lorry drivers in one European country have a direct impact on economic activities in other European countries and beyond.

It is alleged that the demand for decent labour standards reduces the chances of developing countries to compete with low labour costs. A national strike in developing countries receives almost immediate worldwide attention because labour unrest is automatically viewed as reaction to global pressures of introducing policies of liberalisation and flexibilisation in these countries. Although the strike reasons often are local or national in origin, for example a change of national dismissal law or discrimination of trade unions, the protest receives global news coverage because it is perceived as a direct response to social injustices resulting from free market policies.

The reform of legal policies and labour law are increasingly driven by global concerns. Deregulation of employment protection is commonly justified by expectations of an alleged international demand for flexibilisation of workforces. These experiments with massive deregulation of labour law receive much attention, for example the radical abolishing of employment protection in New Zealand in the 1980s and 1990s, and are openly used as means in competition over foreign investments.

If we look at supranational or international law and policy-making, a number of processes can be discerned. In the European Union the so-called social dimension officially accompanies economic integration. It consists of social and labour policies that have led to a number of 'hard' legal rules in areas such as health and safety of workers and equal pay and equal treatment between men and women. These laws are vigorously enforced by European institutions with active support from the European Court of Justice. In addition to the core of hard rules, there exists a variety of 'weak' supranational legal norms in the European Union, many of which have been introduced since 1997 in the context of coordination policies as part of the European Employment Strategy.

European social policy measures are not the outcome of corporatist arrangements, as is characteristic of many national labour law systems. They form part of neo-voluntarist policies following a programme of neo-liberal restructuring of national economies (Streeck 1996). Nevertheless, European social policy and labour law provide a basic frame for transnational private regulation in Europe (Bercusson 1997). This includes promotion of sectoral collective bargaining and European works councils in the European Union (Bercusson 2009a, ch. 9).

In switching from the European to the international level, we notice attempts to add a 'social dimension' to globalisation by establishing a global legal framework of labour standards. International labour law derives foremost from labour standards introduced by the International Labour Organization (ILO). For the development of international labour law the ILO is still the leading source. It has transformed from a pure standard-setting agency for the harmonisation of national labour law to a true international organisation that pursues its own policy agenda. In particular its Decent Work agenda enables the ILO to create global labour law that reaches beyond the confines of national labour law into labour market policies and regulation of multinational corporations. The switch was supported when the World Commission on the

Social Dimension of Globalisation elevated decent work as its key concept for future employment policies. This provided 'political direction' and boosted policy efforts pursued by the ILO (Casale 2011, p. 2).

However, global labour law transcends international labour law. Labour law norms are increasingly created in private settings and result from activities of networks in which ILO standards form part of norm creation. In their project on transnational private law, Gralf-Peter Calliess and Peer Zumbansen (2010) emphasise the importance of networks for the creation of world law. Furthermore, although networks no longer privilege the nation state as source of law, nation states play a role in them in creating transnational law. They rightly point out that major changes have occurred at the domestic level which are related to the use of new forms of governance and soft law. Applied to labour law we can speak of global labour law as a regime emerging from links between the function systems of law, politics, economy and industrial relations at global, regional and domestic level.

A small example of globalisation of labour law resulting from network activities is international cooperation and mutual observation of labour courts and other judicial bodies dealing with labour law matters. These processes are sources for the creation of labour standards in the judicial realm. Although it would go too far to talk of a 'global community' or network of labour courts (on the idea of a global community of courts see Slaughter 2003, 2004, ch. 2), there are signs that labour courts take notice of foreign decisions in their judicial practice and form more or less informal organisational links. For example, labour court judges operating in the European Union and the European Economic Area have formed their own Association of Labour Court Judges, which holds an annual conference and occasionally produces reports on topics of mutual concern and relevance for European discussions.

Global labour law is closely linked to developments of international business and trade law (see Hepple 2005). The legal framework of international trade law develops in incremental processes and is supplied from a variety of sources (Braithwaite and Drahos 2001; Picciotto 2011). There is much less reliance on statutory law or collective agreements. International trade agreements might contain social clauses and other labour law provisions. Furthermore, internal structures of transnational corporations might reflect national company constitutions in which employee representatives enjoy co-determination rights and thus become part of global labour law.

An important means for the development of the so-called social dimension of globalisation are codes of conduct of companies operating at the global, regional as well as domestic level. They regulate, for example, that suppliers of multinational corporations have to observe labour standards. These codes of conduct often refer to ILO conventions. However, they are also sources for the creation of transnational regulation (Backer 2008). Since sanctions for non-compliance, respectively their lack, can generate problems, codes of conduct create opportunities for collective actors, including trade unions and social movements, to engage in campaigns that demand adherence to labour standards.

Fundamental economic and social rights are a further area of law that contributes to the formation of a global labour law regime. The rights include the right to work, which is defined in Article 23.1 of the Universal Declaration of Human Rights in the following way:

> Everyone has the right to work, to free choice of employment, to just and favourable conditions of work and to protection against unemployment.

However, this right has the problem that in order to be effective it has to be viewed as more than just an individual right. In Article 6 of the International Covenant on Economic, Social and Cultural Rights, the right to work is linked to responsibilities of states for vocational training and other measures supporting individual development.

> (1) ... the right to work ... includes the right of everyone to the opportunity to gain his living by work which he freely chooses or accepts, and will take appropriate steps to safeguard this right. (2) The steps to be taken by a State party to the present Covenant to achieve the full realization of this right shall include technical and vocational guidance and training programmes, policies and techniques to achieve steady economic, social and cultural development and full and productive employment under conditions safeguarding fundamental political and economic freedoms to the individual.

The right to work as understood by the International Covenant on Economic, Social and Cultural Rights is intricately linked to employment policies. Modern labour law can indeed not be separated from labour market policies. We witness a worldwide trend of refocusing the regulatory concern of employment policies from employment rights to employment promotion.

An important factor in developing the social dimension of globalisation has been the interaction of regional and global efforts in regulating employment and industrial relations affairs. In particular, the experience of the supranational European social and employment policy and its relationship with collective interest groups has been an important source of innovative labour law making. In the EU collective, industrial actors participate not only in implementing EU law but have an active role in creating European labour law in the context of the so-called Social Dialogue.

However, the so-called social dimension of European integration underwent two transformations. The first transformation occurred in the 1970s when the initial minimalist policy of simply supporting economic integration and the establishment of a common market with a few social policy measures were abandoned and European social policy became a separate policy field in its own right. In fact, with the active support of the European Court of Justice, social integration was declared to be of equal importance to economic integration as a goal of European policy-making. The second transformation occurred in the 1990s with the adoption of employment policy as an official area of policy-making in the European Union. The focus in relation to labour law shifted from employment protection to employment promotion. Increasing employment rates became an overarching goal since 2000 and included initiatives of modernising labour law in accordance with demands for flexible labour markets (see the Green Paper *Modernising Labour Law to Meet the Challenges of the Twenty-First Century*, European Commission 2006a).

Efforts to establish an internal social dimension of European integration were accompanied in the EU by initiatives for an external social dimension. Particularly noteworthy is the inclusion of labour standards in the so-called Generalised System of Preferences (GSP). Since 1 January 1998 a social clause is part of trade agreements of the EU with developing countries. It operates with incentives of trade advantages if labour standards are adhered to but developing countries lose their trade preferences in case of violation of labour standards (further discussed in Chapter 10).

The relationship of labour law and industrial relations is changing in the world society. The new communication technologies encourage new forms of solidarity. They offer social movements, including the labour movement chances of influencing world politics and gaining attention for their causes. Worldwide communication systems enable a rapid distribution of information about local or regional industrial disputes. Industrial disputes over wage bargaining and trade union rights as well as specific labour law problems such as dismissal or statutory minimum wages gain almost immediate international recognition. Furthermore, global communication has increasing importance for initiating and conducting collective industrial disputes. In fact, globalisation has the potential to strengthen industrial relations in this way.

No doubt there are also negative impacts of globalisation on industrial relations. What has been commented on in relation to smaller nation states in world politics is even truer for national industrial relations: they lack an 'address' for international communications. Their voice is often not heard in regulation of social affairs and labour law at the international or supranational level. This can lead to phenomena such as social dumping, when the lowest standards become the point of convergence in regulating social security and lead to a reduction of protection in developed labour law systems. There is also the famous 'pressure from outside' to deregulate national labour law. However, it would be wrong to assume a standard model or pattern of deregulation. The autopoietic nature of industrial relations is often able to resist deregulation pressures (see Chapters 3 and 6).

If globalisation is mainly associated with markets and free trade, the adoption of labour law and collective bargaining at supranational and international level indicates the limits of globalisation. Liberalisation of the world market will not be able to retain growth over a longer period if it is not properly regulated. The world market, like all other markets, requires a re-forming of capitalism in order to achieve growth with stability (Streeck 2009; Boyer and Drache 1996).

Insofar as industrial relations and collective bargaining at international level are concerned, much will depend on the role of collective organisations and their role within the new contexts of corporate codes of conduct and corporate social responsibility. Transnational solidarity indeed faces severe problems for trade unions (Bieler and Lindberg 2010). Since support from an active welfare state and the legal system is largely lacking, traditional trade union internationalism will have to find new partners at the global level. Social movements promoting human rights, in particular those of migrants, are possible candidates. In utopian versions of a law of humankind, which creates the basis of a global community, replacing both the state and the market as regulatory sites, labour might find support and a place in transnational coalitions (Sousa Santos 2002, pp. 365–73). And unions might find a new role in supporting alternative values in civil society (Crouch 2011, ch. 7), but this requires trade unions, as Richard Hyman aptly observes, to diversify their forms of solidarity (Hyman 2010).

However, it is more likely that the globalisation of the labour movement takes place at home. Indeed, increased recognition of the local through global exposure already supports labour movements in their endeavours. Achievements at the workplace and in collective negotiations can rapidly be disseminated in the global world. Furthermore, the global challenge to workplace industrial relations releases new energies to defend and even strengthen existing institutional regimes (Bélanger et al. 1994). Autopoietic industrial relations and reflexive labour law of advanced national economies become mediating forces which protect their achievements through endorsement of their global role. Insofar as collective bargaining at sectoral and company level and national labour law systems are able to accept the global challenge through reflecting their global position, these confident local, regional and national industrial relations will constitute important premises of the world society.

Let us summarise. The theory of reflexive labour law takes seriously the globalisation of labour law. Labour law develops at different levels, which all are influenced by worldwide processes of increasing fragmentation and conflicts between regulatory regimes. These processes pose new challenges to regulation and self-regulation of labour law. Furthermore, labour law plays a part in what Teubner calls societal constitutionalisation as a response to functional differentiation in the world society. This phenomenon of globalisation of labour law will be further discussed in Chapter 10.

Luhmann predicts less dependence of the major function systems on both legal regulation and the availability of the legal code in the evolving world society (Luhmann 2004, pp. 479–90). However, labour law and industrial relations will continue to play an important role in shaping conditions under which businesses engage in activities in the global market. They are relevant forces in creating 'cultures' and 'institutional regimes' which have been considered the dominant factors for economic growth, replacing government policies in the global age (Albrow 1996).

2. Reflexive labour law: a general introduction

This chapter introduces general features of the concept of reflexive labour law. It starts with information on its origin in the theory of reflexive law and then introduces some specific characteristics of reflexive labour law. The chapter contains a first attempt to apply the reflexive law concept to modern labour law and concentrates on theoretical and general aspects of reflexive labour law. The main theoretical topics discussed in this chapter will be further analysed in separate chapters of the book. These topics include the regulation of self-regulation through collective agreements and employment contracts, reflexivity in the regulation of employment protection and labour market policies and reflexive global labour law. The chapter makes an attempt to refute some of the criticism of reflexive law by demonstrating the usefulness of applying autopoietic social systems theory to labour law.

2.1 THE ORIGINS OF REFLEXIVE LAW

The reflexive law theory, as originally developed by Gunther Teubner, was a response to and continuation of Philippe Nonet's and Philip Selznick's concept of responsive law (Nonet and Selznick 1978; see also Zumbansen 2008, pp. 787–95). In his seminal article 'Substantive and Reflexive Elements in Modern Law', published in 1983, Teubner introduced the concept of reflexive legal rationality. He argued that in addition to notions of formal and substantive legal rationality, a complex modern legal system is characterised by reflexive rationality focusing attention on proceduralisation and the fundamental importance of self-regulation (Teubner 1983, pp. 254–7, 270–75).

The early reflexive law concept, which Teubner developed in collaboration with Helmut Willke, was concerned with legitimation, functions and internal structures of the legal system (see Teubner and Willke 1984). In fact it was presented as an approach to combine the social theories of Jürgen Habermas and Niklas Luhmann in an analysis of specific modern trends in the legal system such as proceduralisation and 'contextual' steering via negotiation systems (Teubner 1982). Central topics were the external links of the legal system, societal guidance through law (see also Willke 1992) and in particular the question of legal regulation. The reflexive law concept suggested that special attention should be paid to the limits of legal regulation and to processes of self-regulation in other social systems.

A shift occurred in the debate with Erhard Blankenburg (see Blankenburg 1984, and the 'rejoinder' by Teubner 1984). In response to Blankenburg's positivistic critique of insufficient empirical grounds of key theoretical assumptions of the reflexive law concept (evolutionism and proceduralism), Teubner radicalised the approach. The new focus became the autopoietic nature of the legal system, i.e. the capacity of the legal system to reproduce itself. The core idea relates to Luhmann's concept of an autopoietic social system that 'constitutes the elements of which it consists through the elements of which it consists' (Luhmann 1988b, p. 14; see also Luhmann 1995a, pp. 34–6, 1997a, ch. 1, section VI). The discussion embarked on topics such as the autonomy and the internal constitution of the legal system and system-specific communications as the basic elements of self-reproduction. The influence of Habermas's theory decreased and Luhmann's systems theory became dominant. Indeed, Luhmann himself helped to push the theory in this direction. In a critique of the reflexive law concept, he emphasised the vagueness of the concepts autonomy, reflexivity and self-regulation and compared them with the 'rigorously inflexible' concept of autopoiesis (Luhmann 1992).

In particular in his collection of essays entitled 'Law as an Autopoietic System' (Teubner 1993a), Teubner took up the challenge. Although basically accepting Luhmann's theory of autopoietic social systems, Teubner deviated from Luhmann's approach in one crucial aspect. He asked the question that was carefully avoided by Luhmann: how the origin, genesis and early history of an autopoietic system can be analysed. Teubner introduced the model of a gradual process in which autopoietic systems are created. He called this the hypercycle in which the system's components are not just self-referentially constituted but hypercyclically coupled. In relation to the autopoietic nature of law, he discussed self-reference, hypercyclical self-closure and self-regulation of the legal system as well as its blind co-evolution with other social systems. The concept of reflexive law became subsumed under the theory of an autopoietic legal system and was largely reduced to a discussion of the regulatory capacities of the legal system. The issues that from now on constituted the core of Teubner's thinking about reflexive law as part of his theory of autopoietic law are indicated in Chapter 5 of *Law as an Autopoietic System* entitled 'Social Regulation through Reflexive Law'. The main topics in this chapter are mutual recognition of autonomy and autopoiesis between social systems, proceduralisation, the limits of legal intervention, constructivist internal models of the external social world, 'interference' of the legal and the economic system through contract and rights, and regulation of self-regulation.

2.2 GENERAL FEATURES OF REFLEXIVE LAW

The theory of reflexive law transforms insights of modern sociological systems theory and post-structuralist approaches to law and society into new questions for the sociology and theory of law. The core of its approach is to view the legal system as an autonomous function system, located within society on the same plane as the economy or the political system (Luhmann 1995a, 2004). In common with other societal subsystems, the legal system is ultimately guided by the need to protect its own self-referentiality and self-reproduction, i.e. its autopoiesis. The recognition of this fact provides the basis for a realistic assessment of the limits, but also the possibilities, of law as a mechanism for social change.

The theory of reflexive law argues that the legal system becomes consciously reflexive when it recognises that the societal domains which it purports to regulate, and to which it also seeks to respond, are themselves independent autopoietic systems. In this, law rises to the most important challenge of modern society, which derives from its overarching mode of integration – called functional differentiation. The separation of law, politics and economics creates the possibility of a decentred society and generates the societal background for law to develop as an autonomous system in society.

In Luhmann's theory of society as an autopoietic social system, subsystems such as law and politics are at the same time operationally closed and cognitively open. 'Operational closure' means that the system reproduces itself entirely by reference to its own internal structures and modes of operation: operational closure leads in case of law to a normatively closed system of counterfactually stabilised expectations. Only law transfers normative validity to its elements and this means from the internal viewpoint of those involved in the operation of legal acts such as legislation or adjudication, that only law can produce law. 'Cognitive openness', on the other hand, implies that the system evolves over time by reference to an external context, which consists of other, similarly constituted subsystems (Luhmann 1985a, pp. 281–8, 1990b).

Cognitive openness allows the legal system to remain oriented to its environment while reproducing itself through self-referential linkage of legal communications. In addition to cognitive openness at the operational level, the legal system responds at the structural level to inputs from its social environment to which it is linked by mechanisms of structural coupling (Luhmann 2004, ch. 10). In this way, law, politics and the economy can be said to co-evolve, that is to say, to evolve by response to privileged irritations which each creates for the other. The fit between them is incomplete, since structural coupling can only produce various degrees of perturbation between systems, to which the operational processes of self-reproduction may or may not respond.

In Luhmann's theory of societal development, chances for reflexive processes increase once society has adopted functional differentiation as mode of integration. He demonstrated this in relation to what he calls positivisation of law (Luhmann 1985a, pp. 164–7). The argument goes as follows. Reflexivity occurs in the development of the legal system as an autonomous function system of society. Reflexivity emerges as a by-product of norm application in decision-making. It describes the process of introducing new types of norms for the regulation of norm application. By developing second-order norms, the legal system becomes capable of reducing its function to decision-making based on the application of the binary code legal/illegal. And in this way reflexivity contributes to the closure of the system and to its autonomy.

Reflexivity in the sense of 'norming of norms' is not unknown to legal theory and is discussed there in a number of ways (see Nobles and Schiff 2006, ch. 5). Hans Kelsen's idea of a hierarchy of norms as self-validating mechanism of law in which higher norms lend legitimacy to lower-ranking norms is a prominent example (Kelsen 1967). Another example is H.L.A. Hart's concept of secondary legal rules as means of ordering primary legal rules (Hart 1997).

Reflexivity as a mechanism of self-control of law and stabiliser of positivisation of law can be distinguished from the founding reflexivity related to stabilisation of expectations. Crucial for the development of law as a system is the emergence of reflexive expectations in the form of expectations of expectations (Luhmann 1985a, pp. 26–8). In particular, the processing of normative expectations of normative expectations lies at the heart of the evolution of law as an autonomous legal system in society.

> The legal system as a whole operates normative expectations of normative expectations as its secure base. It differentiates itself on the basis of the reflexivity of its own operations. Only in this way is the competence to make decisions in the legal system socially understandable and acceptable. Only in this way are instances of legal decision-making more than they were in most of the high cultures: alien elements of a corporative kind in a society ordered by families (houses), with the consequence that communication among neighbours or the

community-based justice of the village or guild was always preferable to going to court. Only in this way can confidence in formal law and a differentiated use of law develop to give structure to the problems of everyday life, and achieve this in competition with local structures which are the more probable one as far as evolution is concerned (Luhmann 2004, pp. 159–60).

Luhmann distinguishes between reflexivity as a general principle and reflexion as a process of self-constitution of the system. The concept of reflexion describes and analyses processes of operational self-awareness of the system, 'where system reference and self-reference coincide' (Luhmann 1995a, p. 455). These include basic operations of self-reference, forms of self-observation and modes of self-description (Luhmann 1995a, pp. 455–60). Reflexion is in fact a process at the heart of autopoiesis or self-reproduction of the system. It is 'the self-referential operation ... by which the system indicates itself in contrast to its environment' (Luhmann 1995a, p. 444).

Legal reflexivity on the other hand is not confined to self-reproduction. Reflexive processes can be used to change structures and to overcome rituals. Reflexive operations can lead to reflexive mechanisms (on reflexive mechanism in general, see Luhmann 1970). Modern society operates with a variety of such mechanisms linked to symbolically generalised media of communication. Examples are the conscious use of techniques on how to learn (learning of learning), education of the educator or power controlling power (Luhmann 1995a, pp. 452–3).

Reflexive mechanisms in law are the introduction of legislation that regulates legislation (legislation of legislation or standardisation of standardisation), decisions about how to decide (decision-making of decision-making) and solving conflicts that arise from conflict resolution. Furthermore, there is the case of norming of norms and there is of course also the original reflexive mechanism through which law develops as an autonomous system which is linked to reflexive counterfactual stabilisation of normative expectation mentioned above (see in particular Luhmann 1985, p. 33, 2004, pp. 147–56).

However, the reflexivity of normative expectations of normative expectations is not limited to courts, the legal profession and other legal organisations. The reflexivity of normative expectations is 'equally maintained in the everyday life of non-members of legal organizations. So, for instance, someone whose rights have supposedly been violated will expect normatively that other will support his cause' (Luhmann 2004, p. 159).

Reflexivity is a concept widely used in assessments of modern society and is not restricted to social systems theory. One strand, in the tradition of action theory, is represented by Margaret Archer, who defines reflexivity as 'internal conversation' (Archer 2003) and 'first-person awareness' of the social environment (Archer 2007, 2010). Such human reflexivity is claimed to be a necessary condition of society, in fact an 'imperative in late modernity' (Archer 2012). However, her studies narrow reflexivity to analyses of the exercise of mental ability to consider oneself in relation to the social context and vice versa, focusing in particular on psychological activities and social habits of distancing or embedding (Archer 2007, p. 65). What is missing from this analysis is an application of reflexivity to social structures.

A prominent approach that analyses reflexivity at the structural level of society is the theory of reflexive modernisation (Beck et al. 1994; see also Beck 1992, 1999). Reflexivity is used by this approach to describe fundamental transformations in modern society. According to the theory of reflexive modernisation, modern society enters a second phase when it is not only becoming aware but increasingly occupied with solving problems it has created for itself. Reflexivity of this kind is linked to conscious strategies of reduction of complexity, which are also called 're-modernization' (Beck et al. 2003). However, their understanding of reflexion is limited and deviates from autopoietic social systems theory since it is equated with societal self-descriptions but not analysed as part of society's self-reproduction (Beck and Holzer 2004).

Within system theoretical accounts we can distinguish between internal and external reflexivity. Luhmann was mainly interested in reflexive processes inside systems. Gunther Teubner, with his concept of reflexive law, pays particular attention to external reflexivity in inter-systemic links. Such reflexivity can be called meta-reflexivity, or second-order reflexivity, since it turns attention to processes inside the system that result from external referencing in the form of reflexion of reflexion in other systems.

Teubner's concept of reflexive law is to a large extent a new theory of regulation. Reflexivity refers to law's capacity to reflect on its environment's expectations in relation to its regulatory capacities (Teubner 1984). The theory of reflexive law is not only an abstract account of modern law but has concrete implications for regulatory design. Its starting point is that in seeking to influence other autopoietic systems which are operationally closed to their environment, the legal system must have resort to indirect means of regulation. Legal intervention is dependent for its effects on self-regulation within the systems which are the target of legal initiatives. Thus, the law can only be successful in so far as it facilitates self-reflexion and self-regulation. This implies a shift from substantive to procedural law (Teubner 1983; see also Wiethölter 1986; Ladeur 1995).

However, it is important, in this regard, not to confuse legal forms with their regulatory functions. The form of a legal rule does not determine how the information it imparts will be received and acted on in another systemic context (as has been demonstrated in relation to efficiency of company law in the economic system, see Deakin and Carvalho 2010). Reflexive law as a theory is an interdisciplinary discipline, which combines analysis of internal legal processes with an understanding of law's context drawn from the social sciences. It demands to go beyond legal formalism and incorporate the sociological and economic study of law.

A good example of this kind of analysis is Teubner's well-known regulatory trilemma. He called it ironically a 'strategy for post-regulatory law' but it is in fact a sophisticated account of limits and potentials of legal regulation (Teubner 1988). Hugh Collins aptly describes it as follows: 'This trilemma states: that either the legal rules may fail to have an impact on social practice, or they may subvert the desirable social practices by making impractical demands, or the law may lose the coherence of its own analytical framework by seeking to incorporate sociological and economic perspective in its reasoning' (Collins 1999, pp. 68–9). Reflexive law suggests as a strategy to tackle the trilemma an engagement in second-order regulation, in particular focusing on regulation of self-regulation. This strategy is indeed very relevant for reflexive labour law, as will be discussed on a number of occasions in later chapters of the book. However, what is most important in Teubner's account is that any legal regulation of social practices depends on law's own self-regulation. Reflexive law means that law changes itself so that it becomes capable of actually facilitating self-regulation in other systems. The emphasis is on new procedural instruments that enable law to influence self-regulation indirectly.

The theory of reflexive law has encountered a number of criticisms. Niklas Luhmann observed a tension between the concepts of reflexive law as a new form of regulation and the limits that such an endeavour poses for legal autopoiesis (Luhmann 1992). He is in particular concerned that law might not be capable and is limited in understanding its own autopoietic character, let alone the autopoietic character of other social systems. Nevertheless, he also observes 'trends towards social engineering and the instrumentalization of law' and predicts that 'the response to this will be a profound change in the conception of law' (Luhmann 1988b, pp. 30–31, 32), which, if interpreted constructively, can be understood as an anticipation of reflexive law. However, Michal King is less optimistic in his reading of Luhmann and is worried instead that reflexive law, by adopting an instrumental view of law, undermines the potential of autopoietic system theory and supports in the end dedifferentiation of the legal system (King 2006).

> My problem ... is with those who attempt to co-opt autopoietic theory into this enterprise (of improving society through reflexive law, R.R.) in the

mistaken belief that they are doing society and the theory a huge favour, when in fact the opposite is the case. The only sure consequence of using the theory in this instrumental way is that the theory becomes diminished. . . . They are also helping the dedifferentiation of law (King 2006, p. 49).

Even less sympathetic critics interpret reflexive law in a political economy context and draw conclusions that this theory in fact supports deregulation (Maus 1986) and neoliberalism (Arthurs 2007a). Others are concerned about the usefulness of reflexive law for empirical research and doubt the novelty of reflexive law's understanding of regulation. Hubert Treiber, for example, has argued that self-regulation has a long history of being a concern of public regulators and that informality has always accompanied state regulation and has in fact been constitutive in public law's responses to regulatory problems (Treiber 1985). In a similar vein, Hubert Rottleuthner declared the regulatory crisis to be an invention of reflexive law that is not supported by empirical evidence. In fact, he criticises reflexive law, like Blankenburg, for not being interested in empirical testing of its hypotheses. The phenomena described by Teubner's regulatory trilemma can be understood without resort to autopoietic theory (Rottleuthner 1989).

However, these criticisms are largely misdirected. There are a number of empirical studies that testify that autopoietic legal theories of regulation are capable of generating empirical results. In the area of labour law research, two remarkable studies on health and safety regulations can be mentioned. Ton Wilthagen reported that self-regulation is vital for state regulation and that in order for government regulation and law enforcement to be successful in this area of law they must be based on a reflexive rationality (Wilthagen 1994). In his analysis of health and safety regulations from an autopoietic perspective John Paterson could show that these regulations emerge in interplay of diverse communicative systems that are riddled by constructive misunderstandings of regulatory and scientific signals (Paterson 2000).

In a later, insightful account of different strands of reflexive law, Paterson could show that at least five understandings of regulation are used in this theory that have direct implications for empirical research (Paterson 2006). These understandings range from only punctual intervention of law, to reconstructing non-legal self-reference in law, to interference of communicative legal and non-legal events (Teubner 1993a, pp. 88–95), to formal organisations of coupling of law and other systems (Paterson and Teubner 1998) and direct steering of programming in non-legal systems (Paterson 2006, pp. 25–30). However, probably the most important contribution of reflexive law's understanding of regulation is to emphasise the need for law to focus on regulation of self-regulation. In this respect reflexive law resonates with the theory of responsive regulation (Ayres and Braithwaite 1992) and has enriched both theoretical and empirical debates of regulation. It argues, however, that responsive law's 'enforced self-regulation' needs to be transcended and refined legal instruments are needed for law to be successful in influencing self-regulatory processes (see for further arguments the discussion of responsive regulation in Chapter 6).

Finally, in identifying reflexive rationality in legal regulation, Teubner's concept of reflexive law is combining an empirical and a normative perspective. This is well captured by William Scheuermann: 'Like substantive law, it is guided by the aim of subjecting social and economic activities to broader regulatory purposes. Yet it hopes to do so without dictating specific outcomes and thereby contributing to the rigidity and ineffectiveness of some existing forms of regulatory law' (Scheuermann 2001, p. 84). This can serve as motto for reflexive labour law as well.

2.3 GENERAL INTRODUCTION TO REFLEXIVE LABOUR LAW

In the following an attempt is made to apply the concept of reflexive law to labour law. The concept of reflexive labour law, first introduced two decades ago (Rogowski and Wilthagen 1994), claims to be a new labour law theory that matches the complexity of labour law in the modern society. Reflexive labour law describes a stage in the development of modern labour law when labour law realises its systemic limits with respect to regulation of other social systems. Furthermore, labour law detects at this reflexive stage a source of strength in its capacities for self-regulation.

The concept of functional differentiation can be used to explain the evolution of the modern legal system and the development of the field of labour law. Labour law is the product of differentiation within the legal system and is characterised by specific links with a particular social system, the industrial relations system. In fact it evolves in the beginning as a subsystem of a national legal system, largely in reaction to legal perceptions of the new, facilitative role that law needs to adopt in order to have an impact within industrial and employment relations.

Marc Amstutz (2001) has demonstrated how an evolutionary perspective informed by systems theory can be used to analyse the emergence of commercial law as a new field in law. Crucial in his analysis is the creation of 'sub models' within the legal system with which law observes changes in its environments and then uses them as 'means of self-modelling' (Ladeur

2012, p. 227). Applied to labour law, this view detects in the evolution of the legal system new forms of legal communication about the role of law in the industrial society. It entails a new self-understanding of law in which it accepts its supportive role for industrial relations and company constitutions. This 'self-modelling' leads to internal differentiation of the legal system and to the formation of the subfield or subsystem of labour law.

Such an evolutionary perspective is compatible with the theory of reflexive labour law which offers a new understanding of both the nature and the relation of law and industrial relations. In accordance with general social systems theory, industrial relations and law are conceived not as systems of action (or collective action) but instead as systems of (collective) communication. Self-reference of their system-specific communications forms the basis of self-reproduction or autopoiesis. On this basis both systems have developed structures that render autonomy to each system in society. It is the concern with the internal constitution of social systems rather than exchange relations with the social environment which is prevalent in the autopoietic and reflexive theory.

In conceptualising the social systems of 'industrial relations' and 'law' as operationally closed systems of communication (on social systems as systems of communication, see in particular Luhmann 1995a, ch. 4), it becomes possible to understand how different communication systems operate with different types of regulation. Furthermore, attention can be directed to the important relationship between modes of external regulation and processes of self-regulation. While labour law forms part of the legal system and is thus constituted by legal communication, collective agreements and collective bargaining belong to the self-regulatory structure of the industrial relations system and are foremost constituted by industrial relations communication.

The theory of reflexive labour law has been put to the test by Harry Arthurs in a study that looks at the phenomenon of corporate self-regulation (Arthurs 2007a). In applying the theory to the practice of corporate codes of conduct, the UN Global Compact and the related idea of 'ratcheting' labour standards, he arrives at the conclusion that 'reflexive labour law may be becoming more commonplace, that it may indeed emerge as the characteristic legal form of the future' (Arthurs 2007a, pp. 28–9). At the same time, applying political economy logic in analysing these developments, he argues that the rise of reflexive labour law goes hand in hand with neoliberal economic policy-making and with deregulation of labour law and welfare state regimes.

This criticism is misplaced (see also Deakin and Rogowski 2011). Reflexive law techniques can be found in a wide range of policy initiatives. Their use in fields such as labour law was initially stimulated by concerns that 'command and control' regulation of the sort associated with some of the regulatory initiatives of the immediate post-1945 decades had failed to achieve the instrumental goals set out for them. Critiques of the means used to implement the egalitarian and solidaristic aims of post-1945 welfare states were undoubtedly combined, in some cases, with critiques of those aims. However, the link is not inevitable. The concept of reflexive law has been used, in numerous contexts, as a way into a debate about improving the effectiveness of labour law interventions, and thereby of responding to the neoliberal critique of labour law. Conversely, by no means all or even most neoliberal policy initiatives use reflexive techniques; they just as often involve the use of traditional 'command and control' approaches to the use of law as an instrument of policy. They also make assumptions about the permeability of the legal system, and its openness to economic influence in the form of market pricing and similar effects, which run counter to reflexive law theory.

In her important overview on the transformation in law from regulation to governance, Orly Lobel demonstrates how law participates in confronting the new challenges posed by changes in the political economy and constructing innovative policies to produce socially responsible market practices (Lobel 2004). She identified three domains in labour law that serve as examples of areas in which new governance techniques dominate: vocational training, occupational health and safety and employment discrimination. These are indeed important areas where we find reflexive labour law emerging in national and international labour law regimes.

In the following an attempt is made to use the basic notions of reflexive law and apply them in a discussion of central aspects of modern labour law beyond the areas identified by Lobel. These include the challenge that self-regulation through collective agreements and employment contracts poses for labour law, reflexivity in labour conflict resolution, and deregulation of employment protection as reduction of complexity. All these topics will be discussed in further detail in separate chapters (Chapters 3, 6 and 7).

2.3.1 Regulation of Self-regulation in Industrial Relations

The regulation of industrial relations has been a main area of labour law since its beginnings. In fact the recognition of industrial relations within labour law has been a major reason for the development of labour law as a separate field of regulation. In order to establish proper legal responses to regulatory needs of the industrial relations system, it was necessary for law to realise the nature of the system of industrial relations. In Germany this was achieved with the help of legal academics such as Hugo Sinzheimer, who analysed the special nature of collective agreements as means of collective actors to regulate their own affairs. In Great Britain it was the legislator in response to unwilling courts in 1906 that acknowledged in the Trades Dispute Act of 1906 the special character and capacity of industrial relations as a system of self-regulation.

In both cases the legal system recognised that new legal instruments were needed that do justice to the autonomy of collective bargaining. What became the field of collective labour law was from the beginning confronted with the need to develop regulatory ways that support rather than undermine the self-regulatory mechanisms of industrial relations. In fact, labour law was engaged in regulating a new societal function system.

In Chapter 3 of this book I shall argue that industrial relations are a fully-fledged function system in modern society. Communications between collective industrial actors constitute the basic elements of the industrial relations system and its centre is the self-reproductive system of collective bargaining. Autopoietic industrial relations create specific institutional structures and procedures for the self-reference of collective communications in autonomous collective bargaining, the structures and procedures which establish a social sphere for new forms of collective communication and collective action. This social sphere and its autopoietic closure are the bases of the independence of the industrial relations system from the economic, the political and the legal systems.

In assessing the regulation of the industrial relations system by the legal system, it is important to analyse the mutual limitations imposed by their respective searches for autonomy. The legal system intervenes according to its legally shaped view of industrial relations, and the industrial relations system reacts towards the legal system according to its own perception of experiences with the legal system. Both systems are more or less exclusively guided by their internal models of the external world (Teubner 1989). Thus, successful regulation through interference of the systems depends largely on mutual internal acknowledgement of the needs of the regulating and the regulated system.

Furthermore, the type of legal regulation of industrial relations depends on the kind of perception of industrial relations in law. The legal system, being itself an autopoietic system, is limited in adopting non-legal worldviews. In general it only perceives industrial relations as a regulatory object. However, if labour law and its institutions manage to acknowledge the autopoietic nature of the industrial relations system, it can engage in reflexive regulation.

The reflexive law concept argues that the main problems of modern law derive from the limits of traditional forms of regulation that impose substantive standards on autopoietic social systems without reflecting their need for self-reproduction (Luhmann 1990b, 1997c). The role of law changes in the complex modern society from an authoritative instrument of control into a facilitative instrument of mutual recognition of self-regulation. This has led to a change of focus in legal thought from regulation to governance (Lobel 2004).

The main form of self-regulation in industrial relations is collective bargaining aiming at the conclusion of a collective agreement. Through collective bargaining the industrial relations system fulfils its societal function of providing channels for peaceful interactions between the collective parties. Collective agreements are means by which the industrial relations regulate both important aspects of economic and other social life and their own affairs (Sisson 1987).

Thus, collective agreements have two basic social functions, to paraphrase Otto Kahn-Freund. They are industrial peace treaties and they are sources for terms and conditions of employment, for the distribution of work and for the stability of jobs. Labour law realises this distinction by separating two parts of the collective agreement, the binding contract between the collective parties and the normative rule-making function of the collective agreement which renders it a code and source of rule-making (Kahn-Freund 1983, in particular ch. 6).

The legal regulation of collective bargaining has to be facilitative or auxiliary to be effective. However, this presupposes that labour law acknowledges the societal function of industrial relations. This can be done at different levels of the legal system, including constitutional recognition of autonomy of collective bargaining. Probably the best example where this was achieved is that of *Tarifautonomie* in Germany. It is indeed a prime example of regulated self-regulation (Bender 2006, 2012).

Labour law has the potential to be facilitative as well as destructive for collective bargaining. A good example of the latter's destructive potential was the use of labour law in Great Britain in the early 1970s and 1980s. By imposing legal standards that were not consented by the industrial parties, national, regional and sectoral collective bargaining was virtually annihilated (see Dickens 1994). Behind these labour law measures were not only policies hostile towards trade unions but radical neoclassical economic policies that question the need of an industrial relations system altogether.

However, in general, so-called collective labour law understands itself as supportive of industrial relations by providing a framework in which collective bargaining can smoothly take place. This is particularly true for regulatory bodies that deal with the legal aspects of industrial relations. Labour courts are important labour law institutions that realise the limits of their regulatory capacities by distinguishing types of conflict which are treated in a judicial forum and those which are left to system-specific fora which form part of the self-regulatory mechanisms of the collective bargaining or workplace industrial relations system. This distinction is used in treating employment conflicts which occur in ongoing employment relations in comparison with conflicts resulting from a broken employment relationship. Judicial fora are considered well equipped to handle conflicts after termination of the social relation, where the goal is to balance the interests of the parties to the conflict. The judicial forum provides mechanisms for the discussion of the dissolution of the relation independent of the complex web of personal and social aspects of the relationship. The judicial procedure requires a new form of cooperation to match the legal requirements (see Blankenburg et al. 1979; Blankenburg and Rogowski 1986).

A crucial step in becoming reflexive is the realisation within law that processes of self-regulation within other social systems are best facilitated by regulating itself. Modern legal systems distinguish between their conflict-resolution function and the regulation of other systems. From an autopoietic point of view, the legal system can remain in conflict resolution within its boundaries of self-regulation in applying legal devices (norms, procedures and legal doctrine), whereas the regulation of other social systems requires a sophisticated retranslation of societal needs into legal facilitation. Regulation of other social systems is different because there are no inherent internal guidelines for the legal system to inhibit potentially destructive use of regulations. The legal system has to rely on external sources to assess its impact.

The realisation of the limits of regulatory capacities within labour law can lead to dramatic effects, some of which might be desirable, others may not. When labour law realises that it is used selectively by social actors, this can have the positive outcome of differentiation of forms of regulation within labour law according to different fields of social regulation. In other words, labour law adapts to different ways of self-regulation. However, this can also lead to negative effects. The system of labour law might lose its capacity to influence self-regulation because it over-adapts and loses track of separate regulatory goals. Furthermore, the subfield of labour law might be undermined and lose its unity and identity.

2.3.2   Regulation of Employment Protection as Reflexion and Reduction of Complexity

The idea of regulation of self-regulation in labour law is not limited to the relation between law and industrial relations. It can also be applied to the regulation of employment contracts. However, the employment contract is a particular regulatory object. It is in general characterised by an imbalance in the distribution of power among the parties. Thus the function of labour law in this instance has to be to counterbalance one-sidedness by insisting on adherence to standards of fairness and non-discrimination (Collins 1992).

The history of the regulation of employment relations was for a long time dominated by the tension between a liberal conception of autonomous employment contracts and an industrial pluralist approach seeking a fairer distribution of wealth through collective bargaining. Both approaches share a commitment to legal abstention. As Hugh Collins has shown, the liberal as well as the industrial pluralist approach can at least in Europe no longer claim to dominate the agenda of employment law. Instead, social inclusion, competitiveness and citizenship have become overarching regulatory goals (Collins 2010).

Nevertheless, Hugh Collins (1999) also has convincingly argued that any legal regulation of contracts has to reckon with self-regulation. If contract law wants to be efficient, it has to understand itself as a mechanism of regulating self-regulation. Contract law becomes reflexive regulation when it tries to secure cooperation 'by conferring autonomy upon the parties to demise their own regulation' and 'to express their expectations of the relationship in their own language' (Collins 1999, p. 67). The compliance with standards that regulate contracts depends on granting autonomy to both parties and on facilitating trust rather than imposing sanctions.

This is similarly true for the regulation of the employment relationship. On the one hand, compliance with employment standards requires control and there is a role for inspections of workplaces. On the other hand, these controls cannot substitute the willingness of the employer and the employee to adhere to standards. Labour law can encourage employers to grant employees discretion to define and carry out tasks in exchange for a greater commitment on the side of the employees to obligations of loyalty and professionalism (Collins 1999, p. 22). Or it can create incentives for individual employees to enforce labour standards in the form of rights, for example by granting claims for equal pay. However, reflexive labour law goes a step further by recognising the problem of enforcing rights. For this problem to be addressed, a procedural approach is required that favours negotiations between the employer and the employee at the place of work (Collins 2010, pp. 29–30).

However, there is also the question of the role of labour law in solving disputes between employers and employees if negotiations fail. According to Luhmann, individuals – and this includes employees and employers as well as organisations – have 'the power to decide if law is to be invoked or not. Here lies what I want to call *invocation sovereignty*' (Luhmann 1982, p. 124, emphasis in original). Can reflexive law help in deciding which disputes can be handled by adjudication and which should be left to the market or politics?

Let's consider the famous case of polycentric conflicts, which was prominent in Lon Fuller's theory of adjudication. In disputes that arise within polycentric relationships, 'such that a change to any one relationship causes a series of complex changes to other factors' (King 2012, p. 190), adjudication and arbitration reach their limits (Fuller 1963, 1978–79). Deciding such polycentric disputes requires indeed a reflexive approach to adjudication and arbitration. Fuller argued that in adjudication, participation of the affected parties in the form of 'presenting proofs and reasoned opinions for a decision' is essential for 'the integrity of adjudication' (Fuller 1978–79, p. 364). Fuller's intuition that, if mechanisms of self-regulation exist, these are probably better suited to find solutions than a court seems in general the right approach from a reflexive law perspective. However, reflexive law would add that it requires courts to be able to understand and assess these self-regulatory mechanisms, for example markets, in order to make a decision to abstain. For solving polycentric conflicts within the context of collective bargaining, Fuller proposed mediation as an alternative to arbitration. Mediation only requires a proposal from the third person that assists the negotiations between the parties. Mediation requires the parties to come to an agreement, thus taking responsibility for regulating their affairs.

The regulation of labour conflict resolution is commonly classified as procedural labour law, which comprises a separate body of norms regulating labour court procedure and procedural arrangements of arbitration. However, for reflexive labour law this distinction of procedural and substantive labour law remains rather arbitrary. It disguises the use of procedure within substantive labour law, which is of utmost importance for an account of reflexive tendencies in the labour law development.

Labour law understands procedure by definition as a legal concept both for self-regulation of its own procedures and for the regulation of industrial relations and employment relations. Legal procedures can be described in sociological terms as episodes in which the procedure itself controls its beginning and end. Judicial procedures are distinct from other procedures because they operate throughout the procedure with a high degree of uncertainty about the outcome. A main function of the regulation and organisational design of legal procedures is to motivate the parties to become active participants who lose through their involvement grounds for criticism of the outcome. A legal procedure thus absorbs protest (Luhmann 1969). However, these features often make legal procedures attractive for other social systems that resist substantive regulation but still rely on law as a regulator of procedure. The specific devices of legal procedures for the treatment of conflicts are viewed as more successful in solving conflicts in comparison with system-specific alternatives.

The use of legal procedure in the regulation of other social systems has been interpreted as a form of juridification. Gunther Teubner and Hellmuth Willke (1984) have argued in this context that juridification is in fact a general trend towards proceduralisation, in accordance with the general decline of instrumental law and the disillusion with legal formalisation and materialisation. Proceduralisation has penetrated not only the judicial practice but also the rationality structure of law and has influenced the development of legal doctrine (see Teubner 1983; see also Wiethölter 1986; Eder 1986; and on juridification of labour law, see Simitis 1987).

This has also been observed in relation to employment law. 'Through its historical reliance upon procedural regulation, and in particular, the promotion of collective bargaining as an instrument of self-regulation, employment law has evolved a distinctive character' (Collins 2010, p. 31). However, in modern employment law other forms of self-regulation are as important as collective bargaining. These include for example the involvement of works councils and employee representatives in codetermination schemes as well as health and safety committees that perform important roles in the reflexion processes in which the company detects its public interest in itself (Teubner 1994).

A perennial problem of all social systems in modern societies is internal complexity. Not only do the structures of the system have a tendency to grow but also the amount of system-specific communications that are available for self-referential or other cyclical relations. In the case of the legal system, its structural components of legal norms, procedural rules and legal doctrine as well as case law tend to develop in different directions, leading to differentiation of decision-making programmes (Luhmann 1985a, ch. 4). In addition there is differentiation of the legal system into autonomous subsystems of law such as labour law.

The legal field of labour law is confronted with the same problems of legal complexity as the legal system on the whole. There is an increase in statutory and other norms to protect employees, improved access to judicial and other procedures to find redress for rights violations, and a growing labour law doctrine that supports but also complicates decision-making.

The increase of internal legal complexity is usually accompanied by an increase in legal regulation. Thus, legal complexity is not just a problem for the legal system but also encountered by those other social systems that are regulated by labour law. These problems have led to the allegation that legal regulation leads to juridification of social regulations.

Internal as well as external complexities constitute unavoidable problems for the modern legal system that nevertheless require adequate responses. If one looks at policies that deal with the complexity of labour law, a prominent strategy is deregulation of labour law and in particular of employment protection. However, deregulation policies are motivated by different programmes or ideologies. A conservative programme of deregulating labour law, for example, is usually exclusively concerned with the economic effects of legal rules. It concentrates on 'unburdening business' and the 'needs' of companies. This version of deregulation rests on the neoclassical economic assumption that removing law and lowering levels of employment protection will automatically improve the performance of companies and have a positive impact on the labour market.

A more balanced approach pursues not only economic but also wider social goals in designing deregulation strategies. In many cases these socioeconomic goals are directly linked to labour market policies that try to reduce unemployment. Social deregulation operates with a more balanced view of industrial and employment relations. It takes both sides into account and tries to strike a balance between employer demands of reduced levels of protection and the employees' interests to find and keep a secure job (see Chapter 6 of this book).

There are also cultural aspects underlying some deregulation policies. These relate to changes in general attitudes towards work and commitment, demographic developments and increased female interest in gainful employment. The accompanying type of deregulation tends to focus on flexibility in relation to the forms of employment and reduces barriers and obstacles that limit the use of so-called atypical employment. An increase in female participation rates in the labour market requires liberalising and indeed endorsing part-time work by removing legal and other (for example social security) obstacles.

Finally, deregulation can be motivated directly by legal complexity. This deregulation strategy can be called reflexive deregulation insofar as it is in fact self-regulation of the legal system. Reflexive deregulation balances law's internal requirement for reduction of complexity with wider goals of deregulation in relation to its social environment.

It has to be emphasised that each form of deregulation is more or less a response to legal complexity and is thus engaged in reduction of complexity. Furthermore, in the vast majority of deregulation efforts, they are accompanied by re-regulation measures. In fact, in a reflexive law perspective, deregulation is a predictable event that is almost necessarily leading to new regulation. In any event, deregulation is itself a particular form of regulation.

2.3.3 Reflexive Labour Law, Societal Constitutionalisation and Global Labour Law

Modern labour law is undoubtedly under strain, both as a result of internal developments and external pressures. The theory of reflexive labour law claims that it is able to name the main reasons that explain this situation. Furthermore, by viewing labour law as both reproducing itself and operating within the larger society, propositions can be made about conditions for future developments.

Ruth Dukes has recently reminded us that the debate on constitutionalisation of labour law that took place at the beginning of the twentieth century is still on the agenda (Dukes 2008). This debate dates back to the beginning of forming labour law as a separate field of regulation and was originally linked to Hugo Sinzheimer's proposal of an economic constitution that picked up Beatrice and Sidney Webb's idea of an industrial constitution guaranteeing industrial democracy (Webb 1897). The idea of an economic and industrial constitution being part of the political constitution in the wider sense became reality in the Weimar Republic in the form of a company constitution in which works councils gained rights of participation in company decision-making. In Dukes' view, constitutionalisation of employment relations should nowadays be considered as providing the framework for the debate over combining flexibility and security concerns in reforming labour law, in particular by forcing the regulator to think about collective bargaining as a preferable way of finding flexible solutions that accommodates diverging interests. This view resonates with reflexive labour law's idea of recognition of regulation of self-regulation as key in achieving the regulatory goals of employment protection.

In his reply to Dukes, Harry Arthurs has commented that the notion of constitutionalisation in labour law is no longer synonymous with recognition of labour rights because the global context has fundamentally changed the conditions for constitutionalisation of the workplace (Arthurs 2009, 2010). Arthurs emphasises what he calls the new political-economy context and argues that national economic constitutions are increasingly undermined by globalisation effects arising from the worldwide drive towards neoliberal economic policy-making and the changing workplaces in transnational corporations. Constitutionalisation at the global level transcends a rights-based model of the constitution (see similar arguments raised by Arthurs in relation to comparative labour law in Arthurs 2007b and reflexive labour law in Arthurs 2007a).

It is indeed correct that the discussion of a constitutional frame for any national or international regulator must take a different form in the global age. The globalisation of modern society makes it increasingly difficult for all function systems, including law, to confine their operations within national boundaries controlled by national constitutions. In some function systems national boundaries are virtually obsolete due to globalisation. In the economy or the science system it makes no sense, outside narrow political debates, to talk of a national economy or a national science. As Luhmann has reminded us, modern society is a world society in which normative attitudes are gradually replaced by cognitive orientations (Luhmann 1982; see also Stichweh 1995). And it is this world society dimension with which the reflexive and autopoietic law concept fundamentally challenges traditional legal and industrial relations analyses. Reflexive labour law claims that nowadays modern labour law and industrial relations are challenged and have to cope with problems arising from the world society (see also Chapter 10 and Rogowski 1998, 2000a).

Particular problems are posed in this context by the emerging global labour law. This area of law consists of a heterogeneous set of legal orders which includes international labour standards adopted by international organisations as well as supranational social and employment policy measures adopted by the European Union and other regional bodies (Bercusson 1997; Sciarra 1998). In addition there are social and economic rights (Hepple 2006) and codes of conduct issued by multinational companies and other private law mechanisms regulating labour in the wake of globalisation (Bercusson and Estlund 2007). Global law is no longer dominated by public law regulations and we witness a reflexive turn to new governance mechanisms. As Antonio Cassese and his collaborators have recently argued, this reflexive turn has also reached traditional international law where the promotion of monitoring, supervision and fact-finding missions are increasingly becoming alternatives to judicial review and in fact constitute the future of international law (Cassese 2012).

This reflexive turn can also be detected in developments within international labour law. As will be demonstrated in Chapter 10, the ILO embarked on a campaign of redefining labour rights as human rights in order to strengthen its arsenal of strategies for implementation of labour standards. This can partly be explained as a learning process instigated by enforcement problems. By refocusing on a specific set of labour rights, the ILO followed a general trend of upgrading human rights in international law and became able to coordinate its efforts with other international organisations.

However, this reflexive strategy of defining labour rights as fundamental rights has its limits, which has been a topic of discussion among labour law scholars for a while. A legal strategy that relies on labour rights as human rights encounters problems of justifiability and of not reaching those that are in particular need of protection by a fundamental right. Already more than three decades ago, Bob Hepple raised a typical reflexive law argument in his scepticism about the legal enforceability of the global right to work. In his view such a right does not benefit 'those in low-paid discontinuous employment' who are not supported by strong collective organisations because the welfare state cannot guarantee participation in productive employment but only participation in social security and that 'would in practice be only a right to social assistance. The label of a "right to work" would encourage a false consciousness among workers' (Hepple 1981, p. 81). Guy Mundlak, in commenting on Article 6 (right to work) of the Covenant on Economic, Social and Cultural Rights, comes to the conclusion that it is in fact a right to be exploited and only benefits wage-earners and no other types of work (Mundlak 2007).

A fundamental right such as the right to work and the ILO's core labour rights can also be assessed in a different context and this is the trend in global law which Gunther Teubner calls societal constitutionalisation. The strategy of defining labour rights as human rights has a positive effect on global labour law as an autonomous regime. As will be shown in Chapter 10, identifying fundamental rights can be interpreted as a reflexive trend that is constitutive for the establishment of the regime of global labour law.

Gunther Teubner has argued that the emergence of a multiplicity of legal regimes at the world level is a sign of fragmentation of world law as a legal system. This view is widely shared among international lawyers (see only Koskenniemi 2007). However, the fragmentation itself requires interpretation. It is in Teubner's view an internal response of law to societal differentiation.

> For centuries law had followed the political logic of nation-states and was manifest in the multitude of national legal orders, each with their own territorial jurisdiction. Even international law, which viewed itself as the contract law of Nation-States, did not depart from this model. The final break with such conceptions was only signalled in the last century with the rapidly accelerating expansion of international organizations and regulatory regimes, which, in sharp contrast to their genesis within international treaties, established themselves as autonomous legal orders. The national differentiation of law is now overlain by sectoral fragmentation. In contrast to the constantly reiterated claims, the appearance of global regimes does not entail the integration, harmonization or, at the very least, the convergence of legal orders; rather, it transforms the internal differentiation of law. Societal fragmentation impacts upon law in a manner such that the political regulation of differentiated societal spheres requires the parcelling out of issue-specific policy-arenas, which, for their part, juridify themselves (Fischer-Lescano and Teubner 2004, pp. 1008–9).

The thesis thus is that societal differentiation leads to legal differentiation in the form of a multiplicity of new legal regimes. In applying this interpretation to labour law, the field of global labour law can be understood as a regime that is a product of 'co-evolutionary internal differentiation' of world law. Global labour law is one of the many legal regimes that emerge at the global level. Furthermore, the fragmented global legal order encounters conflicts between legal orders. In fact, Teubner argues that these so-called regime collisions intensify (Teubner 2012, ch. 6; Fischer-Lescano and Teubner 2004). However, it should be added that new problems also lead to new solutions and that, in the regime of global labour law at least, forms of cooperation with other global regimes develop alongside conflictual relations between regimes.

The juridification Teubner talks about takes the form of constitutionalisation when the regimes develop Hartian secondary norms in the form of fundamental principles and regulatory norms of decision-making. For this to happen, Teubner has proposed the concept of double reflexivity. Constitutionalisation does not happen at the level of function systems but at 'social process "beneath" the function systems, at formal organizations and at contractual arrangements' (Teubner 2012, pp. 54–5).

We can now ask what constitutionalisation means in the context of labour law. What Teubner actually has in mind is corporate constitutionalisation. For global labour law these are corporate social responsibility and, in relation to processes of constitutionalisation, codes of conduct of multinational companies. These transnational corporate constitutions are constituted through double reflexivity of secondary legal norms and reflexive social structures (Teubner 2010a, 2011b).

Teubner's concept of societal constitutionalisation through corporate constitutions is not without criticism. A number of concerns have been raised about the appropriateness of the constitutional framework in the global context. Nico Krisch, for example, criticises in Teubner's account that it lacks a critical normative dimension and in fact 'surrenders to the forces to be' (Krisch 2010, p. 77).

Other critics miss in Teubner's concept of societal constitutionalisation the national level (for example Ladeur 2012). In his account of global labour law and its impact, Harry Arthurs voices scepticism about '*lex laboris*' that for him 'does not exist in any functional sense'. However, this does not mean for Arthurs that globalisation of labour law has no impact. In the end he adopts an interpretation which is quite compatible with a reflexive labour law understanding of global labour law. Global labour is for him 'formative, not normative. It changes labour law not by directly amending the substantive rules but by transforming the institutions, structures and processes through which those rules are made and administered' (Arthurs 2006, p. 56). And this includes constitutionalisation at national level.

It is indeed right and an important insight that societal constitutionalisation is not confined or exclusive to global law. In David Sciulli's view, the protection and guarantee of self-regulation of professions, which he calls collegial formations, is the key task of a societal constitution, in particular at the national level (Sciulli 1992). In the early discussion of constitutionalisation of labour law, instigated by Sinzheimer and his students, the constitutional context of labour law, i.e. Sinzheimer's economic constitution, was seen necessary for the development of labour law. However, it is important to add that we now have to understand globalisation of labour law as the driving force of its development and that constitutionalisation lies at the centre of the evolution of global labour law as a legal regime within world law.

3. Industrial relations as a social system

The chapter proposes to adopt a new view of industrial relations as a fully-fledged autopoietic function system operating within the world society. The recognition of industrial relations within labour law has been a major reason for the development of labour law as a separate field of regulation. In Germany, Hugo Sinzheimer's theory of the collective bargaining agreement (*korporativer Arbeitsnormenvertrag*), which he developed in the first decade of the twentieth century, is widely seen as the start of labour law as an academic discipline (Sinzheimer 1977 [1907]). At the same time the British Trades Dispute Act of 1906 was the official recognition of industrial relations as a system of collective laissez-faire and self-regulation. However, it took until the second half of the twentieth century for the academic discipline of labour law to emerge in the United Kingdom, mainly due to Otto Kahn-Freund's efforts, in particular his analysis of collective bargaining and the double nature of collective agreements as codes and contracts which captured well the voluntarist nature of British industrial relations (Kahn-Freund 1983, ch. 6).

Although modern labour law has expanded widely and is nowadays an important means of regulation of individual employment relationships, collective labour law and regulation of industrial relations is still a main focus. It is thus important for reflexive labour law to have an understanding of industrial relations that adequately reflects its role in modern society. In the following a new theory of industrial relations is introduced based on the theory of autopoietic social systems.

Systems theory can claim to have been one of the most influential approaches in both national and comparative accounts of industrial relations since the 1950s (Müller-Jentsch 2004; Bean 1994, pp. 2–3). In particular John Dunlop's *Industrial Relations Systems*, first published in

---

[1] The 1958 edition of *Industrial Relations Systems* was reprinted several times and then republished in 1993 by the Harvard Business School. The 1993 edition contains a new preface and a commentary on industrial relations as an academic discipline, comparing it with labour economics and human resource management. However, there are hardly any alterations to the main text.

1958,[1] has had a lasting impact on national and international industrial relations research (Meltz 1991; see also Schienstock 1982, pp. 32–59; Hyman 1989, ch. 5; Kaufman 2004, pp. 250–5). His approach was based on the then fashionable sociological theory of social systems of Talcott Parsons. However, since the 1950s general systems theory and social systems theory have developed and matured and encountered recently a major paradigm shift in which the structural-functionalist view is being replaced by an autopoietic understanding of social systems. In the following I shall use Dunlop's systems theory approach as the background against which an alternative approach to the system theoretical conceptualisation of industrial relations, based on Niklas Luhmann's work on autopoietic social systems, will be developed.

3.1   A CRITIQUE OF DUNLOP'S SYSTEMS THEORY OF INDUSTRIAL RELATIONS

Dunlop justifies his usage of systems theory with several direct references to Parsons' theory of social systems. He considers systems theory in general, and Parsons' analysis of the economic system as social system in particular, to be 'suggestive for organising insights and observations about the industrial-relations aspects of behavior in industrial society' (Dunlop 1993 [1958], p. 5). For Dunlop, systems theory advances beyond previous approaches in industrial relations research, which he disqualifies as 'classifications in the spectrum of labor peace and warfare'. He expects from an application of Parsons' systems theory that it can 'provide *analytical* meaning to the idea of an industrial relations system' (Dunlop 1993 [1958], p. 3, emphasis in the original).

Parsons' theory of society includes both an analysis of the structure of society and a theory of social evolution. The theory of evolution is based on a concept of societal modernisation, which is characterised as a process of functional differentiation of the social system into subsystems. The social system differentiates subsystems that are specialised to fulfil functions for the system at large. Social systems also create integrative mechanisms, which link the functionally differentiated sub-systems. Primitive societies are characterised according to Parsons by a low degree of differentiation into social subsystems, whereas modern societies are characterised by structural differentiation of the economic, the political, and finally the cultural system, respectively achieved by the Industrial Revolution, the Democratic Revolution, and the Educational Revolution (Parsons 1966 on the theory of the three revolutions separating early from late modernisation).

Dunlop's starting point is to call the industrial relations system 'an analytical subsystem of an industrial society on the same logical plane as an economic system' (Dunlop 1993 [1958], p. 5). This, however, deviates from a Parsonian view in which the economic system is one 'functional' subsystem of the overarching social system when it is decomposed according to the four functional imperatives (see below). For Parsons, the industrial relations system can only be a subsystem of a subsystem, most likely a subsystem of the economy. Thus, the industrial relations system cannot be on the 'same logical plane' as the economic system.

In line with Parsons' theory of social evolution, Dunlop's theory of industrial relations focuses on differentiation and modernisation processes both in society and in industrial relations. Dunlop calls industrial societies 'modern' when relations of managers and workers are formally arranged outside the family, when these relations are distinct from political institutions, and when the industrial relations system has an existence separate from the economic system.

Dunlop is inspired by Parsons' theory after its complete systems-theoretical turn, as outlined in Parsons' and Smelser's 'Economy and Society' of 1956.[2] Social action is conceived after this turn as the result of a combination of structural forces of the social system.[3] These forces derive from four 'pattern variables' which describe functional

---

[2] Parsons' theory developed in three phases: from the study of the structure of social action as voluntaristic, non-deterministic action (Parsons 1937) to an analysis of the structure of social interaction as the basis of society as a social system (Parsons 1951) and then into a theory of so-called pattern variables and generalised media of communication that create the structures of the social system (Parsons and Smelser 1956; and most of the 'late work' of Parsons). Initially, Parsons' analysis of the structure of society was characterised by a tension between action theory and systems theory, a tension which was resolved after the publication of *The Social System* (Parsons 1951), and in particular after *Economy and Society* (Parsons and Smelser 1956), in favour of systems theory. The emphasis shifted from developing a systems theory based on conditions of social interaction to constructing social systems according to functional imperatives derived from a general scheme of pattern variables.

[3] An insightful and informative discussion of Parsons' 'systems-theoretical turn' can be found in Jürgen Habermas's *Lifeworld and System*, Vol. 2 of *The Theory of Communicative Action* (Habermas 1987). Habermas criticises Parsons for his deficit in 'action theory', which Habermas alleges to result in neglecting the analysis of the lifeworld context of social systems. However, Habermas's criticism is ultimately driven by the normative concern to 'defend the subject' in the analysis of society. Thus, despite his integrative theory-building, it is in fact Habermas who limits the theorising of society and excludes theories that are not centred on subjects and their 'communicative actions'.

imperatives: adaptation, goal-attainment, integration and latent-pattern maintenance.

These pattern variables, known as the AGIL scheme, represent not only the conditions for social action but also describe both the functions of the main social subsystems and the functions of the surrounding systems. Thus, the four main social subsystems of society are each characterised by one of the four functions: the economy by adaptation, the polity by goal-attainment, law and other mechanisms of social control by integration and 'the locus of cultural and motivational commitments', for example, family and cultural institutions, by latent-pattern maintenance (Parsons and Smelser 1956, pp. 46–53). Furthermore, the surrounding systems are also characterised by these functions. Whereas the social system is characterised by integration, the cultural system is characterised by latency, the personality system by goal-attainment, and the behavioural organism by adaptation.

In a 'note' added to his outline of basic features of an industrial relations system,[4] Dunlop offers the following application of Parsons' differentiation concept and his four functional imperatives to the study of industrial relations. A quotation from this note demonstrates Dunlop's use of systems theory. In addition, it introduces the main components of Dunlop's own conception of an industrial relations system:

> The functional differentiation of an industrial relations system and the corresponding specialised structures or processes may be defined as follows: (1) Adaptive – The regulatory processes or rule-making in which the specialised output is a complex of rules relating the actors to the technological and market environment and the frequent changes which pose problems of adaptation to the actors. (2) Goal Gratification – The polity or political functions in the subsystem are specialised toward the contribution of survival or stability of the industrial relations system and to survival and stability of the hierarchies of the separate actors which is requisite for the attainment of goals by the actors. (3) Integration – The function of maintaining solidarity among the actors in the system is contributed by the shared understandings and common ideology of the system relating individual roles to the hierarchies and hierarchies to each other in turn. (4) Latent-pattern Maintenance and Tension Management – The function of preserving the values of the system against cultural and motivational pressures is provided by the role of the expert or professional in all three groups of actors in the system (Dunlop 1958, p. 30).

Dunlop uses Parsons' 'pattern variables' as a classification scheme for the presentation of system components ('rules', 'hierarchies', 'ideologies' and 'experts') which he considers relevant to his comparison of national

---

[4]   In the 1993 edition of *Industrial Relations Systems* the 'note' was omitted.

industrial relations systems. However, Dunlop subscribes only formally to Parsons' ideas. In fact, he does little more than presenting his own understanding of industrial relations in the Parsonian language of the AGIL scheme. Neither in the theoretical outline nor in the comparative study do Parsons' insights in the four functional imperatives guide Dunlop's conception of an industrial relations system.

Dunlop's own theory is based on four 'elements' which appear in various constellations in the above quotation: actors, contexts, ideologies and rules. The separate existence or 'autonomy' of industrial relations systems is shaped by these four 'elements'. Dunlop discusses them separately in his theoretical outline, in which he characterises the 'elements' as follows: the three main *actors* are management, workers and government agencies; *contexts* consist of technology, market constraints and the power distribution in society; and the *ideologies* of the actors must resume around a common set of ideas that guides the allocation of acceptable roles to the actors. The last, and most crucial, 'element' in Dunlop's theory of autonomous industrial relations is the concept of *rules* governing the relations of industrial actors. This body of rules, which includes rules on procedures for the establishment and administration of substantive rules, constitutes 'the center of attention in an industrial-relations system' (Dunlop 1993 [1958], p. 13). In Dunlop's view, the specific character of industrial relations systems derives from rule-making independent of decision-making in the economic system.

Dunlop's 'elements' have been widely discussed in industrial relations theory. Shalev, for example, criticises Dunlop for a meaningless use of the ideological factor: '. . . his materialistic theoretical bias, explicitly seeking in "technological and market forces" rather than "political and ideological considerations" the key to national diversity in industrial relations, precluded meaningful utilisation of ideology as an important variable' (Shalev 1981, p. 251). The element 'contexts' has been criticised for lacking any justification for selecting only the three factors of technology, markets and power. Other authors argue that the element 'actors' needs further differentiation. Employees should be divided into organised and non-organised employees and employers into employer associations and single members (for references see Schienstock 1982, pp. 40–46). However, these authors misunderstand Dunlop's abstract notion of the tripartite structure of actors. As part of the tripartite relationship, each actor is conceived in Dunlop's model as a complex and hierarchically ordered entity whereby their respective hierarchies influence – and are influenced by – rule-making and the substance of the rules of the industrial relations system (see also Schienstock 1982, p. 40).

In general, Dunlop's elements must be criticised for a lack of theoretical deduction. There is no definition of 'element' in his theory, and it is probably impossible to find a unifying characteristic of those heterogene-ous factors which Dunlop calls elements. In this respect, Dunlop reveals a lack of rigour in his theoretical model.

Dunlop uses various, not always coherent, approaches to discuss or to classify rules and procedures. His main scheme of rules reflects his distinc-tion of 'elements' and operates with five 'ideal types' of industrial relations rules and procedures, all linked to the three 'actors' and their relation-ships (Dunlop 1993 [1958], pp. 13–16, 34–58, 76–7, 92–3, 127, 342–79). Rules and procedures are determined for Dunlop by: (a) managerial hierarchy; (b) specialised governmental agencies; (c) worker hierarchy; (d) joint management and worker hierarchy; and (e) tripartite rule-making of management, workers and state agencies. In addition, he sometimes uses distinctions which are close to legal classifications when he separates administrative regulations, collective agreements and customs and tradi-tions in the workplace. In a more descriptive fashion he also distinguishes between compensation rules, disciplinary rules and job aspiration rules.

Dunlop's analysis of rules and rule-making can be criticised on a number of points (see also Kaufman 2004, pp. 253-4). In trying to advance beyond descriptions in his analysis of rules, he merely mentions different sources of rule-making. He does not, however, discriminate between those sources that are internal and those that are external to the industrial rela-tions system. Dunlop can be criticised in general for economic reduction-ism, which is expressed in a tendency to over-generalise that 'economic development' is ultimately responsible for rules and rule-making: 'indus-trialization proliferates rules' (Dunlop 1993 [1958], p. 343).

My main criticism is related to Dunlop's lack of analysis of the actual process of rule-making. Although it is emphasised throughout his study that rule-making creates the centre of the theory of industrial relations, he is ultimately unable to analyse within the limits of his methodology how these rules are created by the system. Schienstock rightly criticises Dunlop for neglecting decision-making processes and for conceiving actors only as structural entities (Schienstock 1982, pp. 40–46, 55–9). Dunlop makes no effort to study the actual processes that generate the stable 'grid of rules' at the various levels of national industrial relations systems.

It is both astonishing and revealing that Dunlop's theory of industrial relations systematically neglects not only the contribution of collective bargaining and grievance procedures to rule-making but the analysis of collective bargaining as such (see also Meltz 1991, pp. 13–14).[5] There is

---

[5]   In later studies Dunlop showed some interest in the analysis of negotiations and collective dispute-resolution mechanisms. See Dunlop 1984.

no separate analysis of the process and structure of collective bargaining and arbitration procedures in his analytical study of industrial relations systems. Grievance procedures are only briefly discussed at a late stage of the analysis, where they are conceived solely as mechanisms for the settlement of disputes but not as mechanisms in generating rules (Dunlop 1993 [1958], p. 367).

Furthermore, his approach to procedures is half-hearted. Procedures are not important as an independent object of Dunlop's theoretical and comparative study but only insofar as 'procedures are themselves rules' (Dunlop 1993 [1958], p. 13). Dunlop is preoccupied with the substantive content of rules, which supposedly reveals a higher degree of uniformity than procedural rules. Unfortunately, he makes no use of his observation that institutional rule application or procedures 'particularly well reflect the characteristics of a national industrial relations system' (Dunlop 1993 [1958], p. 367). The general assumption that 'a diversity of procedures may still result in similar substantive rules' (Dunlop 1993 [1958], p. 26) is not backed up with any concrete study of procedures in his comparison.

The theoretical and practical limits of Dunlop's systems-theoretical endeavour to analyse the industrial relations system can be further demonstrated with respect to his analysis of the unity of the industrial relations system. In the last section of his theoretical 'note', Dunlop tries to show how differentiation within the AGIL pattern of Parsons' functional imperatives contributes to establishing the 'unity' of an industrial relations system:

> It can be seen how each of these functional differentiations contribute to each other and to the unity of an industrial-relations system. (A-G) The rule making contributes to the attainment of stability and survival, and stability in turn requires a grid of rules. (A-L) The technical problems involved in rule-making contribute to enhance the role of the professional or expert, and his role in turn produces a reduction of tension (a literal drawing of the 'heat') among the actors and is the repository and defender of the values of the system. (G-I) The attainment of stability and survival requires shared understandings relating the actors to each other, and an effective integration contributes to the achievement of stability and survival. (L-I) The reduction in tensions and the preservation of values contributed by the professionals is a force for integration, and the shared understandings contribute toward enhancing and maintaining the role of the professional or expert. The functional differentiations of the system reinforce each other and unify the industrial-relations system (Dunlop 1958, pp. 30–31).

Dunlop, like Parsons, discusses the problem of unity as a problem of structure. Unity is conceived in this forced application of the four pattern variables as a product of rather static links among the system components which are supposed to reinforce each other and thus to contribute to system maintenance ('stability', 'survival', 'integration'). However, achieving unity does not seem to be a problem for the system. The links among the system components miraculously unify the system.

In fact, unity in this discussion is merely the construct of an external observer. It is not analysed as a vital concern for the industrial relations system itself. Dunlop's analysis conveys the impression that the problems of the system derive from external rather than internal sources. It is beyond Dunlop's sociological imagination that threats to the unity and, indeed, to the existence of the industrial relations system itself could derive from the internal processes and links among the system components.

Dunlop conceptualises the industrial relations system both as a subsystem of society at the national level, as a system of industry-wide collective bargaining, and as a system of work relations in a single enterprise. Although this seems to correspond with common understanding in industrial relations research, it is unclear how this is related to his systems theory approach. Dunlop pays little attention to the relation of these three levels of the industrial relations system. He can therefore be criticised for having acknowledged the scope and the different levels of the industrial relations system only with respect to its external relations but not with respect to the internal structure and processes of the industrial relations system.

Dunlop's approach is an input–output analysis, which places high emphasis on contextual factors that influence the structure of the system. Dunlop shows in detail how the content or substance of rules reflects the various contexts of the industrial relations system. The contextual influence varies inversely with the structural complexity of the industrial relations system: 'The smaller the unit to which the term [industrial relations system, R.R.] is applied, the larger the context, and in general the larger the influence of givens outside the system' (Dunlop 1993 [1958], p. 24). The idea is that workplace rules in a single enterprise are more influenced by technical and market constraints or the distribution of power in society than rules that apply to an industry or a national industrial relations system. The question remains, however, of what constitutes the 'core' of an industrial relations system which is not determined by external forces and which integrates both large and small units.

In summary it can be stated that Dunlop's systems theory remains at a classificatory level. This is probably related to the lack of understanding of the theory of structural functionalism, which he himself admitted.[6]

---

[6] Dunlop thought of his own application of Parsons' system theory that it 'may not be acceptable to Professor Parsons, and it may reflect a lack of understanding of his theoretical system' (Dunlop 1958, p. 30, footnote 30).

Indeed, his systems-theoretical understanding has hardly exhausted the potential of Parsons' systems theory to conceptualise industrial relations systems (see also Wood et al. 1975; Singh 1976). Nevertheless, his classificatory approach, which enabled him to present information on foreign industrial relations systems that otherwise might have been suppressed by adopting a strict deductive approach, should probably also be considered a phenomenological virtue without, however, reducing the criticism on his conceptual weaknesses.

Thus, it seems hardly acceptable that central areas of industrial relations such as collective bargaining, arbitration, grievance-handling, negotiations between worker representatives and management, and political exchanges at national level are either neglected or poorly treated in the study. Although rule-making in industrial relations is central in Dunlop's discussion, his study reveals a lack of interest in considering the real processes of the creation and application of rules through procedures.

It seems due to Dunlop's rather mechanical understanding of systems theory, which tends to conceptualise industrial relations as a trivial machine, that he underestimates problems related to the internal complexity of the system. More than 40 years after the publication of his study, the reader is astonished at the lack of sensitivity to the threats to the system which derive from internal processes. Internal complexity creates problems both for the structure and for the elements of the system. The need to reduce internal complexity is an important reason, for example, for the formalisation of interactions between collective actors or between individual and collective actors. However, only recently have we begun to analyse these interactions as communication processes in which the system reproduces itself.

The theory of social systems has evolved from a closed systems approach into an open systems approach and then into a theory of operationally closed but cognitively open systems. Dunlop applied the open systems paradigm to the study of industrial relations. In taking seriously the 'paradigm shift' in social systems theory, which replaces the focus on structures and functions of social systems with analyses of internal communication processes that are constitutive for the self-reproduction or autopoiesis of the system, we can advance beyond the Dunlopian approach to industrial relations.

3.2   THE SOCIAL SYSTEM OF INDUSTRIAL RELATIONS

The author who stands for the paradigm shift to autopoiesis in social systems theory is Niklas Luhmann. Before a concept of industrial relations based on Luhmann's approach is proposed, I shall briefly indicate basic features of autopoietic social systems theory that I see to be relevant for a discussion of autopoietic industrial relations. In particular, five types of social systems, which can be derived from Luhmann's approach, are discussed as possible candidates to characterise the industrial relations system as a social system. At the end of the chapter, a proposal to define industrial relations as a fully-fledged autopoietic function system operating in the world society is presented.

3.2.1 Basic Features of Autopoietic Social Systems

Luhmann's theory overcomes the Parsonian input-output model or open systems approach by focusing on the social system's capacity of self-reproduction or autopoiesis. Luhmann borrows the concept of autopoiesis from general systems theory. Autopoiesis was originally invented as a concept in biology to describe the essence of living organisms. In discussions within general systems theory, it became a powerful tool in understanding the basic principles of self-reproducing and self-organising systems. In applying the abstract autopoiesis concept, Luhmann distinguishes between elements and structures of social systems. Self-reproduction occurs at the level of elements and not at the structural level. Autopoietic social systems are cognitively open at the structural level, but closed at the operational level. This is a radical solution insofar as no environmental factors can have direct influence on the system's reproduction.

Probably the most startling aspect of Luhmann's theory is his assertion that social systems consist of communications. He rejects the conventional view that sociological analysis has to start from actions or interactions. For him communications are the basic elements and social systems reproduce themselves through self-reference of communications; actions are ascriptions of certain communications and thus cannot function as elements of a system. Function systems operate with system-specific forms of communication and boundary maintenance is achieved within function systems by applying a system-specific binary code.

Luhmann's general theory distinguishes three levels of analysis of social systems as systems of communication: interaction, organisation and society (Luhmann 1982, ch. 4). Furthermore, he distinguishes types of social systems that are characterised by special relations either to specific social systems or to society at large. These are conflict systems and immune systems.

Luhmann describes *interaction systems* as social systems, which are formally characterised as communication between participants who are present. The presence of the participants enables mutual perception.

Communication in interaction systems consists of both verbal and non-verbal communication that can be perceived. The perception of communication among actors who are present is always reflexive: ego's perception can be perceived by alter and vice versa (Luhmann 1975, pp. 23–4). Luhmann distinguishes between communication and structure in interaction systems. The structure of interaction systems arises from mechanisms such as the sequential order of relevant events, the use of topics or factual themes in discussions, and the restriction that participants are not allowed to speak at the same time, but only one after the other. 'When such structures are formed, centered interdependencies emerge' (Luhmann 1995a, p. 415). However, the structure of interaction systems is ultimately shaped by the autopoietic requirement that communication must continue. Structures of interaction systems are not particularly stable. Topics or themes can be changed easily and the participants have time constraints due to other commitments. Structurally interaction systems show a low degree of autonomy. Interactions are episodes with a strong tendency to disappear when the communications among present actors ends. To become interaction systems, episodes must be combined (Luhmann 1995a, pp. 406–7). In addition, interactions must be able to reproduce themselves through self-constituting self-reference.

The second type of social system, *organisation*, is characterised by a form of communication without those communicating having to be present. The most important aspect of organisations is membership. The relationship between the organisation and its members is impersonal. Organisations operate with particular forms of communications. These are decisions. Thus, the autopoiesis of organisations is conceived as the recursive communication of decisions. Only on this basis can structures, such as organisational goals and programmes, internal hierarchies or membership rules, emerge (Luhmann 2000b).

Luhmann introduced an additional third type of social system in his later writings. He called them social or protest movements (Luhmann 1996b). They are specific autopoietic systems with special structural couplings, mainly with the mass media system. Social movements occur in modern society as opposition to society within society, as communication against communication. Protest movements observe society by concentrating on negative consequences. In their reactions to protest movements, function systems often show reluctance in responding to protest for fear of generating further protest (Luhmann 1997a, pp. 847–65).

Conflict systems constitute a fourth type. In Luhmann's theory of social systems as systems of communication, contradictions and conflicts play an important role. Social systems create contradictions through communication of negation. Contradictions form part of the self-reference of social systems. Contradictions are a result of the requirement of unity of the three elements of communication: information, utterance and understanding. 'Only a communication's expectation of unity constitutes a contradiction, by choosing what communication brings together. Contradictions emerge by being communicated' (Luhmann 1995a, p. 365). Contradictions and conflicts operate with negative communication relations either to another social system or to society at large. They create the basis for two types of social systems, which are called conflict system and immune system.

For Luhmann, a *conflict system* is characterised by four aspects: contradiction, conflict, negative double contingency and a parasitic position inside another social system. Contradiction is defined as non-acceptance of a communication or, in other words, a situation in which expectations are not fulfilled. A contradiction only becomes a conflict when the contradiction is voiced and the refusal of expectations is communicated back as negation of the communication. Luhmann acknowledges the possibility of a conflict system, based on recursively communicated negations, which becomes an independent social system of a particular kind (Luhmann 1995a, pp. 388–90). In interactional conflict systems, the situation of double contingency is redefined as one of 'negative' double contingency in which ego refuses to do what alter wishes since ego expects alter not to do what ego wants. In itself, this alternative of a reversed structure of expectations is highly integrative, allowing a wide range of actions to be incorporated within the basic assumption of opposition. Anything that can be assumed to be detrimental to the other party is potentially part of a conflict system. The destructive consequences of the new conflict system are thus felt in the social system in which the conflict system originated. For Luhmann a conflict can develop into an independent conflict system only within another social system. From the covering system's point of view the conflict system is the 'excluded, included third' (Luhmann 1988a, p. 212; see also Luhmann 1995a, ch. 9). Luhmann describes this relationship with a rather unfortunate biological metaphor as a relationship between a non-symbiotic parasite and its host. The metaphor is borrowed from Michel Serres's study on 'social parasites' (Serres 1980). The conflict system is 'parasitic' in the sense that it absorbs attention and resources of the 'host' system.

However, contradictions and conflicts circulate in society and can be activated against societal structures. And to some extent society needs to protect itself from the destructive consequences of conflicts. This is the starting point for Luhmann to conceptualise a different type of social system, which he calls the *immune system*, that protects society at large. The idea of an immune system is not simply to protect society from conflicts. Its function is not to maintain attacked structures and to restore the status quo but to protect autopoiesis. The function of a social immune system lies in the continuation of communication by other means. Thus immune systems do not avoid conflicts but merely offer suitable forms of communication. The overriding aim is to avoid the use of open violence that, among other negative consequences, interrupts communication necessary for the self-reproduction of society (Luhmann 1995a, p. 369).

In Luhmann's theory, society is the overarching social system that includes all other social systems. Society is primarily differentiated into *function systems*. The major function systems are law, politics, economy, science, art, education and religion. Luhmann transcends Parsons' approach of viewing society as being controlled by (only) four pattern variables (Luhmann 1982, ch. 3). For Luhmann the modern society does not consist of a fixed number of function systems. There is always the possibility of new function systems that manage to achieve operational closure. However, this happens increasingly nowadays under conditions established by the emerging world society (Luhmann 1997a, Vol. II, pp. 760–61).

3.2.2   Six Types of Industrial Relations as Social Systems

We can deduce from our short introduction of Luhmann's theory six types of social systems as possible candidates to characterise industrial relations as a social system. First, there are the four types of social system: interaction system, organisation system, social movement and function system of society. Second, there are the two additional types that operate with contradicting communication relations either in relation to another social system or to society at large. These are called conflict system and immune system accordingly.

3.2.2.1   Industrial relations as a set of interaction systems

An analysis of industrial relations as interaction systems focuses on the systems of negotiations in which actors are present. These are in particular collective negotiations, generally known as collective bargaining. The communication in collective bargaining is structured by an agenda, by topics and by a procedure that prescribes formal rules of participation in communications. These negotiations are episodes that are linked through their results, i.e. collective bargaining agreements, which are supposed to be renegotiated after a certain period of time. Indeed, combination of episodes (Teubner 1987b) is a mechanism that equally applies to the industrial relations system. Interactions are episodes in the 'carrying on' of society. Structures created in industrial relations episodes are used in later episodes. Independent industrial relations discourses with elaborate grievance procedures and collective bargaining styles evolve from these structures. In the end an industrial relations culture evolves.

Interaction systems of the industrial relations system have generally achieved a high degree of structural autonomy. Collective bargaining and grievance procedures both define which claim or grievance they can process in procedures that are established by the systems themselves. These negotiation systems define their communicative elements through self-reference and are therefore autopoietic systems.

The industrial relations literature provides many descriptions of the autonomous character of collective bargaining that allude to self-reproductive concerns of the industrial relations system. Wolfgang-Ulrich Prigge, for example, defines collective bargaining as a negotiation system of interorganisational self-governance which is able to determine topics of discussion, processes or phases of negotiations and the roles of the negotiators (Prigge 1987, pp. 33–5).[7] And Walther Müller-Jentsch describes autonomous collective bargaining as consisting of the two related aspects of conflict resolution and rule-making (Müller-Jentsch 1997, ch. 12).

Industrial relations communications are not only the result of interactions but they also describe themselves as industrial relations negotiations. Furthermore, collective bargaining negotiations link as interaction systems through mutual recognition. They form a set of independent interaction systems.

If industrial relations are viewed as a set or combination of interaction systems, it might be asked if the set itself has evolved into a new kind of system through the combination of interaction systems. The set might have achieved the capacity to define the various interaction systems as its elements. In this case negotiations in industrial relations interaction systems are no longer randomly related communicative episodes. These interaction systems might be linked through their communications. Several other system components of interaction systems might be related according to a higher, or second, order which has evolved at the level of industrial relations at large. In this case it would be insufficient to describe industrial relations only in terms of a set of loosely related interaction systems.

3.2.2.2 Industrial relations as a hypercyclically constituted network of organisations

An approach to analyse industrial relations as a second-order system is to use organisation and network theories. Organisation theory can be

---

[7] Prigge's approach is an open systems approach. His input–output analysis focuses on institutional structures rather than communication processes.

applied at two levels: at the level of participants of industrial relations interactions and at the level of the industrial relations system at large.

The organisational account of industrial relations usually focuses on the special characteristics of industrial relations as interactions between organisations of employees and employers. Unions or worker representatives and employer associations or employer representatives carry out collective bargaining on a meso-level of industry or region and on a micro-level in the company or the plant.

The topics of industrial relations communications are the result of organisational processes. Claims in collective bargaining are generated in internal processes within unions and employer associations. However, industrial relations research has shown that the relation between the size of the claim and the outcome of bargaining is rather constant over time.[8] This finding can be interpreted from a systems theoretic point of view to indicate both the separate existence and the links between the claims-generating organisations and the negotiation system. The organisations that are responsible for the claims recognise the separate existence of the negotiation system by referring to experiences with claims in previous negotiations. Unions and employers define their roles by referring to the negotiation system and to its conditions which thus influences the generation of claims.

It is therefore necessary to switch attention to the collective negotiation system as such. There are a few accounts in industrial relations research that use variants of organisation theory to describe the negotiation system. Allan Flanders, for example, characterises it as a political institution. He emphasises the power relationship between organisations and, in particular, the capacity of collective bargaining to establish rules as an alternative to statutory regulation (Flanders 1970, pp. 220–21). One could also think of applying the system theoretical view to autopoietic organisations (see for example Teubner 1987a; Baecker 1999; Luhmann 2000b).

However, certain uneasiness remains in viewing the industrial relations system simply as an organisation system. Most industrial relations systems are certainly capable of communicating their internally achieved results to the external world (Luhmann 1990a, pp. 672–87, discussed in relation to scientific and academic organisations). They define themselves through membership by inclusion of certain collective actors and by exclusion of others. They can isolate themselves from social and psychic conditions in

---

[8]   Hansjörg Weitbrecht reports that the outcome of negotiations in the German metal industry remained at a level of two-thirds of the union claim from 1948 to 1966. See Weitbrecht 1969, p. 145.

order to follow self-generated programmes and they are able to generate their own 'media of positions' (Luhmann 1988a, ch. 9, discussed in relation to economic organisations).

Nevertheless, there is something specific about industrial relations, which is not captured by this description. This is related to the fact that the main instrument for self-regulation and the creation of internal structures is a mutual agreement. Thus, a further qualification of the organisational type of social system seems necessary. Of assistance can be Teubner's research on *networks* as autopoietic systems of a higher order (see Teubner 1993b, 2002, 2011d). For Teubner, networks result from a combination of the two types of social institution 'contract' and 'organisation'.

> By contrast with contract and organisation, networks are higher-order autopoietic systems, to the extent that they set up emergent elementary acts (network operations) through dual attribution, and link these up in circular fashion into an operational system. They are systems which are formed through a combination of contract and organisations and which possess the major features of an autopoietic system (Teubner 1993b, p. 50).

Networks are collective actors that act through other collective actors. Main examples of networks as collective actors are, for Teubner, the 'legal hybrids' franchises and joint ventures.

In applying Teubner's idea of a hypercyclically constituted network, it can be argued that *collective bargaining* develops into an autonomous network system between organisations that becomes able to define both its norms and the status of its members, i.e., the participating collective actors. Collective bargaining creates mechanisms of self-observation and self-constitution and produces its own institutional structures. The network collective bargaining system is a collective actor that acts through other collective actors. Thus, interactions of unions and employer associations form a network which produces norms, defines a space and forms a unity.

3.2.2.3   Industrial relations as a social movement

Luhmann's additional third type of social system, which he calls protest movements, has special relevance for industrial relations. The origins of industrial relations are closely linked to the emergence of labour movements. Zygmunt Bauman, in his *Between Class and Elite* (Bauman 1960), demonstrated the difficult origins of the labour movement in Great Britain. He emphasised in particular differences in the labour movements of craft guilds and factory workers. Craft guilds did not develop into autopoietic systems. They were mutual aid networks that disintegrated with industrialisation. On the other hand, factory workers responded to the negative consequences of industrialisation.

> The factory workers were rejected by society, plunged into an ever deepening abyss of destitution, deprived of civic rights and faced at every step by a wall of indifference, antipathy and fear erected by the politically privileged classes. In consequence, they adopted an attitude of total opposition to society and the complex social relations that characterised it (Bauman 1960, p. 40).

However, this labour movement had great difficulties in establishing itself as a protest movement. It faced severe opposition for official politics and the judicial system, which in turn led to secretive bondage inside the movement. It also created fragmentation and a spread of religious cults. Nevertheless, it led eventually to the establishment of trade unions on the employee side and employer associations on the management side that could engage in specific forms of self-referential communications (on origins of industrial relations, including intellectual sources for its self-awareness, in general see Kaufmann 2004).

In applying Luhmann's theory of social and protest movements (Luhmann 1996b) to industrial relations, we can describe them as an autopoietic system with structural couplings that include special relations to the mass media system and the political system. Strikes and other industrial conflicts are forms of protest that attract attention in the public eye and form special relations with the media. Furthermore, Keith Ewing has observed a shift to 'supply side trade unionism', with a new emphasis on direct involvement of trade unions in governmental and public administration processes (Ewing 2005). This form of structural coupling is recognition by the political system that the labour movement has a special position as observer of the social question and of negative consequences of economic and other societal processes on the social well-being of citizens.

3.2.2.4   Industrial relations as a conflict system

With respect to intersystemic links, Luhmann's theory of social systems offers a unique option to conceptualise the industrial relations system as a social system. This option is the conflict system that develops within another social system. A conflict system takes part in communications of the host system by switching to contradictions, thereby opposing the host system's communication on principle. Contradictions enable the continuation of action in the absence of the certainty of expectations.

Luhmann emphasises the destabilising effects of contradictions on the social system. However, this destabilisation is not considered dysfunctional but rather supportive for the evolution of the system. In certain situations the conflict system achieves that structures of the host system are replaced in order to maintain the autopoietic reproduction of the system. Complex social systems need a certain amount of instability to be able to react towards perturbations both within the environment and within themselves. Examples are changing prices in the economic system, a legal concept in which criticism and even change of the law becomes a normal event and marriages, which can be terminated by divorce. Contradictions are the communication of 'no' and protect the system against petrification (Luhmann 1995a, pp. 388–97).

Luhmann has not directly applied the idea of a conflict system to industrial relations. In his *Die Wirtschaft der Gesellschaft* (The Economy of Society), he only mentions the problem of 'labour' as an example of the general problem of scarcity in economics. In this context 'labour' is described as a 'parasite' of the economic system (Luhmann 1988a, pp. 212–23) and industrial relations are mainly treated as being an old-fashioned semantic of 'Capital' vs. 'Labour'. Although Luhmann does not contest that workers need organised representation of workers' interests (Luhmann 1988a, p. 171), he criticises unions for protecting interests in a mode which leads to inflexible labour markets. Luhmann only discusses industrial relations from an economic perspective, in which trade unions are described as instruments to increase the price of labour without any discussion of their wider role in society (Luhmann 1988a, pp. 223–4).

Nevertheless, conflict systems are conceptualised as interaction systems. Conflict systems endure when the conflict can be interpreted to show signs of general societal relevance beyond the limits of the specific interaction. Luhmann sees law and morality as mechanisms that can operationalise societal relevance of conflicts in interaction systems. Where law and morality fail to upgrade or select individual conflicts as 'socially relevant', specific organisations fulfil this function. Luhmann proposes that trade unions can be seen as organisations that select particular conflicts and enhance their status as relevant for the society at large (Luhmann 1995a, p. 393).

Luhmann's brief analysis of generalisation of the conflict within the conflict system (Luhmann 1995a, pp. 392–3) does not consider repercussive effects of the generalisation on the conflict system as such. In Luhmann's approach there is no possibility that the conflict system might transform into a different type of system.[9] Thus in his account, a conflict system remains a conflict system despite a tendency towards generalisation of conflicts.

---

[9]   In his last major publication, Luhmann adds social movements as a new type of social system (Luhmann 1997a, pp. 847–65). However, he does not view them on the same level as the other types of social system, in particular interactions and organisations (Luhmann 1997a, p. 813). I thus refrain from discussing this option ('a sixth option'), without, however, denying the possibility to describe industrial relations in this way. The labour movement and industrial relations could indeed be analysed in terms of an autopoietic social movement.

However, an alternative scenario can be proposed that assumes a transformation of the very character of a conflict system through generalisation. It assumes that the conflict system can reach a level of autonomy that allows the transformation from negative communication to positive communication. During this process negative double contingency is transformed into positive double contingency. An example can be the development of those industrial relations systems that switch from conflictual communications to joint decision-making. These industrial relations systems change their reproductive basis from negative to positive forms of communication. Thus, the generalisation of conflicts within a particular host system, which no longer defines the reason for conflicts as half-heartedly included thirds but as own system problems of wider societal relevance, not only helps to preserve the conflict system but transforms the conflict system from an interaction system into a different form of social system. The conflict system acquires a new identity during this transformation process and domesticates conflict through limiting negative double contingency to situations of adversary negotiations and collective bargaining.

3.2.2.5 Industrial relations as an immune system of society
Luhmann's theory offers a fourth possibility to conceptualise the industrial relations system. This is to perceive it as an immune system of society.

Luhmann has demonstrated his idea of an immune system with respect to the legal system (Luhmann 1995a, pp. 373–6). The legal system serves as the prime immune system of society, which guarantees communication of expectations even in the case of contradiction. It permits societal communication to resort to legal forms of communication in the case of communicative breakdown in everyday life situations. The legal system operates as an immune system of society by anticipating uncertainties and instabilities internally before these uncertainties and instabilities occur in society. Law is created in anticipation of possible conflicts. It secures the continuation of communication in a modified form in case of contradiction in normal communications. Law selects certain expectations and protects them in case of conflict, which creates the basis of normativity of expectations. Experiences with conflict are generalised for this reason in anticipation of future conflicts. In modern societies law invents new problem constellations which, in fact, nobody would have thought of if law did not exist. And law declares the expectations, which arise from new problem constellations to be law. Thus, law does not serve the function of avoiding conflicts but, in fact, increases the chances for conflict. It simply tries to avoid the violent carrying-on of conflicts by providing a means of communication adequate to the conflict. In Luhmann's words: 'Law serves to continue communication by other means' (Luhmann 1995a, p. 375). Law is societally adequate when it is able to generate enough conflicts and enough internal complexity to manage these problems.

We might ask whether the industrial relations system could be conceptualised as an immune system similar to the legal system. The industrial relations system complements the legal system in its role as the immune system for society. In a way the industrial relations system serves as a second immune system because of the limited capacity of the legal system in handling conflicts. The legal system requires conflicts to be transformed into individual claims before they can be handled within the system. The industrial relations system is the second immune system of society, which handles collective conflicts. It serves to continue communication in the case of collective conflicts. It provides procedures that transform violent collective conflicts into negotiations.

Luhmann's 'social immunology' could be further advanced by applying the concept of immune systems to the study of functional subsystems of society. A good example of immune systems at the level of concrete social systems is the dispute resolution system within the industrial relations system. Thus, in addition to the general character of the industrial relations system as an immune system of society, we find a system-specific immune system within the industrial relations system. This system is the grievance procedure and arbitration system, which serves in the capacity of an immune system in the collective bargaining system.

3.2.2.6 Industrial relations as a functionally differentiated societal subsystem

The four previous characterisations of industrial relations as a social system do not preclude the conceptualisation of the industrial relations system as a functionally differentiated societal system on the same plane as the legal, the economic or the political system.

Teubner's application of the idea of a hypercycle, derived from biochemical theories on the origin of life, is not restricted to the emergence of organisations as autopoietic systems. It is equally applicable to the evolution of functional subsystems of society.

Teubner describes autopoiesis as resulting from a three-step autonomisation of social systems from self-observation to self-description to autopoiesis of social systems. Autopoiesis or self-reproduction emerges from a cyclical relation of cyclical system components (= hypercycle).[10]

---

[10] Teubner 1993a, p. 32: 'Social subsystems acquire increasing autonomy if their components (element, structures, process, identity, boundary, environment,

Teubner proposes a gradual evolution of autopoietic systems. He assumes that self-reference is not limited to elements (parts) but occurs with respect to other system components, i.e., structure (networks), process (production), boundary and environment (space) and the system as a whole (unity). For Teubner the hypercycle, i.e. cyclical combination of cyclical self-description of self-reference, is thus not confined to self-reference of elements but equally applies to the other system components.

Teubner has demonstrated the idea of a hypercycle with respect to the cyclical relations of the four components of the legal system: legal procedure, legal action, legal norm and legal doctrine. In the development of the legal system from diffuse societal law to a state of relative autonomy, and then to full autopoiesis, these components first acquire identity by a process of self-reference, then are used operationally as self-descriptions of the legal system and finally are connected hypercyclically in a third process to form the autopoietic legal system (Teubner 1993a, Figure 1, p. 37).

It is possible to construct an autopoietic industrial relations system in analogy to Teubner's construction of an autopoietic legal system. Procedures, action, norms and a retained body of knowledge can be found in the industrial relations system as well.

Teubner distinguishes three stages in the evolution of a legal system: diffuse societal law, relatively autonomous law and autopoietic law. Industrial relations consist of diffuse societally produced system components. Workplace industrial relations rules, which are not introduced through procedures but are followed repetitiously for reasons of tradition, are examples of such a state of an industrial relations system.

An industrial relations system has become partly autonomous when one or more of its components become self-referential. Examples of this, by analogy to secondary legal rules, are norms of recognition of employee representatives in grievance procedures or collective bargaining, which regulate the creation of norms.

The industrial relations system is hypercyclically structured when its components are not only engaged in self-reference but when the relations of its components become recursive. In an autopoietic system the elements rely on references to other system components to constitute themselves. Elements and structure become two mutually referential system

---

performance, function) are self-referentially defined via reflexive communication (self-observation). The degree of their autonomy is also determined by whether these self-observations are made operational in the system (self-constitution). Finally, their autonomy is dependent upon whether their components are linked together in a hypercycle and produce each other on a reciprocal basis (autopoiesis).'

components. Actions of the industrial relations system (elements) are used to define rules (structure) and rules are used to define industrial relations action (which should not be confused with industrial action).

Teubner's hypercycle concept is thus highly suggestive of a conception of an industrial relations system as a social system. It differs from Luhmann's concept, which insists that autopoiesis characterises all social systems and that social systems are by definition autopoietic and cannot be partly autopoietic and partly allopoietic (Luhmann 1987, pp. 318–19). According to Luhmann, social systems do not differ with respect to autopoiesis. They can only differ with respect to the degree of differentiation from their societal and other environments and with respect to the degree of internal and external complexity.

Teubner's concept has the advantage of discussing the crucial question of the historical origin of autopoietic systems. Luhmann's approach seems contradictory in this respect because he adheres to a theory of differentiation of society in which autopoietic function systems are achievements of evolutionary processes, but he resists conceptualising the historical origins of a particular social system before it has become an autopoietic social system.

3.3 THE INDUSTRIAL RELATIONS SYSTEM AS A FUNCTION SYSTEM OF SOCIETY: A PROPOSAL

I propose to view the industrial relations system as a functional subsystem of society on the same plane as the legal, the economic or the political systems. The industrial relations system has constituted itself as a fully-fledged function system of society. Although it is possible to characterise it as a conflict system within the economic system and as an immune system of society, these characterisations cannot grasp the entire nature of the industrial relations system in modern societies. Thus, in my view the modern industrial relations system is best understood as a functionally differentiated subsystem of society.

This proposal can be demonstrated by discussing the four hypotheses which Luhmann has outlined in his analysis of the economic system as a 'catalogue' for the empirical testing of the existence of a social subsystem (Luhmann 1988a, p. 51). In applying these hypotheses the industrial relations system can be characterised in the following way:

- Form and scope of differentiation have reached a level in modern societies which makes an autonomous industrial relation system possible that is not dominated by other function systems.

- The industrial relations system operates with a specific combination of closure and openness with respect to its elementary operations.
- The industrial relations system operates under a binary code, which represents the exclusive function of the system.
- The industrial relations system has achieved a relative prominence in society at large in its ability to arrange corporatist exchange relations with other function systems to further its autonomy.

The following outline of the proposal for a model of industrial relations as a social system discusses these four hypotheses separately.

3.3.1   Differentiation of an Industrial Relations System

Modern societies are functionally differentiated societies. Such a society has overcome the hierarchical mode of integration which was characteristic of stratificatory societies. A primary mode of integration in modern societies is a vertical order of mutual recognition of functional subsystems. Each function system is exclusively responsible for fulfilling its societal function.

It might be argued that the industrial relations system is not a full-blown autopoietic system. Teubner could argue in analogy to his idea of steps in the autonomisation of the legal system, that the industrial relations system consists of autopoietic interaction systems but lacks the hypercycle of recursive relations of system components and, therefore, has not yet reached the status of a functionally differentiated autopoietic system on the same plane as the economic or the legal system (Teubner 1993a, pp. 36–46). In my view this is partly a question for the theory of an autopoietic industrial relations system and partly an empirical question about the stage in the development in the industrial relations system. My preliminary answer is that more signs point in the direction of a fully-fledged autopoietic function system.

Self-reference of the elements of the industrial relations system is not only a theoretical supposition but also an empirically observable phenomenon. Institutions and the structure of the industrial relations system are based on self-reference. However, self-reference of collective communications is a highly improbable process. Nevertheless, in modern societies industrial relations have developed into autopoietic function systems which are recognised by other function systems. Industrial relations have developed from a conflict system into a societal subsystem, which defines itself with respect to fulfilling a function in society at large. I propose to call the function of the industrial relations system the management of collective violence, which can occur in the relations between industrial interest groups.

Although there are a number of discussions in Luhmann's work which are related to problems of an industrial relations system, he has not directly applied his theory and analyses of social systems to a discussion of industrial relations as a social system. This might have theoretical reasons. But it might also be due to Luhmann's anti-Marxist convictions. Luhmann resents that the 'exhausted' Marxist theory of society dominates both a number of discourses within sociology and descriptions of our system of society (Luhmann 1988a, p. 168). Luhmann's anti-Marxism, however, should not prevent research from describing industrial relations as a social system. In fact, Luhmann's self-inflicted resistance to industrial relations leaves some space for his students to advance autopoietic systems theory and to apply it to one of the rare fields which have not been treated by an exhaustive study by Luhmann himself.

Nevertheless, Luhmann has embarked on problems of industrial relations in two contexts: in his analysis of the economic system and in his semantic studies of self-descriptions of modern societies. In his sociological analyses of the economic system, he discusses the history of 'Labour', as already mentioned, as the history of parasites of the economic system (Luhmann 1988a, pp. 213–23). 'Labour' is a semantic problem related to the economic problem of scarcity. Although Luhmann senses that 'Labour' indicates a different relation to the society at large which cannot be captured by the code of the economic system (Luhmann 1988a, p. 222), he does not analyse 'Labour' apart from the economic system.

Luhmann touches upon 'Labour' and its semantic opposition 'Capital' in his discussion of classes in society. He views class theory as a peculiar form of self-description of the modern society at large. Luhmann admits that the opposition of 'Capital' vs. 'Labour' as representing two classes of society has advanced beyond a mere scientific analysis of society and has achieved the status of a widely shared self-description of society. However, for Luhmann, class society means a self-description of the modern society as a hierarchically ordered society. Thus, the semantic of 'Capital' and 'Labour' represents an inadequate self-description of modern society. It is an attempt of society to resist recognition of its functional differentiation into polycentric, horizontally ordered function systems (Luhmann 1985b, 1988a, pp. 168–76).[11] However, if Luhmann had studied the specific self-descriptions of the industrial relations system, he might have detected that

---

[11]   Luhmann holds the Marxist 'semantic' of 'Capital' and 'Labour' responsible for diverting societal communication from discussing the real problems of modern societies by triggering and perpetuating conflicts which are unrelated to the overwhelming and urgent 'ecological' dangers of our societies. See Luhmann 1988a, p. 169.

it has achieved the status of an independent function system in society. The opposition of labour and capital has formed a negotiation system, which has become self-reproductive.

The industrial relations system is characterised by special forms of inter-actions between collective actors, i.e. strike activities. The understanding of these interactions has changed. These changes in the self-descriptions indicate a development of the industrial relations system. Whereas the modes of regulation of strikes are the main concerns of industrial rela-tions in its pre-autopoietic phase, the nature of its elements, i.e., col-lective negotiations, as conflictual or cooperative becomes prevalent in autopoietic industrial relations. Thus the self-descriptions of the system increasingly relate to the self-reproduction of its basic communications. Industrial democracy is a form of self-description of industrial relations which emphasises co-determination or participation between the collective actors.

These self-descriptions also reflect different forms of regulation of the industrial relations system, and in particular the transformation from external regulation to self-regulation. Regulation of industrial relations has historically evolved from regulation of industrial action to regulation of arbitration and other forms of third-party facilitation to self-regulation of negotiations by self-created agreements. This history of industrial rela-tions is reflected in the order of regulatory instruments in modern collec-tive bargaining. However, it appears in this order in a reversed form: first negotiation, then arbitration, then industrial action (Müller-Jentsch 1983, 1997, p. 206).

Industrial relations fulfil the societal function of managing conflicts between collective actors. From the society's point of view the function of the industrial relations is the management of collective violence. However, modern industrial relations have advanced beyond the status of a conflict system. Interaction of collective actors occurs in the shadow of conflicts, i.e., strikes and lockouts. Negotiations both avoid and make creative use of these forms of collective behaviour or collective violence.

Most industrial relations systems are conflict systems in the beginning of their development. However, once industrial relations systems have developed structures of formalised negotiations, they acquire a function as institutions of conflict resolution for both the host system and society.

Otto Kahn-Freund has provided insightful remarks on how autono-mous industrial relations, which manage conflict to achieve a number of purposes, can nevertheless revert to open conflict systems. In his article on 'Intergroup Conflicts and Their Settlement', he defined as the 'cardi-nal feature of labour-management relations' that 'it is the conflict itself which gives rise to the formation and consolidation of groups and to the establishment of the relevant social relations as group relations' (Kahn-Freund 1978 [1954], p. 42).

For Kahn-Freund it is not so much the aspect of the conflict relation defined as 'negative communication' between the collective actors but the conflict as form of interaction between unions and employers' associations which leads to progress in the industrial relations system. Open conflict is gradually reduced and transformed into an instrument, which becomes 'the sparingly used *ultima ratio* in the arsenal of the groups'. However, he also noticed that intergroup relations are in danger of reversal to 'primitive' forms of conflict behaviour in complex conflict systems:

> Eventually this may lead to a situation in which the element of spontaneity appears in the intragroup rather than the intergroup sphere: The dissatisfaction of the workers may be directed against the union itself on account of the deliberateness and moderation of its action. It may find expression in 'unofficial' or 'wildcat' strikes, i.e., labour conflicts conducted on the workers' side by spontaneous and ephemeral 'strike committees' frowned upon by the recognised unions. At this point the story of the eternal dialectic of spontaneity and organisation in labour relations may return to its beginning: the danger of a relapse into more primitive forms of conduct is inherent in the rigidity of the social patterns of the labour dispute at the highest point of its development (Kahn-Freund 1978 [1954], pp. 44–5).

Thus for Kahn-Freund industrial relations are a conflict system that always has the potential to reverse into open conflict. However, the nature of the conflict system is transformed if joint decision-making is introduced that requires a stable basis of trustworthy communications. The perception of industrial action as disruption of communication with consequences beyond the realm of the industrial relations system leads to a different understanding of industrial action. Industrial relations may open up under these conditions and become responsive to societal needs, expressed in the form of dissatisfaction with certain forms of (irresponsible) collective violence.

Industrial relations maintain the character of a conflict system when the relations of unions and employers are dominated by what industrial relations research has coined the adversarial principle (see Barbash 1979, 1984). Adverse industrial relations operate under the maxim 'what is bad for my enemy is good for myself'. As long as this attitude dominates the behaviour of actors, the autonomisation of the industrial relations system is inhibited. The communication in the conflict system is restricted to negative communications with the 'host' system. However, in reality, industrial relations often create under these conditions alternative forms of communication, which substitute for the dependency on negative links with economic communications.

3.3.2   Operational Closure and Cognitive Openness

Autopoietic industrial relations are operationally closed and cognitively open. The elements of the industrial relations system, i.e., collective communications, are constituted in self-referentially closed operations. Because autopoiesis or self-reproduction is guaranteed by closed communication circuits, the industrial relations system can be open towards its societal environment.

The elements of an autopoietic industrial relations system are communications between collective actors. If collective communications are defined as negotiations, they are perceived as actions of the industrial relations system. Negotiations within an industrial relations system can be called 'industrial relations acts', in analogy to 'legal acts', which Teubner proposes as the self-constituted elements of an autopoietic legal system (Teubner 1993a, p. 37).

Industrial relations acts in the form of negotiations in collective bargaining constitute the core of the industrial relations system as a social system. Luhmann's discussion of the link between communication, action and the social system is directly applicable to an industrial relations system. The industrial relations system defines behaviour of collective actors only as industrial action if it is linked to negotiations within the collective bargaining system. However, this link is entirely an internal affair of the collective bargaining system. Thus collective bargaining is defined as industrial action within the industrial relations system when it is recognised as industrial action in collective bargaining.

Furthermore, each negotiation can be ascribed as a form of action. The collective bargaining system observes and describes itself as a system of negotiations. Negotiations are the communications 'produced' by previous communications relevant to the self-reproduction of the system. Reference of negotiations in collective bargaining to previous negotiations constitutes the self-referential process, which guarantees the autopoiesis of the industrial relations system. Thus the realisation as negotiation system is the mode of self-reference which constitutes the basis of autopoiesis of the industrial relations system. On this basis of operational closure the industrial relations system can be open to establish intersystemic links.

Industrial relations research is used to discuss problems of operational closure and cognitive openness under the heading of the autonomy of industrial relations. The concept of autonomy of industrial relations, and in particular of collective bargaining, has a long history in the debates both of external regulation through state intervention and of self-regulation of the industrial relations system. However, autonomy is usually discussed with respect to the structure of the industrial relations system, and thus with respect to the capacity of its institutions to regulate the system's affairs. Modern social systems theory relates the autonomy of the system to the self-reproductive processes and understands autonomy as a necessary condition for the protection of autopoiesis.

The radical view is that the industrial relations system creates the grievances and claims because it defines which conflict is treated as a 'grievance' or 'claim' in the industrial relations system through reflexive processes. This perspective does not deny that grievances or claims are defined by the individual grievant or claimant or by the union. It only assumes that the occurrence of grievances or claims, treated by the grievance machinery or in the collective bargaining system as products of previous communications inside the system, is influenced by the structure of the system, which operates with a definition of grievances as industrial relations acts.

3.3.3 The Code of the Industrial Relations System and Its Operation

A major precondition for autopoiesis is the ability of the system to distinguish its elementary communications. In order for the industrial relations system to operate as an autopoietic system it must be able to distinguish and select its elements from other societal communications. This requires applying a code, which is specific to the industrial relations system and enables the system to carry out this selection of communication. With a system-specific code it becomes able to draw a distinction between those elements which it considers to belong to the system and those which belong to the environment.

Luhmann calls the invention of codes technically the most efficient and consequential form of differentiation of function systems (Luhmann 2012, Chapter 4, section viii). The main function systems structure their communication with a binary code which claims universality with respect to the respective specific function and also claims the exclusion of third possibilities (Luhmann 1989, pp. 36–7). Luhmann has analysed several binary codes of function systems. He defines the code for the scientific system to be the opposition of truth and untruth; the code of the economy is payment and non-payment; and the code of the legal system is law and non-law or legal/illegal. The binary code reflects the function of the system. Only if the application of the code is guaranteed can the system be called autonomous and autopoietic.

I propose to call the binary code of the industrial relations system *negotiable or non-negotiable between collective industrial actors*. Like other binary codes, the code of the industrial relations system entails a paradox insofar as the code itself cannot be justified by applying the code. The distinction between negotiable and not negotiable is itself not negotiable for the industrial relations system.

It is possible to demonstrate the idea of element and structure of autopoietic industrial relations in reconstructing the definition of industrial relations offered by Walther Müller-Jentsch. This definition includes major features of a definition of industrial relations as an autopoietic social system. Müller-Jentsch emphasises that interactions between persons, groups and organisations are the object of industrial relations from which norms, contracts and institutions result (Müller-Jentsch 1997, ch. 1). In systems theory terms he identifies interactions as relations of communications from which the structure of the system derives. Interactions appear in this definition as abstractions, which inhabited complex relations between management and employees, employers' associations and unions or between persons, groups and organisations; and these relations can be conflictual or consensus-oriented. However, the main radicalisation of autopoietic systems theory in the study of industrial relations lies in the analysis of the self-reproductive process. Interactions and their derivative institutions form conditions and programmes for operational closure and cognitive openness. Interaction in industrial relations is communication, which produces communication. Collective bargaining produces new collective bargaining; grievance processing produces new grievance processing.

The industrial relations system is a complex system, which creates its structure by selecting among certain relations of its elements. The introduction of the criterion collectivity is such a selection. Collectivity is both an abstraction from individual relations and a way to reduce the complexity of relations of employees and employers to those communications in which collective representatives operate on behalf of the employees.

When industrial relations are conceived as social systems that operate in a society consisting of several functionally differentiated social systems, they have to manage both the internal and the external complexity of the system. In fact, industrial relations have to manage a higher internal complexity than most other function systems of society. This is related to its specific form of organisation or, more precisely, the requirement of interaction between organisations. The vast majority of function systems, including the religious, the political, the economic, the legal and the scientific systems, adopt organisation as their form of achievement of function and performance. In his analysis of the economic system (Luhmann 1988a, pp. 302–23) and the scientific system (Luhmann 1990a, pp. 672–80), Luhmann emphasises competition among organisations as a structural principle. Fulfilment of function needs openness, which is usually guaranteed by a plurality of organisations (competition among political parties, universities, corporations). Industrial relations are characterised by reflexive organisation, i.e. organisation of organisation. However, even among reflexive organisations competition is possible. In addition to union competition and competition among employer organisations, a plurality of forms of collective bargaining is possible.

3.3.4 Intersystemic Relations of the Industrial Relations System in Society

The relation of the industrial relations system to other second-order social systems is described by Luhmann as one of performance rather than function. In functionally differentiated societies, the function describes the relation with society. However, social systems relate to each other 'horizontally' through performances and a relation of performance between two second-order social systems is established when the means used by one system to achieve a certain effect in another system are compatible with the structure of the other system (Luhmann 1997, pp. 759–60).

Luhmann's distinction of function and performance enables one to criticise the inflationary use of the term function in industrial relations research. Walther Müller-Jentsch (Müller-Jentsch 1997, pp. 202–11), for example, defines several 'functions' of collective bargaining which are in some cases better described as performances of the industrial relations system. His list of collective bargaining functions – which include protection of living standards, distribution of income and contribution to industrial democracy – are not only benefits for employees but also performances of the collective bargaining system for the economic system. The creation of uniform conditions of production through standardisation of wages and working time and through reinforcement of stable wage structures and working conditions are performances which benefit the whole group of employers. And the autonomy of collective bargaining benefits the state insofar as it relieves the political system from regulating working conditions; it increases rather than decreases the legitimation of the state and the government. Furthermore, what Walther Müller-Jentsch calls 'societal effectiveness' (Müller-Jentsch 1997, p. 205) of collective bargaining describes, in fact, the function of collective bargaining and, indeed, of the whole industrial relations system, namely the containment and canalisation of conflicts.

In describing relations between function systems, Luhmann distinguishes between temporary performance relations and long-term structural coupling. Within the evolutionary process function systems have the chance to become structurally coupled. Important examples are the coupling of the legal and the political system via a constitution and the coupling of the legal and the economic system via contract and property (see Luhmann 2004, ch. 10). In relation to industrial relations, corporatist arrangements involving associations have been suggested as system-specific mechanisms of structural coupling (Brodocz 1996).

Industrial relations systems tend indeed to develop their performance relations with the political and the legal system into intersystemic exchange relations. These exchange relations are often tripartite in nature with the two industrial actors interacting with state officials. If recurrent meetings of the three parties take place on a regular basis, such institution is commonly referred to as a corporatist arrangement. However, the intersystemic relations between the industrial relations system and its surrounding neighbour systems can only flourish when the industrial relations system is secure in its own autonomy and autopoiesis. Corporatist arrangements can only benefit the industrial relations system if it is strong enough to resist direct determination and can use corporatist arrangements for internal creation of structures. And the political and legal systems benefit only from participation in corporatist arrangements as long as the industrial relations system can offer performances, which are useful for their internal communications. The political and the legal system will only maintain their support in the long run when the industrial relations system is strong enough so that the other systems can receive something in return for their participation in corporatist networks. Thus autonomisation and interdependence are not exclusive but co-evolutionary processes (see also Willke 1989, p. 90; Rosewitz and Schimank 1988, pp. 298–304).

PART II

Reflexive trends in modern labour law

4. Reflexive employment protection

Employment protection constitutes the core of what is traditionally known as individual labour law or employment law. Adequate protection against arbitrary decisions of management has for a considerable time been the essential pillar of labour law. Conceived as an individual right, employment protection plays a central role in Otto Kahn-Freund's famous definition of labour law as countervailing force:

> The main object of labour law has always been, and we venture to say will always be, to be a countervailing force to counteract the inequality of bargaining power which is inherent and must be inherent in the employment relationship (Kahn-Freund 1983, p 18).

The justification for legislative intervention, for example in situations of termination of employment, is according to Kahn-Freund the unequal power relation between employer and employee during the termination of employment. Labour law is thus 'an attempt to infuse law into a relation of command and subordination' (ibid.).

However, as a field of legislative intervention, employment protection is currently under attack. In particular it is blamed for negative economic consequences. In this situation reflexive labour law can assist in changing focus in understanding trends in employment law. The argument developed in the following is that modern employment protection law has encountered a number of internal as well as external challenges deriving in particular from the growth of atypical employment. These challenges require employment protection to become reflexive.

Statutory employment protection is the result of historical processes and its scope was gradually enlarged over time. It developed from special protection for vulnerable groups of workers (children and women in particular), first introduced in England in the mid-nineteenth century in the form of factory legislation, to general protection granted to all employees. Modern employment protection has significantly increased the areas of protection. It is no longer confined to health and safety measures and regulations of hours of work, but now includes protection against discrimination and in particular regulations on unjustified termination of the contract of employment.

The chapter proceeds in four steps. After a brief overview of leading theories of employment protection, the chapter discusses in its second part reflexive trends in dismissal law. In the third part the legal response to atypical employment is described as reflexive regulation in the form of 'protection of employment protection'. Finally, in assessing reflexive trends in fields of workplace regulation such as health and safety and discrimination law, the notion of participatory self-regulation is put forward as a strategy in line with understanding modern labour law as reflexive law.

4.1   THEORIES OF EMPLOYMENT PROTECTION

We basically can distinguish three types of theories of employment protection. First, there are economic studies that tend to view employment protection as an external reference system that creates costs for companies. Second, there are legal theories that understand employment protection as a result of dynamics in the legal system and view it as more or less determined by legal factors and constraints. A third type of theory assesses employment protection either from a political economy perspective or an industrial relations view in which it is shaped by collective bargaining practices.

4.1.1   Economic Theories

An influential economic theory that is of relevance for a system theoretical understanding of the labour market is the theory of labour market segmentation (Doeringer and Piore 1971). It argues that important differences exist on the demand side that cannot be explained by individual firm or employee characteristics. The labour market is a dual market that is divided into primary and secondary markets – roughly equalling the sociological and legal distinction into typical and atypical employment. Furthermore, labour markets are segmented according to race, ethnic differences and gender. 'Employers . . . consciously manipulate ethnic antagonisms to achieve segmentation' (Reich et al. 1973, p. 362). Differences in levels of employment security are a direct result of differentiation of the labour market into segments.

This economic view is closer to sociological system theory than traditional neoliberal economic theories that largely ignore such contextual factors. They concentrate instead on individual choices and in general take a hostile view towards unfair dismissal legislation. However, not all neoliberal economic theories argue against employment protection regulations. Neoclassical human capital theory, for example, argues that atypical employment and a reduction in employment security decrease the chances for investments in human capital to be recovered (Becker 1964; Mincer 1974). Both the uncertainty and the risk of unemployment after termination of atypical employment have negative consequences on the returns to investment in education, training and further training. Furthermore, allowing the reduction of employment security as an individual choice has negative macro-economic consequences (Boyer 1993).

An alternative to neoliberal economic theory is the efficiency wage theory. It assumes that an individual's utility is a function of the intensity of the job and the real wage received (Raff and Summers 1987). Wage cuts therefore have negative effects on a worker's productivity and increase costs of production possibly by more than the wage cut saves costs for the firm. In this model it is rational for a firm to pay a wage above the full employment equilibrium wage since workers are expected to reduce shirking because of the high costs of a job loss. This latter effect constitutes the discipline function of aggregate unemployment for individual work efforts (Shapiro and Stiglitz 1984). This theory has been used to explain agreements between managers and workers on lower wages and higher work efforts in exchange for employment security (Aoki 1988).

However, other economic analyses of the relation of atypical employment and employment security maintain that wages should not be the only, or even the main, concern. A classic example is Ronald Coase's theory of the firm. He stresses the cost advantage of permanent work contracts in comparison with 'several shorter ones'. The advantage results from the fact that any other form of work contract would have to specify more precisely the content of the work to be carried out. There is a negative impact of the non-permanent character of atypical employment not only on employment security of the employee but on the firm as well. Permanent, long-term contracts are cost-effective because it is difficult for the firm to foresee which tasks might be required from the employee at a later point in time (Coase 1988 [1937]).

4.1.2 Legal Theories

Legal theories focus on analysing contractual and statutory regulations of employment. In their attempts at finding adequate answers to the erosion of legal protection of employment as a result of increased use of atypical forms of employment, they tend to resort to notions of an employment relationship underlying or characterising the employment contract (Countouris 2007). In the following the theory of the standard employment relationship (SER) will be contrasted with basic assumptions of reflexive labour law about the regulation of typical and atypical employment.

SER distinguishes between the contract of employment and the employment relationship (Mückenberger 1985a, 1985b; 2010; see also Hepple 1986). Whereas the contract of employment refers to express agreements between the employer and the employee, the employment relationship is defined as a status which in legal terms is constituted by a floor of rights (Deakin and Mückenberger 1989). These rights are granted by statutory employment protection, which defines rights independent of the terms agreed upon in the actual contract of employment.

In this view, statutory employment protection aims primarily at the employment relationship and not at the contract of employment. Employment protection measures are thereby understood as means that shape the employment relationship in legal terms and equalise a socially unequal relationship between the employer and the employee. In fact, like Kahn-Freund, the theory assumes a factually unequal relationship between the employer and the employee and this inequality is the main reason for legal measures of employment protection. Since the employment relationship is dominated by powerful employer interests in this view, legal regulation is required to restrict and counter the company interests. Labour law's role is to guarantee at least minimum standards of protection.

This theory conceives the SER both as a factual relationship and as a legal relationship. The legally protected employment relationship is seen as a minimum condition for an adequate participation of employees in social life. The fact that the employment relationship constitutes the economic basis for the employee means that legal protection participates in guaranteeing the subsistence of the employee. The theory assumes a determining influence of factual changes on legal developments. Thus the legal model of a standard employment relationship is threatened by factual changes in the forms of employment.

The theory of the standard employment relationship was originally explicitly normative or prescriptive (Mückenberger 1990). Based on a so-called politico-economic assessment of social processes, it viewed new forms of employment as predominantly expressing employer demands. The function of labour law was therefore to protect employees against one-sided demands of employers of 'flexibilising' employment conditions (Mückenberger 1989; Deakin and Mückenberger 1989). From this perspective, atypical employment, including temporary work, part-time work or fixed-term contracts, is seen as undermining the standards which the law provides for a typical employment relationship. The growth of atypical forms of employment appears as a process of gradual 'erosion' of the standard employment relationship (Mückenberger 1985b).

One weakness of the theory lies in its distinction between typical or standard employment conditions and atypical forms of employment. The notion of a standard employment relationship is increasingly difficult to define (see Dickens 2004). For example, it is unclear how many of the typical elements (permanent, full-time, etc., employment) need to be changed, and to what degree, to turn typical into atypical work. The theory also appears unable to accept variations in the type of employment contracts as being incorporated into the system of employment standards. Probably the greatest weakness of this approach lies in neglecting employee demands for flexibilisation of employment.

There has been a critical discussion among theorists defending the SER and its implications of supporting the preservation of an increasingly unrealistic model of a male wage-earner who is responsible for a family of non-wage-earners. The rigid defence of SER is widely replaced by a pragmatic attitude towards new forms of employment (Bosch 1986; Mückenberger 2010). New forms of employment are no longer seen as inspired exclusively by employer demands, but rather as an expression of general trends and cultural changes in lifestyles. An increased female participation in the labour market means that not only employers but also employees demand new forms of employment, in particular part-time jobs. The task for labour law cannot be to prevent the flourishing of these new types by insisting on a negative appraisal of them as an erosion of a sacred standard employment relationship. Labour law must instead develop notions of social protection compatible with these new forms of employment (Mückenberger 1989; Keller and Seifert 1993, 1997).

In contrast to the theory of SER, which focuses on 'external' factors related to the economic, the political or the industrial relations system in arguing an erosion of the basis for employment rights, the theory of reflexive labour law prefers to focus on 'internal' factors inherent to the legal system in explaining the development of law. Reflexive labour law assumes that the legal development is only indirectly influenced by economic development and postulates that in modern labour law systems, legal innovations are in general resulting from previous legal regulations. This approach is interested in the 'feedback loop from legal norm to social consequences to legal norm' (Teubner 1986, p. 261). For labour law to become reflexive it has to become aware of the limits of legal regulation. In line with this general assumption, reflexive labour law views the regulation of both typical and atypical employment foremost as an internal affair of an increasingly complex labour law system. For example, the regulation of fixed-term contracts is interpreted as a reaction to problems created by the employment protection measures themselves (Schömann et al. 1998, ch. 1).

Furthermore, in the perspective of reflexive labour law, the concept of an employment relationship is an internal legal construction of an external world of social relations. New social constellations have no determining effect on the legal system. Factual changes in the forms of employment can only influence the legal construction if they are recognised as a problem within the legal discourse. This recognition is not a theoretical but a practical affair and happens in legal practice and in the operation of law, in particular legal decision-making.

The theory of the standard employment relationship and the theory of reflexive labour law agree that an analysis of both the legal norms themselves as well as their political and economic contexts is required for an adequate understanding of the development of legal norms. However, they differ with respect to the relative weight each of the theories attaches to legal and non-legal factors in explaining the development of regulation of atypical employment. Nevertheless, they seem compatible if the political and economic analyses of the standard employment relationship theorists are reconstructed as attempts to explain the non-legal use of law and the studies following the reflexive labour law concept as concentrating on the legal view of law.

4.1.3 Political Economy and Industrial Relations Theories

The starting point of assessments of employment protection undertaken by political economists and industrial relations specialists is factual changes in the relationship of the employer and the employee. They tend to conceive employment as a status which is only marginally regulated by the actual employment contract. In their analyses societal factors such as economic changes (post-Fordism) and cultural and value changes determine the erosion of typical and the emergence of atypical employment rather than individual needs. In relation to employment protection, these theories emphasise industrial structures and policy aspects that influence legislation processes and shape implementation of employment protection policies (Streeck 1990).

Particular attention is given in political economy and industrial relations accounts to regulations that aim at flexibilising existing patterns of protective legislation. Some authors have observed a switch in social policies from Keynesian welfare to Schumpeterian workfare policies in a number of member states of the European Communities in the 1980s (Holden 2003; see also Jessop 1993, 2002, ch. 3). Non-standard forms of employment were discovered as instruments that not only benefit human resource management policies of companies by making hiring easier but potentially reduce unemployment in Europe. A forerunner in this respect was the UK, where policies were adopted under the general heading of 'flexibilisation' and 'deregulation' of the labour market in the 1980s. Employment protection was declared to be a 'burden on business' and labour law in general came under attack for neglecting business interests. Governments embarked on policies which aimed at 'liberalising' labour law and 'flexibilising' labour markets (Standing 1993). This free-market version of deregulation has become a global phenomenon (Standing 1999, 2009) and meant both fewer restrictions on personnel policies of companies and a decrease in employment protection for workers, especially for so-called atypical employees. Political economists are worried that these policies lead to a large group of the workforce being in precarious employment, forming a new social class that Guy Standing has coined in a catching fashion the 'precariat' (Standing 2011).

Industrial relations approaches emphasise the role of collective actors in regulating and administering employment protection. They emphasise that in advanced labour law systems, works councils play important roles in finding decisions on dismissals and other aspects of employment protection at company level. In advanced industrial relations systems, collective bargaining is used beyond wage determination in order to regulate crucial working conditions and certain aspects of employment protection. Furthermore, collective actors are involved in implementing and administering employment protection measures, for example as lay members in labour courts. These relations between industrial actors and the state have led in many jurisdictions to stable corporatist arrangements.

A pleasant characteristic of many political economy approaches to employment protection is their comparative methodology. Furthermore, they tend to take an analytical approach by distinguishing, for example, types of protection measures according to level and scope in providing employment security (see Buechtemann 1993a). Such studies tend to link broader views on the development of employment with specific proposals for the reform of labour law. A prominent example for a legal strategy that is informed by political economy approaches is the flexicurity debate (Eurofound 2007).

Simon Deakin has shown in a number of studies of labour law and corporate governance that the legal and the political economy approach are not mutually exclusive (Deakin 1996, 2009a; Deakin and Wilkinson 2005). A good example is his discussion of the employment contract, in which he combines legal and economic perspectives in insightful ways: 'The employment contract is best understood as a governance mechanism which links together work organization with labour supply in such a way as to make it possible to manage long-term economic risk' (Deakin 2002, p. 179). Of particular importance for reflexive labour law is his assessment of employment protection legislation (Deakin 2010, 2012). In these studies he demonstrated the positive relation of employment protection legislation and innovation and training in companies that make creative use of theoretical, methodological and empirical research findings. These findings give insights into reflexive processes at company level in which employment protection can have productive economic impacts.

4.2   REFLEXIVE REGULATION OF EMPLOYMENT PROTECTION

From a reflexive law perspective, employment protection is a unique field of regulation (see also Collins 2000). The object of regulation is employment relations at the place of work and employment protection as a legal field covers a number of areas of vulnerability of employees in the company. These include in particular the regulation of discipline and unfair dismissal as well as health and safety, employment discrimination and the minimum wage. Reflexive labour law thus broadens the field of employment law beyond statutory rights and their judicial enforcement. Central concerns of the reflexive law approach are related to regulatory limits of the rights-based approach and exploring alternative ways of handling conflicts and decision-making at the place of work.

The rights approach leaves enforcement of employment law to the individual employee. In contrasting the individual rights approach with the public law model of labour inspectors, Hugh Collins has identified well the problems of regulating employment protection that are associated with both approaches. The individual rights approach assumes that employees know their rights and are willing to raise the issue in dispute both with their employer, despite their fear of retaliatory action, and with judicial bodies, despite existing barriers to access to justice. The public law model, on the other hand, which used to underlie the approach to employment protection in France and the Netherlands, produces prohibitively high costs for governments because it does 'require a huge army of inspectors, who could credibly threaten stiff penalties, in order to secure full compliance' (Collins 2010, p. 29).

Hugh Collins also gives an idea of what an alternative could look like using the reflexive labour law approach. It would be to understand dismissal law as facilitation of compliance at the place of work, for example by granting 'incentives to employees to enforce labour standards' (ibid.). Reflexive law strengthens mechanisms of self-regulation as measures to improve protection at the place of work. Instead of control by external instances in the form of labour inspectors or labour courts, reflexive labour law deems legal instruments in the form of procedural devices that support self-regulation as more effective than external control. These procedural solutions include collective bargaining at the place of work, including works council involvement, as well as other forms of cooperation, for example negotiations between management and health and safety representatives.

The privileging of procedures over imposition of substantive standards is not entirely new in employment law. Reflexive labour law in fact supports a trend that has been characteristic of modern employment protection law for a while. As will be demonstrated in the next section, we find the proceduralist approach at the centre of the current law of unfair dismissal at the global and the national levels.

4.2.1 Proceduralism in Unfair Dismissal Law

At the global level, the ILO has tried to shape the development of legislative employment protection through a number of conventions and recommendations. Its concern with labour standards and the rights-based approach is widely seen as promoting substantive legal norms. However, if we look closer at the legal instruments proposed, we detect in fact a proceduralist understanding at the centre of the ILO approach.

The ILO started initiatives to introduce international standards in the area of unfair dismissal in 1963 with Recommendation R119 concerning Termination of Employment. It took until 1982 for a second Recommendation, No. 166 concerning Termination of Employment at the Initiative of the Employer, to be issued, which led in the same year to Convention C158 concerning Termination of Employment at the Initiative of the Employer (in force since 23 November 1985). It is widely acknowledged that Convention C158 had a significant influence on the spread and design of unfair dismissal legislation worldwide (Bronstein 2009, ch. 3).

The right to be protected against unfair dismissal constitutes in many countries the main jurisdiction of specialised labour judiciaries. Furthermore, dismissal protection has been granted the status of a fundamental right in the European Union. Article 30 of the Charter of Fundamental Rights of the European Union states: 'Every worker has the right to protection against unjustified dismissal.' However, what is remarkable about dismissal protection from a reflexive labour law perspective is not the legislative basis in national or international law nor the institutional set-up to guarantee rights enforcement, but the degree to which it relies on procedures as a mechanism of job protection.

If we look closer at the right to be protected against unfair dismissal at the global and the national levels, we detect a central concern with procedural devices. In the ILO Convention on termination of employment, we find a main concern with notice periods, which are regulated in Article 11: 'A worker whose employment is to be terminated shall be entitled to a reasonable period of notice or compensation in lieu thereof, unless he is guilty of serious misconduct, that is, misconduct of such a nature that it would be unreasonable to require the employer to continue his employment during the notice period.'

In addition, the Convention provides in Article 7 for a procedure prior to or at the time of the termination. This is in fact a combination of a rights-based and a procedural approach since it is intended to guarantee the employee a right to be heard by the employer before a dismissal decision is taken. 'The employment of a worker shall not be terminated for reasons related to the worker's conduct or performance before he is provided an opportunity to defend himself against the allegations made, unless the employer cannot reasonably be expected to provide this opportunity.'

A third procedure mentioned in Convention 158 is the procedure of appeal against termination. This appeal can be launched with an internal or an outside body, such as a labour court. What has to be guaranteed is organisational autonomy, expressed in the Convention by the requirement that the body has to be impartial (Articles 8 and 9).

4.2.2 Notice Periods

At the centre of the procedural devices with which dismissal law operates are the notice periods. They require that after the dismissal has been officially announced a certain period has to elapse before a dismissal takes effect. The reason for notice periods are to create space for negotiations and find solutions for the conflict underlying the termination of employment while the employee is still in employment. Notice periods are ultimately a form of regulation of self-regulation. They provide space for negotiations between the parties.

National labour laws vary in relation to complexity and detail of regulation of the procedures that need to be followed in case of dismissal. Many countries grant minimum periods of notice that increase to a maximum period of notice after a certain number of years. For example, in the United Kingdom the current (2013) minimum period is one week for a person being employed continuously for between one month and two years and increases by one week for each additional year of continuous employment; the maximum statutory notice period is 12 weeks (s. 86 ERA). Under German law the current minimum notice period is four weeks, which extends with the length of service up to a maximum of seven months for 20 years' employment and above and can be extended by collective agreements (§ 622 BGB).

It is quite common to distinguish notice periods for white-collar and blue-collar employees, granting longer periods for the first category and shorter periods for the latter. For example, countries such as Denmark, Greece and Italy only grant statutory notice periods to white-collar workers. However, notice periods for blue-collar workers may then be regulated by collective agreement. In Belgium, labour law operates with different notice periods not only for blue-collar workers and for salaried or white-collar employees but for employers as well (Schömann et al. 1998, ch. 3).

4.2.3 Dismissal Procedures

In relation to dismissal for reasons of conduct or performance of the employee, the ILO convention provides that an employment relationship cannot be seen as terminated before the employee is given an opportunity to defend himself against the allegations made. At a closer look, we see that this so-called right to be heard is in fact a procedural device.

From a reflexive labour law perspective company procedures provide opportunities for the parties to regulate their affairs. The role of labour law is to offer guidance for conflict resolution carried out by the disputing parties. Reflexive labour law builds on sociolegal insights that effective compliance with employment rights happens not through courts but at the place of work (Dickens 2012). Thus reflexive labour law shifts attention from the judicial level to the company level and views the role of labour law as supporting decision-making at company level – in short, regulation through self-regulation. It focuses on the role of procedures and asks how procedural protection can be regulated.[1]

The exception in which the right to be heard does not apply is summary dismissal. This is a case in which the dismissal is based on a serious breach of the employment contract. In fact, the law stipulates that in such cases of serious breach a continuation of employment is unlikely and thus an attempt to force the parties to find ways of resolving the dispute in order to continue the relationship is inappropriate.

---

[1] Hugh Collins, in his book *Justice in Dismissal*, has suggested that dismissal procedures are based on substantive criteria of fairness. He compares three 'models' of moral justification – respect for dignity, democratic participation and efficiency – and finds evidence that British employment tribunals favour the criterion efficiency in assessing dismissal procedures as reasonable (Collins 1992, ch. 4).

If we look at the legal reality in companies, we find that there exist multiplicities of company procedures in addition to the standard dismissal procedures proposed by the ILO. Among these are procedures that allow employee representatives, works councils or trade union members to be involved in dismissal decisions. In Germany, the law on works councils provides that if an employer wishes to dismiss an employee he must first consult the works council. Without consultation of this body of employee representatives, the employer dismissal is automatically illegal. There is, however, evidence that works councils underexploit their bargaining power in acting on behalf of individual employees in dismissal situations in exchange for participation rights in economic decision-making (Falke et al. 1981).

Employment protection in the form of representation of employee interest is also carried at higher levels of the company in Germany. This is regulated by the law on co-determination under which elected trade union representatives take part in decision-making in the supervisory board. These regulations are an important means for companies to transform into what Gunther Teubner calls 'centres of reflexion' in order to arrive at decisions beneficial to the company as a whole (Teubner 1994, 2010a).

Dismissal law in Portugal, for example, provides that if the employer wishes to dismiss an employee for just cause, both the works council and the employee have to be informed of the offences in writing (report of blame). The employee has a right to be heard and present further evidence (a simplified procedure applies in companies with fewer than 20 employees). After the works council has delivered a 'reasoned opinion', the employer can dismiss the employee within a period of 30 days. The employee can appeal to the labour tribunal and, if successful, can choose between reinstatement or severance payment (Schömann et al. 1998, pp. 56–8).

In the United Kingdom companies are assisted by an elaborate ACAS Code of Practice on disciplinary and grievance procedures (2009). 'The Code embodies notions of natural justice and advocates a "corrective" rather than "punitive" approach to discipline' (Dickens et al. 1985, p. 101). The Code outlines procedural steps to be followed by management in dealing with disciplinary matters leading to a dismissal, including the possibility of a hearing or other form of stating the case for the employee before dismissal.

Special cases constitute so-called redundancy procedures for collective or individual dismissals for economic reasons. In France, for example, the procedure in the case of dismissal for reason of redundancy depends on the number of dismissed employees. The procedure for individual economic redundancy follows the three-phase procedure for disciplinary dismissals. In addition, the employer is required, in the case of economic dismissals, to indicate the possibility of retraining (*convention de conversion*). For economic dismissals of two to nine employees within 30 days, the employer must observe not only the requirements for individual dismissals but must also consult the responsible employee representatives. In collective redundancies of 10 or more employees within 30 days, or 30 employees within six months, the employer has to observe a strict consultation procedure which requires negotiations with the relevant employee representatives (see Domergue 1987; Enclos 1990).

In cases of dismissal for reasons of economic redundancy, the employer must establish a collective redundancy plan if the company employs at least 50 people. The Labour Code requires that the validity of the collective redundancy plan must be assessed based on the size and financial situation of the company or group and the redeployment opportunities available within the company or group. French works councils have to be involved in establishing the redundancy plan and have a right to challenge the plan in court. Furthermore, there is some control of the procedure by the Labour Inspector.

A number of labour law jurisdictions know special procedures or procedural requirements for dismissal of particular groups of employees, for example pregnant employees and disabled workers. The dismissal of works council, trade union and employee representatives at company level, including health and safety officers, is a further case of particular protection through special procedures. In a system theoretical perspective, the legal protection of employee representatives is recognition ('reflection') in law of the needs of the industrial relations system.

In addition to the procedural devices that need to be followed to reach a dismissal decision, the ILO convention demands national labour laws to provide an impartial procedure of appeal once the decision to dismiss the employee is made by the employer. In many countries this procedure means recourse to a judicial body or labour court. However, in some countries, for example the United States, such external appeal procedures are limited to specific areas of employment protection such as health and safety, discrimination and union representation. Appeals are part of the grievance procedures inside the company leading to final and binding arbitration within a private system of justice.

4.3 REFLEXIVE LABOUR LAW AND ATYPICAL EMPLOYMENT

The regulation of atypical employment shows a number of reflexive trends. Probably the clearest case of legal reflexivity in employment protection law can be found in the relation of atypical employment to unfair dismissal. With the extension of dismissal law we see an increase in attempts to circumvent this protection. In particular the use of atypical forms of employment is often seen as motivated by a desire to avoid employment protection granted to so-called standard employment. In a reflexive law perspective, the legal strategy of limiting possibilities of using atypical forms of employment through restrictive legal measures is a reflexive form of regulation, aiming at and being motivated by a concern for 'protection of protection'.

4.3.1 Employment Theory and Atypical Employment

Atypical employment is at the centre of neoliberal reforms of the labour market at national and supranational level. These policies have forced labour lawyers to adapt to a new view of their field. Labour lawyers had to get used to the idea that the main function of labour law is no longer restricting atypical contracts for the sake of employment protection. Instead, atypical employment contracts are to be interpreted as instruments of labour market policies in line with the goals of legal norms which were introduced to facilitate the use of atypical employment.

Furthermore, atypical employment challenges traditional notions of the employment relations because it represents social and cultural change. And these changes occur on both sides of the relationship. The organisation of work and new employer demands as well as new attitudes towards work and employment on the side of the employees are behind the trend towards new forms of employment.

This has led to debates about the fundamental tenets of the employment relationship (see Leighton 2011). A main function of legal scholars is to assist law's recognition of social changes by rethinking the conceptual basis of law that guides legal practice. An example is the lively discussion over the nature of the modern contract of employment. For example, Mark Freedland has proposed to redefine the employment contract as 'personal employment contract' (Freedland 2003). His main concern is to enlarge the understanding of the contract of employment and to capture so-called semi-dependent employees who are formally self-employed but whose working conditions are defined by another party. This seems a good attempt to redefining the notion of employment contract in order to incorporate changes that occur in the reality of employment relations (see also Countouris 2007; Freedland and Kountouris 2011).

The social reality of employment is also the starting point for the theory of reflexive labour law in assessing legal changes in the employment relationship. However, a legal theory inspired by social systems theory emphasises that factual changes or academic redefinitions have to be understood as new challenges within internal legal operations and that this is not an automatic process. Reflexive labour law assumes autonomy of the legal system in shaping legal forms of employment. It focuses on internal problems related to the legal complexity of employment protection and attempts of legal control which influence occurrence as well as the rates of alternative forms of employment. In this view, an extensive use of atypical employment, for example fixed-term contracts, has to be understood as a development within a national system of employment protection. A country's employment system which protects the standard employment relationship is expected to create forced self-employment or a specific group of fixed-term employees and has a potential to promote or discriminate this group of employees. The regulatory need for protection against discrimination, for example, is greater if a national system of employment protection adheres to a traditional model of a standard employment relationship.

In light of the debates over atypical employment, Gerhard Bosch, one of the leading proponents of the theory of the standard employment relationship (SER), has offered a redefinition of SER. He sees a new SER emerging that is based on the notion of flexibility (Bosch 2004). He defends the concept of the SER because it reveals how labour law is informed by a particular logic of protection that rests on certain forms of work. Bosch distinguishes between forms and substance of the SER. The substance of SER is determined by its enduring functions, whereas the form merely expresses how the SER is understood at a particular point in time. The substance of the SER remains built around the model of a stable, socially protected, dependent and more or less full-time job, whereby the basic conditions (working time, pay, social transfers) are regulated by collective agreement or by labour and/or social security law. However, Bosch's new SER offers a framework for self-organised diversity in which the differing interests of individuals, firms and society are balanced. It requires a new institutional framework responding to new needs for flexibility based on the following elements:

- public childcare infrastructure for children under 6 and for those of school age (all-day schooling);
- promotion of internal flexibility in companies;
- promotion of lifelong learning;
- flexibilisation in choosing working hours;
- equal treatment of men and women regarding welfare entitlements, including abolition of derived rights of women, such as pensions for widows (Bosch 2004, pp. 632–4).

In Chapter 5 we shall see that Bosch's understanding of the employment relationship comes close to discussions related to the concept of transitional labour markets.

4.3.2   Reflexivity in the Regulation of Fixed-term Contracts

Since 1999 the area of fixed-term work is regulated in the European Union by a directive.[2] Its stated aims are to prevent unequal treatment of fixed-term workers in comparison with comparable permanent workers, to improve the quality of fixed-term work and to prevent abuse arising from the use of successive fixed-term employment contracts.

In order to improve the quality of fixed-term work, employers must provide fixed-term workers with access to appropriate training opportunities to enhance their skills, career development and occupational mobility. Fixed-term workers must also be taken into consideration when calculating the threshold above which workers' representative bodies may be constituted.

A main objective of the European regulation of fixed-term contracts is to prohibit the continuous use of fixed-term contracts. Successive fixed-term contracts automatically transform into a permanent contract unless there are objective reasons justifying their renewal. However, the directive does not require the employer to state a reason why only a fixed-term contract instead of a permanent contract is offered (Barnard 2012, p. 442). Instead, it lists three areas of regulation:

- objective reasons justifying the renewal of such contracts or relationships;
- a maximum total duration of successive fixed-term employment contracts or relationships;
- a maximum number of renewals.

The European law leaves ample scope for member states for further regulation in this area. The regulation of fixed-term contracts in the member states does indeed take a number of forms. They reach from specific measures to general regulations in their law on employment contracts. For example, Belgian law distinguishes a number of types of contract that are limited in duration. These include temporary employment contracts,

---

[2]   Fixed-term Work Directive 1999/70/EC of 28 June 1999 concerning the framework agreement on fixed-term work concluded by the ETUC, UNICE and CEEP.

contracts for a fixed term, contracts for a specific task and contracts for reasons of replacement. The last type was introduced by the Social Recovery Act of 1985; they are permitted for all categories of employees and can be concluded for a maximum of two years. Typical reasons for a replacement contract are military service or maternity leave. However, replacement of employees who are suspended for economic reasons, bad weather, strikes or lockouts is illegal. A replacement contract which continues over two years automatically becomes permanent (Blanpain and Oversteyns 1993, p. 49).

In other countries, such as France or Germany, replacement is one of the most common legally accepted reasons for concluding a fixed-term contract. Furthermore, like Belgian law, French law assumes a close relationship of fixed-term contracts (*contrat à durée déterminée*) and temporary work (*travail temporaire*). Both types have been the subject of continuous reform and have been used for labour market purposes. A remarkable feature of the French approach is the continuous experimentation with atypical employment as forms of special labour market policies, for example in the form of an employment solidarity contract (*contrat emploi-solidarité*). This policy is supported by industrial relations; statutory restrictions, for example, introduced by the *lois Auroux* of 1982, have been repeatedly modified by collective agreements in order to ease the use of fixed-term contracts (Lyon-Caen 1993; Schömann et al. 1998, pp. 35–7). The result has been that in France so-called temporary workers encounter 'wage penalties, increased exposure to unemployment and repeat spells of fixed-term employment' (Gash and McGinnity 2007, p. 467).

Motivations for regulations on fixed-term contracts reveal different forms of reflexivity. From a reflexive labour law perspective, the close link between two particular areas of law that interact needs to be stressed. These areas are dismissal protection and concerns about fixed-term contracts being used to circumvent dismissal protection. The regulation of fixed-term contracts is indeed a particular case of a reflexive trend in labour law. Many legislative attempts to regulate this type of atypical employment are motivated by labour market policy concerns. Allowing, or even encouraging, fixed-term employment contracts was seen as a policy to combat unemployment through the promotion of non-standard forms of employment (see, for example, Rodgers and Rodgers 1989).

In a country with a strong track record of deregulation of labour law, such as the United Kingdom, promoting the use of fixed-term contracts means in fact operating with low standards of protection for workers employed on this type of contract. There are no statutory restrictions in the United Kingdom to enter a fixed-term contract of employment and its so-called business-friendly approach stipulates that both parties are in theory encouraged to choose freely which form of employment contract they wish (Deakin and Reed 2000a). The employer does not need to justify the use of a fixed-term contract by recourse to a legally prescribed reason and there is no restriction on the length or renewal of the fixed term. The fixed-term contract can therefore take a variety of forms, including a contract for a stated period or until the occurrence of an event which is certain to happen at a definite time. Casual workers who work for relatively short periods in seasonal trades or services are not even considered employees.

The British approach is to avoid special treatment of fixed-term contracts at statutory level and to assimilate this type of contract with employment contracts for an indefinite period. However, it needs to be mentioned that the unfair dismissal rights are only granted to permanent employees if they were in continuous employment for at least one year at the effective date of termination of the employment contract (section 108 ERA). This qualifying period constitutes in fact a one-year probation period and reduces the need for British employers to use fixed-term contracts in order to avoid perceived risks of unfair dismissal law. Employers can freely terminate the employment contract during this period. The British legal situation with respect to employment protection might also explain why fixed-term employees tend to include a large number of relatively well-paid employees who have opted voluntarily for a fixed-term contract (Slater 2011).

A strong link between regulations on atypical employment, in particular fixed-term contracts, and labour market policies can also be found in Portugal and Spain. The use of fixed-term contracts was liberalised in Portugal after the collapse of the authoritarian regime in 1976 in order to ease the allegedly rigid dismissal protection system. It has been reported that these new forms of employment contracts were widely used in practice. Seventy per cent of all new employment contracts were concluded in the mid-1980s on a fixed-term basis (Pinto 1987, p. 348). However, it has also been stated that this meant that permanent employees enjoyed a high degree of security whereas fixed-term employees had very little legal protection (see Pinto et al. 1993, p. 239). Thus in 1989 the dismissal law was liberalised and fixed-term contracts were re-regulated by introducing specific contractual types and a list of official reasons for concluding a fixed-term contract.

The situation in Spain was similar. After the Franco regime, Spanish employers were granted the right to use excessively temporary employment in exchange for trade union freedom (Hamann 2012, ch. 3; Larrea Gayarre 1992). The legal regulations on fixed-term contracts were liberalised in 1984 and fixed-term contracts were permitted under quite general circumstances and without the previous constraints – without, however, changing the comparatively generous dismissal protection for regular employees (see Jimeno and Toharia 1993). The employment effects of regulation of 'flexibility at the margin' were dramatic and led to a dual labour market in which especially young employees were trapped in atypical employment. Legal reforms in 1994, 1997, 2001, 2002 and 2006 tried to improve the situation for young atypical employees getting permanent employment but had little impact (Wölfl and Mora-Sanguinetti 2011). As in Italy, the situation has only been tolerable because the traditional family structure is capable of bearing the negative social impacts of the dual labour market (Malo et al. 2000).

A striking case of legal reflexivity in regulating atypical employment, and in particular fixed-term contracts, can be found in Germany, where, since the 1960s, the courts have virtually reversed the principle of contractual freedom to enter fixed-term contracts for reasons of 'protection of unfair dismissal protection'. The labour courts introduced the 'requirement of reason' (*Begründungspflicht* or *sachlicher Grund*) for a fixed-term contract to prevent circumvention of statutory dismissal protection. According to this requirement, employers should always consider offering a permanent contract unless they have a specific reason for a fixed-term contract.

The German Employment Promotion Act (*Beschäftigungsförderungsgesetz*) of 1985 introduced a change in attitude towards the regulation of fixed-term contracts. In a sense, the protection of protection by the Federal Labour Court had reached a point that its line of decision-making had created a certain degree of legal uncertainty by inflating the number of possible reasons for entering a fixed-term contract. The Employment Promotion Act was, in a reflexive labour law perspective, a statutory reaction to judicial uncertainty. However, politically it was sold as a measure of 'deregulation' and flexibilisation of dismissal law. Labour law was also discovered as a possible instrument of labour market policy. The predominant negative view of fixed-term contracts as circumvention of dismissal protection was amended by viewing them as positive measures to reduce unemployment. However, the Act did not replace the existing regulations of fixed-term contracts, which remained valid for all contracts not covered by the Act (Schömann et al. 1998, pp. 40–42). The Act was in fact an innovative form of legislation. It was originally limited to a five-year period during which an official evaluation of its effect had to be carried out. The results of this research were sobering (Buechtemann and Höland 1989). The employment effect of the Employment Promotion Act was modest at best and the research found that the vast majority of employers were in fact interested in long-term rather than fixed-term relationships (see also Fuchs and Schettkat 2000, p. 232).

A pioneering combination of labour market reform with relaxation of dismissal protection and promotion of atypical employment has been pursued in the Netherlands. The dual system of judicial or administrative authorisation for a dismissal is argued to be a main reason for Dutch employers to encourage temporary employment (Jacobs 2004, pp. 97–119). A characteristic of the Dutch labour market is a comparatively high percentage of part-time employment and temporary work obtained through temporary work agencies (Gorter 2000, pp. 187–8). Furthermore, the key concept used in labour market reforms has become flexicurity (Auer and Gazier 2011). It is a reflexive labour market policy strategy that successfully combines security concerns of employees with flexibility demands of employers (see section 5.4.3 in Chapter 5).

4.4   REGULATING THE PLACE OF WORK

Reflexivity is a trend that can be observed in many areas of regulation of the place of work. It is characteristic of international labour law and national reactions to globalisation through international labour law. And it is particularly apparent in less traditional but booming areas of labour law such as health and safety, discrimination and equal treatment as well as the regulation of the minimum wage.

4.4.1   Reflexive Regulation of Working Conditions

From a reflexive labour law perspective, areas of regulation such as health and safety, discrimination and equal treatment or the guarantee of a minimum wage encounter the same problems as other areas in which the company has to respond to public law demands. Compliance with these demands of external regulation requires capacities for adequate internal responses. It depends on the organisational context how companies respond.

However, working conditions are special since their effective improvement not only depends on management decisions but on the involvement of employees as well. Through interaction with their employees, companies have the chance to develop forms of self-regulation that respond to and are shaped by internal as well as external contexts of the company. Furthermore, through cooperation with employees and their representatives, companies can increase their productivity, as Wolfgang Streeck has demonstrated in relation to so-called producer coalitions (Streeck 1991).

What is necessary from a reflexive law perspective is that both the regulator and the regulated become aware of the public importance of private regulation. The matters regulated are always of both public and private concern. Health and safety, for example, is no longer simply a matter concerned with the health of employees, but touches on issues of internal as well as external environmental protection that are of importance not only to employees but also to the local community in the vicinity of the company and beyond.

Reflexive law demands from regulation that it becomes sensitive to the conditions at the place of work. Using the example of a statutory minimum wage, Hugh Collins has commented in an insightful manner about the complexities and difficulties of regulation of this area that require a reflexive approach:

> ... securing compliance ... can be alleviated by making regulation more sensitive to the differences between industrial sectors, types of working arrangement, and the qualities of the worker. In the case of a statutory minimum wage, for instance, it is possible to create exceptions, to vary minimum wage according to industrial sectors. Or to set different rates according to the qualities of the worker such as setting lower rate for young people. These variations create complexity, however, which tends to reduce levels of compliance, because employers and workers become unsure what detailed rules apply to their relationship. ... In sum, to avoid inefficiency and ineffectiveness, legal regulation of employment must be 'reflexive', in that it must respond and be sensitive to the variety of contexts to which it applies (Collins 2010, p. 28).

In short, reflexive labour law demands from companies and employees to live up to their public duties. They need to engage in self-regulation that benefits both sides as well as the general public. Reflexive labour can facilitate here by encouraging the parties to interact. It advocates what Steve Anderman has called collective consultation over individual dismissals, which recognises the legitimate interests of employee representatives in the exercise of managerial power (Anderman 2004).

With respect to discrimination and equality law a number of authors have argued that the future of this area will depend on a reflexive turn (see, for example, McCrudden 2007b). Bob Hepple (2012) has suggested that equality law can only become effective through initiatives at the workplace. He opts for a reflexive model of regulation of workplace equality that:

> rests on three foundations: strong incentives for internal scrutiny by an organisation; engagement with stakeholders; and an independent enforcement agency which can summon deterrent sanctions where voluntary means fail (Hepple 2012, pp. 64–5).

However, most crucial is the introduction of equality representatives at the place of work. Employers must have a duty to engage with their employees in order to improve workplace equality.

Probably the best formula that is most compatible with a reflexive labour law approach has been coined by Hugh Collins. He argues that 'participatory self-regulation' is needed in order to achieve equality at the place of work:

> The case for a more participatory process is particularly strong in the area of discrimination, because such a process is likely in itself to promote respect for diversity and inclusiveness, and at the same time to facilitate minority groups in asserting and defining their particular needs (Collins 2010, p. 75).

In the above quotes Collins and Hepple have formulated in relation to equality law what is a central insight of reflexive labour law in general. In order to be effective, statutory regulation has to switch from merely granting regulatory agencies command and control competences to facilitative regulation of self-regulation (Estlund 2010). However, crucial from a reflexive labour law perspective is the additional element of involving employee representatives. Procedural regulation in labour law means not just guidance for management to reach decisions, but opening up possibilities for participation of employees and their representatives. The formula of participatory self-regulation is indeed the key concept for a reflexive form of regulation of labour law.

4.4.2   The Reflexive Link between National and International Regulation of Employment Protection

What is remarkable about the relationship of international to national labour law from a reflexive law perspective is its non-hierarchical approach. The facilitative character of international labour law has made it reflexive in nature since its beginning. The standards developed in international labour law are meant to support national labour law and not as imposition.

The ILO operates with a number of legal instruments that aim at influencing law and policy in member states. From a reflexive law perspective, it makes a difference if the instrument aims at formal ratification, such as conventions, or is meant as support of policy-making, such as recommendations. In the area of employment protection we find both types. We might even detect a trend from imposition to facilitation.

The limits of the standard ILO governance method, conventions, can be demonstrated in relation to a major ILO convention in the area of employment protection, C158 concerning Termination of Employment at the Initiative of the Employer of 1982, which came into force on 23 November 1985. It is an important harmonising measure in employment protection and provides the basic legal regulation of dismissal. In Articles 4–6, the Convention outlines the reasons that employers can use for terminating the employment contract. It operates with the presumption that an employment contract cannot be terminated unless there is a 'valid reason'. It outlines three reasons employers can use for dismissal: (a) capacity (or capability); (b) conduct of the employee; and (c) redundancy, which is defined as a reason 'based on the operational requirements of the undertaking, establishment or service'. With the exemption of the US, which proves in this area again its exceptionalism by adhering to the notorious employment-at-will doctrine (for a critical discussion of the US exceptionalism thesis, see Hirsch 2012), the approach of the convention provides the basic structure of national dismissal protection laws around the globe.

However, there are clear limits of conventions as methods of regulating labour laws. In order for the convention to become law in member states, it needs to be ratified. Formal ratification can be slow. The ILO indicates on its website that by the end of 2012, Convention C158 was only ratified in 36 out of 183 countries.[3] Lack of formal ratification does not mean of course that members lack dismissal laws designed along the lines outlined in the convention.

The governance approach of the convention can be contrasted with the regulatory style underlying a recommendation. For example, Recommendation R198 on the Employment Relationship, adopted by the ILO in 2006, abstains from imposing principles and offers instead, according to Article 11, criteria 'for the purpose of facilitating the determination of the existence of an employment relationship'. The criteria include, according to Articles 12 and 13, subordination, dependence or integration of the worker in the organisation of the enterprise; the fact that the work is carried out according to the instructions and under the control of another party; is performed solely or mainly for the benefit of another person; carried out personally by the worker and/or within specific working hours or at a workplace specified or agreed by the party requesting the work; is of a particular duration and has a certain continuity; requires the worker's availability; or involves the provision of tools, materials and machinery by the party requesting the work. Further criteria are periodic payment of remuneration to the worker; the fact that such remuneration constitutes the worker's sole or principal source of income; provision of payment in kind, such as food, lodging or transport; recognition of entitlements such as weekly rest and annual holidays; payment by the party requesting the

---

[3]   http://www.ilo.org/dyn/normlex/en/f?p=NORMLEXPUB:11300:0::NO:11
300:P11300_INSTRUMENT_ID:312303:NO.

work for travel undertaken by the worker in order to carry out the work; or absence of financial risk for the worker.

The approach of the recommendation is in line with a reflexive labour law approach. In its facilitative approach, it implicitly respects not only national legal requirements but also recognises differences among industrial sectors and types of employees. The list of criteria for the assessment of employment relations expresses sensitivity in identifying relevant criteria for the determination of the existence of an employment relationship that takes up many of the suggestions made during the consultation in establishing the recommendation (Casale 2011).

4.5   REGULATING FLEXIBILITY

There is a lively debate about the impact of employment protection legislation, and theoretical accounts and empirical findings paint a diverse picture (Skedinger 2010). The debate has led to legislative reforms, some of which follow an overt deregulation agenda while others aim at flexibilising existing legislation in order to take account of new regulatory needs of atypical employment. In the case of flexibilisation policies, the reforms often consist in easing the recourse to temporary employment while leaving existing provisions for permanent employment contracts mostly unaltered.

In its Employment Outlook 2004, the Organisation of Economic Cooperation and Development (OECD) assessed the evidence on economic impact of employment protection legislation (EPL) and compared its benefits and disadvantages. It found convergence in levels of protection and added:

> Despite this convergence, the relative position of countries across the overall spectrum of EPL strictness, as defined and measured by the OECD, has not changed much since the late 1980s. The overall strictness of EPL continues to vary widely between countries and the regulation of temporary employment remains a key element in explaining cross-countries differences.
>
> Employment protection regulation fulfils its stated purpose, namely protecting existing jobs. Indeed evidence . . . suggests that EPL tends to limit firms' ability to fire workers. At the same time, EPL would reduce the re-employment chances of unemployed workers – thereby exerting upward pressure on long-term unemployment. Indeed, in deciding whether to hire a worker, employers will take into account the likelihood that firing costs will be incurred in the future. In sum, EPL leads to two opposite effects on labour market dynamics: it reduces inflows into unemployment, while also making it more difficult for jobseekers to enter employment (i.e. lower outflows from unemployment).
>
> The net impact of EPL on aggregate unemployment is therefore ambiguous

a priori, and can only be resolved by empirical investigation. However, the numerous empirical studies of this issue lead to conflicting results, and moreover their robustness has been questioned. On the other hand, it is possible to detect a link between EPL and employment rates for specific groups. Some studies, as well as the analysis presented in this chapter, suggest the possibility of a negative link between strict EPL and the employment rates of youth and prime-age women, while there may be positive links to the employment rates of other groups. This is consistent with the above findings of the effects of EPL on labour market dynamics. Indeed youth and prime-age women are more likely to be subject to entry problems in the labour market than is the case with other groups, and they are therefore likely to be disproportionately affected by the effects of EPL on firms' hiring decisions.

Differences in the strictness of EPL for regular and temporary jobs may be an important element in explaining the rise in the incidence of temporary work for youth and the low skilled (this is less the case for other groups, notably prime-age men). This means that facilitating the use of temporary work arrangements, while not changing EPL on regular employment, may aggravate labour market duality. It may also affect career progression and productivity of workers trapped in temporary forms of employment, which are typically characterised by weak job attachments and limited opportunities for upgrading human capital.

Any overall assessment of EPL has to weigh costs against benefits. EPL may foster long-term employment relationships, thus promoting workers' effort, co-operation and willingness to be trained, which is positive for aggregate employment and economic efficiency. In addition, by promoting firms' social responsibility in the face of adjustment to unfavourable economic circumstances, a reasonable degree of employment protection could be welfare-improving, i.e. it can help balance concern for workers' job security with the need for labour market adjustment and dynamism. Thus, some recent studies suggest that an optimal policy would combine some EPL with effective re-employment services and active labour market policies aiming at counteracting the negative effects of EPL on firms' hiring decisions (OECD 2004, p. 63).

The OECD captures reasonably well the mixed impact of employment protection legislation on labour markets from an economic perspective. However, from a reflexive labour law perspective, this economic assessment is too narrow. In addition to economic impacts, other consequences of employment protection on society also have to be taken into consideration. There are advantages and beneficial effects of employment protection that relate to psychological factors. Richard Sennett has demonstrated convincingly for the case of the US how employment insecurity creates negative effects for character formation and the management of personal lives and careers (Sennett 1999, 2006). And there is also the political demand for employment protection as a central element of social policies of advanced welfare states.

Arturo Bronstein emphasises rightly that the labour law reforms mentioned by the OECD have increased the number of exceptions to dismissal protection. In addition to support for fixed-term contracts, these include relaxation of rules for small enterprises and extension of probation and qualifying periods. Nevertheless, these labour reforms do not question the basic right not to be unfairly dismissed without valid reason (Bronstein 2009, ch. 3).

When looking at the political intentions of these labour law reforms, they often follow a deregulation agenda, which in a reflexive labour law perspective is characterised by inherent paradoxes and reflexive tendencies. Deregulation is itself a form of regulation and inevitably leads to new regulation (see Chapter 6). Furthermore, it is statistically wrong to assume that non-standard employment is gradually replacing standard employment.

In any case, for designing regulation it is important to recognise differences in non-standard work. Part-time work, fixed-term work, temporary agency work or forced self-employment, let alone informal, clandestine and illegal work in the black labour market, differ in their regulatory needs. Reflexive labour law realises that these different forms of non-standard employment require different forms of regulation (Schömann et al. 1998, ch. 7).

Furthermore, it is important to understand that the link of typical and atypical employment highlighted in the quote from the OECD is in fact an interaction between legal spheres of regulation. Regulation of atypical employment is a reflection of employment protection in order to protect itself from being undermined. Reflexive labour law suggests in this context moving from negative protection (of protection) to positive standardisation.

The starting point of this discussion is the insight that concerns about security and insecurity of employment are relevant not only for standard but equally for non-standard employment relations. The challenge that atypical forms of employment present to labour law has already led to a discussion of new standard employment relationships (in particular Schmid 2008a, ch.5, 2011). However, the real challenge is to find the right balance between flexibility and security and this indeed has been the central concern of European employment policy for a number of years, as will be shown in relation to the flexicurity debate discussed in Chapter 8.

4.6   CONCLUSION

Employment protection has been in the spotlight for a while. As a field of regulation, employment protection regularly encounters reform discussions. However, economic concerns with allegedly negative impact of employment protection on the labour market tend to dominate these discussions. Suggestions from a reflexive labour law perspective can help to broaden this debate.

A good starting point would be understanding employment protection as a global issue. International and European labour law can help to design new policies and legislation that modernise and coordinate legislation. Reforms of employment protection can have beneficial political and economic effects in levelling the playing field and in releasing productive capacities of welfare policies for economic performances.

In reforming unfair dismissal, aspects of economic security need to be balanced against flexibility concerns of companies. Reflexive labour law emphasises internal conditions and path dependencies of legal reforms. The need for regulation of atypical employment results partly from a reflexive trend of protection of protection within systems of employment protection. However, reflexive labour law suggests treating each atypical form of employment as a separate object of regulation. The right balance of flexibility and security in using these forms of regulation can be achieved through a new standardisation of atypical employment relationships.

For the reflexive regulation of employment protection, it is important to focus on internal conditions of company decision-making. Law can assist through innovative design of procedures that support self-regulation of the company. Such procedures should allow employee representatives to participate in decision-making. The ideal solution from a reflexive labour law perspective is the model of participatory self-regulation in companies that involve employees and their representatives in deciding issues related to employment protection.

5. Reflexive regulation of labour market policies

The chapter deals with legal boundaries and legal opportunities in relation to the emergence, operation and efficacy of labour markets. It concentrates on a particular strategy for the reform of modern labour markets known as transitional labour market policy. The chapter starts with a discussion of legal boundaries under the headings of legal complexity, regulation thresholds and costs of transitions and transactions related to law. It then explores a number of legal and social strategies and reforms that provide opportunities for a legal design of the transitional labour market. These include a strategy of reflexive deregulation of legal barriers to transitions, with particular reference to a re-regulation strategy of introducing vouchers or social drawing rights. The chapter also discusses some examples of reflexive regulation, with particular reference to the regulation of part-time work and training and the policy known as flexicurity.

5.1 THE LEGAL REGULATION OF LABOUR MARKET POLICIES

The investigation of the relationship between labour market policies and legal regulation is of key concern for reflexive labour law. Generally legal regulation of policies has two functions. It marks boundaries for policy-making, which derive from general normative principles and basic rights of individuals. However, it also has the function to provide opportunities for policies, which aim at flexibilising institutional structures. The second function requires law to become reflexive. In fact, in order to be a successful facilitation of policies, law needs to reflect on its own limitations and to engage in the balancing of concerns that derive from established legal structures and new legal demands.

A major aspect of the first function of law is to protect individuals from negative effects of markets. Law does so by conferring rights. In labour law these are employment rights and other measures protecting workers. Labour market policies can be both hampered and promoted by labour law measures. Without security, workers will be reluctant and lack the motivation to engage in transitions, as they will fear that changing status will bear significant risks and might become a change for the worse. These risks include the loss of a job (or a loss of employment in general), a deterioration of the terms of employment (in particular a decrease of income or future incomes such as pensions), diminished career opportunities, the social exclusion from the workplace or from other important spheres of life, an interference with social responsibilities and activities beyond the realm of work and an invasion of privacy and civic autonomy as a result of dependency on social benefits. If confronted with such prospects, employees tend to stick to the 'status quo'.

However, there is also the risk of long-term unemployment and other forms and causes of exclusion from the labour market. Indeed, at the centre of labour market policies lies the political concern with high unemployment that plagues modern society. Labour market policies are conceived as vehicles, instruments or methods to fight both cyclical and structural unemployment. Ideally, their aim is to obtain full employment in terms of flexible, though substantial and enduring, labour market participation for all (Schmid 2008b).

5.2 LEGAL BOUNDARIES FOR LABOUR MARKET POLICIES

Legal boundaries for labour market policies derive from the nature and purpose of law. We can identify internal factors that either limit the capacity of legal regulation, such as legal complexity and the detection threshold, or relate to normative criteria of legal regulation, such as the discrimination and the evaluation thresholds. In addition, there are various costs that occur as a result of legal regulations.

5.2.1 Legal Complexity

Reduction of complexity is the starting point for the emergence of social structure, social systems and society. Without reduction of complexity 'there would be nothing, no world consisting of concrete entities but only undifferentiated chaos' (Knodt 1995, p. xvii). Because a system is inferior by definition to its environment in terms of complexity, it needs to embark on strategies to reduce complexities. This in turn allows the system to build up internal complexity and thereby transform unorganised into organised complexity (Luhmann 1995a, pp. 26–7).

Each function system as well as its subsystems requires autonomy to fulfil its societal function. Reducing complexity is constitutive of law as an autonomous social system. By introducing a specific strategy of autonomous reduction of complexity, law establishes itself as an autopoietic system. However, the legal system produces complexity in its own operations deriving from autopoietic decision-making and the introduction of specific legal structures. The creation of legal complexity implies on the one hand that law 'has to protect the make-up of its own complexity by high thresholds of indifference' (Luhmann 2004, p. 219). On the other, it has to develop strategies to reduce its self-produced complexity.

The legal system, like other function systems, is differentiated into subsystems. These include legal fields such as contract law, company law, administrative law, social security law, tax law and labour law. Each legal subsystem develops its specific internal model of the external world and evolves along trajectories that are dominated by self-created norms and principles. The result is an enormous increase of complexity in modern society at both levels of the function system and its subsystems. In addition, modern law is characterised by a diversity of legal sources that are situated 'below' legislation adopted at the level of the nation state. These sources include collective agreements and customary law, but also standard-setting, informal agreements and norms created by private bodies.

In comparison with other legal subsystems, labour law has to cope with particular problems of external complexity that are related to its regulatory object of industrial relations and employment relations in companies. Normative premises and institutional orders of labour law tend to clash with other legal subsystems and orders. In particular when the social and industrial basis vanishes on which employment rights and collective bargaining rest, labour law regulations based on normative perspectives that are centred on rights of employees and trade unions have a tendency to clash with other normative legal premises (see Supiot 1999; Supiot et al. 2001). For example, workers' rights to take educational, parental or unpaid leave can clash with social security laws that link entitlements to continuous work careers. Another example is pension rights that are lost if a worker switches jobs or moves across sectors and branches of business and industry. Furthermore, informal company or workplace codes can also obstruct legal rights to leave or to work part-time, as full-time or all-time availability of the employee is often considered a prerequisite for prospects of promotion.

A legal design that regulates labour market policy has to be aware of the different logics of legal subsystems. The modern legal system is increasingly confronted with problems that derive from its self-generated complexity and there are many attempts to tackle the problem of legal complexity. A prominent strategy to reduce complexity is deregulation. However, deregulation is path-dependent. Its goals are shaped by national legal, industrial relations and political systems and accordingly vary widely among countries. Furthermore, deregulation is ineffective or detrimental if it is not perceived as a solution within various legal subsystems.

Thus, for reflexive labour law to successfully regulate labour markets, it must embark on a strategy of coordination of legal subsystems that acknowledges the major presuppositions of each order. This approach combines reduction of legal complexity with policies of flexibilisation that support parallel trajectories in different subsystems. Such reduction of legal complexity becomes a form of reflexive deregulation when it realises the limits of deregulation and leaves scope for re-regulation (see Chapter 6).

5.2.2 Regulation Thresholds

Any policy of regulation and/or deregulation has to reckon with regulation thresholds. The concept of thresholds can serve as a method to analyse legal boundaries. A regulation threshold describes the capacity of the legal subsystem to determine its scale of legality. Three types of thresholds can be distinguished: the detection threshold, the discrimination threshold and the evaluation threshold:[1]

1. The *detection* threshold refers to those aspects of the social object that require regulation; it distinguishes between relevant and irrelevant issues. Some issues are simply not (yet) taken up by the legal system. A reflexive legal design for labour markets has to tackle the detection threshold by indicating the legal relevance of unregulated or insufficiently regulated areas. For example, in labour law the legal (*de jure*) or contractual dependency of one person (employee) on another person (employer) is a decisive criterion, whereas the actual (*de facto*) dependency is only relevant in cases of doubt about the legal relationship, for example lack of a written employment contract. This means that the situation of persons who are self-employed, but dependent on one client (for example, the former employer in cases of outsourcing of a job and rehiring the worker as a formally self-employed person), is largely neglected in law.
2. The *discrimination* threshold concerns differences in the description of the social object that may justify qualitative differences in regulation; it distinguishes between the same – that deserves equal treatment

---

[1] The idea of regulation thresholds is based on the discussion of limits of regulation in Sousa Santos (2002, pp. 429–30).

– and the different – that allows unequal treatment. A particular problem is created by legal thresholds that exclude certain employees or non-employees from social benefits or from being covered by social security schemes.[2] Furthermore, in many countries (e.g. Germany and the Netherlands) social protection and employment laws have traditionally been based on the male breadwinner model. This kind of bias does create a barrier for enlightened labour market policies as it produces an insider/outsider distinction. Moreover, legal complexity will be increased if socially excluded groups are (re)entering the labour market. In case of interruption of employment, there are concerns with the continuation of social protection. However, there is also the issue of reversed discrimination. New rights and opportunities can undermine existing benefits and thus lead to new discrimination against those protected by previous regulation.

3. The *evaluation* threshold relates to rights granted to individuals and to principles that underlie legal structures; it distinguishes between the legal and the illegal. In most cases the existing system of rights and institutions provides the frame for new regulation. In addition there are specific rules that derive from non-statutory collective agreements and custom and practice at firm level that limit arbitrary choices. For example, an employer might deny certain career opportunities to an employee who has been on leave, contending that this employee has not shown sufficient commitment and loyalty to the company. In most current legal orders it is difficult to argue on legal grounds that this decision is 'illegal'.

5.3   THE REGULATION OF TRANSITIONAL LABOUR MARKETS

In the following a specific concept of labour market policy will be discussed that is known as transitional labour market (TLM) policy. The multidisciplinary nature of TLMs poses special challenges for regulation. The theory of reflexive labour law is particularly well suited to address these problems (see also Deakin and Rogowski 2011).

---

[2]   This does not merely hold for legislation, but also for collective agreements and 'soft law'.

5.3.1 The Concept of Transitional Labour Market Policy[3]

The TLM concept originates from research undertaken by Günther Schmid and his collaborators at the Research Unit on Labour Market Policy of the Wissenschaftszentrum Berlin (WZB). The TLM approach was the main theoretical concept of the large-scale European project TRANSLAM (Social Integration through Transitional Labour Markets), which was funded under the European Commission's Fourth Framework Programme of Targeted Socio-Economic Research (TSER).[4] TRANSLAM developed the concept of transitional labour markets into a regulatory idea for building institutional bridges which support individual transitions between various employment statuses (unpaid involuntary civil work, part-time and full-time work, continuous adjudication and training, dependent employment and self-employment). A basic premise was that 'making transition pay' enhances the employment intensity of growth and avoids the dilemma of growing segmentation of the labour market into insiders and outsiders. This research came to the conclusion that labour market policy that focuses on transitions transcends a narrow focus on European employment policies and is beneficial for the European economy as a whole.

The idea of transitional labour markets was further advanced in debates and research carried out in the thematic network *Managing Social Risks through Transitional Labour Markets* (TLM.NET), funded under the Fifth Framework Programme *Improving the Socio-Economic Knowledge Base* of the European Commission.[5] In these discussions the TLM approach was combined with the idea of social risk management and transitions over the life course of individuals. It led to a wide range of policy conclusions for both national and supranational employment policies (see Berg, de Gier 2008).

The closeness to policy is indeed one of the defining features of the TLM approach (see in particular Schmid 2002). Its success can be measured in terms of influence in various national and supranational policy debates. In France, for example, it has been supported for a number of years by Bernard Gazier, who actively promoted it in discussions organised for the *Commissariat général du Plan* (before its demise in 2005) (Gazier 2003). It probably had the strongest influence in Germany, due to a large extent

---

[3] The following section is based on the discussion of TLMs in Rogowski 2008a, Section 1.

[4] TRANSLAM lasted officially from 1 February 1996 to 31 January 1999.

[5] TLM.NET lasted officially from 1 December 2002 to 1 March 2006.

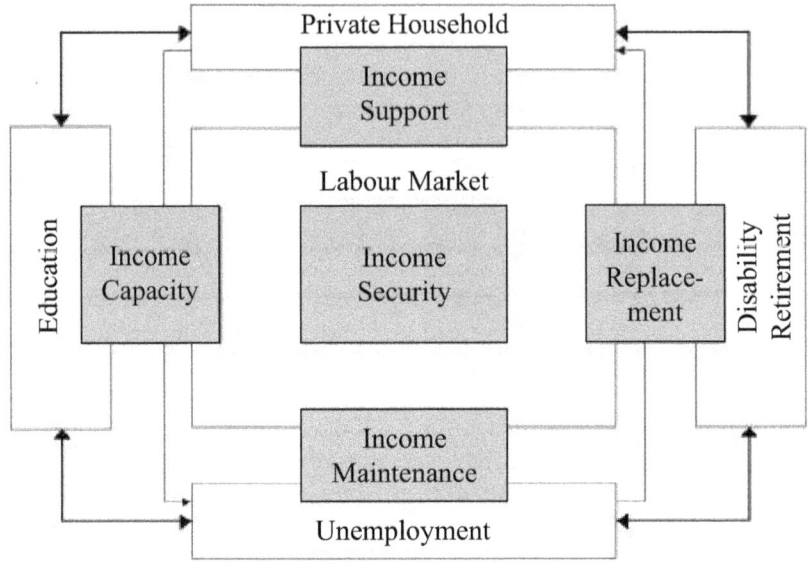

Source: Schmid, G. and K. Schömann (2004), Managing Social Risks Through
Transitional Labour Markets: Towards a European Social Model (TLM.NET Working
Paper No. 2004-01). Amsterdam: SISWO/Institute for the Social Sciences, Figure 6 at p. 21.

Figure 5.1   The transitional labour market and social risk management

to Günther Schmid's membership in the Hartz Commission on labour
market reform. TLM has been a key concept in the Hartz Commission's
fundamental overhaul of German labour market policies since 2002.
Furthermore, the TLM concept has been most influential in designing and
evaluating the European Employment Strategy (EES), as will be shown
later.

The original concept of the transitional labour market operates with
five core transitions within as well as into and out of the labour market.
Figure 5.1 shows how the original TLM approach and the idea of management of social risks can be linked.

Figure 5.1 depicts the modern labour market as consisting of the active
workforce of wage-earners and self-employed. The central idea underlying the diagram is to view the labour market as being embedded in and
linked to four groups and areas of non-wage-earners. The concept of
transitional labour markets analyses five major transitions into and within
the labour market: transitions from education and work, family and work,
work and retirement or disability, employment and unemployment, and
transitions within the labour market, including change from employment

to self-employment and change of type of employment (part-time and other atypical employment). The links between these areas and the labour market are fluid. The idea is that in modern times it is necessary to make the transitions in and out of the labour market more flexible and to concentrate regulatory efforts on these transitions.

The model suggests devising policies that support flexible transitions in the labour market and innovative institutional set-ups including new forms of legal regulation. Figure 5.1 shows in particular how the TLM concept can be linked with a concept of social risk management. Different types of transition are related with different types and aspects of income:

1. First, developing, maintaining and enhancing the *income capacity* (known also as 'employability') for successful transitions between education and employment and during transitions between (continuous) training and employment.
2. Second, guaranteeing *income security* during critical transitions between various employment relationships, especially between part-time and full-time work, between dependent employment and self-employment, and – increasingly important – between high and low wage jobs.
3. Third, providing *income support* during phases in the life course in which the income capacity is reduced due to social obligations such as the care for children or other dependent persons.
4. Fourth, securing *income maintenance* during transitions between employment and unemployment.
5. Fifth, providing *income replacement* in case of disability or retirement, which means in phases of the life-course in which employability is severely reduced or lacking completely (Schmid and Schömann 2004, p. 21).

Günther Schmid has proposed that the core idea of TLM, i.e. flexibilising the boundaries between gainful and non-gainful employment combined with social risk management as outlined above, can lead to a meaningful redefinition of full employment (Schmid 2002). Key is a new understanding of the role of the welfare state as coordinator of economic policies. Furthermore, a focus on transitions requires that active labour market policy becomes 'activating' labour market policy. Such reorientation of labour market policies opens new paths into employment for unemployed and inactive sections of the employment force and bears a large potential for reducing overall unemployment in Europe.

By conferring rights and establishing legal structures, law imposes certain boundaries on TLMs. It defines the scope and form in which transitions can take place. However, it also provides opportunities to explore new forms of transitions. Thus, in some cases legal protection prevents workers from making transitions in terms of a change of the employment status, while in other cases legal provisions trigger and warrant transitions. It depends to a large extent on the form of legal protection – social security and job and employment protection – that legal systems offer workers. Indeed, a legal system that is optimally geared to a TLM requires from most national employment systems substantial reforms of legislation and other legal regulation.

5.3.2 Legal Transition Costs

Legal regulation of TLMs can present a barrier to transitions by raising the costs of transitions for the worker and/or the employer. It can also fail to lower the costs of transitions and transactions when deemed appropriate.

In general the costs of transitions in the labour market, as referred to in the model of TLMs, consist of monetary, psychological as well as legal costs. They can be labelled *transition costs*. Workers who engage in transitions are threatened with the loss of employee benefits, such as pensions and health insurance, or access to the 'inside track' on future promotions. They might even risk the loss of their job. On the part of the employer, transition costs consist of loss of productivity, loss of income, lost investments in firm-specific training, extra hiring and training costs for replacements. From an economic point of view, transitions are only likely to take place once the benefits of a transition are higher than the costs of that transition. In that case, it is optimal for the employee and the employer to transact or reach an agreement on the transition.

A specific type of cost that might prevent the transition from taking place is constituted by so-called *transaction costs*. Transaction costs are associated with the cost of acquiring information about exchanges; in fact, any exchange, including those in the labour market, has a 'price'. The theory of transaction costs argues that it can at times pay to use the market as a coordination mechanism, while at other times it is less expensive to use hierarchical organisations such as firms to coordinate actions (Williamson 1994). A firm represents a set of long-term contracts between owners of labour and entrepreneurs, which, once these contracts have been established, no longer responds to price signals. Instead, the employee transfers certain user rights over his labour resource to the entrepreneur. Long-term/standard employment contracts reduce transaction costs because they relieve employers from spot-market exchanges, i.e., repeatedly having to hire and fire employees to perform single tasks. A standard employment, which is to a certain extent 'unspecified' with respect to the tasks that are to be performed and with respect to the working conditions – this is where the concept of hierarchy comes in – could, in this way, be cheaper and more efficient. Transaction costs, in the case of transitions, are information production costs.

Managing transitions within a company or in the labour market as a whole causes specific transaction costs. In general, these costs comprise information production costs, drafting costs, communicating costs, negotiation costs, agency costs, litigation costs, enforcement costs and costs of opportunistic behaviour. Legal transition costs occur both *ex ante* and *ex post* of an agreement. Typical costs after the agreement are costs of maladaptation and adjustment that arise when contract execution is misaligned as a result of gaps, errors, omissions and unanticipated disturbances. Furthermore, there are costs that derive from new legal requirements that actually aim at stimulating transitions. For employers, customised employment contracts and individual fiscal and social security arrangements increase administrative costs, in particular in relation to US-style contractualism. A voucher system or the introduction of default terms, which will be discussed later in this chapter, could possibly be one of the solutions to this problem.

Finally, even if the legal intention is reducing transition costs, the law is limited in this respect. Some costs/barriers for workers are related to internal human resource management policies of the employer, e.g. the policies with respect to promotion and career opportunities within the company. In these areas law can, at present, hardly or only marginally affect the employer's prerogative. In other areas the legal norms tend to be too general, such as the norms of 'the good employer' or 'good faith', and their implementation depends on the interpretation by case law or collective agreement. Other instruments and strategies than law, such as education, or informal agreements with trade unions and works councils are often more adequate.

5.4 REFLEXIVE REGULATION OF TRANSITIONAL LABOUR MARKETS

There are a number of reflexive strategies that aim at removing the types of legal boundaries or thresholds identified in section 5.2.2. Examples of reflexive regulation include conscious reforms of existing regulations and facilitative regulations of self-regulation. These strategies are often characterised by sophisticated ways of balancing different (social and economic) interests, carried out at the national, regional or local levels.

Reflexive regulation is not confined to legislation but can also be pursued via collective bargaining. Collective agreements are an important source of labour law, in particular when declared generally applicable. There are many interesting cases of trade-off between competitiveness and employment goals that reveal social responsibility and cognitive openness of collective bargaining (Meer 2000). However, collective bargaining and industrial relations, which are, like labour markets, self-referential systems and constrained by their autopoietic needs (see Chapter 3), are limited in their 'social responsiveness'. The trade-off possibilities of collective bargaining represent both barriers and opportunities to strategies of reflexive regulation.

In a number of countries, most prominently in Denmark but also in the Netherlands and Germany, social partners enjoy significant regulatory powers and are capable of entering agreements at the national level. This is still a basic feature of the Danish situation and of the so-called Dutch 'Poldermodel' (Visser and Hemerijck 1997; Heijden 1998) and a line of policy pursued on various occasions in Germany (for example in the *Bündnis für Arbeit* between 1998 and 2002; see Streeck 1998, 2009, ch. 4). However, the effect of recommendations of national corporatist arrangements is in general fairly limited to economic and financial issues; social policy issues are, with the exception of Denmark, to a much lesser extent taken up by national corporatist arrangements. In the case of Germany, the focus shifted in the last decade from macro-corporatist arrangements in the form of national alliances to firm-specific workplace alliances (Streeck 2009, pp. 85–6).

From a reflexive labour law perspective, law not only establishes boundaries for policy-making but also creates opportunities and steers politics into pursuing certain avenues. Not only new legal forms such as soft law, but also established legal principles such as discrimination or proportionality can be used for purposes of rethinking existing policies, of starting policy-making in new fields and designing innovative regulatory strategies. Furthermore, law's structural coupling to the political system is a continuous source of irritation that instigates both legal and political dynamics.

Opportunities mirror to some extent the legal barriers outlined in the previous part of the chapter. There are a number of options for creating legal opportunities. These include what I shall call reflexive deregulation and strategies of introducing vouchers or social drawing rights. Furthermore, there exist a number of legal strategies to level out discrimination thresholds, to implement measures that support the development of transitional labour markets and to foster training. It ends with a discussion of new labour market initiatives in the Netherlands and in Scandinavia.

5.4.1   Reflexive Deregulation

Deregulation policies are attractive for policies that focus on TLMs. Where regulations create obstacles to transitions, and their removal incurs no unbearable costs, a policy of deregulation seems feasible. Such a strategy becomes a form of reflexive deregulation if it involves coordinating different regulatory logics that govern labour markets. Furthermore, reflexive deregulation is usually accompanied by attempts to re-regulate the labour market. In the following, general aspects of deregulation are discussed under the heading of reduction of complexity and a specific example of re-regulation, the voucher system.

5.4.1.1   Reducing legal complexity

A general strategy to create legal opportunities that ease transitions is directly related to reduction of legal complexity. Modern labour law systems, like other social systems, are continuously forced to look for strategies of reducing complexity. When these systems realise that internal complexity is, at least partly, self-generated, they might turn reflexive and develop their own system-specific strategies of reduction of complexity. It is in this context that a new view on deregulation might emerge (see also Chapter 6).

There exists a variety of deregulation policies and analyses of deregulation of Western labour law systems reveal their divergent nature. In Great Britain, for example, deregulation focused in the 1980s and 1990s on some reduction of employee protection combined with severe legal restrictions on trade union activities (Dickens 1994). In Germany, deregulation involved adaptations to the complex structure of the autonomous labour law system in order to achieve certain necessary reforms, particularly in the use of fixed-term contracts (Buechtemann 1993b; Fuchs and Schettkat 2000). In France, the main purpose of deregulation in the 1980s was to reduce the powers of the labour inspectorate while at the same time strengthening the representation of employee interests at establishment level and making employment relationships more flexible, particularly through new or atypical forms of employment contract (Lyon-Caen 1993; Malo et al. 2000). And in the USA, deregulation meant the *de facto* loss of employee rights because of the decline in trade union membership and the consequent decline in protection provided by collective agreements (Gould 1993).

Despite its divergent nature, there are some common patterns of deregulation of labour law. An example is the debate on atypical employment contracts. A number of deregulation policies aim in similar ways at flexibilising the available forms of employment and support atypical

employment contracts, in particular by overcoming the so-called legal discrimination of fixed-term contracts of labour. However, it has to be said
that each of the deregulation policies is path-dependent, i.e., the form and
the actual process of deregulation is determined by the specific character
of national labour law systems and their relationships to national industrial relations systems (see Schömann et al. 1998).

The varied experiences with deregulation make it impossible to speak of
a uniform trend. The objectives range from radical free-market approaches
of abolition of employment protection to piecemeal reforms of existing
labour laws. However, it is important that deregulation policies are always
conducted within the framework of existing legal and other normative
structures.

Alongside deregulation, there are attempts to re-regulate the labour
market. These are legal strategies that combine reducing complexity
and enhancing individual preferences. Such strategies become reflexive
regulation when linked to self-regulation (for details see Chapter 6). In the
following, an example of such reflexive re-regulation is discussed. This is
the market-driven but collectively controlled strategy called the voucher
system (see on experiments and studies of voucher systems in the area of
education and training Levin 1980, 1983, 1991).

5.4.1.2   The voucher system and social drawing rights

A voucher system (also referred to as a quasi-market) can be defined as a
system that enhances (or restores) the (free) market as well as the freedom
and preferences of individual persons (i.e. workers) within the regulatory
framework of the labour market. At the same time, a voucher system
serves to allocate (public and/or private) resources (Van Gendt 1980).
Voucher systems can be seen as solutions for collective failure (in the case
of public or quasi-public goods).

However, from a reflexive law perspective, they are means to complement, supplement, endorse or implement public regulation. In the context
of privatisation of public services, they both pose a threat to public
employment services and provide new opportunities. Petra Kaps and
Holger Schütz are certainly right that there are still many ways to improve
public employment services that 'represent alternatives to market-type
instruments such as performance contracting and vouchers' (Kaps and
Schütz 2011, p. 92). Nevertheless, vouchers, if regulated properly, are
a useful means to promote transitions from a reflexive labour law
perspective.

The basic function of a voucher system within a transitional labour
market would be to enable workers – financially, but also in other respects
– to engage in transitions and to *manage* their own transitions adequately

(Schmid 2008a, p. 291). A voucher system grants legal entitlements. Alan Supiot argues that the entitlement of the worker to switch from one work status or situation to another has already emerged as a new legal figure which reconciles freedom and security. He mentions special leave schemes, timesaving schemes and training vouchers. The main thrust of these schemes is that the workers are granted rights which are exercised within the bounds of a previously established claim, but bring them into effect by free decision rather than as a result of risk. Therefore these rights are referred to as 'social drawing rights' (Supiot et al. 1998, pp. 48–9).

If successfully implemented, the voucher system is able to contribute to reversing juridification of the labour market, to reducing legal complexity and to lowering transition and transaction costs. It also enhances labour market flexibility and allows for a sound form of deregulation. Social drawing rights impinge on fundamental aspects of the employment relationship and the relationship of law and the labour market. Vouchers or social drawing rights enhance chances of flexibilising employment and support transitions in employment through:

- entitlements to (a certain amount of) training and education (e.g. in hours, days or qualification levels);
- entitlements to the reduction and extension of a person's working hours during his or her career (enabling a person to switch from full-time to part-time schemes);
- entitlements to certain fiscal subsidies, advantages or benefits which, e.g., enables a person to switch between employment and self-employment;
- entitlements to pre-retirement schemes (e.g. in hours per week), which enables a person to (partly) retire and at the same time preserve his or her employment (within certain limits);
- entitlements to a variety of leaves (parental leave, special leave, calamity leave, unpaid leave);
- entitlements to childcare arrangements (e.g. in number of hours, days or years per child);
- entitlements to holidays and to (a certain amount of) leisure time, e.g. in the form of a leisure time account (comparable to a bank account).

A voucher system contributes to workers' empowerment and, by allowing an exchange of vouchers (within a company or in an exchange market), enhances individual preferences. Moreover, by allocating funding on the basis of workers' vouchers to labour market institutions, such as training and education services, public employment agencies and childcare centres, a voucher system contributes to dynamic efficiency. A voucher system allows individuals to exercise rights, not as a result of risk, but as a free decision. It thus differs fundamentally from a social security scheme based on the payment of premiums (Supiot et al. 1998, p. 49). Social drawing rights can be used for specific social purposes and enable 'drawers' to (collectively or individually) build up reserves that cover the use of the drawing rights.

However, the question remains to what degree it is efficient and fair to have individuals freely choose both the purpose and the moment for exercising their rights. Voucher systems have to find ways to balance and reconcile collective and individual interests since not all (individual) purposes are necessarily socially gainful activities. Although the moment for exercising the rights will be decided by the individual in general, there will be social and organisational constraints that need to be acknowledged. Certain timing will be attractive from an economic and social point of view. For example, workers might have to use their drawing rights to education during a period of recession rather than at times of economic boom.

A major question in setting up a voucher system is the financing. It is likely that some government funding is needed, but employers and perhaps trade unions will probably have to contribute as well. In any case, the time during which workers exercise such rights will have to count as 'working time' for labour law and social security purposes (Supiot et al. 1998). Furthermore, a special issue is the time limit of entitlements. According to the general concept, the use of vouchers should not be limited in time. However, the absence of time limits poses great difficulties to organisations and institutions, notably in the field of education and training, in estimating the demand for their services. As a consequence it is difficult to allocate budgets. Moreover, if individuals are allowed to save up their entitlements over a long period of time and if the entitlements are based on units in hours, days, months, courses or similar quantities, it should be noticed that the actual price and worth of these units could change over time. This also has an impact on budgets and reserves. It might thus be necessary to limit the time for the use of entitlements by so-called default terms.

An important aspect of voucher or social drawing schemes is their capacity to enhance collective bargaining of labour agreements. Many existing collective agreements already allow for differentiation and individual choice. Regulating voucher systems by collective agreements, combined with statutory minimum standards, makes it easier to take collective interest into account and to adjust them to the peculiarities and established practices in sectors of industry and companies. A good example of a collectively agreed labour market measure is the Community Initiative in the German region of Saarland (*Saar-Gemeinschaftsinitiative*). Formerly unemployed persons are granted a reduction of social security premiums if they accept a job; this premium is 'paid' in the form of rights to training (Scherer 2006, pp. 94–5).

5.4.2 Levelling out Discrimination Thresholds

An important aspect of reflexive regulation of labour law is levelling out discrimination thresholds, mentioned in section 5.2. Relevant legal and social policies in this context include the promotion of part-time employment and paid leave schemes that make it possible for men and women to combine and balance work and (family) care. Part-time work has facilitated in many countries the transformation from an industrial economy to a service economy that has contributed to growth of employment and is predominantly based on female labour (O'Reilly and Fagan 1998). In the following, the Dutch example of levelling out discrimination through promotion of part-time work is contrasted with the Scandinavian policies that favour paid leave schemes.

Part-time work presents a good example of levelling out concrete discrimination thresholds (on international efforts to regulate part-time work, see Murray 1999). In the Netherlands most discrimination thresholds in this area were removed at end of the 1990s. The Dutch government started with recommendations to the collective bargaining partners to use collective agreements for the promotion of part-time work through differentiation of working-time patterns. This was followed in July 2000 with a Law on the Adjustment of Working Hours. It introduced a right for workers employed in companies and services with 10 or more employees to adjust their contractual working time by either working *more* or *fewer* hours. Employers can only deny workers an adjustment of working time if major company or services interests are negatively affected.

An alternative strategy to overcome discriminatory regulation threshold is pursued in Scandinavia (see Pfau-Effinger 1998), where the preferred policy choice is that men and women work full-time. Legal and social reforms accordingly tend to concentrate on paid leave schemes and support for childcare. Paid leave arrangements were first introduced as labour market policy measures to combat unemployment in Denmark in 1994. The paid leave programmes were labelled as job rotation programmes, allowing a wage-earner to leave work for a certain amount of time (usually fewer than 26 weeks and 52 weeks maximum) and pursue other activities, while being replaced by an unemployed person during the leave period. Paid leave was extended to three types in Denmark: educational leave, sabbatical leave and childcare leave. However, the types of

paid leave differ in their legal forms. Paid leave is only a legal right in relation to childcare, whereas the other types of leave need to be negotiated
between the employer and the employee.

Per K. Madsen argues that, although all types of leave have their pros
and cons, educational paid leave is the most beneficial type for both
parties as well as the economy as a whole in Denmark. Educational paid
leave programmes have short- and long-term effects, which can be summarised in two extremes. On the one hand, these programmes carry the
risk of creating bottlenecks and wage pressures (in case only a certain
segment of the labour market makes use of them). On the other hand,
educational paid leave schemes have positive effects in terms of improved
qualifications of the workforce. In addition to beneficial macroeconomic
effects, paid leave has a potentially beneficial macro-social effect in terms
of personal relations and mobility. This is particularly true for work-
sharing arrangements (Madsen 1998a, 1998b).

5.4.3   The Strategy of Flexicurity

Reflexive strategies of regulation that aspire to trigger, facilitate and safe-
guard transitions within the labour market need support from employees
as well as employers and their representatives. The political and social
feasibility and success of legal reform of transitional labour markets
depends on the ability of reflexive law to convince not only workers but
also employers that they gain something from transitional employment.
For both parties the benefits need to outweigh the costs. In this context
attempts of creating a positive trade-off between linking – and rebalancing
– flexibilisation of the labour market, favoured by employers, on the one
hand, and increased (employment and social) security in particular for
atypical workers, on the other hand, is a key example of reflexive regulation of labour markets.

Flexicurity has been defined as a policy strategy that attempts, syn-
chronically and in a coordinated way, to enhance on the one hand the
flexibility of labour markets, the organisation of work and labour relations, and to enhance on the other hand employment security and social
security, in particular for weak groups in and outside the labour market
(Wilthagen and Tros 2004; Bekker and Wilthagen 2008). Flexicurity
is a new labour market policy that flexibilises rigidities (Dore 1986) by
addressing paradoxes and dilemmas of existing labour law and labour
market policy (Elster 1979). In particular it deals with an aspect that
labour lawyers such as Spiros Simitis have called the negative consequence
of traditional labour law, namely the exclusion of atypical employees
from employment protection (Simitis 1994b). In other words, flexicurity

is a strategy of reflexive deregulation combined with positive attempts of re-regulation.

The first country to introduce a legislative programme on flexicurity was the Netherlands (Auer 2001). Although initially introduced as a new labour policy measure, it was also part of attempts to reform the Dutch dismissal system. Dutch dismissal law requires prior consent from either a judge or the labour office to end an employment relation (see Chapter 4). Employers have for a long time viewed this prior check of the employer's decision to terminate the employment relationship as unreasonable. Circumvention of dismissal protection has been a major reason for the rise of atypical employment and a high rate of disability claims (see Blankenburg et al. 1985). Over the last 30 years there have been repeated attempts to reform Dutch dismissal law. However, their success will depend to a significant degree on agreement to these reforms by the social partners (Blanchard, Tirole 2004).

A key role in the creation of the Dutch flexicurity law was played by the Dutch Foundation of Labour. This unique macro-corporatist institution used to be a key player in the 1970s' Wage Control Policy and still plays an important role in advising collective bargaining parties, companies and the government (in particular the Dutch Ministry of Social Affairs and Employment) on social and economic policies. It fosters bi-partite agreements between the confederations of employers' and employees' organisations and tri-partite agreements involving the government, which elaborate or complement legislation or serve as a substitute of statutory regulation in the field of industrial relations and labour law. Since the pursuit of so-called 'win-win' strategies (Levine 1995) constituted for a considerable time the core of the Foundation's policies, it is not surprising that this institution was a key player in preparing the bill on flexibility and security.

The trade unions, the employers' confederations and the government were much committed to the Foundation's proposals. However, there was also criticism alleging that more weight was put on the flexibility than on the security part, in particular the proposal to extend fixed-term employment contracts three times without having the obligation to apply for a permit to give notice was seen as a significant weakening of dismissal protection. Besides, it had become clear that the trade unions' and employers' organisations' interpretations of the covenant on a new collective agreement in the temporary agency business are very much at odds with each other. The negotiations on the intended collective agreement did not proceed as smoothly as assumed. However, after some debates, the new legislation came into force on 1 January 1999 (on the legislative history of the Dutch flexicurity law, see Wilthagen 1998).

The new law had a significant impact on Dutch labour market policies.

The flexicurity strategy was not limited to legal reform in the area of atypical work, dismissal law and social security. Trade unions and employers engaged in experiments combining internal and external flexibility.
So-called 'job pools' or 'flex pools' and other hybrid forms of organising
employment were either reformed or newly created in order to increase
the employability of workers and to prevent redundancies. Older forms of
job pools that can be found in the Amsterdam and Rotterdam harbours
were successfully reorganised. In fact, Dutch employment policies know
two types of job pools: a *banenpool*, or 'labour pool', which creates additional jobs for the hard-to-place unemployed, and an *arbeidspool*, which
constitutes an 'employment pool' or 'flex pool'. This is a new private or
public-private organisation (or cooperation of organisations) that allo-
cates workers, including temporary and other atypical workers within
a company, to a network or cooperation of several companies within a
certain region or sector, depending on the actual demand for labour. In
many cases temporary work agencies take up the role of coordinating
these pools and recruitment for these pools is accompanied with offers of
training and education for the unemployed.

The flexicurity strategy became a key part of the European Employment
Strategy when it entered its second phase in 2005. Building on the Dutch
experience, but also on the Danish policy of combining flexible employment laws with high levels of social security and active labour market
policy measures (on this so-called 'golden triangle' see Bredgaard et al.
2008), flexicurity became the key policy concept in European employment
policies and was widely regarded as encapsulating the main virtues of the
European Social Model (see Chapter 8 and Rogowski 2008b). In order
to support the development of national flexicurity strategies, common
principles on flexicurity were adopted in December 2007 (European
Commission 2007).

5.4.4   Reflexive Regulation of Atypical Employment and the Training Paradox

Regulating training and education can be regarded as typical and illustra-
tive for the dilemmas, paradoxes and problems of modern labour markets,
including TLMs. Modern labour markets consist of a growing number of
employees who are not likely to permanently work or be actually present
in one particular company or workplace. Of course, the reason for this
will vary and can be judged either negatively or positively. On the one
hand, a large part of so-called contingent workers are deemed to remain
deprived of a permanent job and a decent career, regardless of their own
preferences. They belong to the peripheral workers in a bifurcated labour

market. Workers who engage in transitions as envisaged in the model of TLMs, on the other hand, repeatedly change horizons out of free will and for good individual and social causes. Nevertheless, the existence of both groups does raise similar problems when it comes to investing in training and education.

The paradox at hand here can be termed the flexibilisation versus training paradox. Modern societies are being viewed as 'knowledge-driven economies', and vocational training and education and provision of skills are very much on the political and economic agenda. The EU's 2020 initiative, for example, puts the new skills at the centre of labour market reforms (European Commission 2010a, 2012a). The acquisition of knowledge and skills is both the main challenge and the central opportunity for achieving a return to full employment. However, at the same time, further flexibilisation of the labour market is being pursued vigorously in many countries. And the question, put on the agenda by human capital theory (Becker 1964), has to be asked: why should firms or individuals invest in the production of knowledge and skills if they cannot exclude others from the final gains of these investments? More specifically, it is argued that employers are not likely to invest in general, transferable training.

A strategy that is popular in countries such as the Netherlands is to use temporary work agencies that provide employees for particular kinds of skilled jobs. However, training their employees is usually not high on the list of obligations of temporary work agencies. At best they function as transitory institutions from non-employment to regular employment for persons that would be confronted with less stable employment conditions under any circumstances (Osterman 1994). However, the willingness of temporary work agencies to invest in training is likely to increase if the employment relationship between worker and agency is turned into a more or less permanent contract.

Can the training paradox be solved by using reflexive labour law? A non-reflexive way would be to make it mandatory for employers by legislation to invest in training for the flexible and 'transitory' workforces they deploy. However, such a strategy is likely to encounter resistance. An alternative would be leaving it to collective bargaining to regulate training arrangements for flexible workforces. This strategy encounters the problem of atypical employees being outsiders in general and not covered by collective agreements (Crouch 1997).

A strategy more in tune with a reflexive approach would be to grant flexible workers or workers in transition certain entitlements to training and education, more or less independently from the companies that hire or deploy them. These entitlements could be built up in individual training accounts. However, such market-type strategy still requires the state to participate because of a number of risks related to limited savings, risk of failure of capital markets and a lack of equity. However, purely state-subsidised schemes also encounter problems and there are a number of alternatives. Günther Schmid argues convincingly that flexibilising existing social institutions such as social insurance schemes or tax credits has a large potential for stimulating continuous vocational education and training (Schmid 2008a, pp. 286–92).

5.5   A EUROPEAN STRATEGY OF REGULATING TRANSITIONAL EMPLOYMENT

Reflexive regulation starts from the assumption that a multiplicity of institutions might be involved in administering labour market policy. Furthermore, there are a number of strategies that can be used in a complementary way to regulate labour markets. Probably the most advanced, although abstract form of regulation of TLMs would be to introduce a constitutionally protected right to transitional employment. It would create a legal basis for entitlements to transitional employment (Gazier 2002; Gazier and Lechevalier 2008). This legal innovation could be added to the fundamental social rights protected in European treaties, social charters and international conventions (see Weiss 1996). The European Social Charter of 1963 is an obvious starting point.

A number of ILO conventions and recommendations and European directives regulate atypical employment at the international and the European level (further discussed in Chapters 9 and 10). They contain valuable support for securing transitions in employment. They not only contain several rights for part-time workers and anti-discrimination clauses, but also demand that, where relevant, states should facilitate changes in working hours, i.e. transitions from part-time and fixed-term employment to full-time employment and vice versa.

Many countries have experimented with interesting legal initiatives (including provisions in collective agreements) to adjust the traditional wage-earning status which has traditionally been the central reference point in labour law but has become problematic now that the transitions within a working life are no longer 'linear', for example these transitions are no longer guaranteed to follow a straight line. However, no country seems yet able to present a clear-cut alternative to the traditional wage-earner status. In any case, an encompassing design to promote atypical employment and transitions requires a new legal and social interpretation of the concepts of 'standard employment'. Such a design should adopt a lifecycle perspective, already discussed in the social sciences (Lyon-Caen 1996).

An interesting proposal for a strategy of 're-institutionalising the employment relationship' has been suggested by a working group chaired by Alan Supiot (Supiot et al. 1998). They argue that the basic outline for re-institutionalisation is already present in national legislation. The new employment status should be 'based on a comprehensive approach to work, capable of reconciling the need for freedom and the need for security' (Supiot et al. 1998, p. 45). The prime aim should be 'to protect workers during transition phases between jobs'.

From a reflexive law perspective, their approach to establishing rules is remarkable and includes an allocation of negotiating fora for these rules that enable collective parties to intervene. New legal instruments must be developed 'to guarantee the continuity of status above and beyond different and non-working cycles. The worker should be in favour of abandoning the linear career model. Career interruptions and occupational reorientation should come to be considered normal incidents in on-going employment status. Such continuity may be ensured by law or collective agreement' (Supiot et al. 1998, pp. 183–4).

A crucial point in Supiot et al.'s analysis is to extend the concept of employment to include non-marketable forms of work, requirements of equality of men and women, continuing training and the undertaking of activities of common benefit and career choice. The concept of *work* is thought to fulfil these requirements. Work is distinguished from 'activity' in that it stems from an obligation, whether imposed or voluntarily agreed. Therefore, domestic work for example, is rightly considered work. Law should thus apply in all cases of work, but the protection may vary. For that purpose four circles of social law (protection) are proposed: a first circle that covers universal rights that apply to anyone irrespective of the type of work (e.g. health insurance); a second circle that comprises rights based on unpaid work/socially useful activity (such as retirement benefits and accident coverage for volunteer work); a third circle that pertains to the common law of occupational activity whose base can be found in European Union law (such as equal treatment); and, finally, a fourth circle that covers rights that are related to paid employment directly connected with (degrees of) subordination. This typology replaces the paradigm of employment by a paradigm of occupational status, covering the various forms of work that a person may perform during his or her life.

A number of regulatory strategies are possible to respond to such a new typology of work 'beyond employment' (Supiot et al. 2001). One option would be to simply declare it illegal by European law to discriminate against a person that is or has been engaged in making transitions in the labour market. Such a provision could be directly added to non-discrimination and equal treatment law that has developed at the

European level and has been proven of paramount importance in fighting discrimination thresholds (Ellis and Watson 2012). However, for the macro European strategy of a social right to transitional employment to be effective, it must be accompanied by strategies at the micro level of specific legal regulations. Indeed, the coordination of existing laws in the areas of labour law, social policy and social security in order to remove concrete and overt barriers to transitions is already a core concern of coordination policies pursued under or accompanying the European Employment Strategy. Probably the greatest challenge in this context will be the coordination of different legal orders that are located at different levels of regulation. An increase in legal complexity within the legal system and subsequent strategies of reduction of complexity are unavoidable consequences of introducing a right to transitional employment protected throughout the European Union.

5.6 CONCLUSION

From a reflexive labour law perspective, both legal barriers and opportunities can be identified for labour market policies such as TLM. When addressing needs for transitions in employment, labour law is confronted by several normative orders which are characterised by a distinct rationale and a high degree of complexity and entail a variety of regulatory thresholds. Moreover, legal regulations produce or raise certain costs of transitions. However, there should be a clear understanding that many of the boundaries labour law presents to policy innovations derive from important normative concerns with protection of the basic rights of individuals, aiming at shielding individuals from the negative effects of markets.

Nevertheless, law can contribute in significant ways in creating opportunities for policies that aim at flexibilising institutional structures and facilitating transitions in the labour market. Reflexive labour law can offer a number of promising legal strategies based on existing trends. First, there is the strategy of reflexive deregulation to create opportunities that ease transitions. A promising proposal to reduce legal complexity and to lower the costs of transitions is the introduction of a system of vouchers or social drawing rights that grants people entitlements to transitional employment. Second, combating discrimination thresholds, in particular on the basis of equal treatment law, is a successful policy strategy. And third, flexicurity policies originating from the Netherlands and Scandinavia show that reflexive regulation can lead to innovative legal reforms of labour market policies.

Finally, reflexive regulation takes the multilevel governance approach seriously. Analysing the interplay between policies pursued at the supra-national level of the EU and national labour market policies is crucial. From a reflexive labour law perspective, a European strategy of regulating transitional employment that combines a rights-based approach with specific measures adjusting existing regulations seems feasible.

6. Reflexive deregulation of labour market policies and labour law

Labour market deregulation is a policy pushed at the global level by mainstream economic monitoring institutions such as the OECD, the IMF and the World Bank. The labour market is viewed by these international organisations as performing optimally if cleared of dismissal protection, wage determination through collective bargaining and regulations on working time. Linked closely to a neoliberal understanding of the functioning of the economy, this employer-oriented and employer-supported labour market policy is sold as the only successful solution for the emerging world society. Not surprisingly, it is resisted worldwide by trade unions and to some extent by the international organisation dealing with labour policy, the International Labour Organization (ILO).

Historically, this push for deregulation by employers rather than trade unions was not always the case. In a pioneering book, published in 1916, Hugo Sinzheimer, the 'father of collective labour law' (Kubo 1995) proposed a statute for collective bargaining based on the 'Idea of Social Self-Determination in Law' (*Ein Arbeitstarifgesetz – die Idee der sozialen Selbstbestimmung im Recht*). In it he put forward the essence of what became, with the establishment of the right to free collective bargaining in December 1918, one of the most important social achievements of the Weimar Republic, the social and legal recognition of autonomous collective bargaining as a source of regulation of industrial affairs.

> The machinery of the modern economy is too complicated to be regulated solely by norms laid down by the State. In order that the law can evolve effectively, the State must transfer some of its legislative powers to certain groups in society who will then look for and discover the legislation best suited to their changing needs and circumstances (Sinzheimer 1976 [1916], p. 174, translation R.R.).

This idea is still valid today. However, the significance of free collective bargaining as a form of deregulation accepted and indeed vigorously fought for by workers is increasingly undermined in the post-industrial society (Wedderburn et al. 1994). A great deal is at stake here: not only greater labour market mobility, widely seen as key to economic growth, together with a monetary and financial policy that encourages more job creation in order to eliminate mass unemployment and to improve competitiveness in the world society, but also democracy itself in an extended Europe, which may be at risk unless new forms of solidaristic interest representation are developed that accurately reflect not only the changing needs of the industrial partners but also the unemployed.

One of the forces driving for changes in the modern labour market is the emergence of new groups that Sinzheimer probably hardly thought of, in particular women, whose labour force participation rate is likely to soon match those of men. According to the World Development Report 2012 issued by the World Bank, the female labour market participation rate has increased sharply overall since 1980 at all levels of income (World Bank 2012; see also Lewis and Lewis 1996). Another driving force is individualisation, as a result of which the diversity of needs is increased exponentially in the wake of constantly changing preferences among employees themselves. Individual differences in consumption and lifestyle have become a status symbol in the age of the information society (Bauman 2000; Beck and Beck-Gernsheim 2001).

However, there are also clear negative trends. Luhmann's observation on the emergence of a metacode of inclusion and exclusion in the world society (discussed in Chapter 1) is reflected in the growing number of unemployed or poor people, excluded from full participation in social life, whose interests are neither fully represented in political processes nor adequately legally recognised in law. The growing diversity of needs and trends towards social exclusion are not met by neoliberal deregulation that focuses on employer needs. These social trends create reasons for a new impetus of engaging in deregulation in the tradition of Sinzheimer's social self-determination supported by law.

Ultimately, the world society and the information society also mean that the present unequal distribution of income that is impinging ever more on people's consciousness is increasingly called into question. Whereas real incomes in the 80 poorest countries in the world decline, in some cases dramatically, real incomes in the 20 richest countries have risen, in some cases considerably (OECD 2011). Irrespective of the manifold causes of these developments, modern democratic societies will come under increasing pressure to account for these unequal relationships.

From a reflexive labour law perspective this means that the use of regulatory instruments to exclude certain groups or countries from access to global wealth (protectionism) is doomed to be challenged. For the labour market, particularly the European labour market, a process of negative integration, meaning deregulation in the form of abolition of national barriers to labour mobility, has been under way since the 1950s. This process seems irreversible. However, the success of deregulating further legal regulations will depend on reflexive strategies of combining deregulation and re-regulation at the European level.

The political significance of a properly managed process of deregulation can be gauged by historical assessments of the institutionalisation of free collective bargaining. Ernst Fraenkel rightly spoke of a 'Copernican revolution in the working classes' perception of the law and the State' following the implementation of Sinzheimer's notion of collective labour law. Indeed, 'the discovery by lawyers of the normative effect of collective agreements constituted one of the most important theoretical foundations in the incorporation of the labour movement into the State' (Fraenkel 1973 [1958], pp. 139, 142; see also Hartwich 1996). In the light of its significance, it is scarcely surprising that the abolition of free collective bargaining was one of the first outrages committed by the Nazi regime and its reintroduction after the Second World War one of the first major achievements of the legislature in the newly founded Federal Republic of Germany.[1]

Sinzheimer's notion of 'social self-determination in the legal sphere' is of course a reminder that the purpose of further deregulation cannot be the dismantling of rights, as the neoliberal battle cry of deregulation often suggests or even intends. On the contrary, what is required is reflexive deregulation that is a controlled assessment of regulation that reduces complexity through a combined strategy of elimination and re-regulation of law and supports further delegation of legislative power in order to improve regulatory effectiveness through self-regulation.

The chapter discusses the concept of reflexive deregulation in three steps. After a few comments on the deregulation debate from theoretical perspectives, the chapter gives a comparative overview of deregulation policies in four developed countries. In its third part it outlines strategies of reflexive deregulation and re-regulation of labour markets with particular reference to the concepts of high-velocity labour markets and transitional labour markets.

6.1   THEORIES OF REGULATION AND DEREGULATION

Most of the theories and concepts of regulation agree that regulation operates with a set of authoritative rules that include rules on how to make

---

[1]   In fact, the West German Law on Collective Bargaining came into force on 31 March 1949 before the Constitution (*Grundgesetz*) was passed on 23 May 1949.

rules and how to enforce regulation. These rules include not only commanding rules but also incentives as means to achieve regulatory goals. However, theories of regulation differ widely around scope and style of regulation.

There are schools of thought that transcend the realm of public policy. These include the so-called regulation school (Boyer 1990) for whom all mechanisms of social control, not just state activities, are regulations. This structural theory of regulation in fact equates regulation with social norms. However, in the context of policy research, a narrower concept of regulation is usually preferred. These theories view regulation as providing conceptual tools for empirical research and tend to favour actor-oriented models (see for example Baldwin et al. 2010; Ogus 2004). Furthermore, most common nowadays is to assess regulation in the context of governance. In this view, regulation provides the instruments for governance, and these instruments include not only legal instruments but also administrative techniques and financial incentives.

By no means do all theories of regulation support an increase of regulation. There are a number of approaches that actively advocate deregulation. The most vociferous supporters in this respect are neoliberal economists who have been successful in the US since Jimmy Carter's presidency in influencing governments in adopting deregulation programmes (White 1981). The heyday period of deregulation as ideological and political strategy was certainly the 1980s when Ronald Reagan was US President and Margaret Thatcher Prime Minister in the UK. However, even during this period there have always been as many critics as there were proponents of deregulation. The critics argue that deregulation is not a purely economic affair and social scientists have on many occasions critically analysed the practice of deregulation efforts.

It is therefore not surprising that theories of regulation vary widely in their approaches to deregulation. In their path-breaking study *Responsive Regulation: Transcending the Deregulation Debate* (1992), Ian Ayres and John Braithwaite put forward a new approach to understanding both regulation and deregulation that is based on ideas of delegation of decision-making and participation of interest groups. This study has been refreshing insofar as it showed a way beyond the ideological deregulation debates of the 1980s by assessing the reality of regulatory practices carried out under the heading of deregulation. Their conclusion was that '[w]e have not, and are not, experiencing an era of deregulation so much as an era of regulatory flux – an era when dramatic regulatory, deregulatory, and re-regulatory shifts are occurring simultaneously' (Ayres and Braithwaite 1992, p. 7).

At the core of the concept of responsive regulation lies the idea of enforced self-regulation. The state demands from companies that they introduce modes of self-regulation which are monitored by regulatory bodies (Ayres and Braithwaite 1992, ch. 4). Ayres' and Braithwaite's concept of responsive regulation tries to argue against neo-corporatist strategies of regulation by favouring so-called democratic republicanism. However, their concept of community, which in fact means participation of a wide range of public interest groups (PIGs), is an idea quite close to the neo-corporatist concept of private interest governance (Schmitter and Streeck 1985).[2]

A reflexive labour law approach can agree with Ayres' and Braithwaite's basic view on regulation and deregulation, in particular their central concern with self-regulation. However, reflexive labour law goes a step further. Deregulation viewed in system theoretical terms is a strategy for reduction of internal complexity. Deregulation becomes reflexive when it is used as an alternative regulatory strategy to achieve public goals. Deregulation then becomes a regular affair and is almost always accompanied by strategies of re-regulation. From a reflexive labour law perspective, it is mainly a question of pragmatic choice which regulatory strategy is used to achieve certain public goals.

Furthermore, the weakness of the theory of responsive regulation is its understanding of law. Gunther Teubner made the point in his response to 'responsive law' (Nonet and Selznick 1978) that law has its limits in responding to society's needs which derive from its autopoietic nature (Teubner 1983). Ayres and Braithwaite are certainly on the right track when they emphasise the central role of self-regulation. However, responsive regulation asks too much from law, and remains a command-and-control type of regulation, when it demands regulatory strategies of 'enforced self-regulation'. Law has to become reflexive by regulating itself or, in Christine Parker's words, has to engage in 'meta-regulation' (Parker 2002, ch. 9, 2007) before it can be responsive. Self-regulation of law is a precondition for regulation of self-regulation in other systems.

Labour law is often itself the object of deregulation and this can be a result of its engagement in reflexive processes as reaction to economic and political challenges. An example is the development of a reflexive mechanism of 'protection of employment protection' by German labour courts in their regulation of fixed-term contracts (discussed in Chapter 4).

---

[2] The concept of responsive regulation is openly normative. However, republicanism is no longer high on the agenda. Braithwaite nowadays uses the concept in a typical business school manner as a tool for the design of regulatory strategies for 'capitalism' so that 'it works better' (Braithwaite 2008).

This reflexive mechanism in labour law was recognised by other function systems as detrimental to their objectives and fed into demands for deregulation (see on the German debate over the employment promotion act (BeschFG 1985) as deregulation measure Rogowski and Schömann 1996).

In their report *Why Deregulate the Labour Market?* (2000) Gøsta Esping-Andersen, Marino Regini and their collaborators gathered valuable evidence about employment effects of deregulation policies in Western Europe. They identified five main areas of regulation targeted by deregulation policies, which include unfair dismissal, atypical employment, working time, wage settings and unemployment benefits. They came to the conclusion that deregulation has no effect on the overall employment or unemployment rate but does have consequences regarding who is made unemployed and who has chances to find employment (Esping-Andersen and Regini 2000).

> There is very little evidence that 'rigidities' of hiring and firing, or of wage structures, have anything to do with Europe's chronically high unemployment levels, nor with Europe's apparent incapacity to fuel job growth. There is, however, substantially more credible evidence that 'rigidities' of this sort influence *who* are the unemployed.
> . . .
> One of the clearest results from our study is that various forms of regulation do, or at least may, have some impact on who is unemployed, but they cannot explain overall unemployment levels. Generous social benefits, highly egalitarian wage structures with high fixed labour costs, and strong job protection can be shown to negatively affect the employment chances, and thus increase the risks of unemployment, of three groups: youth, women workers and the low-skilled work force (Esping-Andersen and Regini 2000, pp. 2, 337, emphasis in the original).

These findings can be interpreted from a social systems theory perspective. The problem of labour market deregulation is not its economic irrelevance but that it has societal effects related to social inclusion and exclusion. Deregulation influences who gets included and who is excluded from the labour market. Furthermore, it rearranges the relation and the composition of the core and the periphery of the labour force.

Esping-Andersen and Regini rightly emphasise the importance of 'institutions that surround' the labour market for deregulation policies. They emphasise in particular collective bargaining and families as such institutions. For deregulation to be successful it has 'to persuade' collective bargaining and families to support it (Esping-Andersen and Regini 2000, pp. 5–6). Indeed, deregulation, be it intentionally or unintentionally, regulates families and industrial relations systems. However, things are a bit more complicated. From a systems theory perspective, deregulation policies have to deal with a high degree of complexity resulting from clashes of different system logics. Deregulation of the labour market has to deal with at least five different system references. Deregulation policies are attempts of the political system to influence economic processes through change in the legal system. These changes have direct impacts on the industrial relations system and for families.

In all these systems deregulation has to find a willingness to engage in changing established ways of dealing with problems. Deregulation has to link into and be compatible with system-specific ways of reducing complexity. In other words, deregulation has to understand itself as a form of regulation of self-regulation.

Deregulation is a global trend that contributes to the denationalisation of labour law (Simitis 1994a). Important drivers for deregulation in Europe are EU law and policy. In order to establish a common market, EU law demands from member states an opening of borders and a removal of trade barriers. The ECJ applied this logic of deregulation through negative integration in the *Viking*[3] and *Laval*[4] cases to national labour law, leading to a range of negative implications (see Deakin and Rogowski 2011). However, an alternative EU law strategy would be to embark on reflexive policy-making in which deregulation efforts are accompanied by measures of positive integration. Trends in this direction can already be seen in policies pursued under the European Employment Strategy, in particular in the form of flexicurity policies (further discussed in Chapter 8). Characterising these EU policies as 'targeted and partial deregulation' (Esping-Andersen and Regini 2000, p. 339) misses the point because they are in fact reflexive regulatory strategies that combine deregulation with a re-regulation agenda aiming at a positive combination of flexibilising labour markets and improving security for employees at the same time.

6.2 HABERMAS AND LUHMANN ON REGULATION AND DEREGULATION

Whereas the debate over regulation and deregulation in Anglo-Saxon countries tends to be dominated by economic theories, the discussion in

---

[3]   Case C-438/05 *The International Transport Workers' Federation and The Finnish Seamen's Union v Viking Line ABP and OÜ Viking Line Eesti* [2007] ECR I-10779 (hereinafter 'Viking').

[4]   Case C-341/05 *Laval un Partneri Ltd v Svenska Byggnadsarbetareförbundet, Svenska Byggnadsarbetareförbundets avd. 1, Byggettan, Svenska Elektrikerförbundet* [2007] ECR I-11767 (hereinafter 'Laval').

Germany over the nature of the relationship between law and economy is to a considerable extent influenced by leading schools of social theory. Major contributors in this philosophical or theoretical debate have been Jürgen Habermas and Niklas Luhmann. Both schools take the view that the framework of substantive law governing the welfare state and its development through judicial interpretation are increasingly inhibiting structural change and have undesirable side effects or are, at best, totally ineffective. However, they draw different conclusions as to the future development of the legal system.

6.2.1 Discursive Theory of Law and Regulation

Habermas recognises the historically positive function of the law governing the welfare state. For Habermas, private law traditionally guaranteed individual self-determination in terms of a negative freedom or laissez-faire to engage in autonomous action. This is guaranteed above all through freedom of contract and the right to own property. With the advent of substantive rights conferred by labour and social-welfare legislation, private law acquired a public role in protecting weaker parties, thereby contributing to achieving equality and social justice in modern society.

Habermas nevertheless recognises problems with interventionist regulation. The spectrum of legal forms has been extended to include special legislation, experimental temporary laws and broad regulatory directives of uncertain prognosis, and the influx of blanket clauses, general clauses and indefinite statutory language has given the judicial bureaucracy undue scope for interpretation and increasingly marginalised the democratically legitimated legislature. Furthermore, the shift in the focus of the law towards matters of social welfare has led to a one-sided concentration on the goal of distributive justice which, in conjunction with the tendency towards bureaucratisation, has created the travesty of 'welfare-state paternalism': 'The welfare paradigm of law is oriented exclusively towards the problem of the just distribution of socially produced life opportunities. By reducing justice to *distributive* justice, it misses the freedom-guaranteeing meaning of legitimate rights' (Habermas 1996a, p. 418, emphasis in the original).

According to Habermas, this travesty can be countered in contemporary society only through procedural law, which replaces or supplements the autonomy of the private individual with the 'social autonomy of participants in the procedures of law-making'. True, the institutionalisation of free collective bargaining was a step in this direction. However, it needs to be developed further, since that very freedom of collective bargaining also provides 'examples of how individual self-determination can be undermined by collective powers' (Habermas 1996a, p. 413). Spiros Simitis, for example, in his investigations of rigid and gender-specific age limits, protective norms for female employees, regulations on part-time work and data protection at the workplace and, more generally, the legal elaboration of the so-called standard employment relationship, has shown that collective and company agreements, in the same way as the labour law passed by the political legislator, satisfy social claims at the cost of dictating schemata and behavioural patterns from above (Simitis 1994b).

> These normative controls can have the effect of *normalizations that restrict freedom*. For example, they unreasonably restrict the private life plans of ben-eficiaries insofar as they promote traditional social roles instead of involving the affected persons themselves in the interpretation, differentiation, or reor-ganization of these patterns. As a result, Habermas perceives a need to warn his audience of the danger of the increasing 'colonization of employee behaviour' (Habermas 1996a, p. 413).

Habermas illustrates his critique by reference to the feminist theory of law. To the extent that legislation and adjudication remain wedded to tradi-tional interpretative patterns, regulatory law will consolidate the existing stereotypes of gender identity. And so long as the standard employment relationship for male, full-time workers serves as the criterion for 'diver-gences' that have to be compensated for, women will be required by com-pensatory regulations to adjust to employment relations that disadvantage them structurally.

> The pressure towards assimilation that is exerted on women by both the social-welfare and the liberal politics of equality – a pressure felt precisely where these programs succeed – ultimately stems from the fact that gender differences are not conceived as relationships involving two *equally* problematic variables and *in need of interpretation*. Differences are instead seen as deviations from sup-posedly unproblematic male standards (Habermas 1996a, p. 424, emphasis in original).

However, feminist critique misses its real target for Habermas if it throws out the idea of realising rights in any way. The real source of error lies not in the law but in the absence of public discussions, which can clarify the aspects under which differences between the experiences and living situa-tions of (specific groups of) women and men become relevant for an equal opportunity to take advantage of individual liberties. Gender identity and gender relations are social constructions that crystallise around biological differences but vary historically (see Benhabib 1992; Minow 1990; Rhode 1989; Young 1990). 'According to this proceduralist understanding, the realization of basic rights is a process *that secures the private autonomy of equally entitled citizens only in step with the activation of their political autonomy'* (Habermas 1996a, p. 426, emphasis in original).

It should be noted by way of criticism that Habermas does not list the institutional conditions under which the 'activation' of the private autonomy of equally entitled citizens is to take place. In fact, in his rights-based and proceduralist approach, Habermas adheres to a rather traditional notion of legislation and an impractical theory of legal reasoning. This has been criticised by Niklas Luhmann on a number of occasions (see, for example, Luhmann 1996a; Luhmann 2004, pp. 306–7, in particular footnote 7). But what is Luhmann's alternative?

6.2.2 Systems Theory and Regulation

In contrast to Habermas, Luhmann's account of law as a social system is not impelled by an overarching desire of reforming legal practice. His intention is to describe and analyse the legal system, in particular the ways it operates, including the ways it observes and describes itself (Luhmann 2004, ch. 1). On the other hand, Luhmann's decoding of law's practical and theoretical 'black box' points to a fundamental crisis similar to the diagnosis propounded by Habermas, which in Luhmann's view partly derives from undermining tendencies of social and welfare law.

The theoretical approach Luhmann favours in studying regulation is structural coupling. This approach analyses the conditions of regulation by theorising inter-systemic links. In considering law's role in regulating the economy, he starts with an analysis of the freedom to enter into contracts, which he views as the main foundation for structural coupling between law and the economy. With the concept of contract as private, autonomy law achieved its modern form. After considerable internal struggles, law became free in developing specific legal interpretations of the contract. However, of equal importance was the consequence for the economy, which could now arrange transactions without having to give consideration to a dense network of possible forms of contract. And it could do this even when invoking the far-reaching legal privilege of causing intentional damage to others, because law accepted the primacy of competition as a regulatory principle (Luhmann 2004, pp. 400–402). Luhmann cites in this context Roscoe Pound's remarkable analysis of how the freedom of contract doctrine was used in US courts in order to reject employment protection legislation and the strong criticism the courts encountered for doing so (Pound 1908–09). Indeed, structural coupling of the law and the economy via contract law and practice has implications for political regulation. Luhmann's analysis emphasises limits in the regulation of employment relations that derive from autopoietic needs of the three function systems of law, economy and politics.

In Luhmann's view, institutionalised property and contract rights have been increasingly restricted through political intervention. The instrumental use of law by the political system has put at risk the 'self-generative power' both of money and of the law. This tension is inherent in the modern constitutional state and with an increase in the amount of regulation, the sociologist Luhmann predicts an increasing trend of non-compliance with law and circumvention leading to destabilisation in the function systems:

> It becomes increasingly clear that one can abide by every statute but not by all. Infringements of the law become necessary to survival if living means existing to principles of self-determination. This is no longer the classic problem of ignorance of the law. Phenomena such as tax evasion or moonlighting in the black economy are indications of the fact that life is impossible without infringements of the law. . . . Considerable areas of the economy would collapse if the law were to be enforced. Above all, numerous possibilities for individuals to give their lives a meaning would be cut off if the bureaucracy succeeded in its attempts to enforce the law (Luhmann 2004, p. 478, translation adjusted, R.R.).

Although not explicitly, at least implicitly Luhmann confirms by numerous illustrations and examples that the practical recommendation of the systems-theoretical approach to law amounts to engaging in reflexive regulation and deregulation. Legal regulation needs to become reflexive in order to understand the limited conditions of enforcement and to find ways of adjusting its programmes accordingly. Luhmann's analyses emphasise paradoxes and dilemmas in using law for the realisation of social-welfare goals. Furthermore, as already indicated in Chapter 1, Luhmann emphasises that if inclusion through regulation increases, exclusion takes on more dramatic qualities.

> Exclusion from one functional area prevents inclusion in others. In contrast, inclusion makes a *lesser* integration possible, which means more freedom, *thus* corresponding to the logic of functional differentiation. Functional differentiation requires loose coupling of the function systems, and a curb on inferring the role of one from that of another' (Luhmann 2004, p. 489, emphasis in the original).

In a systems-theoretical perspective, there is much to be said in favour of a conscious and sparing application of legal norms. Deregulation is no surprise for Luhmann given that intervention is often fruitless or even counterproductive due to the autopoietic nature of systems. At best, Luhmann sees the alternative of 'procedural steering', in which discursive legal theory places so much hope, as a stopgap arrangement. In his view, its ineffectiveness can already be foreseen. Like all positivists, legal positivists have to guarantee the future in the present and must therefore work on the assumption that adherence to certain procedural criteria will one day give rise to a rational consensus on the outcome. This may work under the laboratory conditions constructed by Habermas, 'but not in the lifeworld reality determined by organisations and the human factor. A return to legalism, once categorically rejected, is now becoming apparent, with the implementation of state-enacted legal procedures providing the basis of the law's legitimacy, in the manner of a legal fiction' (Luhmann 1993, p. 558).

Habermas's and Luhmann's views on the future role of the law can be summarised as follows. Habermas's discursive legal theory sees the future of the world of work in a moderated welfare state. The moderation consists of the partial deregulation of substantive and collective social-welfare law (particularly as it relates to free collective bargaining) in favour of a discursive ethic, based itself on procedural law, that strengthens individual autonomy. Although the diagnosis of crisis is similar, Luhmann's systems theory approach advocates further differentiation of the legal system and support for the logic by which it operates: it should be confined to norms for which there are no functional equivalents and systematic infringements of the law should be tolerated in favour of greater individual and regional freedom and permanent learning through trial and error.

6.3   LABOUR MARKET DEREGULATION IN COMPARISON

Before an attempt is made in section 6.3 to transcend Luhmann's hesitation to engage in policy discussion from a reflexive labour law point of view, a brief overview is provided in this section of policies of deregulation of labour markets since the 1980s. The aim is to illustrate differences in deregulation approaches. The comparison is based on information for four advanced countries with significantly different labour law jurisdictions: Great Britain, Germany, France and the United States.

In all four countries the target of labour-market deregulation has been statutory regulations suspected of hindering labour market flexibility and dynamism. The concept of flexibilisation is often used as justification of deregulation. It represents an attempt to respond, at the economic and political levels, to the trend towards individualisation; in this context, individualisation denotes not only the increasingly 'chaotic' nature of individual lives (Beck and Beck-Gernsheim 2001) but also, and perhaps primarily, the increasing divergence between enterprises and their individual conditions. One of the key elements in the policy of flexibilisation through labour market deregulation is reform of national labour legislation.

Labour legislation is a product of differentiation within national legislative systems. From the systems-theoretical point of view, labour law regulates the zone of structural coupling between the social subsystems law and industrial relations. It has gained its autonomy within law largely as a result of the special relationships that exist between this area of the law and national systems of industrial relations and/or collective bargaining. However, national labour law systems differ in both complexity of their objects of regulation and the extent to which the sources of legislation are decentralised.

The following comparison takes as its starting point the assumption that the autonomy and complexity of national labour legislation are the decisive factors in shaping national experiences of deregulation. The level at which national labour law and its relationship with the industrial relations system are regulated determines the nature and scope of deregulation policies and the speed with which they are implemented. To put it another way, attempts to respond to a cultural process of individualisation and global economic pressure to adjust must necessarily take different forms in different countries.

6.3.1 Great Britain

Great Britain can be regarded as the classic example of the deregulated labour market. The history of British industrial relations and labour law is shot through with attempts to foster self-regulation in the sphere of industrial relations, and hence in the labour market, by discouraging state intervention.

Their experience of the close cooperation between the courts and employers in the nineteenth century made the trade unions deeply suspicious of state regulation in general. Although Parliament made regular attempts in the latter half of the nineteenth century to curtail the use of the criminal and civil courts to counter trade union activities, the trade unions were never fully integrated into state and society. However, the tension between trade unions and the state did give rise to a specific set of relationships between the economic, political and legal systems. The most important characteristic of this British liberal-corporatist arrangement, which found its clearest expression in the Trades Dispute Act of 1906, was the extensive autonomy granted to the industrial relations system by the political and legal systems in the form of immunities (Wedderburn 1986, pp. 21–5). Four structuring factors can be listed: the *voluntarism* of management and labour, i.e. the willingness of employers and trade unions to regulate industrial relations on a solely voluntary basis; the ideology of *collective laissez-faire*, according to which collective agreements voluntarily entered into can be terminated at any time on grounds of flexibility and rapid changeability, with no possibility of their being enforced by state legislation; the political doctrine of *abstentionism*, according to which the state declines to use the law in order to intervene in matters of industrial relations; and the legal principle of *immunity* from criminal proceedings and claims for damages in civil law for trade union activity (Flanders 1974; on the legal and political aspects, see Deakin and Morris 2012, ch. 1, and Wedderburn 1986, ch. 1).

Work in Britain continued to be regulated largely by this system of liberal-corporatist industrial relations until the 1970s. In consequence, the state declined to use its legislative powers in order to create a regulatory framework and collective agreements became the preferred instrument of regulation. Only the lowest income groups in certain industries were protected by a legal minimum wage set by the wages councils (for a comparison of the British with other forms of liberal corporatism, see Rogowski and Tooze 1992).

Furthermore, the crucial legislation that led to the establishment of the welfare state after the Second World War did not include the introduction of a legal framework for cooperative employment relationships or an incorporation of industrial relations into state welfare policy. The Beveridge system of social security legislation, which was introduced after the Second World War and named after the author of the report that formed the basis of the new system, took the radical step of establishing a welfare system solely financed from taxation (Beveridge Report 1942). It was a deliberate departure in this respect from the German system of statutory social security financed by employers and employees known as the Bismarckian system (on the Bismarckian system see Hepple 2010 [1986]), pp. 133-42). Even at an early stage, the British welfare state favoured a three-way combination of: (1) basic state provision, (2) the benefits derived from occupational schemes; and (3) private insurance against social risks, with this last element becoming increasingly important over time.

Publication of the Report of the Royal Commission chaired by Lord Donovan was followed in 1968 by a change in industrial relations and labour legislation, although not in social-welfare law. The report proposed a two-stranded approach to industrial relations: statutory regulations should be introduced to protect the rights of individual workers while at the same time support should be provided for the voluntarist system of industrial relations (Donovan Report 1968).[5] The Industrial Relations Act of 1971, introduced subsequently by Ted Heath's Conservative government, failed initially because of massive protests, not only from trade unions but also from employers, against the restriction of the voluntarist system through the compulsory registration of associations and the incorporation of the collective bargaining system into a legal framework (see Weekes et al. 1975). The legislation introduced by the Labour governments of 1974–79 was more successful, because it confined itself essentially to regulating individual rights. The Labour governments succeeded in introducing a minimum level of statutory protection for employees, including dismissal protection, maternity protection and anti-discrimination laws.

The Conservative governments of Margaret Thatcher and John Major (1979–97), with programmes that sought to shift the balance of power decisively in favour of employers, advocated radical deregulation of labour legislation in order to remove so-called 'burdens on business' (Department of Trade and Industry 1985; Department of Employment 1985). The deregulatory legal measures introduced by successive Conservative administrations were no longer intended to bolster self-regulation but, on the contrary, to weaken the rights of trade unions, with the paradoxical result that, under the guise of deregulation, more legislation was in fact enacted. Individual protection was scarcely altered by the new laws, with the important exception of the increase in the minimum qualifying period of employment for dismissal protection, which was raised in 1979 from the six months customary elsewhere in Europe to one year and then in 1985 to two years. This procedural measure had the dramatic effect of excluding more than one-third of all British employees from dismissal protection (Dickens 1994, pp. 230–31).

The deregulation of British labour law decreased the level of employment protection that was already comparatively low even before the Conservatives' accession to power in 1979. The liberal regulations on agency work, for example, were introduced in the Employment Agency Act, which came into force as early as 1973. The employment effects of deregulation in the 1980s and 1990s are complex. On the one hand, significant reductions of unemployment occurred after 1993 when levels of unemployment were rising in other parts of Europe. However, this was not true for all categories of unemployed and was accompanied by a growth

---

[5]   As an official member of the Donovan Commission, Otto Kahn-Freund, the leading academic teaching labour law at the LSE in London and later Oxford, who served as a judge in the Berlin labour courts before emigration to Britain, had a considerable influence on the Commission's labour law proposals.

in earnings inequality. And it can be questioned if the structural changes in the British labour market during this period were actually the effect of regulatory reform (Deakin and Reed 2000a).

Support for a deregulated labour market with only limited rights for employees did not fundamentally change under the Labour governments that were in power from 1997 to 2010. Despite far-reaching proposals for reform supported by the trade unions (Ewing 1996), the Labour governments were cautious and in general supported the deregulation programmes of their Conservative predecessors. The main change was dropping the previous open hostility of the Conservatives towards European labour legislation by replacing it with a more neutral approach that accepts but does not actively support new initiatives for a Europe-wide employment policy. In fact, new deregulation efforts were started in the area of health and safety (Hampton Report 2005) that introduced a 'risk-based' approach, leading to a reduction of inspectorial scrutiny and declining levels of enforcement (Tombs and Whyte 2012). The Conservative/Liberal Democrat coalition, in office since May 2010, has returned to a hostile political rhetoric in relation to European labour law and started a number of deregulation initiatives in the area of employment protection and in relation to dismissal law, working time and powers of employment tribunals.

6.3.2 Germany

In contrast to Great Britain, German labour law was established as a separate part of the legal system as early as the 1920s. Since then, a wide range of legislation and a great deal of judicial interpretation, particularly in the labour courts of the Weimar Republic, the Third Reich and in the Federal Labour Court (*Bundesarbeitsgericht* – BAG) after the Second World War, have led to the establishment of a regulatory apparatus of considerable scope and depth. The authority of the BAG to make final judgements is now a fundamental characteristic of the autonomy of German labour law (Blanke 1994).

One disadvantage of the high level of regulation is that it is difficult to gain an overview of the regulatory apparatus as a whole. Despite several attempts, it has so far proved impossible to adopt a systematic, integrated labour code. Rather, substantial areas of individual labour law are governed not only by a multiplicity of separate laws but also by the German Civil Code. Collective labour law includes not only wide-ranging legislation on co-determination and workplace labour relations but also important rules that have been developed on the basis of judicial interpretation when legislation has proved inadequate (particularly in the area of labour disputes). In addition, collective agreements and company agreements are recognised as independent sources of legislation (see Rogowski 1999).

German labour law is embedded in an industrial relations system that not only grants trade unions and employer associations considerable freedom in collective bargaining but also involves associations in a variety of ways in the administration of the labour market and the welfare state. As a direct result of the involvement of industrial partners, the Deregulation Commission that was set up by the Federal Government confined itself in its 1991 report to a number of individual proposals for labour market reform (Deregulierungskommission 1991; for a discussion of individual measures and their implementation, see Keller and Seifert 1997). The aim of the reforms proposed by the Commission was to inject greater flexibility into the existing system without articulating any fundamental critique of the system. The Commission particularly advocated that regulation at plant or establishment level should be strengthened through open clauses in collective agreements, allowing for more detailed arrangements to be negotiated at the lower level, without calling into question the regulatory power of collective agreements or the solidaristic organisation of social security.

Among other things, the Commission proposed that the Federal Labour Office should lose its monopoly in employment-related services and advocated deregulation of individual labour law, a process that had already begun with the Employment Promotion Act of 1985 (Buechtemann 1993b, pp. 272–96). The approach to deregulation adopted in the Employment Promotion Act served to a certain extent as a guideline for the Commission. According to this approach, deregulation should be implemented in a way that not only accommodates existing legislation but also brings a new slant to the law. The element of accommodation in the Employment Promotion Act lay in the link that was expressly made with the principles governing the justification of fixed-term employment contracts that had already been developed through judicial interpretation. At the same time, the new act also defined situations in which those judicial interpretations would no longer apply: according to the amended version that came into force in October 1996, fixed-term employment contracts can be concluded for periods of up to two years without any justification being required.

The new element was the incorporation into labour law of a reform that was intended to create jobs, a purpose that had until then not played any role in German labour law. From the point of view of reflexive labour law, this constituted a meeting of two separate areas of law, namely employment protection and labour market regulation, which required mutual recognition of the different regulatory approaches within both legal fields.

Research could show that the employment effects of this deregulation measure were minimal and did not meet expectations in terms of reduction of unemployment (Buechtemann and Höland 1989; Schömann et al. 1998). The evidence that labour law and labour market regulations, in particular the explicit deregulation measures, had either negative or positive effects on employment or unemployment levels in Germany is inconclusive at best (Fuchs and Schettkat 2000).

There were attempts of deregulation of provisions relating to dismissal protection throughout the 1990s, for example the relaxation of general provisions governing dismissal protection in September 1996, which raised the minimum number of employees required for application of legal protection from 5 to 10. The labour market orientation of these measures, in particular the new type of fixed-term contract called integration contract (*Eingliederungsvertrag*) allowing co-financing of the employment cost between employers and the employment office, caused legal problems for existing notions of dismissal law (Joost 2000, pp. 61–2). However, the most significant development in terms of deregulating the labour market was the so-called Hartz reform of 2002. With the backing of union officials, a programme of significant reduction of labour costs was introduced that helped to strengthen the competitiveness of the German economy on the world market through the creation of a large low-wage sector. It caused major structural changes of the German economy that not only undermined the traditional German model of welfare corporatism (Streeck 2009, ch. 4) but led to a massive decline in real wages (Akyol et al. 2012), and the creation of a sizable group of working poor in Germany (Eurofound 2010b).

One trend that runs counter to the desire for deregulation is the debate on strengthening the basic rights of individual employees, for example the incorporation of the constitutionally guaranteed right to protection of the private sphere into labour law. Protection of the private sphere includes the right of access to personal files, legal regulation of access to computer data held by employers and the public employment service as well as anti-discrimination law (e.g. the 1994 Act on the Protection of Employees from Sexual Harassment at the Workplace). Together the protection afforded by basic individual rights and the principles of social policy upheld in European law, particularly equal treatment, are increasingly forming the framework for statutory and contractual regulations at the workplace in Germany.

The analysis of experiences with deregulation in Germany comes to the apparently paradoxical conclusion that, in the light of the scope and depth of the regulatory apparatus, there should be a considerable demand for deregulation. However, the proposals put forward and the measures actually taken have been limited and intended for the most part to accommodate the established basic structures of labour law. This can be explained by the theory of reflexive labour law. Labour law in Germany has become so autonomous that the traditional relationship between law and politics has been reversed. The law is no longer a subordinate sphere with executive powers only. The evolution of labour law is now being determined primarily by impulses that have their origin within the labour law system itself. Labour law reforms are to a large extent shaped by demands for intervention that derive from judicial interpretation, collective agreements and legal doctrine (Blanke 1994, pp. 207–24). In view of the complexity of the system, it is incumbent upon the political sphere to stress the need for overall coherence and to respond by putting in place policies for coordinating differing social logics.

6.3.3   France

French labour law is embedded in an industrial relations system in which the political fragmentation of the trade union movement has traditionally limited the scope for regulation through collective bargaining. State dominance of the regulation of work has led to a split between the private and public sectors, with special conditions applying to the latter, particularly in relation to social security benefits. The history of French labour law is run through with attempts to curb state dominance and to strengthen the self-regulation of industrial relations.

The deregulation policy introduced at the beginning of the 1980s is one such attempt. According to Antoine Lyon-Caen, it had three objectives: to strengthen self-regulation at plant and sector level, to curtail the autocratic powers of government factory inspectors and to improve the functioning of the labour market by making employment relationships more flexible (Lyon-Caen 1993). In its initial phase, the deregulation policy was decisively influenced by the so-called Auroux laws, named after the socialist Minister of Labour. The primary purpose of these laws was to strengthen the enfeebled system of interest representation by setting up joint works councils and employee representatives at plant or establishment level. These innovations went hand in hand with a reduction of the powers of the factory inspectorate. French law traditionally required the approval of the factory inspectorate for all dismissals. After 1975, this preventative dismissal protection was restricted to redundancies for operational reasons. The deregulation policy pursued in the 1980s aimed to abolish the factory inspectorate's powers of direct intervention in redundancies altogether and to replace them in the event of so-called economic redundancies with negotiations at plant or establishment level and qualitative adjustment measures for personnel threatened by redundancy, for example retraining (Lyon-Caen 1993, pp. 347–57).

In the second phase of deregulation, initiated by conservative governments from 1986 onwards, the main emphasis was on deregulation through flexibilisation. Atypical employment relationships in the form of agency work and fixed-term contracts were particularly encouraged. As in Germany, the underlying consideration was to combine the reform of labour law with labour market policy objectives. These also included various attempts to help young unemployed people and the long-term unemployed to gain access to in-firm training and employment by introducing a range of special employment contracts (Moreau 2000).

From a comparative perspective, it is striking how much deregulation in France has been preoccupied with problems of jurisdiction or competence within the labour administration. It is true that there would be ample reason to simplify the legislation. Despite appearances to the contrary, the comprehensive Code of Labour Law is extremely unsystematic. However, the main problems continue to lie in the powers of intervention wielded by the state. With this in mind, the purpose of deregulation should also be to develop an understanding within the state apparatus of the heterogeneity and regulatory capacity of industrial relations. Ideally suited in this respect would be bipartite industrial tribunals (*conseils de prud'hommes*). However, the elected lay courts are increasingly treated as alien elements within the French legal system and professionalisation of these tribunals is meeting with considerable resistance (Richard and Pascal 2010). The industrial relations system has yet to find an appropriate place within the French state and judicial apparatus.

The employment effects of regulatory changes in dismissal rules, working time and unemployment benefits during the 1980s and 1990s are reported to have been minimal. It is inappropriate, according to Marie-Ange Moreau, 'to use the term "deregulation" as it was in Great Britain in Mrs. Thatcher's years' (Moreau 2000, p. 43) in characterising the relatively minor changes in French labour law. Thus, the French labour law and labour market policies of this period were, according to employment experts, a 'deregulation that never existed' (Malo et al. 2000).

6.3.4 USA

Deregulation of labour law and industrial relations in the USA in the 1980s and 1990s was a *de facto* rather than a politically controlled process. The erosion of the industrial relations system, in particular the dramatic decline in trade union membership rates in the private sector, changed the effective basis of American labour law, the principal purpose of which, at least at federal level, is to protect trade union activity and thus to support collective bargaining. It is true that there was little change in the legal framework formed by the National Labor Relations Act (NLRA) of 1935 or in the way it was implemented by the National Labor Relations Board (NLRB), despite the appointment to it of well-known conservatives during the Reagan and Bush presidencies. However, its influence was increasingly confined to the ever diminishing segment of the labour force employed in the manufacturing industry and *de facto* deregulation affected the major-ity of American workers because of the weakness of the American trade unions, particularly in the booming service sector.

In the USA, legal protection at the workplace is generally provided through company agreements. These collective agreements determine not only wages but also all other basic conditions of employment. Individual employees in union shops can have recourse to the grievance procedures laid down in the company agreement in order to defend themselves against disciplinary measures or dismissal. There is no provision for the binding decisions that constitute the endpoints of these procedures to be examined in the courts. Thus, when the collectively negotiated regulations enshrined in company agreements cease to apply because of de-unionisation, the result is a dramatic loss of rights for employees, in both practical and legal terms.

In other respects, apart from its function of supporting the indus-trial relations system, American labour law is part of the welfare state. Implementation of the law is the responsibility of federal officials, whose procedures are governed by administrative law. The significance of the civil law governing employment contracts is minimal in comparison.

The two core areas of federal labour law, namely protection from dis-crimination and health risks at the workplace, have to date remained more or less unaffected by deregulation, whether *de facto* or legal. As far as dis-crimination is concerned, the grounds have even been extended to include not only race and sex but also religion, disability and age. However, the anti-discrimination authorities (the Equal Employment Opportunities Commission, or EEOC) and the health and safety authorities (the Occupational Safety and Health Administration, or OSHA) are faced with implementation problems. Their procedures and the small number of cases limit the legal protection offered to workers.

This does not apply to the same extent to the Department of Labor's sphere of responsibility. Its genuinely effective efforts to ensure compli-ance with maximum working hours and minimum wages are nevertheless subject to regular criticism. Debates on deregulation in these areas are not uncommonly linked with the astonishingly widespread general criticism of the federal government and its power.

In some states, an increase in employee protection has been obtained through the judicial route, in a way as a reaction to the *de facto* deregulation that has followed the loss of trade union control. In the area of dismissal protection in particular, the principle of unrestricted dismissal ('for good reasons, bad reasons or no reasons at all') has been replaced in California, for example, by the need to establish just cause in certain cases; failure to do so may lead to high compensation payments (Gould 1994, pp. 165–79). Because of the risk of incurring high costs, cases do not often come before the courts and are usually brought only by senior managers or executives. However, the effect of the signals sent by judgements in favour of employees should not be underestimated.

A further development that runs counter to state development is the new legal protection in the event of mass redundancies on grounds of plant closures. The WARN Act – the 1988 Worker Adjustment and Retraining Notification Act – states that in large establishments with more than 100 employees, at least 60 days' notice must be given if more than 50 employees are to be laid off. However, numerous exceptions restrict the law's effectiveness (Ehrenberg and Jakubson 1994). The legislation has a public function over and above worker protection, since notice of layoffs also has to be given to the local authorities in the areas in which the affected plants are located. This requirement is an expression of a public interest in the protection of local labour markets.

There are particular labour markets where privatisation was accompanied by deregulation of labour laws. A study of privatisation in the telecommunications and transport sector, including trucking, railroads and in particular airlines, found significant labour market effects. Privatisation and deregulation in these service industries had an impact on earnings and rates of employment and on the influx of non-union firms (Peoples 1998). Other areas of privatisation in the USA include health, education and prisons in which welfare privatisation in the form of delegation raises concerns about their constitutionality because of lacking public control (Metzger 2003).

The debate on the future of American labour law and labour market regulation is split between advocates of, on the one hand, a stronger collective approach through the industrial relations system and, on the other, of individualised protection through the legal system. Rising union membership rates in the 1990s have raised hopes for a stronger collective approach. A number of authors see signs of a revival of existing institutions that were undermined by anti-labour appointments, like the National Labor Relations Board (NLRB). It has been proposed that litigation strategies like those used in the civil rights movement can turn around this organisation (Dannin 2006).

Other suggestions focus on the company. One of these has been the introduction of so-called employee participation committees along the lines of the German works council model (Weiler 1990, pp. 282–306). Other proposals want to enhance the status of employee participation in human resource management systems, including profit-sharing schemes (see Block et al. 1996, pp. 35–9). Alternative proposals derive from concerns with gender relations, sexual harassment and discrimination at the workplace. These have led to suggestions of strengthening the collective voice in companies in order to foster cooperation, sociability and the existing 'constitutions' at the place of work as the basis for improved equal protection (Estlund 2003).

However, the biggest challenge for US labour law has been the rise of new types of employment and the introduction of non-union human resource management systems on a large scale. The 'New American Workplace' operates with radically transformed work systems in the United States (Appelbaum and Berg 1994). It is strengthening the trend of the *de facto* deregulation of employees.

For an assessment of deregulation from a reflexive labour law perspective, it is important that deregulation patterns vary significantly by country. In Great Britain, deregulation has focused on preventing any extension of the already low level of employee protection while at the same time placing legal restrictions on trade union activities. In Germany, deregulation has been adapted to the complex structure of the autonomous labour law system in order to achieve certain necessary reforms, particularly in the use of fixed-term contracts. In France, the main purpose of deregulation was to reduce the powers of the factory inspectorate while at the same time strengthening the representation of interests at establishment level and making employment relationships more flexible, particularly through new or atypical forms of employment contract. And in the USA, deregulation has involved the *de facto* loss of employee rights because of the decline in trade union membership and the consequent decline in regulation through collective agreements.

These divergent experiences of deregulation make it impossible to speak of a uniform trend. The actual processes of deregulation have been determined to a large extent by the specific problems of national labour law systems and their relationships to national industrial relations systems. There are only a few similarities or functional equivalents that might be indicative of a common pattern of adjustment or point to instructive connections between different patterns of regulation and performance. One example is the relaxation of restrictions on fixed-term contracts for reasons of labour market policy in both France and Germany.

6.4 REFLEXIVE DEREGULATION AND RE-REGULATION OF LABOUR MARKETS

In the following examples, combining reflexive deregulation and re-regulation will be discussed in relation to two types of labour markets. These are high-velocity labour markets and transitional labour markets. They respond in different ways to two major trends: the proliferating use of information technology in an increasingly globalised economy and the growing diversity and variability of patterns of economic activity.

6.4.1 High-velocity Labour Markets

Labour markets are undergoing radical change in the information society in which the rapid change of information technology has profound effects on employment patterns. When economic behaviour is determined essentially by innovation and information, it is not only company forms that are changed but working conditions and the status of employees as well. Traditional labour law based on collective agreements and statutory norms providing a minimum level of worker protection are becoming less important in the regulation of the labour market. In many cases, legal rights laid down in individual contracts are replacing general employee protection and the application of homogeneous social standards. As a result, the law is increasingly becoming the strategic factor in individual bargaining.

The problems of regulating labour markets in the information society can be illustrated by legal developments in the computer industry. In this area of the economy, fundamental innovations are increasingly taking place in small firms in which the boundaries between dependent and independent work are becoming increasingly blurred. These firms not uncommonly have their origins either in the break-up of larger companies or in spin-offs from state or private universities or other educational institutions. Their organisational structures are characterised by a high degree of individualisation and adaptation among those working in them. As a result, working conditions in these firms differ significantly from those in traditional companies.

The labour market in this industry has been characterised by the American labour lawyer Alan Hyde, quite accurately, as a high-velocity labour market (Hyde 1998, 2003), whose basic structural characteristic is the rapidity with which workers change jobs. In this niche labour market, the relationship between organisation and employee is being reversed. The most important resource is no longer the organisational capacity for innovation but the information and ideas in employees' heads. It is the organisation that has to make special efforts to retain workers. A change of employer, or the establishment of a new firm, is becoming the norm.

Nowhere in the world can this change be observed more clearly than in Silicon Valley in California, where the labour market is characterised by specific niche conditions. The small firms that dominate Silicon Valley are enmeshed in a dense social network that fosters collective learning and flexible adjustment on the part of specialised producers. This network of small firms has proved to be a significant job creator. A comparison between Silicon Valley and the Massachusetts computer industry located along Route 128, which tends to be dominated by larger firms, revealed that between 1975 and 1990 the Californian industry had generated three times as many jobs as its Massachusetts counterpart (Saxanian 1994).

High-velocity labour markets make new demands on labour law. Chief among these demands is the fluid transition from dependent employment to self-employment and vice versa or a combination of the two (Hyde 2002). The rights of individual workers and small entrepreneurs are laid down in individual agreements. As a result, contracts rather than laws are becoming the basic sources of employee rights. This suggests a deregulation of existing protective norms, which restrict the 'velocity' of change and thus reduce the dynamism of the industry in macro-economic terms.

However, high-velocity labour markets also give rise to specific new legal problems, for example in relation to the applicability of discrimination law and post-employment legal obligations (Hyde 2002). If pressure to innovate is great and dependent on new information and new discoveries, utilisation of the knowledge contained in employees' heads becomes a legal problem involving intellectual property rights (Hyde 2003, chs. 2–4). From the traditional legal perspective, an employee's knowledge becomes his firm's property when that knowledge can be designated a trade secret; in that case, any employee leaving a firm can be prevented from making use of that knowledge and his new employer can be threatened with an action for damages. In Silicon Valley at least, specialist lawyers in this area have created a new contract-based law that operates at a level lower than the prevailing statutory norms and the principles based on judicial opinion and precedent (see Hyde 2002). And this new situation seems also to have given rise to a renewed need for collective interest representation. However, this does not involve traditional trade union activity but new, specialist forms of interest representation for computer professionals.

High-velocity labour markets are not confined to the computer industry. Deindustrialisation places new demands on labour law worldwide. The adaptation of labour law to the conditions in high-velocity labour markets requires a mix of deregulatory and re-regulatory measures. Labour law must become reflexive by developing mechanisms through which it can observe itself and thereby detect its own limits. The assimilation of comparative legal, social scientific and economic perspectives into labour law would allow that law to be properly contextualised. This would include a reappraisal of traditional instruments from the point of view of labour market policy and an opening up of labour law that would make it possible to incorporate into it elements from other areas of the law, such as intellectual property law. The protection of basic rights, for example against discrimination and the misuse of personal data, would be elevated as a function of labour law, and this would lead in turn to a critique of the traditional use of the law and collective agreements as instruments for enforcing those rights (Simitis 1994b, pp. 183–205). It would then be possible to switch to indirect guidance through procedural law and to foster forms of self-regulation. This would include the individually controlled transfer of company pension rights and share holdings. Labour law can become reflexive by developing a self-understanding aimed primarily at opening up space for a range of options and only secondarily at juridical prescription.

6.4.2 Transitional Labour Markets

Whereas reflexive regulation of high-velocity labour markets is concerned with the needs of the individual as employee or self-employed person, the concept of transitional labour markets focuses on welfare state institutions and their capacity to adapt to new needs of employees as well as the labour market. However, both concepts operate with a combination of removal of certain labour law conditions via deregulation and the introduction of new legal strategies supporting labour market developments.

The transitional labour markets approach (TLM), as conceived by Günther Schmid, pays attention to internal as well as external changes to the conditions under which labour markets operate (see also Chapter 5). These include general developments that force labour markets to open up space for new options. First, TLM looks at social risks that result from known external risks such as market changes, technological change, labour migration, or birth cycles as well as internal risks, such as serious management errors on the employers' side or personal disasters or crises on the employees' side, such as a partner's enforced move, divorce, chronic illness, occupational disease and the birth of a first child. TLM's answer to coping with these risks is support for sophisticated social risk management (Schmid and Schömann 1994; Schmid 2006, 2008a, ch. 6, 2008b).

Second, the world of work is not viewed by TLM as a commodity market but a social institution (Schmid 1994, 2006; see also Solow 1990). The greater the need for adjustment, the less likely it is that it can be realised solely through wage flexibility. For TLM, cultural notions of fair or just wages restrict the ability of wages alone to control the adjustment process. Although civil status, solidarity and the principle of equal wages for work of equal value prevent wages in general to fall below a certain threshold, a reflexive regulation of the labour market does not exclude the possibility of minimum wage legislation (Schmid 2008a, p. 231). In consequence, labour markets require not only effective but also socially legitimated institutions for adjustment to internal or external shocks.

Third, TLM views periodic involuntary (and sometimes also voluntary) unemployment as becoming increasingly less predictable. These periods are linked to the 'post-industrial' syndrome of discontinuous patterns of economic activity which accounts for one-third of unemployment of modern societies (Mutz et al. 1995). In a TLM perspective, sufferers from this syndrome experience relatively short periods of unemployment as they switch from one employer to another or adjust to changes in family circumstances; these changes often lead to better employment conditions and earnings. In the golden age of manufacturing industry, it was agriculture, small-scale artisanal work or the extended family that offered, as it were, natural institutional buffers and social space for productive activities not destined for the market. These natural buffers are either long gone or disappearing rapidly. The theory and practice of transitional labour markets argues that they need to be replaced by socially constructed buffer zones, new social spaces capable of absorbing the unpredictable shocks to which the labour market is exposed, and putting some order into discontinuous patterns of labour force participation (Schmid 2001).

What is crucial from a reflexive labour law perspective is that the increasing fluctuations in working time and in employment relationships require well-ordered, coordinated agreements reached in the industrial relations system to prevent them from leading to renewed segmentation and exclusion in the labour market. Thus, it is the task of the legal, the industrial relations as well as the political systems to develop institutional arrangements through which the transitions between various working times and employment forms can be organised in ways that do not push individual careers into a siding or permanently condemn workers to inferior employment relationships. Such institutional arrangements constitute the core of the TLM approach.

TLM policies *à la* Günther Schmid include planned periods of full-time and part-time work, alternation between (further) training and employment or between dependent employment and self-employment, a combination of work and training for a second or even third career, a combination of 20–30 hours' dependent employment offering a stable income and self-employment providing top-up earnings, a combination of paid work and family work and phased retirement. They form organisational 'bridges' between gainful employment and other productive activities and contain rights to planned and negotiable crossing of these 'bridges' safeguarded by collective agreements, company agreements, courts and legislation. Transitional labour market policies combine low or erratic earned income with transfers or investment income and overall they finance work, not unemployment (see Schmid 2008a, chs. 5–6).

TLM policies pose particular challenges to labour and welfare law. Crucial elements of the employment relationship are targeted to be rearranged through deregulation combined with re-regulation measures. These include pay, working time, duration of working time during the working life, job security and training which need to be adjusted for flexible employment relationships. Furthermore, the labour and social-welfare legislation governing employment relationships needs to be deregulated and re-regulated in such a way that the economic and social advantages of stability are not lost. The model is based on labour law reforms carried out in the Netherlands and in Denmark, where active labour market policies and legislation supporting 'flexicurity' exist that had significant impacts in reducing unemployment (Schmid 1997). Flexible employment relationships and a high level of social security are the result of a reflexive labour law strategy of 'coordinated flexibility' (Schmid 1992, 2008a, ch. 8).

(1) In matters of pay, the principle of coordinated flexibility means strengthening wage determination by incorporating performance and profit-related elements into collective agreements that would subsequently be given concrete form in company and individual agreements. TLM policies encourage interfaces to be created by the legal system so that collective bargaining policy becomes able to transcend the mere focus on wages and act as collective labour market and employment policies. Collective bargaining would in this way share the burden of economic policy with government and would shoulder the responsibility for employment policy. TLM promotes deregulation of entitlements to passive wage replacement benefits accompanied by the creation of rights to the active use of such benefits in exchange.

An option favoured by TLM is to link finance and pay policy through investment wages. These are savings from collectively agreed wage restraint placed in investment funds, which receive favourable tax treatment. With the agreement of trade unions or employers, they are used to set up new companies and to introduce innovations; once a certain employment objective had been achieved, the shareholders in the fund (i.e. the employees) receive profit-related bonuses.

Furthermore, from the perspective of TLM, the question of the connection between income distribution and labour market dynamics acquires considerable importance. The notion of income from work is extended to include investment income. Such income, for example from investments or ownership of land or property, serve as buffers in lean times. The TLM approach assumes that an equitable income distribution helps to make flexible employment relationships more acceptable. The employment policy potential of incomes policy, and particularly of wealth distribution, is proposed to be an important factor for modern labour market policy.

However, the greatest potential for reform is seen by TLM in flexibilising existing welfare policies through improved coordination, in particular by improving the interface between labour market policy and social policy. An example would be reducing marginal taxation for taking a job for those who are in receipt of income support or unemployment benefit. This would be attractive to single parents, for example, who can only work part-time. Roads pursued in Denmark are wage subsidies paid to employers for taking on workers recognised as less efficient. TLM claims also that costs for benefits can be reduced over the long term if entitlements can be used by claimants as vouchers to be exchanged for wage subsidies (in the case of older long-term unemployed people, for example) or training grants (in the case of younger long-term unemployed individuals).

(2) A further area of labour law reform advocated by TLM is greater flexibility in the scheduling of working time. In particular, suggestions are made to overcome the system of bonus payments for night and weekend work that increase costs and sometimes damage the competitiveness of firms. Both labour legislation and collective agreements are encouraged to make greater use of extra time off as a means of compensating workers for unsocial hours or overtime (see also Chapter 9 on European initiatives regulating working time).

The TLM approach also advocates job creation by temporary employment agencies and public labour pools in order to meet both the demand from employers for increasing flexibility and employees' need for greater security of employment. However, conditions for this strategy are employment contracts between the temporary work agency and its employees that guarantee basic rights of employment protection. Furthermore, the TLM approach supports the establishment of public labour pools, the model for which is the Dutch START employment agencies that are suitable to minimise personnel problems of small firms (see Chapter 5). They can lower risks of staff absences due to parental leave or the need to care for relatives, training leave, sabbaticals, unpaid leave and attendance at vocational training courses, as well as fluctuating but unpredictable needs for extra personnel that cause particular problems for small firms (Semlinger 1995, pp. 54–6).

(3) Another area of reform of labour and social-welfare law proposed

by the TLM approach is flexibilising the duration of working time in order to create more opportunities for employment. Law can reduce employees' anxieties to cooperate by establishing individual rights to negotiate preferred working times. For the law to be successful it needs to be tailored more closely to conditions in the new world of work, in particular in relation to the service economy and demands of the information society. For example, employment promotion legislation has to realise that it is no longer possible to speak of regular economic cycles in modern service industries, where slumps in demand are chaotic (as in the fashion industry), demographic (caused by fluctuations in birth rates) or downright political in nature (provoked by government budgetary policies). TLM proposes that new 'bridging' instruments are developed that, like the short-term allowance, help to avoid the transaction costs associated with hiring and firing. It advocates transition allowances, granted to the service sector as well, and particularly to the public services, which are facing major restructuring problems. A few examples in relation to the teaching profession can demonstrate this proposal. In order to avoid redundancies, or a complete ban on the recruitment of teachers, in response to a sharp decline in the birth rate and political decisions, temporary reductions in working time for all teachers could be introduced or additional hours during periods with high numbers of students are remunerated with extra time off at a later date, when it is expected that there will be a teacher surplus or teachers can accumulate time credits over a period of several years and then cash them in for a one-year sabbatical with a guarantee of a job. In the USA, university teaching staff are usually paid only for the nine months during which they teach and examine; for the rest of the year, they seek additional sources of income, such as consultancy work and research funding.

TLM proposes to make creative use of the interface between collectively agreed and government labour-market policy. In countries with national or industry-wide bargaining, the regulation of annualised or lifetime working-time arrangements in collective or company agreements can have positive employment effects. In a truly reflexive labour law fashion, TLM proposes that government authorities make a financial contribution to the cost of implementing such arrangements proportional to the volume of unemployment thereby avoided.

TLM also supports the establishment of working-time accounts, which have been underused so far (Wotschak 2011). A legal innovation suggested by TLM in support of this instrument of job creation is favourable tax treatment for the credits accumulated on working-time accounts. Furthermore, the law would guarantee the right to transfer such credits in the event of a change of job.

(4) In the sensitive area of employment security, TLM adopts a complex approach. It adopts a number of distinctions that include the differentiation between employment security in the inclusive sense (the employment relationship in its totality) and in the narrow sense (duration of individual employment relationships) and between *de facto* and institutional (i.e. legal) security, while at the same time bearing in mind both the micro and macro levels (for a suitably differentiated approach, see Walwei 1996, pp. 219–29 and Buechtemann and Walwei 1996, pp. 652 93). It views as the fundamental problem of dismissal protection its negative impact on particular groups of employees, in particular older and disabled workers. Their exclusion has severe negative consequences because their dismissal often means permanent exclusion with little or no hope of re-entering the labour market.

A deregulation in the form of relaxation of certain provisions on dismissal protection is justified from a TLM perspective if more attractive regulations or fair procedural rules accompany deregulation. For such accompanying regulations, TLM suggests long-term wage subsidies or support for the investment required to adapt jobs in the event of workers becoming less efficient as they age or their health begins to fail. An example would be so-called adjustment groups, which were introduced by Swedish law and consist of company representatives and rehabilitation experts; they negotiate the required adjustments for disabled employees and seek corresponding financial support from local employment offices (an example discussed in Semlinger and Schmid 1985). The Danish example is used by TLM to argue that the need for universal dismissal protection diminishes if active labour-market policies accompany deregulation; increased flexibility is in fact a result of active labour-market policies.

(5) Of particular importance in meeting the challenges of the labour market of the future is for TLM the maintenance and constant renewal of human capital, i.e. training, skills, competences, experience and integration into social networks. If reflexive deregulation aims at an increase in employability, TLM constitutes the institutional approach to the maintenance and renewal of employability in an increasingly chaotic labour market. However, mere deregulation will not suffice to secure employability. Re-regulation in the form of legislation and new rights is needed that extends social autonomy on both the collective and individual levels, which in turn removes some of the burdens from the state and government labour-market policy.

In its institutionalist approach, TLM has a high regard for collective solutions that involve industrial partners and labour-market authorities. Collective agreements are seen as instruments that can make available blocks of time for training as a means of stabilising or increasing employment. Enlarging the agenda of collective bargaining beyond wage determination and including public bodies to take part in negotiations would allow arrangements such as sharing costs for training to be borne by employees in the form of reduced pay increases, while labour-market authorities provide financial support in proportion to the volume of unemployment thereby avoided. In this way unemployment insurance contributions become employment insurance contributions that also confer entitlement to the improvement or preservation of employability.

A good example of deregulation combined with re-regulation is the job rotation scheme that was put into practice successfully in Denmark. Under such a scheme, employees are given leave to undertake further training outside the firm and their jobs are taken by unemployed people. The job rotation system is complemented by a right to training or further training for the long-term unemployed, as well as an entitlement to a sabbatical of up to one year for further training if a replacement can be negotiated individually with the employer. In the ideal case, a successful job rotation scheme generates an upward spiral of further training and employment. And as the example of Denmark shows, the chances of this happening are particularly good in periods of economic upturn (Höcker and Reissert 1995; Madsen 1997).

The integration of the long-term unemployed into structural policy is regarded by TLM as the promotion of employability in the wider sense of the term. In line with a reflexive labour view of encouraging self-regulation, TLM promotes greater decision-making powers to be devolved to local actors at this interface between labour-market and structural policy. It supports the notion of productive employment promotion, according to which unemployment benefit can be used jointly to finance the creation of new jobs, in the spirit of cooperative labour-market policy. However, the kinds of jobs that can be financed should be confined to environment, social projects or youth work, as envisaged by traditional employment promotion laws, such as the German BeschFG of 1985. Moreover, the fact that rates of pay are lower than the collectively agreed rates gives projects that attract financial support the reputation of being part of the 'second labour market', which is counterproductive if the funds provided by the labour-market authorities are intended to contribute to the creation of permanent, competitive jobs.

6.5 CONCLUSIONS

Globalisation and individualisation have produced two types of reaction in modern industrial societies, both of which are socially unacceptable:

persistent unemployment is the European counterpart of the persistent poverty found in the USA (see Dahrendorf 2012 [2008], ch. 7). If the American labour market is not the kind of deregulation to be emulated, what form of deregulation might reproduce its amazing dynamism without its undesirable side effects? At the beginning of this chapter a reference was made to Hugo Sinzheimer and his assessment of the introduction of free collective bargaining in the 1920s as an epoch-making achievement in the process of deregulation. Today, this collective form of social autonomy is no longer sufficient. Trade unions can no longer rely on being embedded in corporatist structures that give them legal, representative and institutional functions. They have to recognise in their strategies pluralisation and differentiation on the employees' side and the diversity of company and regional structures on the employer side. It must be complemented by a strengthening of individual social autonomy and the introduction of minimum protective rights for individuals. It is true that collective agreements still have the decisive advantage of being capable of defining and putting into practice the basic conditions laid down in labour law. However, collective agreements must, like the legal norms laid down in statutory law, become more procedural in character. In other words, they must create negotiating space for the actors at local level, i.e. for firms and individuals, which they can adapt to suit their own needs. In future, the 'customers' of the social partners will not be employees whose needs have to be tended to but members of a free labour force.

Such a radical change in state and collective regulation requires a reflexive labour law able to assess realistically its own limits and capabilities and the role of the enabling state (Gilbert and Gilbert 1989; see also Gilbert and Etzioni 2004; Schuppert 2005) in the interplay between the social partners. Reflexive deregulation recognises the need to dismantle restrictive or outdated protective norms in order to trigger new dynamics for local and individual solutions. However, it also stresses the need for establishment of new rights (such as a right to further training), the details of which should be open to negotiation, legal provisions (such as the promotion of productive work) and tax incentives (see Schmid 2008a). In this way, the state would become an effective and financially powerful partner in the process of labour market regulation. It will of course no longer be the dominant partner in the industrial relations system of the cooperative social state but just the enabling junior partner acting as moderator.

Reflexive labour law teaches deregulation that it is dependent on the willingness of the targeted social systems to respond to its demands. Reflexive deregulation links with system-specific ways of reducing complexity. In other words, reflexive deregulation understands itself as a form of regulation of self-regulation. Furthermore, deregulation is a global trend contributing to the globalisation of labour law. Reflexive deregulation in this context is a normal, necessary and regularly occurring strategy for reduction of complexity opening up advanced national labour law jurisdictions. Deregulation is unlikely to be successful as a general strategy. However, as targeted deregulation, it can become reflexive and serve as part of re-regulation programmes that aim at finding the right balance of flexibility and security in improving labour market performances.

7. Reflexive regulation of labour and employment conflict resolution

Reflexive law can offer research on labour conflict resolution a new paradigm. Niklas Luhmann's and Gunther Teubner's insights in autopoietic social systems and conditions of legal regulation shall be utilised in the following to rethink some basic features of labour and employment conflict resolution.

7.1 REFLEXIVITY IN CONFLICT RESOLUTION

Labour and employment conflict resolution differs in relation to the social system in which it takes place. A basic insight that can be derived from systems theory for a theory of labour and employment conflict resolution is that types of conflict differ according to their system reference and that their resolution is shaped by the social system in which they occur. In applying this insight we can distinguish three 'arenas': collective conflict resolution in the industrial relations system, employment conflict resolution, respectively the handling of disputes between an employer and an employee at company level, and judicial decision-making.

The thesis of this chapter is that the modern approach in regulating labour and employment conflict resolution is characterised in all three contexts by reflexive processes of regulation of self-regulation and recursive decision-making. This shall be demonstrated with respect to examples of regulation of self-regulation in industrial relations and in company contexts, regulation of decision-making at the judicial level, and the recognition of labour market concerns in labour and employment conflict resolution.

As suggested in Chapter 2, an analytical distinction can be made between processes of reflexivity and processes of reflexion. Reflexivity is a concept widely used in assessments of modern society, for example by theories that describe major transformations in modern society as reflexive modernisation (Beck et al. 1994; see also Beck 1992, 1999). Reflexivity is used in these accounts to describe processes in which modern society is not only becoming aware but increasingly occupied with solving problems that it has created for itself. Reflexivity of this kind is concerned with reduction of internal complexity in modern society.

The theory of reflexion on the other hand is closely linked to autopoietic systems theory. It describes and analyses processes of self-awareness of the system that are linked to the autopoiesis and to processes of self-constitution of the system. These include basic operations of self-reference, forms of self-observation and modes of self-description. Through reflexion systems become autonomous. Reflexion uses reflexive mechanisms (Luhmann 1970) and examples are the conscious use of techniques on how to learn (learning of learning), the introduction of legislation that regulates legislation (legislation of legislation or standardisation of standardisation) and deciding how to decide (decision-making of decision-making).

In our context of labour and employment conflict resolution, we can add the attempt to solve conflicts that arise from conflict resolution. Reflexivity, reflexive mechanisms and processes of reflexion characterise a stage in which labour and employment conflict resolution becomes mature. A reflexive process in conflict resolution occurs when it distinguishes itself from conflict regulation (see Dahrendorf 1959). In other words, conflict resolution becomes reflexive when it perceives itself as conflict regulation. Regulation of conflict is in this view a form of conflict resolution that uses its mechanisms to regulate itself.

The distinction between conflict resolution and regulation of other systems is a well-known feature of the legal system (Teubner 1993a, ch. 5). However, the line between conflict resolution and regulation as two distinct results of procedure can be less clear empirically. Whether conflict resolution also means regulation depends on the scope of the conflict, the characteristics of disputants involved and the issues of the conflict. Procedures serve different functions for individual employment disputes and collective labour conflicts. Arbitration procedures for collective conflicts form part of the immune system of the industrial relations system. Labour courts, on the other hand, are judicial bodies for employment disputes which belong to the institutional structure of the legal system.

7.2 SELF-REGULATION IN INDUSTRIAL RELATIONS AND IN COMPANY CONTEXTS

National, sectoral and workplace industrial relations operate with a host of alternative dispute resolution mechanisms. These include arbitration, mediation and conciliation as well as grievance and dispute procedures which are prevalent modes of labour and employment conflict resolution in companies. These procedures are regulated by law or by collective agreements; often by both. If regulated by law, bipartite procedures usually have to adhere to basic democratic principles, for example election of representatives.

In relation to the industrial relations system, the regulation of industrial action is most important for the development of industrial relations as a social system (Müller-Jentsch 2004). In a sociological perspective, three stages can be distinguished in the evolution of industrial relations and collective bargaining: a conflictual, a cooperative and a participatory or collaborative stage (Müller-Jentsch 1993; Rogowski 1994). These stages are characterised by different styles of communications between the collective parties. Mechanisms of labour conflict resolution and their functions not only change while the industrial relations system advances from one stage to the next, but also contribute in decisive ways to these changes.

In the early stages of the development of an industrial relations system, the institution 'collective bargaining' is hardly distinguishable from arbitration (Müller-Jentsch 1997, p. 206). Industrial conflict is the prevalent mode of interaction; negotiations only take place in the context of conflict resolution. In response, the law of industrial conflict develops which encompasses limitations on the right to strike and lockouts (Jacobs 2010; Blanpain and Ben-Israel 1994) and provisions regulating liability for collective action (Goldman 2010).

In order to enhance stability, the industrial relations system tends to introduce in the second stage a body of norms which aims at a non-conflictual and cooperative basis of collective bargaining (Kahn-Freund 1978 [1954]). This is supported by the introduction of the distinction of conflicts of interest and conflicts of rights (Gladstone 2010; Jacobs 2010). The development of norms for the resolution of industrial conflict is facilitated by the state in a number of industrialised countries, including Germany, France and the United States. The development in Britain was different because the system of voluntary industrial relations (see Flanders 1970) prevented active state participation; however, procedural and institutional means were offered to support autonomous self-regulation (Davies and Freedland 1993, ch. 1).

In the third phase of the development of collective bargaining and industrial relations, the treatment of collective conflicts is often delegated to procedures which are separated institutionally from collective bargaining over collectively negotiable issues. Collective bargaining becomes a process of co-decision-making in which both parties realise that they rely on each other to achieve a common goal. The parties begin to define themselves as parts of the industrial relations system. The participating organisations transform into intermediaries who serve their members through representation in collective bargaining and other forms of collective cooperation (Streeck 1982).

A good example of self-regulation of conflict resolution in industrial relations is the German practice of regulating mediation and arbitration procedures in separate collective agreements. This differentiation of collective bargaining procedures into negotiation and conflict resolution is an important evolutionary achievement of the industrial relations system. It is also a good example of using the reflexive mechanism of resolving the conflict of how to solve a conflict or of deciding how to decide. In fact, it is a reflexive mechanism specific to the industrial relations system.

There are a number of ways in which a labour law system realises the needs of the industrial relations system for self-regulation. An example is the proceduralisation of arbitration as a result of judicial policies in Germany (Goll 1980). Both the legal doctrine and the judicial policy of the Federal Labour Court have created legal structures of conflict resolution and collective bargaining which favour procedural requirements over substantive conditions (Rogowski 1999). In particular, the concept of power parity (*Kampfparität*) indicates a withdrawal of substantive welfare state intervention in favour of procedural solutions which are not only acceptable to the negotiating parties but also compatible with major structures of the collective bargaining system and principles of the welfare state representing the public interest. In addition, 'power parity' based on the principle of proportionality is a legal concept which appears to establish a 'sound' basis for judicial review of industrial actions accompanying collective bargaining. Inherent in the concept of power parity is the tendency to favour compromise over 'all or nothing' decisions.

The use of reflexive mechanisms and reflexion can also be observed in the company context. Grievance and dispute procedures at company level form part of a system of shop floor rules. However, the legal nature of shop floor rules and their institutional contexts vary among countries.

Shop floor rules have been a major concern in British labour law for some time. Since the issuing of the Donovan report (Donovan Report 1968), employment policies have placed high emphasis on these rules. The legal approach was supposed to reflect the voluntarist tradition to rely on self-regulation at company level. The reflexive solution was the so-called Code of Practice, which was designed by a government agency (ACAS) as a model procedure to be implemented by companies. Self-regulation through disciplinary and grievance procedures has been further supported by the introduction of the employee right to be accompanied in attending a disciplinary or grievance hearing (Clancy and Seifert 2000).

From a reflexive labour law point of view, the Codes of Practice and the introduction of a right of representation are forms of legal recognition of self-regulation. The status of the legal provisions is facilitative. Employers are forced by circumstances and conditions over which they have control to implement the code, but not by force of law. By not following the code or ignoring the right of representation, employers take the risk of losing in an employment tribunal.

There were a number of attempts to use company dispute procedures to relieve employment tribunals, mainly from increased caseloads, starting with the Employment Rights (Dispute Resolution) Act 1998 and leading up to the interesting experiment that began with the Employment Act 2002. This statute provided that an employee, before being able to make a claim to the employment tribunal, had to begin statutory grievance procedures. The grievance had to be submitted in writing to the employer at least 28 days before submitting a claim to an employment tribunal. However, the practice of these procedures proved a failure because they had unintended negative consequences, became too formalistic and an administrative burden for both employees and employers (Morris 2004; Pollert 2005). The Employment Act 2008 repealed the procedural requirements and replaced them with less stringent, softer provisions that nevertheless allow tribunals to adjust awards in the event of non-compliance with a grievance procedure required by a Code of Conduct (Deakin and Morris 2012, pp. 88–91).

Reflexivity also characterises US labour law in its attempt to regulate grievance arbitration. US labour law is characterised by sophisticated forms of regulation of self-regulation. In the unionised sectors, it delegates decision-making powers in employment conflicts to private arbitration. This system of grievance procedures with final and binding arbitration concentrates the settlement of disputes on an intra-company, on-the-spot and private level, free from both state intervention and judicial review. Supported by the courts and by administrative agencies, the grievance arbitration system is given a high degree of autonomy. Its main actors, i.e. management, unions and arbitrators, actively engage in maintaining private decision-making at local company level (Herding 1972).

There is plenty of research on unionised grievance procedures in the US that uses a variety of theoretical perspectives (for an overview see Lewin 1999). This research includes studies that are inspired by the work of John Dunlop (for a discussion of Dunlop's system theory, see Chapter 2). It views grievance procedures as a system resulting from cooperative labour relations of unions and management. Research carried out using this perspective found that grievance filing and processing as well as settlement and post-settlement outcomes are affected by characteristics of the grievance procedure system. Feedback from prior grievance cases positively related to subsequent grievance settlement (for findings on grievance procedures using psychological, sociological and economic perspectives, see Lewin and Peterson 1988; Peterson and Lewin 2000).

It has to be mentioned, however, that, since the US system of labour and employment conflict resolution has witnessed over a number of decades an almost continuous decrease of union-management controlled systems and an increase of human resource management (HRM) systems without union participation, employment dispute resolution in the non-union sector has become a booming field (Lipsky et al. 2003). It has been argued that employment dispute procedure systems should essentially be understood as a response to the union-supported grievance arbitration system (Freeman and Medoff 1984). However, other research has provided alternative explanations for the introduction of non-union dispute resolution systems. According to Catherine Stone, cost of litigation, in particular high compensation awards in discrimination cases and a willingness of courts to grant compensation for unfair dismissals (just cause requirement) have been important factors for an increase of non-union disciplinary and grievance procedures (Stone 1999).

There is also the interesting case of worker cooperatives that have their special ways of handling disputes. They value informal handling of disputes, but as Stuart Henry analysed critically in *Private Justice* (Henry 1983, ch. 6), they rely on and enforce self-discipline through peer-group sanctioning as a powerful mechanism of social control. However, worker cooperatives offer their employees 'more options for addressing their workplace disputes' than conventional workplaces. This was the overall conclusion of Elizabeth Hoffman's comparison of dispute resolution in cooperative workplaces, although the mixture of informal and formal procedure as well as the amount of 'toleration' of conflicts varied significantly among the industries compared (Hoffmann 2012, ch. 8).

In Germany collective conflicts are handled at company level in special procedures that are closely linked to the system of German works council and firm-level collective bargaining. It allows works councils and unions to enter into company agreements (*Betriebsvereinbarung*) or firm-level collective agreements (*Firmentarifvertrag*). In case of disagreement over these agreements or over their enforcement or interpretation as well as redundancy decisions, the works council or management can request that a tripartite arbitration panel is used (*Einigungsstelle*). These arbitration panels at company level increasingly handle conflicts which could go to the labour courts. They have adopted judicial standards and show tendencies of legalism which derive not least from the participation of labour court judges as arbitrators (Bünger and Moritz 1983). A survey revealed that works councils increasingly oppose management hostility by using arbitration panels (Behrens 2007).

Arbitration panels can become sites of reflexion in companies. Dispute resolution provides opportunities for considerations of the 'company interest' and the 'public interest of the enterprise in itself', in particular in relation to its internal and external social environment (Teubner 1994). In internally controlled dispute procedures, a range of stakeholders engage in defining and redefining the company's self-understanding, albeit with a strong focus on the social responsibility of the company. Furthermore, in the context of co-determination, bipartite or tripartite collective decision-making at company level creates a potential for producer coalitions (Streeck 1992). Labour conflict resolution offers models for decentralised economic decision-making in corporate networks and it seems to fit the trend of involution of neo-corporatist arrangements from macro corporatism to micro corporatism that Gunther Teubner has observed (Teubner 1993a, p. 138, 1987a).

7.3   REFLEXIVE REGULATION OF DECISION-MAKING AT THE JUDICIAL LEVEL

In looking at the judicial level, a number of trends can be identified. These are related to specific characteristics of labour courts and equivalent judicial bodies in terms of professionalisation, appeals and procedure.

The oldest labour courts are the French councils of wise men (*Conseils de prud'hommes*), which until today are lay courts with no professional lawyer on the bench. The first *Conseil* was introduced in 1806 in Lyon and its task was to adjudicate and enforce a complex set of economic, legal and social norms of the local silk industry. Since 1848 *Conseils* are bipartite with an equal number of employer and employee representatives serving as judges and the employee judges being elected. The court's procedure is divided into an obligatory conciliation phase and a judgement phase. Despite a number of reforms, notably in the 1970s, the reputation of the *Conseils* is rather low. A good indicator for low esteem is the fact that it has become standard practice for employers who lost their cases to appeal. The rate of appeals has steadily increased, with currently over 60 per cent of all cases being appealed (Burgess et al. 2012, p. 34). Appeals are handled by appeal courts of the ordinary judiciary (see contributions in Lyon-Caen and Jeammaud 1986).

Like their French counterparts, German labour court proceedings are divided into an obligatory conciliation phase and a judgement phase. However, the bench is tripartite, with a legally qualified chairperson and an employer and an employee lay judge. The first labour courts were introduced in 1926. They handle all disputes arising from the employment relationship and, in addition, statutory claims of collective industrial actors, mainly works councils. The German labour court system is autonomous and creates an independent pillar within the German judicial system. The appeals go first to the State Labour Court and then for a final decision to the Federal Labour Court. Despite a high rate of judicialisation of labour and employment conflict resolution in Germany (Blankenburg and Rogowski 1986), the judicial practice is characterised by a high rate of settlements in court, which often are the result of direct intervention of labour court judges using elaborate non-legal settlement strategies (Blankenburg et al. 1979, ch. 8).

In Great Britain, labour courts were first introduced as industrial tribunals in 1964 and were renamed employment tribunals in 1998. Like their German counterparts, the employment tribunal bench is tripartite with a legally qualified barrister or solicitor serving as chairperson and two lay members representing the employer and the employee side. The procedure differs significantly from their continental counterparts and is modelled on the rather cumbersome adversary common law model with lengthy cross witnessing and a rather passive bench. There are no attempts to conciliate the case by the tribunal. Conciliation is handled prior to the hearing by the government agency Advisory, Conciliation and Arbitration Service (ACAS) (see Wood 1992, Harris et al. 2012). Appeals go to the Employment Appeals Tribunal and then to the Court of Appeal and finally to the House of Lords.

There are no courts in the United States comparable to European labour courts. However, the private system of final and binding grievance arbitration constitutes a functional equivalent. In addition, there exist agencies for the protection and enforcement of union rights, anti-discrimination laws and health and safety standards. Some of these agencies, in particular the National Labor Relations Board (NLRB), operate with quasi-judicial forms of decision-making.

If we analyse recent developments in labour courts, we can detect examples of reflexive regulation of decision-making at the judicial level. Advanced labour courts discover that they are most successful in regulating social relations by regulating themselves. Judicial procedures are a preferred target. The reform of procedures in terms of procedural differentiation is largely a result of legal self-regulation. Since they are internal affairs of the judicial system, we are in Teubner's realm of internal 'variation mechanisms' related to conditions of access to justice (Teubner 1993a, p. 95).

In addition, the legal system regulates other subsystems through procedural requirements. Resort to procedural regulation is a main form of recognition of self-regulation of the industrial relations system by labour courts. However, labour courts facilitate industrial relations for their own purposes of extending legal autonomy in their field of law. There are several examples of how labour courts have tried to instrumentalise industrial relations procedures for their purposes.

In their formative period in the 1970s, British industrial tribunals went beyond mere recognition of industrial self-regulation and actively endorsed and directly controlled the employer's use or non-use of dispute procedures; they developed a reasonableness test linking the judgement of dismissals to procedural fairness (*Earl v. Slater and Wheeler (Airlyne) Ltd.* [1972] ICR 508). The Court of Appeal reversed this line of decision-making, thereby arguing that such a direct linkage would lead to formalistic results (*British Labour Pump Co. Ltd. v. Byrne* [1979] ICR 347) and a middle ground was then found by the House of Lords (*Polkey v. Dayton Services Ltd.* [1988] ICR 142). In effect, the courts stopped instrumentalising company procedures for purposes of judicial decision-making and this can be seen as enhancing the autonomy of industrial relations decision-making.

Labour court procedures tend to be flexible in finding suitable solutions for ending a case that satisfy the disputing parties. French and German labour court proceedings start with an obligatory conciliation session and are required to seek conciliation at every stage of the procedure. Although only the parties can ultimately decide on this option of a conciliated or mediated settlement, they often do so with the active encouragement of the judge (Blankenburg and Rogowski 1986). This to some extent delegates decision-making to the parties themselves. A settlement reached in conciliation cannot be appealed, and therefore removes the dispute from the legal system at this stage.

During conciliation German labour courts engage in active recognition of other forms of regulation. In conciliation about the dismissal of an employee, it is not uncommon for labour courts to propose a solution which suits the regulation of the unemployment agency to secure the dismissed employees an immediate payment of unemployment benefits, and to adopt the agency's view as terms of the settlement. However, labour courts encourage the reference to an absent third party in their own interest. The judges can more easily convince the parties to agree to a settlement when there is an option of calling in a third party. And settlements relieve the court of the obligation to produce a written decision.

Labour courts in general encourage the use of procedures in company contexts. However, it makes an important difference if procedural regulation means support of participatory self-regulation or control of unilateral decision-making by a small entrepreneur. Whereas early judicialisation of employment conflicts in large companies might only disturb self-regulation, in small firms often it is the only option and can rapidly lead to overcoming the stalemate and the loss of communication in the personal re-employment relationship resulting from the disciplinary or dismissal action.

The finding that employment conflicts of small firms are over-represented in German labour courts led to demands for procedural differentiation. For example, it was suggested that special judicial procedures for claims arising from small and from large companies should be introduced (Blankenburg et al. 1979). This proposal favours experiments with proceduralism by demanding from the regulation of conflict resolution at the judicial level that attention is paid to procedural differentiation according to the degree of prior juridification of employment conflicts. A developing field of reflexive decision-making in European labour courts is their interaction with the European Court of Justice (ECJ). European Union law offers, with its preliminary ruling procedure under Art. 267 TFEU (formerly 177 EEC and 234 EC Treaty), any court or publicly recognised arbitration panel the possibility to refer a question of interpretation of European Union law to the ECJ. Research has found that there are remarkable differences in the use of the procedure among labour courts in Europe. A study of developments in six member states in the area of gender equality shows that German labour courts and British industrial and employment tribunals have been more active than their French and Danish counterparts, not to mention the very low activity rates of courts in Italy and Spain (Kilpatrick 2001). Although there are a number of factors that influence the practice, differences in the labour court systems are decisive. The German labour courts are used to judicial activism and repeated references if a decision of a higher court is not workable (Kilpatrick 2001). They indeed engage in reflexive decision-making to pursue their own judicial policies.

7.4 EXCURSUS: MESO-CORPORATIST STRUCTURES IN LABOUR AND EMPLOYMENT CONFLICT RESOLUTION

A specific feature of labour and employment conflict resolution is the participation that representatives of labour and management take in decision-making. Through their involvement, lasting relationships between the state and interest groups are established. The outcome of these relationships has been studied in a number of ways. A common concept used in studies of these relationships is societal corporatist structures (Schmitter 1974; Schmitter and Streeck 1985).

From a reflexive labour law perspective, participation of interest group representatives in the judiciary and in other decision-making bodies of the welfare state is an example of structural coupling between the industrial relations and the legal system. It is a particular form of tripartism in which the state and the two specific interest groups – employer associations and trade unions – form stable arrangements for continuous cooperation with the state (for other forms of tripartism involving public interest groups, see Ayres and Braithwaite 1992, ch. 3). In meso-corporatist arrangements, industrial relations representatives take an active part in the functioning of the welfare state and these interest group representatives thereby not only serve public interests but maintain service functions for members at the same time.

Through participation in corporatist arrangements, associations gain influence in social fields where direct associational control is lacking. In exchange, the public bodies absorb political criticism through integration of professional critics, and, thereby, conciliate antagonistic interests. In meso-corporatist arrangements, associations act politically only in the formal sense of representation; looking at actual decision-making processes with participation of associational representatives, a de-politicisation of issues can be observed as the main effect of the incorporation of interest groups.

Corporatism is in fact a feature that characterises labour and employment conflict resolution in a number of ways. In an earlier study I have characterised these features as meso-corporatist structures (see Rogowski 1985). Meso-corporatist structures are a common feature of employment conflict resolution at the judicial level. Participation of lay judges is supposed to guarantee that expertise of industrial relations practitioners is made available for judicial decision-making. The concept of meso-corporatism as intermediation was used in my analysis of judicial employment conflict resolution at two levels. First, corporatist cooperation of the state, trade unions and employers was analysed in the establishment process of employment protection institutions. Second, meso-corporatist arrangements were compared in the organisational structures of four judicial and quasi-judicial institutions.

Findings were that industrial relations policies always had to be balanced against the interests of the legal profession and the ordinary judiciary. The influence of tripartite cooperation on political decision-making during the establishment of institutions for employment conflict resolution varied considerably. In the United States, the legal profession was successful in resisting specialised courts as alien to the American judicial system and could prevent the establishment of courts with meso-corporatist arrangements (Tomlins 1985; Aaron 1985; see also Klare 1978;

Stone 1981). In France, the bipartite *Conseils de prud'hommes* are generally treated as creatures of the industrial relations sphere. The civil judiciary exercises hierarchical control through judicial review that displays signs of rejection of this lay judiciary on professional grounds. In Great Britain, the compromise has been to call the labour judiciaries 'tribunals' rather than courts, an expression of their inferior status in comparison with 'real' courts, which are permitted to review tribunal decisions. If the tripartite bench in employment tribunals, as they are now called, plays a role is an open question. Finally, in the Federal Republic of Germany, the legal profession insisted, from the beginning of the labour courts, that only lawyers could become professional labour court judges, although it took the legal profession until 1960 to succeed in this.

The degree and the level of participation of lay judges vary according to national jurisdictions. In Germany, meso-corporatist arrangements can be found in relation to the appointment of professional judges; to lay participation on the bench; and special rights of legal representation for trade union representatives. In British employment tribunals, such arrangements are found only at the level of lay judges and trade union or other lay representatives, whereas the French *Conseils* are characterised by meso-corporatist arrangements only at the level of representation. Interestingly, the bipartite bench of lay judges in the French *Conseil* is elected locally, but, in cases of impasse in decision-making, one discovers a residual tripartite structure, in that a professional judge may be called upon to overcome the deadlock (Rogowski 1985, pp. 157–8).

Little is known about the actual influence of lay judges on decision-making in labour courts or tribunals. Studies have questioned their actual influence on final decisions (Burgess et al. 2012). Indeed, formal participation of industrial relations representatives in judicial settings does not automatically guarantee acceptance by the legal profession and in particular trained judges.

7.5 REFLEXIVE LABOUR AND EMPLOYMENT CONFLICT RESOLUTION AND THE LABOUR MARKET

The biggest challenge for current labour and employment conflict resolution results from fundamental transformations of the labour market (see Supiot et al. 2001). Both collective bargaining and decision-making in labour courts is increasingly confronted with problems of dynamic labour markets and changing forms of employment. These challenges require from labour courts and collective bargaining systems a reflexive understanding of their regulatory capacities and their role and impact on the labour market.

In collective bargaining we find a worldwide trend to broaden negotiation agendas to include working conditions. Collective actors increasingly engage in labour market policy. The reference to labour market conditions (high unemployment) can be used to shape the collective bargaining agenda in a certain direction. A prominent example is reduction of working time. By shortening the normal working time, companies are forced to hire additional employees, at least in theory. Furthermore, although an issue that belongs traditionally to the canon of collective bargaining topics, it also fits into political and legislative efforts to raise the employment rate. For example, with its Working Time Directive, the EU not only provides a level playing field for its member states in terms of employment protection, but also pursues the policy of employment promotion and increasing the employment rate pursued under the European Employment Strategy (EES).

In the US, state courts used favourable labour market conditions in the 1980s and 1990s (low unemployment) to engage in compensatory judicial policies. In response to the decline of unionisation and subsequent loss of protection by collective agreements, some state courts have introduced the concept of just cause for dismissals of employees. Employers who dismiss without just cause face high awards of damages issued against them. Furthermore, the courts are prepared to issue high damage awards in cases of discrimination in employment (median recovery of around US$2000000 in the early 1990s in, admittedly, few cases in which the employee won, see Stone 1999, p. 29). The threat of high liability costs has resulted in a growth of non-union grievance arbitration. The US Supreme Court has supported this trend in a decision (*Gilmer*)[1] in which private arbitration for a statutory claim was allowed.

German labour courts have dealt with labour market problems in relation to atypical forms of employment. In the 1960s fixed-term contracts were assessed exclusively as ways to circumvent the existing dismissal protection system. The Federal Labour Court in particular saw its role in a peculiar reflexive fashion. It argued that it was necessary to protect the system of employment protection from being undermined (protection of protection). It introduced the requirement that fixed-term contracts were only legal when covered by one of the reasons permitted by the court. However, with an increasing need for fixed-term employment, the court was forced to allow more and more reasons for engaging in fixed-term

---

[1]   *Gilmer v Interstate/Johnson Lane Corp.*, 500 U.S. 20 [1991].

employment (Schömann et al. 1998). It reached a point that its decision-making created a source of legal uncertainty. In this situation the legislator introduced a law that removed the requirement of reason for new employment contracts, without however replacing the judicial policy. The statute that regulated fixed-term employment, the Employment Promotion Act 1985, was deliberately seen as an attempt to support the labour market by reforming labour law. Removing legal restrictions that derive from employment protections was meant as support for the flexibilisation of forms of employment.

The German Employment Promotion Act 1985 is just one example of a wider trend of deregulation of employment systems in Western jurisdictions. In accordance with neoliberal economic policies, labour law is assessed as to whether it has a positive or negative impact on employment rates. The labour law system as well as labour and employment conflict resolution are forced to assess themselves in relation to their impact on the labour market. At least since the adoption of the Amsterdam Treaty, this trend is supported at the level of the European Union by prioritising employment policies over traditional labour law issues. Policies such as transitional labour markets and flexicurity that balance employer and employee interests are key concepts in this context (Deakin and Rogowski 2011; Rogowski 2008a).

However, deregulation might be seen in a quite different light when it is linked to developments in labour law and labour conflict resolution that are a result of internal reflexive processes. In this perspective, deregulation can be understood as a regular event, intricately linked to the perennial problem of reduction of legal complexity. Regulation and deregulation are different systemic modes in dealing with complexity. Deregulation can be used both for purposes of reflexive self-regulation of law and support of self-regulation of the labour market (see Chapter 6).

7.6 CONCLUSION

Regulations and practices of conflict resolution in industrial relations, companies and labour courts will have to deal with ongoing transformations of employment relations. They have to cope with the needs of modern transitional labour markets and policies designed to support them. The success of these policies will at least to some degree depend on the extent to which labour conflict resolution and labour law can become reflexive in handling the new complexity that arises from the fundamental changes in developed labour markets.

It will in particular depend on corporations to engage in reflexive responses to their various structural couplings with societal systems when designing internal procedures. In his system theoretical analyses of the internal law of organisations and associations, Gunther Teubner found scope for the emergence of new ways of handling disputes and norm production in companies (Teubner 1978). In particular grievance procedures are mechanisms of self-regulation in this view that provide a 'rich source' to be regulated by official law.

> At the center are the decisions of formal organizations. In the internal law of associations and organizations, the law is bound to the self-reproductive processes not only of the economy, but of quite different social sub-systems like health, the mass media, religion or culture. Here it is the entry/exit mechanism that is fundamental for the cyclical linkage, which the law in turn creatively misunderstands as a law-producing mechanism. Organizational structures in economic enterprises, interest associations, trade unions, press organizations, hospitals, and cultural organizations are through this legal fiction made into a rich source of 'social law' that can be taken up, disciplined and controlled by official law (Teubner 1991, p. 137).

One should add that among the relevant societal systems for the production of internal norms and procedures, the industrial relations system occupies a privileged place. The interplay between internal organisational processes and external judicial interpretations leads not only to new forms of dispute resolution but to 'a private machinery for norm production' and a plural production of law. This analysis seems particularly appropriate for the unionised sector in the US but seems equally applicable to management-controlled human resource management systems in the non-union sector.

> The dramatic extension of 'due process' in US private organizations since the sixties supplies illustrative material of the new introduction of this sort of 'plural' production of law. . . . Without statutory provisions here having prescribed the introduction of procedures under the rule of law, a self-accelerating process got under way in which courts misunderstood previously 'law-free' internal organizational decisions as legal decisions and the organizations in turn formalized the grievance procedures and continually extended them. The end of the development is a private machinery for norm production supported by the official law, representing a new 'source of law', comparable with the contractual mechanism. In the ultracycle of the mutual misreading of law and organization, the law gained a new source of law and the organization a new source of legitimation (Teubner 1991, p. 138).

Teubner gives a good example of what can be achieved by companies through reflexive labour law.

PART III

Reflexive European and international labour law

8. Reflexive coordination of European social and employment policies

The law of the European Union and labour law have a chequered relationship. At the beginning of the process of European integration in the 1950s, it was decided that in order for a common market to be established it was not necessary to grant supranational bodies legislative powers in the area of labour law. The influential Ohlin Report stipulated that the common market did not presuppose a harmonised level of labour standards but would more or less automatically lead to convergence of national standards (Ohlin Report 1956). However, some provisions regarding social and employment policy were included in the Treaty establishing the European Economic Community of 1957, for example the equal pay clause and coordination of social security entitlements for migrant workers. These provisions constituted cornerstones for the gradual development of a social dimension of European integration (see Barbier 2008; Barnard and Deakin 2012).

For a reflexive labour law perspective, the last stages in the development of European social and employment policies since the early 1990s are of particular interest. In these stages the European Union embarked on a new approach to labour law by linking it to wider employment policies. The previous focus on employment protection was replaced with a new focus on employment promotion (see Deakin and Rogowski 2011). In this context new legal instruments were introduced in order to conduct and coordinate employment policies pursued in the member states.

The chapter evaluates the soft law instruments in the European Union that accompany the new governance approach adopted for the pursuit of European social and employment policies. It pays particular attention to the open methods of coordination used in the European Employment Strategy (EES) and in core areas of European social policy such as health, pensions and social inclusion. It interprets the development of new forms of governance in social and employment law as a result of three processes: spillover of coordination of economic policies into employment and social policies; efforts of the European Commission to develop a European Social Model; and the emergence of reflexive policy-making. The central thesis is that in order for soft forms of governance to be effective, European law and policy must become reflexive. The chapter aims at showing that since the mid-1990s, forms of reflexive coordination are emerging in European law and policy-making.

8.1   EVOLUTION OF COORDINATION OF EUROPEAN SOCIAL AND EMPLOYMENT POLICIES

European employment policies as well as social policies were given a new direction in the context of the introduction of the European Economic and Monetary Union (EMU) during the 1990s. An economically oriented employment discourse replaced a rights-focused social policy discourse (see Ashiagbor 2001, 2005, ch. 3). In White Papers on Growth, Competitiveness and Employment issued in 1993 and on European Social Policy issued in 1994, employment protection and social policy were evaluated in terms of having positive or negative effects on economic processes and employment rates (see European Commission 1993, 1994). The White Papers endorsed policies of combating unemployment through flexibilisation of existing laws and policies as well as support for businesses in their hiring efforts.

Since the European Council summit in Essen in December 1994, the Commission and the Council play an active role in monitoring labour market and social policies at the national level. A decisive step in relation to employment policies was taken at the 1997 Intergovernmental Conference in Amsterdam. In it a discussion took place of establishing a specific EU unemployment criterion, similar to the four EMU convergence criteria. However, this was rejected and a compromise was reached to adapt for employment policy-making the 'multilateral surveillance process' originally set up to monitor member state economic policies in order to ensure economic convergence in the run-up to the EMU (Trubek and Mosher 2003, p. 38; Mosher and Trubek 2003). Finally, at the extraordinary summit on employment in November 1997 in Luxembourg, the process envisioned by the new Employment Chapter of the Amsterdam Treaty was launched under the name of the European Employment Strategy (EES).

The EES, under which labour market policies of member states are monitored by the Commission, constitutes an ongoing process of negotiation and adjustment between the member states and the European institutions. Of particular interest for reflexive labour law are the new governance mechanisms introduced by the EES and in particular the use of soft law methods that link in new ways the EU level to the national and local levels.

This new governance approach, called the 'open method of coordination' (OMC), has been adopted as a general model to be used in a number of policy areas, including social policies, and it was clearly designed on the model used to introduce the EMU (see Hodson and Maher 2001; Pochet 2005). Through peer review and exchange of best practices, each member state is directly confronted with the plans and experiences of others, thus acquiring benchmarks by which they can measure their own performance.

The essence of the new governance approach was outlined in the White Paper on Governance that the European Commission issued in 2001 (European Commission 2001a). In it a new style of regulation was promoted that favours soft measures of coordination over hard regulation. Four steps can be distinguished in relation to the OMC:

1. setting up of guidelines supplemented by timetables for achieving the goals in the short, medium and long term (the Commission makes proposals on the guidelines);
2. introduction of quantitative and qualitative indicators and benchmarks as a means of comparing best practices (the Commission organises the exchange of best practices and makes proposals on indicators);
3. translation of the European guidelines into national action plans by setting specific targets and adopting measures, thereby taking into account national and regional characteristics;
4. follow-up system: monitoring and evaluating combined with peer review (this provides support to the processes of implementation and peer review). In their review of the national action plans the Commission and the Council regularly provide comments and recommendations that are often based on comparisons with the best performers and create additional benchmarks for each member state.

In a formal legal sense, the OMC is non-binding and ultimately voluntary in nature. The OMC is meant to be flexible. Its voluntary nature allows member states to adjust reforms in accordance with the structures of their regimes, institutional networks and specific circumstances (see Barbier 2005; Heidenreich and Zeitlin 2009). It enables wide-ranging participation of social partners (see Rogowski and Schömann 2002; Goetschy 2012). However, if a member state decides not to cooperate or chooses *à la carte* which policies it wants to follow while resisting others, there are no hard sanctions that can be imposed (see Regent 2003, p. 210). In the end, the effectiveness of the OMC depends on the participants' willingness to cooperate or, to use the language of reflexive law, to engage in self-regulation.

The instruments used by the OMC are known as soft law instruments that for labour lawyers lack the advantage of legally enforceable hard law. However, policy-oriented labour market specialists widely share a belief that in areas such as employment and social policy, the OMC is the appropriate method because member states are largely unwilling to transfer sovereignty beyond coordination (see De la Porte 2002, p. 43). The soft law approach of the OMC seems to have advantages for national governments because they might receive impulses for the reform of their systems without losing sovereignty (Borrás and Jacobsson 2004, p. 191).

In theory the OMC instigates a learning process in which member states are subjected to benchmarking, peer review and evaluations of their progress (see Kajtár and Rogowski 2005). The results of the 'OMC in action' display few examples of successful learning (Zeitlin 2005). However, there seems to be some evidence of learning from negative experience. The outcomes of evaluations and benchmarking can lead to open criticism of member state governments. So-called soft sanctions of 'naming and shaming' can harm the reputation of member states that score less favourably and put their governments under pressure to conform (see Scott and Trubek 2002).

The new governance approach was adopted by the EES for employment policies. The EES envisages a cyclical process in accordance with the approach outlined in the White Paper on Governance. It requires the Commission and Council to issue a Joint Employment Report which provides guidelines for member state policies. The Report is the result of evaluations of the National Action Plans which create the basis for the design of new guidelines. While drawing up the guidelines the Commission consults a number of actors, including the member states, the European Parliament, the Employment Committee, the Committee of the Regions, the Economic and Social Committee as well as the relevant social actors, i.e. trade unions and employer associations. The first employment guidelines were introduced in 1997 and contained 19 separate guidelines, falling under four pillars:

1. *employability*: measures to endorse active labour market policies and to increase skill levels among workers;
2. *entrepreneurship*: support for small, innovative businesses, including tax reform, in order to encourage them to create jobs;
3. *adaptability of businesses*: bridging the need for modernisation of work organisation and increasing the flexibility of workers through training;
4. *equal opportunities for women and men*: promoting gender equality in employment.

8.2 FROM OPEN TO REFLEXIVE COORDINATION

The early EES showed a reflexive design from the start. The use of guidelines was meant to support and not impose the adoption of objectives for national labour market policies. The Commission had great hopes in actually increasing employment rates through this new form of dialogue that respects the legislative limits of European policies while at the same time allowing the Commission to take an active role during monitoring of performances at national levels. However, there have been critical voices since the inception of the EES that warned against over-optimism on the part of the Commission for revealing a tendency of supporting the creation of unsustainable atypical employment while neglecting job quality (Ball 2001).

Partly in response to these criticisms, an effort was made after the first cycle of five years to refine the original guidelines. New objectives and a set of new targets were introduced, indicating a shift from 'passive' to 'active' unemployment-reduction policies. Particular emphasis was given to modernisation of member state public employment services. Other refinements of the original strategy which seem to be the result of learning at the European level are the introduction of incentives for persons aspiring to become entrepreneurs, of efforts to eliminate poverty traps by changing tax and benefit policies, and support for lifelong learning initiatives as well as improvements of procedures for skills certification.

A new and revised EES gained shape in 2000 when at the Lisbon European Council Summit an ambitious employment rate target was adopted according to which 70 per cent of employable European citizens should actually be in employment by 2010. This reorientation of employment policies demanded from active labour market policies privileging measures that encourage the creation of new jobs and the removal of unemployed from being dependent on unemployment benefit.

On the basis of an evaluation of the first five-year EES cycle, the Barcelona European Council in 2002 called for a reinforced, simplified and streamlined process in order to meet the Lisbon target. Further improvements were suggested in 2003 by the Commission in its Communication on the Future of the Employment Strategy (see European Commission 2003b). The new strategy adopted a more focused approach and replaced the four pillars with three overarching objectives that were especially geared to reinforce the Lisbon agenda: (1) full employment; (2) quality and productivity at work; and (3) cohesion and an inclusive labour market. 'Full employment' called for both demand- and supply-side policy measures. 'Quality and productivity at work' reflected the call of the Lisbon agenda for the creation of not only more but also better jobs. 'Cohesion and an inclusive labour market' aimed at reduction of unemployment and promotion of equal access for everyone to the labour market.

The new EES was aimed at specific sectors of the labour market, such as young and elderly workers, women, minorities, third-country nationals and disabled workers. It favoured activation policies that promote training and lifelong learning and support institutional innovations such as employment agencies that view themselves as service providers and treat the unemployed as clients. The renewed EES also encouraged mutual 'learning' between the member states, suggesting that governments and enterprises should see themselves as 'learning units'. An important learning instrument in this context is peer review, which is meant to identify, evaluate and distribute useful active labour market practices that could be transferred between member states (Schmid and Kull 2004).

A further redirection of the EES was introduced in spring 2005 after a thorough evaluation of the OMC and the EES (European Commission 2003d (Kok I), 2004b (Kok II); see Jørgensen 2005; Bulmer 2012). The very ambitious Lisbon target of creating 22 million jobs was reduced to 6 million and new 'streamlining' efforts are undertaken in order to align economic, employment and social policies. The new approach called for joint economic and employment reports. The annual cycle was from 2005 onwards replaced by a three-year cycle. In line with the original Lisbon criteria and agenda for a successful competitive European common market, the main concern of employment policy became competitiveness.

The use of soft law coordination in the form of the OMC was not confined to economic and employment policy. The OMC increasingly played an important role in the modernisation of European social and welfare policies as well and we witness similar transformations in the use of the OMC in these areas (on the OMC and social inclusion, see Armstrong 2010; on indicators for social inclusion, see also Atkinson 2002; Atkinson et al. 2004). The OMC was used in social policy since 2000, first in the area of social inclusion at the Lisbon Summit in March 2000, then in the area of pensions at the Stockholm Summit in March 2001 and finally at the Gothenburg Summit in June 2001 in the area of healthcare and care for the elderly (see De la Porte 2003, p. 340). A streamlining of social policy OMCs occurred at the same time when economic and employment OMCs were merged (see below for further comments on streamlining from a reflexive law perspective).

The final report of the Working Group XI on Social Europe of the European Convention on the Constitution, issued on 30 January 2003 listed a number of areas for further use of the OMC. These included the areas of education, tax harmonisation and the establishment of minimum social standards (European Convention on the Constitution 2003). However, with the demise of the Constitution and the onslaught of the economic and financial crisis of 2008, the extension of the OMC to all these areas was no longer a top political priority. But it has not lost its prominent role as governance mechanism in the current Europe 2020 agenda.

The OMC is said to be capable of acknowledging the diversity of welfare states (see Scharpf 2002, p. 653). However, the range of options can only fall within a certain band. What is fundable in Scandinavian countries might not be achievable in the new Central and Eastern European member states. In the case of countries with less developed economies, the restriction on benefits is often a result of financial difficulties and not the lack of social awareness. Thus, whether the band of reasonable options can be maintained remains to be seen. Furthermore, there exist ideological differences among member states that seem at certain times almost irreconcilable (Britain and Sweden have often been cited as archetypical antagonists in this respect; see Scharpf 2002, p. 650).

By adopting the OMC in the employment and the social policy field, a double shift occurred (Pochet 2003). First, there was a shift in protagonists in the sense that 'traditional' actors such as the Commission, Parliament and the ECJ have become less dominant, while member states and the social partners have turned into 'front-line players'. At least in theory the OMC supports functional participation of interest groups (Smismans 2004; Kjaer 2010, ch. 5) and industrial democracy in a transnational community (Fetzer 2010). Under the aegis of democratic participation, the OMC also involves local and regional forces and other civil society representatives.

Second, and most importantly from a reflexive labour law perspective, there was a shift in the legal nature of the instruments regulating social policy. Soft law is the main form of law used in the OMC. Some authors see a tension between soft and hard law, and in particular between the OMC and proper employment protection. Conventional labour lawyers such as Silvana Sciarra (Sciarra 2004) and Manfred Weiss (Weiss 2004) fear crowding out of hard law by soft law. It is indeed the case that the hard law measures, mainly framework directives, which have been adopted since the introduction of the EES, are all more or less subsumed under the heading of combating unemployment. It is significant that they are concerned with issues such as fixed-term and part-time work or parental leave. These are issues of employment promotion rather than employment protection.

On the other hand, sociolegal scholars such as David Trubek and his colleagues (see Scott and Trubek 2002; Trubek and Mosher 2003; Mosher and Trubek 2003; Trubek and Trubek 2005; Trubek et al. 2006; Trubek and Trubek 2010) are more optimistic about the future use of soft law and predict rather innovative new combinations of soft and hard law measures.

The second scenario seems more realistic in depicting the future of the OMC. Fritz Scharpf's suggestion (Scharpf 2002, pp. 662–6) of combining the OMC with framework directives indicates complementarity of hard and soft law measures in European Union law (see also Smismans 2011). As framework directives are binding, national policy-makers are less likely to ignore the policy discourses of open coordination. His proposal of designing the OMC for subgroups of member states with more or less similar welfare states and similar economic and institutional challenges seems particularly promising. These subgroups would not constitute solid blocks but rather overlapping clusters.

However, from a reflexive law perspective, it seems more appropriate to look at the potential of self-regulation of the OMC. Kenneth Armstrong (Armstrong 2010) and Mark Dawson (Dawson 2011) have convincingly argued that there is a future for the OMC precisely in this respect, at least in the case of the OMC on social inclusion. 'Instead of looking to hard law models of governance as a means of strengthening the OMC, a more appropriate approach would be to consider "harder" EU policy coordination models' (Armstrong 2010, p. 287). Mark Dawson sees the future of the OMC in various ways of 'constitutionalising new governance' (Dawson 2011, ch. 5), thereby continuing the previous debate on the OMC and constitutionalism (Kilpatrick 2006; Klosse 2005) on a new level and opening up the discourse to insights from debates on societal constitutionalism.

The OMC has been criticised by political scientists for a number of inherent weaknesses. Daniel Wincott sees dangers of overextension in using the OMC in areas where it is unlikely to have a strong impact, thereby undermining the credibility of the process as a whole (see Wincott 2003, p. 550). Another issue is transparency of the process. The lack of knowledge among average citizens about the open method of coordination and relatively little media coverage indicates a democratic deficit (Büchs 2007, ch. 7), as does the general lack of national parliamentary debates of the Lisbon Strategy (see European Economic and Social Committee 2004). In a certain sense, the OMC depoliticises the unemployment issue and turns it into a matter for labour market experts (see Goetschy 2003, p. 73). Nevertheless, the OMC is considered to be a democratic process because it inherently promotes a decentralised European Social Model (ESM) (see Feronas 2004, p. 16), suits multilevel governance and prefers negotiated reforms (see De la Porte 2002, pp. 44–5 and the critical assessment in Bulmer 2012).

An interesting proposal has been put forward by Stijn Smismans. He suggests combining reflexive law with new forms of democratic participation which he calls, using a terminology introduced by Joshua Cohen and Jonathan Zeitlin, 'directly deliberative polyarchy' (Smismans 2005, referring to Cohen and Sabel 1997; see also Gerstenberg 1997; Gerstenberg and Sabel 2002). In his proposal, reflexive-deliberative polyarchy serves as a normative frame for the OMC. One can add that prominent participants in democratic deliberations of reflexive policy-making are not just citizens and governments, but ideally social partners, interest organisations and actors at local and regional level (see Rogowski and Schömann 2002). In this way the OMC fits the European approach to partnership and local policy-making that is potentially closer to the citizens. Its 'multi-level dialogue' (see Regent 2003, p. 206) is supposed to increase the role of regions, support the emergence of a European civil society and strengthen the legitimacy of the European Union as a whole, although the reality of a low rate of participation of actors with 'hands-on experience' in the OMC might be somewhat sobering in this respect (Smismans 2008; Kjaer 2010, pp. 97–101).

The OMC can be assessed in terms of reflexive law at two levels. The method itself is reflexive in the sense that it provides a regulatory frame at the European level for regulatory processes carried out at member state level. The regulatory frame has to be facilitative and capable of respecting the logics of member state regulation. In short, for the OMC to be successful, it has to develop an understanding of itself as regulation of self-regulation. Furthermore, the 'methods' used to reform the OMC show signs of reflexivity at a higher level. Streamlining and simplification can be interpreted as processes in which the method is applied to itself in the sense that different forms of coordination are coordinated.

This 'coordination of coordination' can be demonstrated in relation to social policy. Streamlining social policy OMCs is meant as promotion of effective operation of the policy triangle of economic, employment and social policies. The Communication on 'Strengthening the Social Dimension of the Lisbon Strategy: Streamlining Open Coordination in the Field of Social Protection' (see European Commission 2003a) proposed the linkage of the various social policy OMCs. The goal was to modernise social protection systems by making coordination of social protection more effective; decrease the burden on the actors through a reduction in the numbers and the frequency of reports; rationalise and simplify the procedure; and put greater emphasis on implementation of results.

In the beginning, streamlining and simplifying the use of the OMC was confined to the method itself by providing a clearer definition of the scope of the OMC. However, streamlining of policy coordination was expanded and started to become an ambition linked to the overarching goal of improving the quality and the stability of socioeconomic governance of the EU as a whole. The right policy mix was supposed to create a 'virtuous circle' of economic and social progress. The idea was that by linking social, economic and employment OMCs, these policies develop a propensity to mutually reinforce each other (see European Commission 2000, p. 6). Social policy streamlining followed the model of streamlining of economic and employment policies. In these areas, streamlining involved the creation of a unified timetable and the adoption of a switch from one-year to three-year cycles (the first cycle started in 2003).

A major innovation as a result of the streamlined process has been the Joint Social Protection Report of the Commission and the Council. The new report replaced the Social Protection in Europe Report as well as the joint reports on social inclusion, on pensions and on policy cooperation in healthcare and long-term care. Since 2006, one comprehensive and forward-looking Joint Social Protection Report has been issued for three years with lighter updating reports in intervening years. Member states prepare National Action Plans that cover all three social policy fields together and the streamlined processes are based on a set of indicators that increase visibility and comparability of developments in the areas of pensions, health and long-term care (see European Commission 2000).

However, the various efforts of the Commission to strengthen the OMC should not obscure the limited regulatory capacities of soft law. A reflexive assessment of its use has to emphasise that the OMC is non-binding coordination. As such, it is a means to foster compromises in the absence of substantial agreements (see Schäfer 2004). In the end, the member states have to regulate their social and employment policies. European initiatives and coordination efforts can only be facilitators of their self-regulation. At best, the effort of streamlining the OMC leads to a new awareness among the parties involved that coordination gains its strength through accepting its limits. Such awareness could form the basis for reflexive coordination and there are signs indicating that European coordination is developing in this direction. However, if reflexivity is understood in a normative sense as dialogue, there is also evidence of limited reflexivity so far:

> . . . as it stands – the policy of 'streamlining' has been a failure. There is neither (i) consistent evidence of feeding in and feeding out between the different coordination processes, nor (ii) an equal and balanced synergy between them (Dawson 2011, p. 218. A more nuanced account can be found in Armstrong 2010, ch. 4).

8.3   THE EUROPEAN SOCIAL MODEL AND REFLEXIVE COORDINATION

It is simply a fact that economic integration and social protection systems are closely interlinked. Social security regulations provide protection to millions of workers moving within the European Union. It is not hard to imagine that the absence of coordination of social security systems would prevent workers from effectively exercising the right to free movement. Workers would find themselves in a situation of not being entitled to benefits despite many years of continuous employment in different member states if there was no coordination of social security systems (negative conflict of laws). On the other hand, member states would face the problem of double benefit payment without coordination of social security systems (on this positive conflict of laws, see Pennings 2010, p. 6; see also Crevits and Van Buggenhout 2003).

In the early stages of European integration, coordination of social security was almost exclusively linked to enabling free movement of workers. Nowadays, this is no longer the only reason for coordination of social security at the EU level. In particular, the extension of rights granted to all citizens of the European Union beyond the group of migrating workers has led to the reform of coordination of social protection policies (see Fuchs 2002). This extension of rights can be interpreted as linked to the general move from negative to positive integration in the European integration process that requires the 'reconsideration of the legal scope of negative integration in the light of social and political goals other than the maximisation of market competition' (see Scharpf 1999, p. 160). The Commission has indeed expressed the view that European integration and coordination policies 'must . . . be seen from the perspective of European citizenship and the building of a Social Europe' (see European Commission 2003c).

However, already the original approach, which viewed social security coordination as merely supporting the free movement of migrant workers, was dependent on a common understanding of goals and basic welfare provisions in the member states. Although there was no need to make these goals explicit, largely due to the fact of lacking competences in the field of social and employment policies at the European level, this hard coordination of social security rested on a shared set of social values. The anti-discrimination approach that granted migrant workers the same rights as domestic workers formed the key element of early social security coordination. It assumed that there existed rights in all participating member states and that these rights were of a somewhat similar kind, aiming at a similar level of welfare protection.

Since the beginning of the 1990s the situation has changed and the call to define the core elements of social protection could no longer be avoided. A discussion of the meaning of a European Social Model (ESM) started. A number of factors that have influenced this debate can be delineated. The ESM is prominently linked to the ambitious project of a political European Union that is capable of coordination of economic policies as well as foreign and security policies of the member states. The EMU that forms the core of the new EU has become the driving force behind new coordination efforts in employment and social policies.

What is still largely lacking, however, is a common understanding of the function or of the core elements of the model. Some view it as an ideal type, some as a reality, some as a political project (Adnett 2001; Ebbinghaus 1999; Ferrera 2004; Jepsen and Serrano Pasqual 2005, 2006; Kleinman 2002; Lynch-Fannon 2006; Martin and Ross 2004; Offe 2003; Rogowski 2008a, 2008b; Scharpf 2002; Schmid and Schömann 2004; Sisson 1999; Streeck 1999; Tharakanl 2003; Vos et al. 2004; Wickham 2002). It is often contrasted with a US model of a neoliberal minimalist welfare state (Hay et al. 1999). However, the ESM became particularly prominent when the European Commission started referring to the ESM as the underlying goal of European social integration, without however clearly defining its elements.

What seems clear is that the function of the ESM is to capture an important aspect of the reality of European integration that derives from the unique interlinkage of economic integration and social protection systems. The discussion of the ESM is also influenced by a new rivalry between the EU and the US. The EU is criticised by neoliberal economists who are in favour of US-style economic job growth of maintaining inflexible labour markets by supporting an outmoded ESM. In response to this ideological challenge, the discussion of the ESM has turned into a debate over values such as solidarity, social justice and public responsibility for social hardship which are shared among European nations and explain the high esteem in Europe for welfare policies (see Vos et al. 2004, pp. 336–7). The simplistic presumption of neoliberal economists that high economic growth rates will automatically lead to social improvements is not shared among the wider European public.

The European Commission adopted the rhetoric of working towards an ESM and argued that the modernisation of this model has to be an important future target in the European Union. A number of official documents of the EU and the Council of Europe referred directly to the ESM. These comprise 'benchmark documents' (see ETUI 2000, p. 54) such as the 1989 Charter of Fundamental Rights of Workers, the Charter of Fundamental Rights proclaimed at the Nice summit, the Lisbon social agenda as well as the Council of Europe's revised Social Charter. In these official documents and statements, the ESM is characterised as a unique blend of economic and social aims. Competitiveness is said to be coupled with social justice and improving living and working standards, more jobs with better jobs. Elements of the ESM can be found in the EC Treaty, which states that a high level of social protection and promotion of social cohesion are amongst the major aims of the EU, and is also encapsulated in the dual Lisbon aim of 'growth with more and better jobs and greater social cohesion'.

A short quote from a speech given in 2003 by the Employment Commissioner at the time during a visit of a prospective new member state in Tallinn, Estonia, can serve as an example of the Commission's rhetoric:

> From the outset, the EU treaties spoke of rising living standards and higher levels of social protection. Improving working conditions. Promoting a greater quality of life. More than fifty years later, we remain true to that vision of the European Social Model (see Diamantopoulou 2001).

In the rest of the speech the Commissioner lists the various initiatives undertaken by the Commission and the EU in general in the areas of employment and social policies. What is missing, however, is any analytically meaningful definition of the ESM. The reference to the ESM lacks coherence and theoretical distinction and resorts instead to enumeration and description of competences and policies pursued by the European institutions. In the Commissioner's own words, 'it escapes precise definition', nevertheless 'the notion of "model" is significant because it is "anticipatory" or "aspirational"' (see Diamantopoulou 2003).

The EU's official version of the ESM acknowledged a number of stakeholders that include employees and employers as well as social partners. The direct participation of social partners in Community decision-making via the Social Dialogue and indirect participation through 'partnership' in models of corporate governance formed integral parts of the ESM according to the Commission. The architecture of the ESM was seen shaped by a policy-making process that involves decision-making at multiple levels ranging from the European to the national, the regional and the local level.

In academic debates about the distinct character of the ESM we can distinguish two approaches. One approach argues that social and employment policy coordination is needed for the sake of solidaristic social values. The alternative approach emphasises its role in relation to economic efficiency. A prominent example of the second type of argument is Claus Offe's account of the ESM. He has argued that notions related to the ESM constitute the very core of the distinct European character of the political economy of the EU (see Offe 2003). It might indeed be contended that the success of further economic integration of the European economy depends on increased attempts to coordinate social protection and to combat social and economic insecurity and social exclusion, albeit only on a 'neo-voluntary' basis as Wolfgang Streeck sceptically points out (see Streeck 1996). At stake is the unity of the European Union in economic terms and the protection of Europe as an economic community. Despite his criticism of the OMC as disguised support for deregulation (see also Jepsen and Serrano Pasqual 2006), Offe realistically argues that the disparity in social protection systems and in particular in the resulting labour costs disadvantage certain states and is harmful for the Community as a whole, thus providing further incentives to coordinate social policies (see Offe 2003, pp. 458–60).

Anton Hemerijck has gone a step further in his analysis of the ESM. He has argued that the EU's main function in bringing about social integration is that of a facilitator in reforming welfare, assisting processes of self-transformation of national welfare policies through coordination (see Hemerijck 2004). The key idea is that of a close link of economic and social development. This approach represents a shift from a normative to a cognitive understanding of the ESM. In cognitive terms the ESM not only promotes social justice but contributes to economic growth. Social policy is no longer considered an obstacle but a beneficial economic factor that creates security for economic activities and provides, among other benefits, incentives to pursue collective goods (see Hemerijck 2002, pp. 173–4). If this cognitive understanding is shared widely, it creates the ideal basis for the development of reflexive coordination of welfare reforms and other reflexive policy-making.

An insightful comment on the ESM and in particular the new focus of the ESM on new governance and the OMC has been made by Milena Büchs. She has argued that the ESM pursued by the Commission bears resemblance to social democratic policies and in particular the 'third way' politics adopted by New Labour under Tony Blair and the German Social Democratic Party (SPD) under Gerhard Schröder (Büchs 2007, ch. 3). This approach favours a governance approach that promotes social partnership and the use of targets as quantitative measurements of policy success. She comes to the conclusion that the ESM underlying the EES shares the basic values of third-way politics:

> This analysis demonstrates that the most important features of 'third way' labour market policy reappear in the European Employment Strategy: supply-side labour market policy which focuses on improving the fit between supply and demand of labour through 'activation' and training, widening labour market participation through 'making work pay', active ageing and anti-discrimination policies, and combining flexible labour markets with job security (Büchs 2007, p. 48).

Büchs is historically wrong in associating the whole discourse of the ESM closely with the emergence of so-called third-way politics in the 1990s. The ESM discourse at the European level goes back at least to the Delors presidency in the 1980s. However, by analysing the ideological core of the current debate over the ESM, she is right to emphasise that the ESM and the EES share an understanding that 'social policy can contribute to economic success' (Büchs 2007, p. 44) and foster an integrated economic and social policy-making approach.

It is apparent that the ESM has to combine contradictory sets of values. On the one hand, there are reduced public expenditure for social services, financial sustainability, competitiveness, deregulation, flexibility, privatisation and individual responsibility – key concepts in neoliberal economic policies. In appraisals of the ESM, these values are often combined with, on the other hand, values such as security, inclusive society and adaptability. Or in the language of the Presidency Conclusions of the Barcelona European Council: 'The ESM is based on good economic performance, high level of social protection, education and social dialogue' (see European Council 2002, p. 8).

However, a proper assessment of the European Social Model has to look not only at its contradictory content but at its function as well. The ESM has a number of specific characteristics in this respect that delineate it from any national welfare model. Three functional aspects of the ESM can be highlighted: its multi-layered structure, its decentred and plural nature and its reflexive style of policy-making.

First, the ESM consists of a multi-layered structure. The European Union as such is not the main player in devising and carrying out social and employment policies; the responsibility for carrying out and financing these policies rests with the member states and they stay ultimately in control. The European Union only assists the member states and acquires competences beyond coordination only in rather specific areas. Decision-making and the provision of welfare and protection is inherently decentred in the European Union. Even the most sophisticated coordination efforts at the centre cannot change this fact and decentralisation is widely viewed as a positive feature, and indeed appreciated as a major virtue of the model. Coordination is not disguised harmonisation. It is deliberately designed to preserve the right of the member states to be the ultimate decision-makers, captured by the subsidiarity principle.

Second, the ESM is decentred and plural. It does not consist of one but of several models. The plural nature of the ESM supports both homogeneity and diversity. The ESM does not favour a European federal welfare state that replaces national welfare approaches but encourages instead 'competitive federalism' (see Barnard 2000) in its coordination policies. Depending on the intensity of the role of state intervention, it is possible to distinguish four basic social security models that are in operation in a variety of combinations among the member states. In the *statist model* the state is responsible for providing welfare financed out of general taxes. In the solidarity-based *social insurance* model, the role of the state is to provide general regulation under which employees are insured against social risks and employers and employees are obliged to pay contributions. In the *corporatist model*, the state supports the regulation of welfare through collective agreements or company agreements between trade unions, respectively, employee representatives and employer associations or companies. Finally, under the individualist solution, favoured by neo-liberal economic policies, protection against risks is left to the individual seeking it through *private insurance*, thereby reducing the role of the state to granting tax relief or other concessions.

The third and final functional aspect of the ESM is that it is at its very core characterised by reflexive policy-making and the use of reflexive law instruments. In practising the OMC, the EU makes creative use of its limits, in particular limited legal competences. The OMC is policy-making in the absence of hard legal competences. In fact, the EU takes advantage of lacking hard law in order to become innovative in introducing new soft law instruments. This self-awareness makes the European Union's understanding of the ESM particular and reflexive. It reflects on the needs for reform of the member states' welfare policies and understands its role as being a facilitator. Since the 'idyllic vision of symbiosis' (see Lindbeck 1996, p. 20) of welfare and full employment has long been abandoned and the post-war combination of 'strong economic growth, low inflation, confidence in public affairs as well as in individual rights' (European Commission 2004d, p. 28) is no longer reality, reform of welfare systems has become inevitable. Indeed, new risks have emerged and these new risks require welfare states to adopt a reflexive approach and undergo processes of self-transformation. Reflexive modernisation of welfare states is demanded in order to cope with the challenges that both the risk society and globalisation pose (see Beck 1992). In this context, the EU becomes itself reflexive by acting as the coordinator of the welfare state's self-transformation.

The theories of reflexive law and reflexive governance provide tools to understand this form of policy-making. Reflexive law emphasises a transformation in the rationality structure of the modern legal system from formal and substantive rationality to procedural rationality. Policy-making becomes multilevel governance and is embedded in an ongoing dialogue based on mutual learning and policy transfer. This is supported by peer review and benchmarking. However, crucial is the respect for autonomy and self-regulation. European regulation has to turn into regulation of self-regulation. Soft law instruments are often more appropriate than conventional hard law. The theory of reflexive governance adds that this form of policy-making turns the vertical relationship of the EU and its member states into a dialogue (Dawson 2011, p. 60; Lenoble 2005; Lenoble and Maesschalck 2010, ch. 4).

Furthermore, the ESM as practised by the EU is increasingly becoming reflexive in another sense. Social policy-making using the OMC is confronted with problems that arise from using different OMCs for different social policies. The EU embarked on reforming the method by realising the limits of the OMC itself. The rhetoric adopted for these reforms has been OMC simplification. However, from a reflexive labour law perspective, this can be interpreted as an attempt to cope with self-created complexity and engage in 'coordination of coordination', a typical form of reflexivity using the very idea of the OMC to reform the method itself. This is true reflexive coordination.

8.4   CONCLUSION

Coordination of employment and social policies forms part of what is known as the social dimension of European integration. The field of social and employment policy consists at the European level of a social acquis that comprises core employment and welfare policies which have developed for over 50 years by using hard law instruments such as regulations, directives and decisions. Over the last 15 years we have also witnessed a new approach in employment and social policies that uses fairly successfully soft law mechanisms for coordination of policies in member states. However, these new policies have undergone major transformations in recent times that display clear signs of reflexivity.

In fact, the OMC as the key instrument in the new governance architecture has arrived at a crossroad. The OMC has been used in different social policy fields with differing success. In some fields, such as employment policy and social inclusion, it was attested by the High Level Group on the Future of Social Policy in an enlarged European Union to be 'remarkably successful' and having had positive effects during the enlargement process as it helped in catching up and benchmarking new member states (European Commission 2004d, p. 36; see also Zeitlin 2005). In other fields, the impact has been less pronounced (Heidenreich and Zeitlin 2009). There are remarkably few critical academic voices. In some praises of the OMC, the resort to moral or political pressure loses the character of being only the second-best solution to proper legal regulations. Nevertheless, the lack of binding legal instruments can very well turn out to be the crucial weakness of the new governance approach characteristic of the (new) European Social Model.

Labour law has no other choice in this situation than to become reflexive. The chequered history of the relation between European law and labour law took a nosedive with the recent hostility expressed by the ECJ in the *Viking* and *Laval* cases. The way out is a rethinking of the relationship between hard and soft labour law and in particular what Kenneth Armstrong (2010) calls the 'hardening' of EU policy coordination models or what in our language can be called reflexive coordination policies.

What seems clear is that the future of the ESM will depend on coordinating its inherent tensions. Experimentalist policies are needed (Sabel and Zeitlin 2008). The Europe 2020 project is driven in different directions by economic and financial objectives of growth and creation of jobs on the one hand and wider employment and social objectives of policy integration and mutual interaction on the other. One can predict in this situation with some certainty an increased demand for reflexive coordination of policies at the European level and a transformation from the governance of coordination to the coordination of governance (see also Armstrong 2012) .

9. Reflexive implementation of EU employment law – a case study of the Working Time Directive

The assessment of the European Working Time Directive (WTD) and its implementation will be used in the following as an example for an analysis of reflexive trends in the governance of the European Union. The WTD can serve as a model of legislation enacted under the so-called community method of governance.[1] The analysis of the WTD and its implementation reveals strengths and weaknesses in the current system of regulation of the European Union.

The analysis proceeds in five steps. The first section contains a short account of the community method and European labour law. The second section gives a brief overview of the main features and structural deficits of the community method in regulating labour law from a reflexive labour law perspective. The third section outlines the Working Time Directive and efforts to reform it. Section four presents results on implementation of the WTD in four member states of the EU. The final section draws conclusions from the case studies for a discussion of reflexive elements of the community method as a method of governance.

9.1 THE COMMUNITY METHOD AND EUROPEAN LABOUR LAW

The community method has been for a long time the main instrument of regulation of labour law at the European level. However, at least for academic observers, this method of regulating European social and employment policy has never been without tensions. The original neglect

---

[1] The notion of community law was officially replaced by union law when the Lisbon Treaty came into force on 1 December 2009. Accordingly the official name of the governance method discussed in this chapter should be called the union method. However, community method is the common term used in the literature and will be maintained as *modus vivendi* in the following.

of labour law in the 1950s from coverage by the community method was severely criticised as being based on false assumptions of a common market automatically leading to harmonisation of labour law standards (Sypris 2000). The reversal of this policy in the 1970s was hailed when, with the support of the ECJ, a change of attitude occurred in the Council and the Commission was able to adopt a Social Action programme that led to important legislation at the supranational level (Barnard 2012, pp. 8–11; Bercusson 2009a, pp. 107–20). This period culminated in the adoption of the Charter of Fundamental Social Rights of Workers in 1989 (also known as the Social Charter), leading to hopes among trade unions and employees in general that by using the community method, a floor of rights would be established at the European level that is capable of improving the situation for workers in the EU as a whole by forcing member states to adopt adequate measures of protection and by harmonising national legislation (see Bercusson 2006). Even the transformation of the policy focus from employment protection to employment promotion in the 1990s and the introduction of new forms of governance of employment did not fundamentally alter the positive attitude of the trade union movement towards European labour law (on new forms of governance, including the concepts of the OMC and flexicurity, see Rogowski 2007).

Regulatory attempts under the broad heading of workers' rights and European Social Policy were in the beginning centred around the two concerns of enabling the free movement of workers between member states (Art. 48–51 of the original EEC Treaty) and overcoming discrimination in employment in the areas of equal pay for equal work and equal treatment between men and women (Art. 117–22 of the original EEC Treaty, and in particular Art. 119 and subsequent directives). During the 1970s the focus of European Social Policy was gradually expanded. A number of directives were introduced in the areas of employment protection and health and safety. The employment protection measures included directives on collective redundancies, employee rights in case of the transfer of an undertaking, and employee rights in case of insolvency of the company. However, these legislative activities were not particularly concerned with regulating new forms of work or atypical employment at the European level.

The community method has played an important role in the regulation of atypical employment that forms part of the Social Policy of the European Union. The initiatives for European regulations in the area of atypical employment started in the 1980s. Draft directives on atypical workers, i.e., workers employed part-time, on fixed-term contracts and by temporary employment agencies, were first proposed in 1981 and 1982. These attempts were unsuccessful, mainly due to resistance from the United Kingdom (see Gold 1993, p. 24). However, the discussion of introducing regulations on atypical employment became a major concern with the adoption of the Single European Act (SEA), in force since 1987, and the Community Charter of Fundamental Social Rights of Workers of 1989. The social provisions of the SEA and the Social Charter were implemented at the EC level by the 'Action Programme' of the European Commission, which contained 47 separate initiatives. As part of this Action Programme, the Commission prepared three draft directives on atypical employment in 1990 which aimed to ensure the same level of protection for atypical employees as so-called typical workers. They concerned working conditions, distortion of competition and health and safety of atypical employees.

It took until 1997 for the first directive on atypical work to be successfully introduced. Like the following employment directives on atypical employment it paid particular attention to issues of discrimination. This first Directive 97/81/EC on part-time work embodies the non-discrimination principle. Similarly, the second Directive 1999/70/EC on fixed-term work focuses on the right to equal treatment. And finally, almost a decade later, temporary agency work, which had been excluded from the directive on fixed-term work, became protected from discrimination in comparison to ordinary employment by Directive 2008/104/EC that came into force on 5 December 2008.

The Achilles' heel of the community method is implementation in national contexts. Reasons for non-compliance vary. On the one hand, European labour law is viewed suspiciously and rejected in some member states because it is perceived as intrusion of constitutionally protected freedom or autonomy of collective bargaining. On the other hand, there is the traditional, notorious neglect of employment discrimination and protection of atypical work by some national legislators that extends to EU law. In the latter cases EU law has often been welcomed.

National labour law, including industrial relations and collective bargaining, co-evolved more or less happily with community (now union) law. They were seen as operating in different realms. Except for the outsider voice of the UK, the fact that European law might pose problems for national labour legislation, administrative practices, company policies and employee rights was for a long time neglected. However, this coexistence has been challenged by recent case law of the European Court of Justice of the European Union. The *Viking* and *Laval* cases and their judicial aftermath brought into sharp focus that national social and employment protection systems are not exempt from scrutiny and can be declared illegal if not compatible with EU law (see Davies 2008; Deakin and Rogowski 2011).

As a result, central actors in the field, in particular the trade unions and also the employer associations, increased their engagement with EU law. They began to realise that European law and policies may create specific risks and general uncertainty regarding their status, their rights as well as the nature and quality of employment protection they defend by their policies. Ideological and political battles that target privatisation and negative consequences of rampant competition policies are likely to increase.

9.2   THE COMMUNITY METHOD AS A REFLEXIVE MODE OF GOVERNANCE

What characterises the community method in a political science perspective is that it is a unique form of governance based on the principle of 'balanced representation of national and supranational interests' (Majone 2005, p. 59). Majone's assessment of the Community Method (Majone 2005, ch. 3) concentrates on aspects of legitimation and democracy and in particular on problems of cooperation of European institutions and member states in creating legislation. What this view largely neglects is the implementation perspective.

However, from a legal perspective, the community method is the main legal technique in creating so-called hard law. Its main difference from soft law is the binding character of the law created in this way and the fact that it can be enforced. Hard law is enacted by using standard legal instruments regulated in the Treaty on the functioning of the EU (TFEU). The three binding legal instruments that constitute the core of the community method are regulations, directives and decisions. They are considered hard law because the Commission can take legal action in case of non-compliance. Thus, from a legal perspective, implementation is a central issue. Once a legal act comes into force, member states can be forced to obey it. Here lies the main difference with soft law.

Aspects of implementation and enforcement are central for a legal analysis. According to Art. 17 (1) of the Treaty on the European Union (TEU), the Commission is formally responsible for overseeing the 'application' of the law of the European Union. Once it has received information on non-compliance, it has powers to start the enforcement procedure outlined in Art. 258 TFEU. The first step of the procedure is informal. The Commission approaches the member state with an informal letter that warns about a possible violation of its obligations under EU law. Usually the member state will be given a time limit of two months to respond to the initial letter.

The relatively clear and straightforward formal enforcement procedure aims to create certainty for member states in terms of what to expect from the Commission and how to respond. The Commission will start the formal procedure by sending a so-called Letter of Formal Notice. This letter contains a brief legal summary of the alleged infringement that should provide enough information for the member state to prepare its legal defence. Under normal circumstances the member state is given two months to respond. If the Commission considers the member state's response to its Letter of Formal Notice insufficient, it issues a Reasoned Opinion. This is the binding legal statement in which the Commission lists in detail the allegations of infringement of EU law. The Reasoned Opinion constitutes the formal indictment (the Commission now acts as the prosecutor) and has to indicate all legal arguments the Commission intends to use in front of the ECJ. It is in fact the document that the Commission must use if it decides to go to the ECJ. The Reasoned Opinion also spells out clearly the measure the Commission expects the member state to take to end the infringement. Usually the member state will be given a further two months to respond or react. After this period elapses, the Commission has to decide if it will proceed to the ECJ.

However, it has to be emphasised that the Commission occupies a hybrid position as prosecutor as well as administrator of policies in operating the enforcement procedure. On the one hand, the Commission is responsible for avenging non-compliance of EU law, but on the other there is total discretion on the part of the Commission in pursuing an infringement. It can decide to abandon the procedure at any stage. The Art. 258 procedure aims at cooperation and recognises the fact that there is an ongoing relationship between the Commission and the member state which is based on dialogue. Here we can detect an element of legal uncertainty in the very nature of the enforcement procedure. The member state cannot simply rely on the Commission to use its discretion to stop the procedure. The member state has to show at least willingness to continue the dialogue with the Commission in order for the threat of being dragged in front of the ECJ to disappear. What actually convinces the Commission to stop the procedure, in case it is difficult for the member state to obey, remains uncertain (see Tallberg 2003).

However, there are a number of shortcomings of the enforcement procedure. In a sociological perspective it is characterised by a capacity deficit that leads to decisional outsourcing and functional differentiation. According to Poul Kjaer, the capacity deficit results from the EU's severe limitations of competences, a relatively low level of cognitive resources and a lack of real control mechanisms. In his conclusion, reflexive structures, in particular new forms of governance, are 'nurtured by the EU in order to off-set its structural deficits' (Kjaer 2010, p. 48).

On the other hand, these deficits can also be seen as strengths insofar as they force the Commission to become creative in influencing implementation processes. We can detect features of reflexive implementation strategies that promise greater success than formal legal enforcement (see also Deakin and Rogowski 2011). Reflexive implementation forms part of strategies of reflexive harmonisation.

> Reflexive harmonisation operates to induce individual states to enter into a 'race to the top' when they would have otherwise have an incentive to do nothing (the 'reverse free rider' effect) or to compete on the basis of the withdrawal of protective standards (the 'race to the bottom'). This is done by giving states a number of options for implementation as well as by allowing for the possibility that existing, self-regulatory mechanisms can be used to comply with EU-wide standards. In these ways, far from suppressing regulatory innovation, harmonisation aims to stimulate it (Barnard and Deakin 2001, p. 38).

The concept of reflexive harmonisation emphasises that the design of directives reveals reflexive elements in their support for self-regulation in member states (see also De Schutter and Deakin 2005; Deakin 2009b). It captures well the essence of a reflexive understanding of European law. The perspective of reflexive implementation can add to this view that there is a particular role for the Commission to influence regulatory innovation. In order to be successful, the Commission must understand the limits of its role as enforcer by realising that it is dependent on the member states' efforts to regulate themselves. Reflexive implementation is a two-way process of regulation of self-regulation. It is an ongoing process that includes revision of the legislative programme adopted at the EU level as a result of interactions with member states during implementation.

9.3   THE WORKING TIME DIRECTIVE (WTD)

In the following the problems of governance and implementation of European labour law created by the use of the community method will be discussed in relation to the example of the Working Time Directive (WTD). This directive regulates weekly hours of employment and is situated in between health and safety regulations, employment protection and labour market policy. It also crosses over to the field of industrial relations insofar as regulation of working time falls in some member states, for example Germany, into the constitutionally protected domain of 'autonomy of collective bargaining'.

The WTD was first introduced as Council Directive 93/104/EC on 23 November 1993. It was amended by the so-called Horizontal Amending

Directive 2000/34/EC of 22 June 2000 and adopted in its current form on 4 November 2003 as Directive 2003/88/EC concerning certain aspects of the organisation of working time. The WTD is officially a measure to protect the health and safety of workers and regulates specifically hours of work.

9.3.1 Scope and Content of the WTD

Key features of the WTD are the limitation of the maximum length of a working week to 48 hours in 7 days, a minimum rest period of 11 hours in each 24 hours, at least 4 weeks' paid holiday a year and protection in the case of night work.

The 1993 Directive was stated to apply to all areas of economic activity as defined by the Framework Directive on Health and Safety,[2] but then went on to exclude certain sectors: 'air, rail, road, sea and inland waterway and lake transport, sea fishing, other work at sea and the activities of doctors in training' (Art. 1(3) WTD). These excluded sectors were removed by the Horizontal Amending Directive of 2000, and additional directives were put in place for specific sectors. This resulted in special rules for mobile workers in sea, road and air transport. With effect from 1 August 2003, non-mobile workers in these sectors, in addition to all workers in rail transport and all workers in other forms of work at sea (such as offshore oil and gas workers), gained the full protection of the 1993 Directive, and mobile workers in road transport received the benefit of the provisions governing paid annual leave and health assessment for night work. Furthermore, Directive 2003/88/EC extended the coverage to doctors in training but granted member states transition periods for introducing national legislation in this area. In effect Directive 2003/88/EC only enlarged the scope of Directive 93/104/EC; otherwise the provisions are materially identical to those of the 1993 Directive.

A special and controversial feature of the WTD is the possibility of an individual opt-out. According to Article 22(1)(b)(i) (former Article 18(1)(b)(i)) WTD, member states can grant workers the right to opt out of the 48-hour rule on a voluntary basis. The fact that this opt-out is often presented as an individual right of the employee disguises the fact that it is companies and employers who have an interest in the opt-out and who are the real beneficiaries (on the open pro-business attitude of conservative British governments in rejecting European working time regulations, see Grant et al. 2009).

---

[2] Council Directive 89/391/EEC of 12 June 1989 on the introduction of measures to encourage improvements in the safety and health of workers at work.

The 2010 Report of the European Commission on the implementation of the WTD provides the following assessment of the use of the individual opt-outs by member states:

> In 2000, the UK was the only member state to make use of the opt-out. However, by 2003, other member states (France, Germany, the Netherlands and Spain), had introduced, or were introducing, opt-outs. These were limited to workers who performed extensive on-call work, and were thus intended to alleviate in the short term the problems posed for health systems seeking to absorb the implications of the Court of Justice's rulings regarding on-call time in *SIMAP* and subsequent cases.
>
> Following recent enlargements, the use of the opt-out within the EU has expanded further, and a total of sixteen member states now explicitly provide for use of the opt-out (including one which is currently legislating to allow its use).
>
> Bulgaria, Cyprus, Estonia, Malta, and the United Kingdom allow use of the opt-out, irrespective of sector. The Czech Republic, France, Germany, Hungary, Latvia, the Netherlands, Poland, Slovakia, Slovenia, and Spain allow for use of the opt-out in certain jobs which use extensive on-call time. Belgium is currently legislating to allow use of the opt-out by doctors and some other health professionals (see European Commission 2010d, pp. 87–8).

9.3.2 ECJ Case Law on the WTD

The above quote from the 2010 Commission report on implementation of the WTD refers to case law of ECJ interpreting the directive. It indicates that ECJ case law was the driving force behind the expansion in the use of individual opt-out clauses. In general, this case law has to be distinguished into two types of cases: those that challenge the legal basis of the WTD and those seeking interpretation of specific WTD concepts.

The Conservative UK government under Major sued the Council in the mid-1990s, arguing that the WTD had a defective legal basis (see Case-84/94 *United Kingdom v Council of the European Union* [1996] ECR I-5755 and Industrial Relations Law Reports (IRLR), Vol. 26, No.1, January [1997] 32). The UK government claimed that the directive should have been adopted on the basis of former Articles 100 or 235 EC Treaty, which required unanimity within the Council, rather than Article 118a EC Treaty which allowed a health and safety measure to be adopted by majority vote. According to the UK, the connection of the areas regulated by the WTD with the health and safety of workers was too tenuous and not supported by scientific evidence. In the UK's view, the WTD contributes to the improvement in living and working conditions of employees and thus is part of the Community's social policy; it went further and called the WTD disguised labour market policy. The ECJ rejected the UK view and held that the principal objective of the WTD was the protection of the health and safety of workers within the meaning of Article 118a EC Treaty. 'It does not follow from the fact that the directive falls within the scope of Community social policy that it cannot properly be based on Article 118a, so long as it contributes to encouraging improvements as regards the health and safety of workers' (see ibid., IRLR at 36).

Specific provisions of the WTD were clarified and interpreted in a number of rulings of the ECJ, for example the calculation of the duration of working time. However, the most notable cases have been the *SIMAP* judgment of 2000 (Case C-303/98 *Sindicato de Medicos de Asistencia Publica (SiMAP) v Conselleria de Sanidad y Consumo de la Generalidad Valenciana* [2000] ECR I-7963) and the *Jaeger* judgment of 2003 (Case C-151/02 *Landeshauptstadt Kiel v Norbert Jaeger* [2003] ECR I-8389I), both concerning on-call duties of doctors in hospitals. In the *SIMAP* judgment the ECJ defined, for the purposes of work and rest calculations, all time when a worker is required to be present on site as actual working hours. Times when the worker is on call, but not on site, do not count as working time. The *Jaeger* judgment confirmed that all time doctors spend at their place of work counts as working time, even if workers are allowed to sleep during their services, although periods when the doctor is not working should be treated as rest periods. These judgments have had practical effects, particularly for junior doctors and care home workers who traditionally work on nightshifts and are required to be resident on site when on call. They were confirmed in later judgments, for example the *Dellas* case (Case C-14/04 *Abdelkader Dellas and others v Premier Ministre*, [2005] ECR I-10253).

In addition to on-call work, the ECJ clarified on a number of occa-sions WTD requirements that need to be met for an individual opt-out to be legal. It decided in *Fuß* (Case C-243/09 *Fuß v Stadt Halle* [2010] ECR I-09849), a case in which national laws at regional (*Land*) level required fire fighters to work a standard 54-hour working week, that the WTD did not apply because the *Land* had not transposed it adequately by creating measures for the use of the individual opt-out. In *Pfeiffer and others* (Joined Cases C-397/01 to C-403/01 *Pfeiffer and others* [2004] ECR I-8835), emergency workers working for the German Red Cross chal-lenged work rosters regulated by a collective agreement. The collective agreement permitted a working week of up to 49 hours if time spent on call at the workplace amounted to at least three hours per day. The Court argued that 'the worker's consent must be given not only individually but expressly and freely' (ibid., para. 84). Consent granted collectively in a col-lective agreement is not sufficient (see Barnard 2012, pp. 549–50).

Summarising the case law on individual opt-out, the following condi-tions must be met for the opt-out to be legal: the member state must have clearly introduced the 'necessary measures' for the use of the opt-out mentioned in Art. 22 (1) WTD. The individual workers concerned must have expressly and freely granted their consent to the opt-out; a blanket endorsement by collective agreement is not sufficient, unless the collective agreement expressly regulates the measures mentioned in Art. 22 (1) WTD. The employer must keep records for all opted-out workers, available for inspection on request of health and safety inspectors.

9.3.3 Reform of the WTD

The attempt of the European Commission to reform the WTD since 2004 reveals interesting reflexive strategies. The Commission has been put under considerable pressure by member states and other interest groups. It is particularly concerned about reactions in member states to ECJ rulings on on-call work which led to the adoption of opt-out provisions in the majority of member states. The Commission has tried to find a way to reconcile general opposition to the WTD – for example regularly voiced by the UK, which insists on maintaining a strong opt-out clause – and efforts, for example by the European Parliament, to strengthen the WTD by abolishing any opt-out clause.

The Commission put forward a proposal to amend the WTD in 2004 (European Commission 2004c). In it the Commission suggested among other things that inactive on-call time should be excluded from being considered working time. This proposal was blocked by the European Parliament with a counter-proposal which suggests removing the possibility of opt-out from the WTD altogether and that the entire period of any time spent on-call, including the 'inactive part', should be considered as working time.[3] The Commission reacted with an amended proposal, which considered some of the amendments suggested by the European Parliament but did not accept the Parliament's proposed amendments regarding the two contested issues: namely, the individual opt-out clause and on-call time.

It took the Council until 2008 to reach a political agreement on amending the WTD. During 2005 and 2008 the Commission tried a number of strategies for a compromise. For example, it proposed a time limit for the opt-out to run out. When this idea encountered massive opposition, in particular from the UK, it was abandoned and replaced with a proposal

---

[3] Opinion of the European Parliament A6/2005/105. The European Parliament was not opposed to the possibility of exempting inactive on-call time from coverage by the WTD if this was accepted in collective agreements.

to strengthen the reporting and evaluation requirements for member states that use the opt-out. An agreement was finally reached by qualified majority at the EPSCO Council in June 2008 (for details on the negotiations, see the analysis in Nowack 2008).

However, this agreement was again rejected by the European Parliament, which continued to insist on removing the opt-out clause from the WTD. A second reading of the amending proposal under the co-decision procedure became necessary. A Common Position was formally adopted by the Council in September 2008 and transmitted to the European Parliament. The Parliament adopted a Resolution in response in December 2008, proposing a number of amendments to the Common Position, some of which were in turn accepted by the Commission in its Opinion issued in February 2009.[4] The Council, however, decided to reject the changes proposed by Parliament. In the following conciliation procedure, an agreement could not be reached between the Council and Parliament within the required six weeks. The result was that the legislative proposal lapsed.

In September 2009, the Commission changed its strategy. The Commission announced its intention to carry out a new review of the WTD, based on a detailed impact assessment (European Commission 2010c) and on a consultation of the European social partners in accordance with Art. 154 TFEU. In fact, it started exploring the possibility of using the Social Dialogue for the reform of the WTD. It launched the first phase of the consultation of the European social partners in March 2010, asking whether they saw a need for action at EU level, what in their view could be its scope, whether they considered that the Commission should launch an initiative to amend the Directive, and whether they wished to consider entering a dialogue of the European social partners under Article 155 TFEU on any of the issues raised. The second stage of consultation started in December 2010, leading to a formal agreement of the social partners in November 2011 to negotiate on EU working time rules. These negotiations are conducted by the main cross-sectoral social partners at EU level, which are BUSINESSEUROPE, CEEP and UEAPME, representing employers, and the ETUC, representing employees.

---

[4] *Opinion of the Commission pursuant to Article 251 (2), third subparagraph, point (c) of the EC Treaty on the European Parliament's amendments to the Council's common position regarding the proposal for a Directive of the European Parliament and of the Council amending Directive 2003/88/EC concerning certain aspects of the organisation of working time amending the proposal of the Commission pursuant to Article 250 (2) of the EC Treaty COM(2009)57 final.*

9.4   IMPLEMENTATION OF THE WORKING TIME DIRECTIVE: CREATION OF UNCERTAINTY IN MEMBER STATES

The troubles of reforming the WTD at the European level are in many ways linked to difficulties related to implementation in member states. For reflexive European policy-making it is necessary to understand and productively use insights on implementation in improving European legislation. In fact, such ability constitutes a core element of reflexive implementation. The continuous revision of the programme based on evaluation and new contextual insights is an integral part of the overall implementation process.

In the following, the implementation of the WTD will be assessed in terms of how receptive member states have been in having working time regulated by European law and in particular how much uncertainty the WTD has created in member states. The latter question, if the community method creates uncertainty in member states, is rarely asked in European labour law. Since hard law, including directives, is designed to send out clear expectations, its objective is to create certainty. Indeed, problems of uncertainty are usually not encountered at the level of formal legal transposition of directives, which are the main legal instruments used in EU labour law. However, if we use the standard model of three phases in implementing law (transposition, enforcement and application), used for example by Gerda Falkner and her team in studying compliance with EU social and labour law directives (Falkner et al. 2005; Falkner et al. 2008), uncertainty is more likely to occur at the levels of enforcement and application of EU measures at national level (see also Hartlapp 2005; Treib 2005).

For a study of enforcement and application of EU law, contextual information on general characteristics of the national labour law system and on the national approach in implementing EU law is necessary. Also important are the assessment of behaviour and attitude of national courts and problems in specific industries. And last but not least, the reaction of the political system can play a crucial role.[5]

---

[5]   The following information on contextual factors is based on case studies on the implementation of the WTD in four EU member states: the Czech Republic, France, the Netherlands and the United Kingdom. The case studies were carried out for the work package on European Governance of the EU-financed research project *Governance of Uncertainty: Tensions and Opportunities* (GUSTO) covering processes until mid-2012. Results of research undertaken for this work package will be published in Barbier et al. (forthcoming).

The labour law jurisdictions of member states of the European Union constitute quite diverse conditions for the implementation of European law. Some have Communist or socialist legacies and have been receptive to international law for many decades, such as the Czech jurisdiction; others, such as French labour law, are characterised by elaborate statutory regulations on employment contracts and working conditions compiled in a separate code (*Code du travail*) and are less flexible compared with the Dutch or the German jurisdictions, which often operate with specific legislation in response to new labour market developments. However, the latter approach might also lead to an arrogant attitude, leading to non-compliance with European regulations because the national laws are viewed as superior to the European regulations. A special case is UK labour law, which is based on a common law tradition with a rather scattered system of statutory regulations on working time at the time of implementation of the WTD in 1998.

The UK is also a good example of an instrumental approach to transposition of EU law. A noticeable split exists in the UK between political and legal attitudes towards implementation of EU law. A considerable political reluctance co-exists with an uncritical legal obedience. The WTD was implemented via secondary legislation, the Working Time Regulations (WTR), a statutory instrument that has equal effect to primary legislation in UK law. Such use of secondary legislation is not unusual since most EU directives are implemented in the UK by delegated legislation in accordance with the Statutory Instruments Act 1946. This form of implementation avoids parliamentary debate but it has the disadvantage of creating a patchwork of legislation that neglects the unity of the legal system. The technocratic minimalist approach to implementation also risks being 'out-of-line with Europe' and invites litigation in front of the European Court of Justice (Bercusson 2009b, pp. 571–84).

However, the UK is not alone in its instrumental approach to implementation. More or less all countries investigated had no problem with formal transposition of the WTD into national law. In the Czech Republic, the implementation of the WTD was part of the overall change of legislation during the process of accession to the EU. Directives were adopted uncritically and implementation became a rather technical ('copy and paste') affair (Sirovátka, forthcoming). Despite the hot debate in France over working time ('35-hour week'), the WTD was implemented in a straightforward manner by simply amending the *Code du travail* and the *Code de l'action sociale et des familles*. Only the Netherlands took the opportunity of introducing new legislation on working time in the Working Hours Act (*Arbeidstijdenwet*) 1996, which regulates maximum hours of work, breaks and minimum rest periods in accordance with the original WTD, including a limited possibility of an individual opt-out (Sol and Ramos, forthcoming).

Due to the mechanical transposition process, the impact of EU labour legislation is often hard to assess. Nevertheless, there is evidence of a gap between formal transposition of EU law and enforcement and application. Problems have been reported in relation to enforcing the law in the courts and in specific industries.

An interesting reaction to the WTD at the level of application and enforcement can be found in the UK. Unlike the political system – represented by fundamental opposition to the WTD expressed in the political programme of the Conservative Party, which dominates the current government – there is no outright opposition towards the WTD or its implementing measures in UK courts. A remarkable trend is that employees have taken up the opportunity to launch working time claims in British employment tribunals. These claims have been consistently among the highest group of applications since 2005 and outnumbered all other areas of jurisdiction during the last statistical periods (Rogowski, forthcoming).

A further implementation issue are judicial reactions to the interventions of the ECJ in the cases *SIMAP* (2000) and *Jaeger* (2003) mentioned above (section 9.3.2). The ECJ addressed an issue that constitutes a particular problem for junior doctors in a number of countries. However, its interpretation of on-call working time, regulated in the WTD, led to interactions between judicial bodies, which from a reflexive labour law perspective are a potential source for reflexive trends. Noteworthy in this context is the strategy of the French *Conseil d'Etat*. In the wake of the ECJ decisions, it referred a case to the ECJ under the preliminary ruling procedure (*Dellas* case), thereby successfully challenging the French law on calculating working time.

In terms of implementation, EU labour law has the advantage over other policy areas of possessing a second legal route of implementation through collective agreements. This so-called Social Dialogue is particularly important in those industries that have specific problems in complying with the WTD. In the Netherlands, there are several specific sector regulations, which in principle can only be applied by collective agreement. Derogations and exceptions to the general rules on the organisation of working time by collective agreements are found in a number of sectors, i.e. healthcare and mining (Sol and Ramos, forthcoming).

The limits imposed on overtime work brought specific problems for several industries, such as transport, restaurants and hotels as well as hospitals and emergency services. For hospitals, a specific problem emerged in 2006 when the provisions of the WTD regulating on-call duty were amended following the *SIMAP* and *Jaeger* cases. In the Czech Republic, for example, hospitals reacted by adding an overtime work clause to the labour contract of doctors or through additional so-called free agreements outside the labour contract, both routes enabling the total working time to transcend the legal limits on the length of working time. Some hospitals even went so far as establishing a separate legal entity within the hospital for staff working on-call so that they cannot be considered being 'at the workplace' (Sirovátka, forthcoming). In the UK the medical profession has been vociferous in its opposition using a number of sometimes phony arguments, for example that not using junior doctors for more than 48 hours in hospitals would undermine their training requirements (Rogowski, forthcoming).

There is evidence that the intervention of the ECJ created uncertainty in member states. This is even truer for the difficulties in reforming the WTD at the EU level. In countries in which the attitude switches from pro-European to Euro-scepticism depending on a liberal or a conservative government being in power, such as in the Czech Republic or the UK, the EU uncertainty over the future of the WTD transmits into national politics.

A special case is the strategy pursued by the UK government in implementing the WTD. Although the implementing measure, the Working Time Regulations, follows in legal terms relatively closely the text of the WTD, the fact that it expressly includes the possibility of an individual opt-out somewhat contradicts and undermines the aim of the WTD. This fact also expresses the general hostile attitude towards regulation of working time in British politics. The Conservative Party openly opposes this regulation, and this view is, although less vociferously, shared by the dominant market-friendly core of the Labour Party ('New Labour'). The UK government announced repeatedly in 2011 and 2012 that it will propose further exemption from EU social and employment law as part of their overhaul of British employment laws. It is likely to use future negotiations with the European Union to pursue its objective of limiting the application of the WTD in the UK.

9.5 SUSTAINABILITY AND UNCERTAINTY IN THE GOVERNANCE OF WORKING TIME IN THE EUROPEAN UNION

From a reflexive labour law perspective, the hard law created by the community measures needs to be assessed in the context of other legal instruments. Of particular importance are soft law measures central to the new governance approach. They often try to influence economic developments and respond directly to new labour market demands.

Reflexive labour law thus suggests viewing the WTD in the wider context of governing working time in the European Union. Working time policies play a central role in European labour market policies. They reach far beyond regulations on the limitation of the maximum length of the working week, the focus of the WTD. We can distinguish in this respect the supranational governance context and the labour market policy context, including the regulation of new forms of employment.

9.5.1   The WTD and Methods of Governance

The community method constitutes only one of four methods of governance of employment law at the supranational level (on the four 'strategies' to govern European labour law, see Bercusson 2009a, Part II, pp. 99–255). In addition to (a) the community method, which is traditionally seen as the ordinary route of legislation and was used to create the WTD, there are (b) the Social Dialogue, (c) governing employment through fundamental rights, and (d) governing employment through new forms of governance, in particular the use of soft law such as the open method of coordination in the context of the European Employment Strategy.

The Social Dialogue is a governance method to create legislation through agreements between social partners. The Social Dialogue is the responsibility of the European social partners (BUSINESSEUROPE, CEEP and UEAPME, representing employers, and the ETUC, representing employees). Once the social partners have established a so-called framework agreement, the Commission will use it to create a proposal for a directive, which is usually endorsed by the Council without discussion (and no input from the European Parliament!). As we saw above, this second route of legislation is currently explored by the Commission for the revision of the WTD. A number of important directives regulating working time arrangements, such as the directives on parental leave, fixed-term contracts and part-time work, originate from the 'collective route' (see Barnard 2012, pp. 67–87) of legislation.

Governing employment through fundamental rights has been significant since the adoption of the Charter of Fundamental Social Rights of Workers in 1989 and became a great hope for reform with the adoption of the Charter of Fundamental Rights in 2000. With the introduction of social citizenship, constitutionalising employment rights is seen to enlarge Social Europe to 'the excluded peoples of Europe . . . the poor, the unemployed, the old, the ethnic minorities and others whom the common market has excluded' (Bercusson 2006, pp. 19–20). Art. 31 (2) of the Charter of Fundamental Rights states one of the rights to fair and just working conditions: 'Every worker has the right to limitation of maximum hours, to daily and weekly rest periods and to an annual period of paid leave'. It has been suggested that upgrading the WTD regulations to fundamental rights puts the possibilities of excluding certain sectors of employment and derogations in the directive and in national implementing laws into question (Blanke 2006, in particular pp. 374–5).

Probably the most promising way to influence working time policies at member state level is through soft law. The European Employment Strategy establishes through the use of the open method of coordination (OMC) an ongoing dialogue between member states and the Commission about objectives of labour market policies. Guideline 21 of the Employment Guidelines 2008, for example, states as an objective of European employment policy the promotion of flexibility combined with employment security. In this context, flexibilising working time arrangements has been identified as an important policy goal. However, if this transition from protection to promotion in European employment policies (Rogowski 2008b) will be successful still remains to be seen. The economic crisis of 2008 has certainly revealed its limits (see Rogowski et al. 2011).

9.5.2 The WTD and Working Time Arrangements

A reflexive labour law perspective on the WTD emphasises that it has to be seen in the wider context of regulating working time arrangements that provide employees with real autonomy over their working times. Measures created by using the community method and in particular its reform must become able to take into account not only changes in the labour market but, crucially, other regulatory attempts embarked on at the EU level in regulating working time arrangements (see also Barnard et al. 2005). Many new demands for more flexible working time arrangements result, for example, from an increased participation of female employees in the labour market and the introduction of new technologies at the place of work. This can be demonstrated by listing some of the types of working time arrangements that have been in practice. In addition to the two cases of part-time employment regulated in the Part-time Work Directive 97/81/EC, which aims at prevention of discriminatory treatment in part-time work, and fixed-term employment regulated in the Fixed-term Directive 99/70, both of which were mentioned above (section 9.1), there are a number of other working time arrangements, some of which are supported by policies surrounding the WTD, such as the European Employment Strategy (EES).

9.5.2.1   Overtime

Overtime, i.e. hours worked above a certain threshold of working time for an extra payment, is an important flexibility tool, favoured in particular by employers. It is often an important source of extra income for employees. The WTD establishes a threshold for the maximum of allowable overtime by establishing a weekly limit for working hours that cannot be exceeded.

9.5.2.2   Flexitime arrangements

Flexitime arrangements are promoted within the EES as forms of flexibilisation of employment. They are working time arrangements with no fixed start and end of a working day. They include working time banking, i.e. a system of accumulation of hours around the standard number of weekly or monthly hours. It can mean that an employee can work more hours in exchange for taking the equivalent time off at some time in the future. Two options can be distinguished: working time banking with the possibility to take only hours off, and working time banking with the possibility to take full days off. Flexible working time arrangements include the option of a flexible start and end of working day and the possibility to fully determine the own working schedule. In addition, there is a category of 'other', which often includes the case of a fixed start of the day until the work is finished (see European Foundation 2010a).

9.5.2.3   Annualised hours and working-time accounts

Working time accounts are growing in popularity among EU member states (see Wotschack 2011). Annualised hours' schemes are an accepted means of achieving working time flexibility. They allow working time (and pay) to be calculated and scheduled over a period, for example a year. Art. 18 WTD, which creates scope for derogations by means of collective agreements, including the length of the reference period which may be extended by up to 12 months, opens up the opportunity to implement annualised hour schemes in order to adapt to changes in demand.

9.5.3   Reflexive Implementation of the WTD

The WTD is a good example of the paradox that characterises law in modern society according to social systems theory. Any attempt of creating certainty by reducing complexity automatically creates new complexity and new uncertainty. In fact, 'reduction of complexity serves to increase complexity' (Luhmann 2004, p. 317). It is the irony of reflexive law that it understands this paradox but continues engaging in regulatory efforts, albeit with new legal instruments.

There are a number of ways in which law produces uncertainty. Three ways can be highlighted. First, vague legal programmes may render law merely symbolic without becoming effective in society. Second, statutory law can become uncertain if it is not, or only partially, enforced or implemented. Third, statutory provisions can become ambivalent due to legal or judicial interpretations or failure to learn from implementation problems.

The example of the WTD can provide evidence of legal uncertainty on all three levels. The WTD has increased uncertainties in national law (see Sypris 2007, pp. 141–2). The failure to reach agreement on reforming the WTD at the European level has created anxiety and uncertainty at the national level.

Furthermore, legal uncertainty can be the result of ECJ rulings. Insofar as labour law in general is concerned, the *Viking* and *Laval* cases are the most prominent examples of creating uncertainty. And legal uncertainty has certainly been the result for employers and national governments regarding the organisation of on-call work after the intervention of the ECJ in *SIMAP*, *Jaeger* and other cases on behalf of junior doctors and care workers.

However, despite these uncertainties, it has to be emphasised that law is a key, probably the most important, means to guarantee sustainability in European social and employment law and policies. In particular, the community method has this function. Its success depends on it being able to become reflexive. As the case of the WTD shows, in order for hard law to be effective it has to be reflexive, both in the sense of realising its limits as a regulatory instrument and the context in which it operates. Political opposition as well as labour market developments shape its application and limit its effectiveness. Regulation of working hours is part of a wide range of regulations of working time arrangements at member state level. The Dutch example shows that focusing regulation on part-time employment is an alternative way of reducing long working hours.

The context at the European level consists not only of other directives regulating working time (for example, fixed-term and part-time employment, temporary work and parental leave), but also of other modes of governance used for reducing uncertainty in employment. From a reflexive labour law perspective, it is remarkable that European law and policy have achieved introducing a meta-level of governance at which different routes of governance can be chosen. The Social Dialogue is currently used for the resolution of the political deadlock over the WTD, which has been reached by using the community method.

The regulation of the length of working time, including holiday pay and rest periods, has to be interpreted in the context of a wide range of issues related to working time. Working time has become an important matter for labour market policy. This policy area has witnessed significant transformations related to changes in work organisation and labour market composition. The traditional model of a male breadwinner working an eight-hour day is no longer the dominant model. Increasing female labour market participation has led to more flexible forms of work organisation and changing working-time preferences. To tackle the regulatory problems that derive from these trends, the focus of the WTD has to be transcended. In fact, a mix of methods of governance is necessary to address problems arising from demands for new working time arrangements. And for this, further reflexive laws and policies are needed.

Furthermore, reflexive implementation in member states would ideally view European law as an opportunity for broader reform discussions. The proper transposition of EU law is not a technical, mechanical or instrumental affair. It should lead to broad political discussions that involve all relevant stakeholders. In this way reflexive implementation makes productive and creative use of the uncertainty created by the requirement of transposing European law.

10. Reflexive global labour law

10.1 INTRODUCTION: IS LABOUR LAW BECOMING MORE INTERNATIONAL OR MORE GLOBAL?

The final chapter discusses reflexive trends in global labour law. It begins with an assessment of international labour law and its response to globalisation. It will argue that international labour law as part of public international law is limited and does not cover all or even the most important aspects of the globalisation of labour law. From a reflexive labour law point of view, it is necessary to distinguish between international and global labour law.

In discussing this distinction we can return to topics introduced in Chapter 1 on the world society context of labour law. The creation of labour law at the global level is no longer confined to the traditional legal sources of agreements between nation states which establish international labour law norms and legislative competences for international organisations. Labour law in the world society globalises worldwide and global labour law derives from a multiplicity of sources. Thus, international labour law has lost the position of being an exclusive or a hierarchically superior source of labour law at the global level.

The chapter pays particular attention to the interaction of international and (other) global labour law. In fact, international labour law is part of plural global labour law and is itself responding to developments outside the realm of public international law. Realising this interaction and making creative use of it constitutes the core of reflexive global labour law.

The chapter progresses in four steps. It starts with an analysis of reflexive elements in the law-making process of the International Labour Organization (ILO), in particular in relation to the ILO's move to identify core universal labour standards and the combination of labour standard-setting with new forms of governance within the ILO's Decent Work Agenda.

The second section discusses reflexive trends in international labour law beyond the ILO. Major regulatory efforts that support the establishment of universal labour standards have been undertaken by a variety of international organisations. These include OECD Guidelines, the UN's Global Compact, and more or less successful attempts by the WTO and the EU to introduce social clauses in international trade agreements.

The third section is devoted to a key aspect of reflexive global labour law. This is labour norm-creation as a result of self-regulation in multinational companies. Main topics are policies and practices pursued under the heading of corporate social responsibility (CSR). A particular focus in this section will be codes of conduct of multinational corporations.

The final section addresses global labour law within the wider context of constitutionalisation of global labour law in the world society. It includes a discussion of labour rights as human rights and suggests viewing global labour law as a regime.

10.2 REFLEXIVE ELEMENTS IN INTERNATIONAL LABOUR LAW

The main international organisation responsible for the regulation of labour law at the global level is the ILO. It was created in the aftermath of the First World War, in a period in history that reflected a new belief, at least in Europe, that a lasting peace can only be accomplished if it is linked to concerns with social justice. The powerful President of the American Federation of Labor (AFL), Samuel Gompers, was a strong supporter, although he tried to export his US concept of apolitical unionism onto the international level. Gompers 'wanted to create an international organization to strengthen workers' rights to organize and collective bargaining. . . . He strongly opposed, on the other hand, any international organization that would get involved in politics' (Kaufmann 2004, p. 204). However, there was a broad consensus that politics mattered. The ILO was ultimately founded with an understanding that industrial peace and international peace were closely related and that the recently achieved world peace would not be sustainable if countries were allowed to undermine labour standards and promote social dumping.

10.2.1 Reflexive Trends in Labour Standard-setting of the International Labour Organization (ILO)

The ILO was officially founded in 1919 and the original constitution established it as a permanent organisation to address problems relating to labour conditions. The preamble listed eight areas of activities in which it was granted competences for the creation of international labour law:

Table 10.1   The main areas of activities of the ILO

---

1. Regulation of the hours of work, including the establishment of a maximum working day and week;
2. regulation of labour supply, prevention of unemployment and provision of an adequate living wage;
3. protection of the worker against sickness, disease and injury arising out of his employment;
4. protection of children, young persons and women;
5. provision for old age and injury, protection of the interests of workers when employed in countries other than their own;
6. recognition of the principle of equal remuneration for work of equal value;
7. recognition of the principle of freedom of association;
8. organisation of vocational and technical education, and other measures.

Establishing international labour standards in these eight areas became the primary objective for the founders of the ILO. The ILO's constitution did not attempt to impose substantial obligations on member states. The approach adopted was to set up an institutional framework for the definition of rather general standards and provide some enforcement measures. From the beginning, the approach the ILO took in standard-setting was legalistic. Standards are established in legal procedures and need to be ratified by the members of the ILO in order to become binding law. Standards only establish minimum thresholds.

Officially the ILO has three main areas of activity, two of which are closely related to establishing labour standards. The first and most important is standard-setting in the narrow sense of establishing, negotiating and supervising the ratification of standards. The second is technical cooperation, in particular providing technical assistance to developing countries. Technical assistance is an important means of implementing labour standards, occasionally combined with elements of conditionality. Finally, the ILO's third major course of action is conducting research and producing studies in the areas of employment, labour markets and industrial relations.

The ILO operates with three legal instruments, of which conventions are the most important when it comes to setting labour standards. Conventions are binding if ratified by member states. The two other instruments, recommendations and declarations, are not binding. As of September 2012, the ILO had introduced 189 conventions, of which eight are considered 'fundamental' and four have 'priority' for governments, and 202 recommendations. In comparison, the number of declarations is small. The ILO has only adopted four:

Table 10.2   The ILO Declarations

- Declaration of Philadelphia, 1944
- Declaration concerning Action against Apartheid in South Africa, 1964
- Tripartite Declaration of Principles concerning Multinational Enterprises and Social Policy, 1977
- Declaration on Fundamental Principles and Rights at Work, 1998

ILO declarations have high symbolic value and are programmatic in nature. They reflect a broad consensus on minimum labour rights. The 1944 Declaration of Philadelphia, which became part of the constitution of the ILO, took a bold step in establishing a constitutionally important fundamental principle of international labour law by declaring that labour is not a commodity. This principle was reiterated in Article 23(3) of the Universal Declaration of Human Rights and later in Article 4 of the European Social Charter.

The ILO has had problems with ratification of its law since its inception. The binding force of ILO conventions is limited because it is not mandatory for member states to ratify them. Trying to convince member states to adopt and implement ILO law has occupied the major part of the ILO's agenda. In addition, mainstream economists took a negative view on labour standards and provided arguments for political opposition to ratification, although this orthodoxy has been challenged more recently by other leading economists such as Amartya Sen and Joseph Stiglitz (on the economic debate, see Sengenberger 2006).

In the approach which the ILO adopted to improve effectiveness of its labour standards we can detect reflexive elements. In order to enhance the awareness of labour standards, the ILO gradually began to prioritise certain standards.[1] The turning point was 1998 when this tactic became fully adopted in the Declaration on Fundamental Principles and Rights at Work.

This policy symbolises an effort in becoming more effective through reflexivity. In realising its limitations, the organisation turns them into strengths. The reflexive move was to admit problems with ratification and then concentrate on core standards as a solution. The core standards are regulated in eight key conventions, also called the four human rights treaties: the abolition of forced labour (Conventions No. 29 and 105), the freedom of association and collective bargaining (Conventions No. 87 and

---

[1]   Prioritisation was a strategy proposed by Clarence Wilfred Jenks, who served as Director-General of the ILO from 1970–73. See Jenks 1960, 1969.

Table 10.3 The four core Labour Standards and the eight Fundamental ILO Conventions

Labour Standards	Fundamental Conventions
Freedom of Association and the Right to Collective Bargaining	● ILO Convention No. 87 – Freedom of Association and Protection of the Right to Organize, 1948 ● ILO Convention No. 98 – Right to Organize and Collective Bargaining, 1949
Forced Labour	● ILO Convention No. 29 – Forced Labour, 1930 ● ILO Convention No. 105 – Abolition of Forced Labour, 1957
Equality of Opportunity and Treatment	● ILO Convention No. 111 – Discrimination (Employment and Occupation), 1958 ● ILO Convention No. 100 – Equal Remuneration, 1951
Child Labour	● ILO Convention No. 138 – Minimum Age Convention, 1973 ● ILO Convention No. 182 – Worst Forms of Child Labour, 1999

98), discrimination in the workplace (Conventions No. 100 and 111), and the elimination of child labour (Conventions No. 138 and 182). Table 10.1 lists the core standards and their conventions.

The attempt to strengthen labour standards through prioritisation became truly global with the explicit acknowledgement of the world society context. This happened when the ILO started an initiative in February 2002 that led to the establishment of the World Commission on the Social Dimension of Globalization. The Commission demands in its final report, entitled *A Fair Globalization: Creating opportunities for all* (ILO 2004), respect for core labour standards, in particular in so-called export processing zones. It was a response to criticism of developing countries that labour standards deprive them of their competitive advantage in a globalised economy (Novitz 2010). The report addressed the issue by, on the one hand, acknowledging that more policy autonomy of developing countries is needed with respect to global rules on trade and finance, but, on the other, pointing at the danger of unacceptable relaxation of labour law standards, especially in export processing zones.

The system of Export Processing Zones (EPZs) has become a prominent issue. Over 50 million workers are now employed in such zones worldwide. Persistent concerns have been expressed that EPZs are sometimes given exemptions from national labour laws, or that there are obstacles to exercising rights in practice, and that they engage countries in a competition for foreign investment which leads to damaging tax and subsidy policies. By their nature, EPZs are linked closely to the global economy. However, they often have few linkages back to national economies, thereby creating international enclaves. Outside such zones, similar concerns are expressed about employment and working conditions in a variety of smaller enterprises in international subcontracting chains, both formal and informal (ILO 2004, p. 21).

The ILO has a number of powers to influence the effectiveness of its law. In relation to conventions and recommendations, the ILO operates with regular supervisory procedures. The two main tools that monitor adherence to the core conventions on the four fundamental rights are an annual report on situations in countries where the core conventions have not been ratified; and each year a global report gives an overview of the situation concerning one of these rights for all countries.

These procedures do not apply to declarations. The instrument to make declarations effective is the follow-up procedure. The purpose of this procedure is to encourage the efforts made by member states to promote the fundamental principles and rights at work and to offer technical cooperation. Article 19(5) of the constitution gives the ILO the authority to request information from non-ratifying countries. Countries that have not adopted a declaration have to submit reports.

While the monitoring process is purely promotional and thus does not operate with sanctions, the number of ratifications of the eight ILO fundamental conventions has nevertheless significantly increased since the adoption of the ILO Declaration on Fundamental Principles and Rights at Work in 1998. The current ambitious goal is universal ratification by 2015. However, major countries still have to join the ILO efforts. In 2012 the ILO reported in its General Survey on ratification of the core conventions that 'out of 183 member States, 135 have ratified all eight fundamental Conventions. Therefore, 48 member States have yet to complete ratification of all eight Conventions. These include member States with the highest populations' (ILO 2012a, p. 2).

10.2.2   The ILO's Decent Work Agenda

Probably the best example for reflexive trends in ILO law-making is the ILO's Decent Work initiative. The new agenda allowed the ILO to broaden its range of legal instruments and procedures. The ILO opened up to experimenting with new governance techniques, including the use of soft law. In discovering alternative legal or non-legal procedures for implementing labour standards, it adopted a proceduralist approach.

The Decent Work initiative started with the 1998 Declaration on Fundamental Principles and Rights at Work, which marked the beginning of the already mentioned ILO campaign to promote core labour rights. The ILO launched its Decent Work initiative in 1999. It added a qualitative dimension to labour market policy: 'The goal of decent work is not just the creation of jobs, but also the creation of jobs of acceptable quality. The level of employment (quantity) cannot be divorced from its quality' (ILO 1999). The ILO report recognised that all societies had a notion of decent work, but that the quality of employment could mean many things. It could relate to different forms of work, and also to different conditions of work, as well as feelings of value and satisfaction. The ILO saw the need to devise social and economic systems that ensure basic security and employment while remaining capable of adaptation to rapidly changing circumstances in a highly competitive global market.

The concept of decent work marked a watershed for the ILO since it aimed at overcoming organisational boundaries between its policy-oriented and its legal departments. Labour market policy was upgraded and became a strategic goal of the ILO. The decent work concept puts labour rights in a broader context: 'It is not adequate to concentrate only on labour legislation since people do not live and work in a compartmentalized environment. The linkages between economic, political and social actions can be critical to the realization of rights and to the pursuit of the broad objectives of decent work and adequate living for working people' (ILO 2008, p. 7).

The Decent Work programme focuses on four principal, strategic objectives: standards and fundamental principles and rights at work; employment; social protection; and social dialogue, with gender and development as cross-cutting priority themes. The following descriptions summarise the four objectives.

10.2.2.1 Rights at work

Rights at work have been the traditional domain of the ILO. They include fundamental rights associated with dignity, equality, freedom, adequate remuneration, social security and voice, representation and participation for all categories of workers. The ILO has legislative competences for establishing labour standards in relation to these rights. These labour standards provide the legislative framework for policies relating to all four components of decent work in countries around the world. In addition, the ILO promotes rights at work, employment, social security and industrial relations through issuing thematic reports, giving policy advice, and providing training and operational activities.

10.2.2.2 Employment

Employment in the Decent Work Agenda covers work of all kinds, including wage employment, self-employment, and work from home as well as full-time, part-time and casual work and work carried out by women, men and children. The Decent Work Agenda is particularly concerned with precarious work and the unemployed and refers to active labour market policies as means to address their concerns. For example, research conducted by the ILO supports as a target of decent work 'protected mobility', which squares reduced employment protection compensated by labour market security (Auer 2006). However, employment goals of the Decent Work Agenda aim at providing opportunities for productive and meaningful work and, most importantly, decent working conditions, which include adequate working time and work intensity, a living income and opportunities for the development of personal capabilities (on capabilities and employment policy see also Nussbaum 2000; Rogowski et al. 2011).

10.2.2.3 Social protection

The Decent Work Agenda describes the purpose of improving security in particular for those in irregular, temporary or physically risky employment as well as those outside paid employment and the labour force. This understanding of social protection deliberately transcends the more limited notion of security for work-related situations. Social protection can be achieved in a variety of ways: through formal social insurance systems which provide for contingencies such as illness, unemployment or old age; through informal mechanisms of solidarity and sharing; through investment in workplace safety; and through labour market institutions and policies which protect workers against fluctuations in employment – legislation or collective agreements to discourage layoffs, for instance, or training systems which offer routes back into the labour market. The effectiveness of these systems varies widely, and ILO estimates suggest that only a fraction of the world's workers have truly adequate social protection (Ghai 2006, pp. 14–18).

10.2.2.4 Social dialogue (industrial relations)

The Decent Work Agenda recognises that, in addition to legislation, regulation through industrial relations is an important goal in itself. Industrial partners provide an alternative way of enforcing labour standards through collective bargaining and other forms of negotiations and discussions, which can also include public authorities engaged in labour market and other social and economic policies. From a reflexive labour law perspective, the ILO – although attentive of its facilitative role for industrial relations and conscious of the vital contribution of social dialogue for politics and a representative and participatory democracy – lacked a sophisticated set of legal instruments to grant proper support for self-regulation through collective bargaining. With the Decent Work Agenda the ILO is empowered to promote an institutional framework for collective bargaining or for local level decision-making in which protection of weaker parties and other common goals can be identified and agreements reached. Social dialogue provides support so that the other three dimensions of decent work may be built.

The Decent Work Agenda also aims at improving the situation for workers who are either excluded from or under-represented from meaningful social dialogue (ILO 2000, p. 6). In this respect it seems to have a beneficial impact on the global industrial relations system. Leah Vosko identified a 'new emphasis on extending protections to workers on the periphery of formal systems of employment' in the Decent Work Agenda; 'trade unions of informal workers, emerging labour organizations in the informal sector, women's groups and other NGOs are receiving a greater hearing inside the ILO' (Vosko 2002, p. 38).

The implementation of the Decent Work programme shows signs of a reflexive labour law approach. Member states are encouraged to make creative use of soft law instruments in establishing so-called Decent Work Country Programmes (DWCPs). These programmes define priorities in responding to the Decent Work programme and provide a structure for ILO assistance. The ILO supports these DWCPs with a wide range of technical assistance that includes the development of employment and work-related policies and legislation, labour market systems, social dialogue, industrial relations, social security, skills and vocational training, labour migration, working conditions and occupational safety and health. In addition, the ILO supports the collection of labour market data and analyses economic and social indicators, so that policies and programmes can respond to evolving and emerging labour market trends.

10.2.3 The OECD Guidelines

The internal rethinking within the ILO that led to a reflexive concentration on core standards did not happen in a vacuum. A number of other international organisations were engaged in strategies of increasing the awareness of labour standards and social impacts. The Organisation for Economic Co-operation and Development (OECD) adopted in 1976 a Declaration on International Investment and Multinational Enterprises (MNEs) that aims at preventing and mitigating adverse impacts resulting from the activities of multinational enterprises operating abroad. The impacts addressed in the Declaration include social impacts as well as economic and environmental impacts. The Declaration outlines a set of voluntary rules of conduct for MNEs that are referred to as guidelines. Both the Trade Union Advisory Council (TUAC) and the Business and Industry Advisory Council (BIAC) supported the Guidelines. The Guidelines have been amended five times: in 1979, 1984, 1991, 2000 and 2011.

The Guidelines are a classic case of soft law and their purpose is to encourage MNEs to respect international as well as national labour law rather than impose legal standards. In Sol Picciotto's assessment, the growth of new forms of soft law in the international arena was a direct response to globalisation pressures and he identified, in addition to guidelines, 'Codes and cooperation between regulatory bodies' as examples of the new soft law approach emerging at the global level (Picciotto 1999, p. 15).

Soft law has a number of advantages and disadvantages. The obvious problem is their non-binding character, which has led to questions about their effectiveness. In the case of the OECD Guidelines, trade unions recommended that OECD bodies should be empowered to make specific comments on MNE conduct in relation to compliance with the Guidelines. However, this proposal to give bite to the Guidelines was rejected (see Picciotto 2011, p. 194, Fn. 54, referring to Blanpain 1979, 1983).

The strategy pursued by the OECD Guidelines is to call on companies around the world to observe and advance the principles of corporate social responsibility (see 10.3 below). The Guidelines lay out a code of conduct that targets all main areas of business ethics, including general policies, information disclosure, human rights, employment and industrial relations, environment, combating corruption, consumer interests, science and technology, competition, and taxation. In Chapter 5 on employment and industrial relations, the Guidelines formulate the aim that the operations of MNEs live up to the expectations of host countries by establishing a baseline of labour rights. In this context, the Guidelines refer directly to ILO labour standards.

In this collaboration of the OECD and the ILO we can detect a clear case of reflexivity. The international organisation OECD understands itself as an enforcer of law established by another international organisation. The OECD views its Guidelines as means to implement ILO standards, as can be seen from the following extracts of the official commentary notes 48 and 49 of the 2011 OECD Guidelines.

48. The International Labour Organization (ILO) is the competent body to set and deal with international labour standards, and to promote fundamental rights at work as recognised in its 1998 Declaration on Fundamental Principles

and Rights at Work. The Guidelines, as a nonbinding instrument, have a role to play in promoting observance of these standards and principles among multinational enterprises. The provisions of the Guidelines chapter echo relevant provisions of the 1998 Declaration, as well as the 1977 ILO Tripartite Declaration of Principles concerning Multinational Enterprises and Social Policy, last revised in 2006 (the ILO MNE Declaration). The ILO MNE Declaration sets out principles in the fields of employment, training, working conditions, and industrial relations, while the OECD Guidelines cover all major aspects of corporate behaviour. The OECD Guidelines and the ILO MNE Declaration refer to the behaviour expected from enterprises and are intended to parallel and not conflict with each other. The ILO MNE Declaration can therefore be of use in understanding the Guidelines to the extent that it is of a greater degree of elaboration. However, the responsibilities for the follow-up procedures under the ILO MNE Declaration and the Guidelines are institutionally separate.

49. The terminology used in Chapter V is consistent with that used in the ILO MNE Declaration. The use of the terms 'workers employed by the multinational enterprise' and 'workers in their employment' is intended to have the same meaning as in the ILO MNE Declaration. These terms refer to workers who are 'in an employment relationship with the multinational enterprise'. Enterprises wishing to understand the scope of their responsibility under Chapter V will find useful guidance for determining the existence of an employment relationship in the context of the Guidelines in the non-exhaustive list of indicators set forth in ILO Recommendation 198 of 2006, paragraphs 13 (a) and (b). In addition, it is recognised that working arrangements change and develop over time and that enterprises are expected to structure their relationships with workers so as to avoid supporting, encouraging or participating in disguised employment practices. A disguised employment relationship occurs when an employer treats an individual as other than an employee in a manner that hides his or her true legal status.

The Guidelines abstain from a precise definition of MNEs. However, their application is regulated in separate norms. In case of conflict between international human rights and national labour laws, MNEs are required in the first place to comply with the rules of their host country (Muchlinski 2007, pp. 476–8). They emphasise the importance of negotiations between employee representatives, trade unions and companies and thus support collective bargaining as the means to regulate company affairs. Companies are encouraged to conclude agreements on wages and working conditions. Furthermore, employment effects of any restructuring of companies should be discussed and negotiated in advance with employee representatives and government authorities.

The Guidelines are an example of reflexive law insofar as they recognise and support modes of regulation used by MNEs for internal decision-making. They represent a clear case of regulation of self-regulation. 'Given that many multinational enterprises have established internal codes of conduct and that supervisory authorities in different areas of business have abandoned their former authoritative approach in favour of self-regulation procedures, the Guidelines encourage the application and the further development of self-regulatory practices' (Breining-Kaufmann 2007, pp. 164–5).

Although companies cannot be sanctioned in case of non-compliance with the Guidelines, there exist procedures to bring complaints against companies that violate the Guidelines. These complaints can be brought by labour unions or business organisations, other companies or affected parties and are handled by so-called national contact points (NCP). In specific instances, the NCP can suggest conciliation or mediation proceedings as a means of consensual and non-adversarial dispute resolution in order to assist the parties in dealing with the issues. The results of the procedures are published in statements and can be accessed on the OECD's website.[2] These procedures operate in a genuine reflexive manner since their aim is dialogue and support for negotiations in order to reach lasting outcomes.

Nevertheless, a widely recognised weakness of the OECD Guidelines is their approach in relation to the discrepancy of standards in developing and developed countries. MNEs that apply lower employment and industrial relations standards in less developed countries must obey only the minimum requirements of standards in the host country.

10.2.4 The UN Global Compact

Around the time when the ILO began its internal rethinking and embarked on reflexivity by gaining strength through concentration on core standards, an external route opened up for reinforcing these standards. This was the UN Global Compact, which included in its 10 core principles labour standards. The Global Compact complements the OECD Guidelines, which only apply to companies that operate in the 39 mostly developed countries that are members of the OECD. The Global Compact aims particularly at developing countries and is open to participation by all companies, not only multinational corporations.

The Global Compact was launched in July 2000 and it is hailed as an organisational innovation to realise UN Principles, including labour standards (Waddell 2011). The Global Compact asks companies to embrace, support and enact, within their sphere of influence, a set of core

---

[2] The OECD has dedicated a special website on NCP procedures where the statements can be accessed. See http://www.oecd.org/daf/internationalinvestment/guidelinesformultinationalenterprises/ncpstatements.htm.

Table 10.4   The UN Global Compact principles

General

Principle 1:   Businesses should support and respect the protection of internationally proclaimed human rights; and

Principle 2:   make sure that they are not complicit in human rights abuses.

Labour

Principle 3:   Businesses should uphold the freedom of association and the effective recognition of the right to collective bargaining;

Principle 4:   the elimination of all forms of forced and compulsory labour;

Principle 5:   the effective abolition of child labour; and

Principle 6:   the elimination of discrimination in respect of employment and occupation.

Environment

Principle 7:   Businesses should support a precautionary approach to environmental challenges;

Principle 8:   undertake initiatives to promote greater environmental responsibility; and

Principle 9:   encourage the development and diffusion of environmentally friendly technologies.

Anti-corruption

Principle 10:   Businesses should work against corruption in all its forms, including extortion and bribery.

Source: http://www.unglobalcompact.org/aboutthegc/thetenprinciples/index.html

values in the areas of human rights, labour standards, the environment and anti-corruption. These values are listed in the Compact's 10 principles (Table 10.2).

The 10 Global Compact principles are derived from the Universal Declaration of Human Rights; the International Labour Organization's Declaration on Fundamental Principles and Rights at Work; the Rio Declaration on Environment and Development; and the United Nations Convention against Corruption. The management of the Compact is the responsibility of the Global Compact Office.

The idea of the Compact is that the allegedly universally accepted Compact principles not only give stakeholders such as trade unions and other non-governmental organisations tools for their campaigns, but also that the principles become an integral part of business strategies. On the side of the UN, six of its bodies are involved in the Compact. These include the ILO and, in addition, the UN Industrial Development Organization, the Office of the High Commissioner for Human Rights, the UN Office on Drugs and Crime, and the UN Environment Programme.

The businesses participating in the Compact are not limited to large companies but include small and medium-sized enterprises from all industrial sectors and regions. Companies must publicly declare their willingness to participate in the Compact and engage with the United Nations. There are a number of engagement mechanisms for business and other societal actors that the Global Compact offers at the global, regional and local level, such as assistance for finding practical solutions and projects on the ground as well as identification of good practices.

The Global Compact offers a variety of engagement opportunities for its participants: networks, dialogues, learning, initiatives and partnership projects. Companies and other Global Compact stakeholders are encouraged to take an active role in country networks. Global Compact networks support implementation of the Global Compact in a local context through dialogue, learning and projects, and provide support for quality assurance. In policy dialogues, the Global Compact supports action-oriented local, regional or international meetings that focus on specific issues related to globalisation and corporate citizenship. To promote learning, the Global Compact fosters the development of tools and publications to assist participants with the process of implementing the principles and sponsors opportunities for participating companies to share best practices and lessons learned. As a voluntary initiative, the Global Compact seeks to establish the business case for responsible corporate citizenship. In furtherance of this aim, it has, for example, facilitated a number of initiatives with the financial community to promote responsible corporate practices.

The Global Compact has been called weak because governments do not play an active role in it. The Compact is meant to be an alternative to hard law in the form of national or international regulation.[3] 'As a merely aspirational tool, however, the compact includes no enforcement or accountability mechanisms, and companies can only demonstrate their adherence to it by taking (corporate) action' (Breining-Kaufmann 2007, p. 161). Reports by companies on the measures taken are published on the UN Global Compact website. In order to improve the effectiveness of the Compact, an advisory Global Compact Board was established in 2006.

---

[3] In a speech at the World Economic Forum in 1999 the then UN Secretary Kofi Anan introduced the idea of the Global Compact as a response to the failure at the Singapore summit and the Social Clause not becoming part of international trade law. He also emphasised that the Compact operates with a type of law that is an alternative to hard law, see http://www.un.org/News/Press/docs/1999/19990201.sgsm6881.html.

10.2.5 Social Clauses

There are clear limits to a reflexive strategy of international organisations supporting each other in achieving their objectives. In particular, the international organisations dealing with finance, the World Bank and the International Monetary Fund (IMF), and with trade, the World Trade Organization (WTO), have proven to be friends at best but not allies (Neff 1990). They could potentially have a vital impact on labour standards but have so far shown a rather poor record of interaction with the ILO (O'Higgins 2002) and have revealed clear limits as protectors of labour rights (Hepple 2005, p. 131).

A lively discussion has taken place about linking trade and labour (see only Myrdal 1994). It has been argued that we witness unilateral departures from multilateral WTO trade law in favour of 'social trade regulations' (Schefer 2010, pp. 314–15). The evidence for this is the inclusion of so-called social clauses in international trade agreements. These clauses demand from trading participating partners the observance of labour standards.

10.2.5.1 The WTO and social clauses

The WTO is indeed a particular case when it comes to regulating social clauses. After heated debates, it resisted including social clauses in trade agreements as a means of enforcing labour standards. In fact, the main measures of the reflexive strategy of strengthening labour standards discussed so far – the 1998 ILO Declaration on Fundamental Principles and Rights at Work, the OECD Guidelines and the Global Compact – can be interpreted as responses to the dramatic failure of attempts to include social clauses into WTO law.

First efforts to link trade and labour rights were made in the draft Charter of an International Trade Organisation (Havana Charter) in 1948, which for a number of reasons did not come into force. The issue of social clauses re-emerged during the Uruguay negotiations (1986–94) over the General Agreement on Tariffs and Trade (GATT) that led to the establishment of the WTO. International trade unions lobbied for an inclusion of social clauses. However, when the United States, supported by the European Union and other European countries plus Canada, Japan and New Zealand, requested a working group to study the issue of social clauses, no agreement could be reached (Hepple 2005, p. 130). Social clauses were not mentioned in the Final Act signed in Marrakesh in 1994, mainly because it was strongly challenged by developing countries. They feared that behind the use of social clauses were protectionist policy motives of developed countries.

The issue was postponed and put on the agenda of the first regular biennial meeting of the WTO at ministerial level in Singapore in December 1996. Here it was finally made clear that the WTO does not favour social clauses as a means of enforcing labour standards. The rather convoluted passage of the Declaration rejecting the use of social clauses reads as follows:

> 4. We renew our commitment to the observance of internationally recognized core labour standards. The International Labour Organization (ILO) is the competent body to set and deal with these standards, and we affirm our support for its work in promoting them. We believe that economic growth and development fostered by increased trade and further trade liberalization contribute to the promotion of these standards. We reject the use of labour standards for protectionist purposes, and agree that the comparative advantage of countries, particularly low-wage developing countries, must in no way be put into question. In this regard, we note that the WTO and ILO Secretariats will continue their existing collaboration.[4]

This statement meant in practice that the WTO is not responsible for labour standards and that the WTO and the ILO may collaborate but not through the use of social clauses in trade agreements. The WTO sees its role in protecting developing countries from having to observe labour standards as a condition for trade because they supposedly undermine their alleged comparative advantage in world trade. 'This provision . . . represents a considerable shift since the Philadelphia Declaration of 1944, which emphasised the equality of free trade and labour rights and the need for the integration of free trade into labour standards. Now, it is the protection of free trade that has priority' (Breining-Kaufmann 2007, p. 71). Free trade has priority because the WTO policy is based on the neoliberal belief that promoting free trade leads to economic growth, which in turn is seen as the best way of promoting labour standards.

Employers are particularly worried that the WTO dispute settlement procedure could be used to force companies to adhere to labour standards. The International Organisation of Employers has put forward the legal argument that fundamental differences in handling disputes constitute reasons for separating trade and labour standards.

> . . . any efforts to formally link trade and international labour standards . . . would inevitably encounter a number of substantive legal problems. Prominent

---

[4] The 1996 Singapore WTO Ministerial Declaration (WT/MIN(96)/DEC) is available at http://www.wto.org/english/thewto_e/minist_e/min96_e/wtodec_e. htm.

amongst these would be the coherence and content of the different legal streams, the different fora (labour standards are the domain of the ILO, while trade law is that of the WTO) and the appropriate forum to receive complaints (again, the ILO or the WTO). There is also a fundamental difference approach between the two organizations. The WTO's dispute settlement mechanism was created solely to deal with trade disputes, primarily through the withdrawal of measures that are inconsistent with WTO agreements. An argument of those calling for structured linkages between trade and standards is the potential recourse to the formal dispute settlement mechanism of the WTO, which contrasts with the absence of comparable enforcement procedures within the International Labour Organization. While it is true that the WTO has the capacity for formal enforcement procedures under its Dispute Settlement Mechanism and the ILO's processes are less strident and binding, a great deal of effort and resources are required by governments in terms of ILO supervisory processes (i.e. the Committee on Freedom of Association and the Applications Committee) (International Organisation of Employers 2006, pp. 3–4).

There are nevertheless a number of ways to reconcile social clauses with WTO law, as Bob Hepple has shown (Hepple 2005, ch. 6). They are in the main techniques of interpreting WTO law, for example referring to principles listed in the preamble of the WTO Agreement or invoking general rules of treaty interpretation. They suggest broadening the jurisdictional basis of the WTO's Dispute Settlement Mechanism. However, it is clear that WTO law is a major obstacle for the promotion of voluntary means of improving labour standards, especially if this promotion is supported by governments or local authorities. WTO law in general establishes barriers for global reflexive labour law.

10.2.5.2 The Generalized System of Preferences, the North American Agreement on Labor Co-operation (NAALC) and US labour law

As response to the WTO's refusal, the US government has used unilateral social clauses since the early 1980s. Unilateral social clauses are clearly an alternative to social clauses in multilateral agreements. They were included in a number of trade relations schemes initiated by the US government, among them the important Generalized System of Preferences (GSP), established in 1976, which since 1984 has operated with a labour clause.[5] The GSP allows the US government to withdraw exemptions of custom duties if countries do not respect labour standards. The threat of losing custom preferences granted by the United States has proven to be successful in bringing about labour law reforms, for example in Costa Rica,

---

[5] Other US trade schemes containing labour clauses include the Caribbean Basin Trade Partnership Act of 1983; the Andean Trade Promotion and Drug Eradication Act of 1991; and the African Growth and Opportunities Act of 2000.

the Dominican Republic, El Salvador and Guatemala. These reforms improved in particular the right to freedom of association.

However, unilateral social clauses bear the risk of being biased and used for protectionist purposes. When 'a country that has established a GSP labour clause is the sole judge in determining when and which country would be subject to a GSP investigation and may eventually be deprived of trade benefits . . . risks of having double standard practices are not to be ruled out' (Bronstein 2009, p. 110). In summarising the criticism of the US GSP that can be found in empirical and evaluative studies, Bob Hepple identified three main problems with this 'aggressive' unilateral trade policy (Hepple 2005, pp. 91–101). These are the problems of legal inconsistency in the US GSP system and deviation from international law in interpretations of labour standards. Second, the procedures for handling violations of labour standards were found to be ineffective. Finally, decisions under the US GSP were politically motivated and revealed indeed a bias in favour of protectionism.

Similar criticisms have been launched against the North American Agreement on Labor Co-operation (NAALC), the side agreement to the North American Free Trade Agreement. Although its approach is multilateral, there are a number of severe limitations. The interpretation of labour standards in NAALC is narrower than international standards and weakens international understandings of levels of protection, procedures for bringing cases and dispute resolution is ineffective and the approach is based on a model of unilateral extra-territorialisation of US labour law that at best leads to interpenetration but resists harmonisation and multilateral regulation of labour law (Stone 1999; Piquer 2006).

> The NAALC labor commitments themselves, while seemingly simple and clear, upon examination, are extremely difficult to interpret and apply. The procedures for raising claims that a Party country has violated the NAALC are diplomatic and negotiatory, rather than adjudicatory, failing rudimentary criteria for transparency and due process. Both in terms of procedures and in terms of remedies, the NAALC seems designed to thwart effective enforcement (Weiss 2003, p. 299).

Nevertheless, from a reflexive labour law perspective, it is not just the efficiency of regulations that matters. Transnational labour regulations open national labour law orders to external concerns. Unlike comparative labour law, which only provides information on foreign laws, transnational labour regulation changes the existing legal order and has a greater chance for national labour law to be reconfigured in light of foreign experiences and international law. It has the potential to be an irritating factor within national labour law orders (Teubner 1998). However, if transnational law is only meant to extend the reach of US law, the potential for reflexive processes to occur within US labour law is limited.

10.2.5.3 Developmental policy and the Generalised System of Preferences (GSP) in the European Union

An alternative to aggressive unilateralism can be found in the European Union's approach to international labour standards (Novitz 2002, 2005). The EU has used them in conducting its development policies. The Cotonou Agreement of 1990 introduced a social clause referring to the ILO's core labour standards (Art. 50) that need to be adhered to in trade between the EU and least developed countries in Africa, the Caribbean and the Pacific (ACP). Since the 2001 Communication on labour standards,[6] there has been a debate in the EU about extending the use of this clause beyond trade ACP countries. The communication proposed two principles. First, any developmental aid of the EU is made conditional on compliance with core labour standards. Second, the EU supports directly the ILO in the promotion of core labour standards. This approach is a clear case of a reflexive measure in support of international labour law.

In addition, the EU also runs a system of granting preferences in trade with developing countries (EU GSP), which includes special incentive arrangements for the protection of labour rights that go further than the ILO core standards by adding slavery and prison labour (Hepple 2005, p. 103). It is indeed an interesting case of reflexive labour law because it operates with incentives for developing countries and these trade privileges in terms of reduced or zero import tariff may be temporarily withdrawn for serious and systematic violations of core human and labour rights conventions or failure to incorporate or not effectively implement relevant ILO conventions. The European Commission monitors its trade partners in the developing world by examining available information from relevant monitoring bodies (such as the UN and the ILO). The EU, through its own monitoring efforts, contributes to a strengthening of international labour law (see Orbie and Tortell 2009).

In the operation of the system of EU GSP we can find reflexivity at work in the form of continuous monitoring of monitory mechanisms. The EU regular revises its legislative basis and the impressive list of countries that are beneficiaries of the EU GSP. The latest revised list of countries entitled to reduced or zero import tariff rates focuses on fewer beneficiaries

---

6   Communication of the European Commission on Promoting Core Labour Standards and Improving Social Governance in the Context of Globalization (COM(2001)416 final, 18.7.2001).

and grants more support for those that respect human and labour rights, the environment and good governance rules. The new EU GSP will come into effect on 1 January 2014, for 89 nations, 49 of which are listed as least developed countries. The regulation removes 20 nations from the list which the World Bank has declared to be 'high or upper middle income' economies and which the EU considers very rich.[7]

However, despite the EU's efforts, it seems fair to conclude with Lord Wedderburn that the 'use of "social clauses" has not won a strong place in global regulation or practice' (Wedderburn 2002, p. 51). The WTO's refusal to endorse social clauses and the US approach to use them for protectionist purposes are not encouraging. Nevertheless, it is also hard to disagree with Bob Hepple's account of the soft unilateralism approach of the European Union and its system of generalised tariff preferences that 'it avoids most of the criticism which have been directed at the "aggressive" US unilateralism' (Hepple 2005, p. 105). In fact, the EU's understanding of its role as complementing and supporting ongoing monitoring by the ILO and the approach followed by the European Commission of seeking an ongoing dialogue with developing countries on issues in relation to an effective implementation of ILO conventions contain clear signs of reflexive labour law.

10.3   GLOBAL LABOUR LAW AND CORPORATE SOCIAL RESPONSIBILITY

Global labour law transcends public international labour law. For an account from a reflexive labour law perspective, it is important to pay particular attention to the many attempts of introducing labour standards in private contexts. The expansion of labour standard-setting from public to private forms of labour regulation provides probably the best case for reflexive labour law at the global level. It also highlights the problems and challenges that 'privatising regulation' (Hepple 2005, ch. 3) faces in practice.

---

[7]   The new EU GSP was introduced in Regulation (EU) No 978/2012 of 25 October 2012. 33 of the beneficiary countries are in Africa, 10 in Asia, including Myanmar, five in the Pacific and Haiti in the Caribbean. A further 40 'low and lower middle income' nations, including China, India, Iran, Iraq and Syria, are also listed to benefit from the GSP scheme. The countries that were removed are considered very rich or so-called upper-middle income nations. The very rich include Saudi Arabia, Brunei, Macao and the five Gulf states and the so-called upper-middle income nations Argentina, Brazil, Cuba, Uruguay, Venezuela, Belarus, Russia, Kazakhstan, Gabon, Libya, Malaysia and Palau.

The most prominent form of private labour law-making is corporate social responsibility (CSR) and the use of codes of conduct in companies. CSR forms part of corporate governance and is a means by which companies create internal structures of decision-making through privatised application of labour standards (Kearney 1999). It is in fact a classic form of self-regulation (Rudolph 2003). The regulation of this form of self-regulation is closely linked to initiatives of creating frameworks that are suitable for influencing the behaviour of the most powerful organisations operating at the global level.

The development of CSR and the use of codes of conduct in companies are of particular interest for reflexive labour law. In a certain sense, these developments can serve as the model for a reflexive type of regulation. It requires the acknowledgment of the key role of internal regulation in companies and the concept suggested by reflexive labour law, the theory of regulation of self-regulation, seems particularly well suited for an analysis of these modes of governance. What is characteristic of these attempts of regulating multinational companies is a linking of public and private efforts of regulation of employment conditions. International organisations have recognised internal labour policies of multinational companies as promising ways of implementing their standards and have undertaken efforts of regulating CSR by developing new instruments in international labour law. Multinational companies, on the other hand, have begun to view the design of human resource policies in accordance with international labour standards as a beneficial productive factor.

10.3.1 Corporate Social Responsibility, International Labour Law and the Problem of Monitoring

CSR can be defined in accordance with the widely acknowledged portrayal of the European Commission as 'a concept whereby companies integrate social and environmental concerns in their business operations and in their interactions with their stakeholders on a voluntary basis' (European Commission 2006b, p. 3). Important features of CSR in this portrayal are their voluntary nature and that these schemes are instruments of self-regulation at company level. The social environment referred to in the definition includes trade unions, interest groups, non-governmental organisations and other stakeholders.

For reflexive labour law, it is of interest that these private forms of regulation are recognised in public policies and legal strategies. CSR has received strong public support from international law. Although dating back to discussions in the United States during the 1950s, the debate over CSR at the global level started in earnest during the 1960s and 1970s when multinational enterprises were recognised as objects of regulation in international labour law. The ILO and the Organisation of Economic Co-operation and Development (OECD) were important drivers; particularly noteworthy are the ILO's Tripartite Declaration of Principles concerning Multinational Enterprises and Social Policy (MNE Declaration) of 1977 and the previously mentioned OECD Guidelines for Multinational Enterprises.

The ILO's Tripartite Declaration advises MNEs on principles deriving from international labour standards. These include employment practices, training, conditions of work and industrial relations. In addition, the ILO has issued a range of codes of practice on health and safety issues. These codes of practice take a distinctive reflexive approach in that they only set out practical guidelines for public authorities, employers, workers, enterprises and specialised occupational safety and health protection bodies (such as enterprise safety committees) without being legally binding instruments. The ILO is explicit that they are not binding and should thus be considered as soft law measures:

> ILO Codes of Practice ... are not intended to replace the provisions of national laws or regulations, or accepted standards. Codes of Practice provide guidance on safety and health at work in certain economic sectors (e.g. construction, opencast mines, coal mines, iron and steel industries, non-ferrous metals industries, agriculture, shipbuilding and ship repairing, forestry), on protecting workers against certain hazards (e.g. radiation, lasers, visual display units, chemicals, asbestos, airborne substances), and on certain safety and health measures (e.g. occupational safety and health management systems; ethical guidelines for workers' health surveillance; recording and notification of occupational accidents and diseases; protection of workers' personal data; safety, health and working conditions in the transfer of technology to developing countries) (ILO Codes of Practice at http://www.ilo.org/safework/info/ standards-and-instruments/codes/lang--en/index.htm).

The real problem with codes of conduct is of course uncertainty over their actual impact. Although the enforcement of the ILO Declaration aiming at establishing codes of conduct in MNEs is voluntary and it is formally not subject to the reporting and monitoring systems of ILO conventions and recommendations, the ILO nevertheless carries out its own monitoring through reports and studies of the use of codes of conduct by MNEs (see, for example, Mamic 2004). In analyses of the content of codes of conduct, the ILO found reference to main ILO conventions in the codes, in particular those regulating child labour, forced labour, harassment and abuse, occupational safety and health, wages and benefits, and working hours. Some but not all codes also mention non-discrimination, freedom of association and the right of collective bargaining.

However, there is only sketchy evidence to determine the actual impact of codes on labour practices. Empirical studies report a selective approach in addressing labour issues and an uneven implementation of fundamental labour rights and, as Bob Hepple emphasises, codes vary significantly among industries and countries (Hepple 2005, p. 73). A factor limiting impact is a restriction in scope when codes are not, or only insufficiently, covering suppliers and so-called supply chains. Research found that codes rarely cover every link in the supply chain and rarely encompass workers in the informal sector, for example home-workers or unregistered workers of subcontractors. They often only cover the companies' main suppliers and their workers.

In order to increase effectiveness, codes of conduct might include clauses on mechanisms for the monitoring of their implementation. In these cases the monitoring of multinational enterprises is either carried out in-house or is delegated to a consultancy firm. Monitoring means assessing the conformity of the core organisation and its suppliers with key provisions of a code of conduct (Santoro 2003). Research has found improvement of working conditions as a result of successful monitoring of the implementation of the code (see, for example, the case of Nike, analysed and reported by Locke et al. 2007a; see also Locke et al. 2012). In certain industries, corporate social responsibility has contributed to a spread of global norms (see Dashwood 2012 in relation to the mining industry). However, research also found that monitoring and auditing is often seen as the sole responsibility of management and does not involve worker representatives.

Monitoring enables civil society organisations and trade unions to engage in controlling the conduct of multinational enterprises. In fact, it offers trade unions a new field of activity. In addition to management audits, trade unions can participate in monitoring of conformity with a code of conduct that is carried out at a country level. This is known as social audit and is necessary for producers who want to be accredited as suppliers to a particular market. Social audits are often subcontracted and carried out by specialist consultants and should be of particular concern for trade unions.

10.3.2 Regulation through Collective Bargaining: International Framework Agreements and Other Negotiations between Unions and Corporations

A more traditional and direct form of bilateral participation of trade unions in regulating codes of conduct is offered by collective agreements. Multinational enterprises have begun to enter so-called international framework agreements (IFAs) with globally operating trade unions. These agreements aim at establishing an ongoing and stable relationship between MNEs and trade unions and offer in particular sectoral trade unions from the MNE's home country to participate in the negotiation of the agreement. In framework agreements, multinational enterprises commit themselves to applying the same labour standards to their employees in all the different countries in which they operate. Since framework agreements result from negotiations between companies and international trade unions, they are viewed by the ILO as ideal instruments to promote industrial relations in the world society (Papadakis 2011a, 2011b). However, so far they are geographically biased because the majority are concluded between European MNEs and European unions (Stevis and Boswell 2007, p. 194).

Research found that international framework agreements vary according to the type of companies and trade union involved and according to industrial relations traditions and practice of the parties involved. In general, framework agreements include the ILO's four fundamental labour principles but differ in covering other ILO standards, such as the protection of workers' representatives, wages, occupational safety and health, and skills training. Most framework agreements make reference to the entire supply chain, even if supplier companies are not parties to them. Companies usually commit to inform all their subsidiaries, suppliers, contractors and subcontractors about the agreement (Eurofound 2009, pp. 6–7).

It has been argued that framework agreements depend on strong global unions in order to be successful (Fairbrother and Hammer 2005). However, in order to guarantee that trade unions are involved the agreements have to be designed appropriately, for example by including follow-up mechanisms. There are good examples of agreements that set up procedures for joint implementation of the agreement through joint action of management and unions or employee representatives. Examples of such joint action are joint responsibility for company-wide dissemination of the agreement or the development of joint training programmes. In any event, crucial for joint responsibility of implementation are procedures that allow global unions to make a complaint if the company violates the terms of the agreement.

In addition to international framework agreements there is evidence that corporate social responsibility schemes are the result of negotiations and not unilateral management initiatives. This is particularly the case in industries in which trade unions are strong (Edwards et al. 2007). Furthermore, the European Union has been supportive in launching three corporate social responsibility initiatives. The first initiative in 2002 was called 'Corporate Social Responsibility: A Business Contribution to Sustainable Development' (European Commission 2002) and explicitly encouraged companies to adopt ILO labour standards and the OECD's Guidelines as minimum standards in their codes of conduct. It was followed in 2006 by an attempt to encourage companies by 'Implementing the Partnership for Growth and Jobs: Making Europe a Pole of Excellence on Corporate Social Responsibility' (European Commission 2006b). The recent third initiative supports employee involvement through 'Transnational Company Agreements: Realising the Potential of Social Dialogue' (European Commission 2012b).

Karen Buhmann has shown in her analysis of the Commission's policy-based approach to regulating CSR that the procedural design of reflexive multi-stakeholder regulatory processes was central in the EU's initiatives (Buhmann 2011). She argues convincingly that further attention to reflexive law could lead to improvements in the EU's regulatory technique. However, her plea for normativity and substantive juridification of CSR, especially in the formation and definition of CSR, is less convincing and hardly seems compatible with the procedural self-understanding of reflexive law. Although reflexive law is not adverse to substantive or normative policy considerations, as argued in Chapter 1 and demonstrated throughout this book, it does not claim to be a normative approach itself.

10.3.3 NGOs and Social Accountability Standards

In addition to unilateral corporate codes of conduct and bilateral collective agreements, there exist a number of so-called social accountability standards which are promoted by non-governmental organisations (NGOs). These need to be taken into account from a reflexive labour law perspective since they form part of spontaneous and plural creation of standards, norms and principles. NGOs such as Oxfam have developed long-term strategies of engagement with transnational companies. They actively promote companies to adopt voluntary codes of conduct. It has been observed that in their consumer campaigns they switched from 'the confrontational tactic of consumer boycotts' to promoting 'long-term positive engagement aimed at winning continuous improvement in company practice' (Mayne 1999, p. 241). And these practices include labour standards and labour relations in transnational companies.

However, NGOs are not the only players in the field of social accountability. In fact, there exists an industry of creating and implementing social accountability standards, often linked to accreditation or certification processes. The logic behind certification is that MNEs seek to conduct business only with certified factories, and this creates in turn an incentive for factories to obtain certification. The established International Organization for Standardization (ISO) developed in 2010 the ISO 26000 standard, which addresses corporate social responsibility. It includes, among others, rules on labour practices. However, unlike some other well-known ISO standards, the rules on labour practices cannot be certified. Instead, ISO standards only clarify the meaning of social responsibility in practical terms and support the sharing of best practices relating to social responsibility. Nevertheless, research could show that advertising adherence to ISO 26000 achieves higher brand awareness (Matteraa et al. 2012).

A well-known example of social certification is the voluntary standard SA 8000, initiated by the Council on Economic Priority Accreditation Agency and now administered by the New York-based NGO Social Accountability International. SA 8000 can either supplement or replace company codes of conduct and it is particularly concerned with conditions of work. It includes reference to the ILO conventions, and sometimes also other ILO standards relating to conditions of work and hygiene and security. Research on SA 8000 comes to the conclusion that, although impressive in its reach and showing signs of having some impact on working conditions at the micro-level of MNEs and their suppliers, given the current dimension of international business activity, voluntary corporate responsibility initiatives such as SA 8000 'are simply a drop in the ocean' (Rasche and Gilbert 2012, p. 77).

10.3.4   The Reflexive Nature of CSR

Both CSR schemes and the regulation of CSR show many characteristics of reflexive regulation. Successful regulation of codes of conduct is dependent on the acknowledgment of the particular conditions of the regulated object, which often is the result of reflexivity in the company. In order to be successful, any attempt at external regulation of CSR has to understand itself as facilitative rather than authoritative. The regulator has to reveal an understanding that self-regulation in MNEs and other companies is central in improving conditions in organisations.

The regulation of CSR can be considered an archetypal example of soft law. The regulation of CSR and codes of conduct takes the form of guidelines and the main form of sanctioning is blaming in case of non-compliance. The process of monitoring is in fact a central element in the design of CSRs. It can be carried out by management or a professional organisation hired by management but, if sufficiently transparent, it also opens up possibilities for NGOs and trade unions to exercise control.

In his assessment of research on codes of conduct, Gunther Teubner comes to the conclusion that codes have improved labour conditions, increased environmental protection, and pushed through human rights standards. In his optimistic view, NGO monitoring and binding contracts with civil societal certification bodies enhance the likelihood of success (Teubner 2010a, 2011b, referring among others to case studies in Locke et al. 2007a, Locke et al. 2007b, Dilling et al. 2008). However, empirical analyses of codes of conduct also found a rather selective approach that codes of conduct take in addressing labour issues. This selective approach can be interpreted from a reflexive labour law perspective as at least partly related to the function of these codes as a hybrid mechanism of internal control and external symbol responding to demands of self-regulation. The selection of labour issues in codes often reflects the nature of the public debate over problems in the industry or service sector rather than internal regulatory agendas (Didry 2011). By making the topics regulated in codes a matter of internal debate and consensus among stakeholders, the codes can strengthen their impact. From a reflexive labour law perspective, they should be the result of participatory self-regulation.

Christine Parker has suggested theorising the legal regulation of self-regulation as meta-regulation. Her idea of regulation of the corporate conscience as the main aim of meta-regulation of CSR resonates with the reflexive law concept of supporting 'reflection centres' in companies (Teubner 1994). Colin Scott has rightly emphasised that for meta-regulation to achieve the desired learning effects in companies, it is necessary to transcend regulation of self-regulation by government and to explore non-governmental forms of meta-regulation (Scott 2008). Nevertheless, Parker's response to the critique that meta-regulation is merely procedural regulation reveals remarkable similarities with the reflexive law approach. Like meta-regulation, reflexive labour law aims at creating conditions in companies so 'that substantive conflict between social values and corporate ways of doing things is forced to be dealt with and resolved inside the organisation' (Parker 2007, p. 231). This requires not only change at the company level but a transformation of the concept of law that includes recognising standard-setting (Schepel 2005) as law-making and most importantly 'the recognition that law itself is regulated by non-regulation, and should therefore seek to adapt itself to plural forms of regulation' (Parker 2007, p. 213). A reflexive labour law perspective would only add that it is necessary to guarantee that a sufficient number of labour issues are on the agenda of 'values' that make up the corporate conscience.

Both the regulation of CSR and CSR mechanisms themselves have been criticised by labour lawyers. Their main concern seems to be that self-regulation should not replace state regulation and that it is incapable of providing similar degrees of protection (Kolben 2011). Alan Neal has pointed out that 'at a time when corporate governance is addressed increasingly in terms of a loss of faith in self-regulation, it is a matter of concern that social policy (including health and safety of workers, and protection of the environment) should apparently be treated in a diametrically opposed manner'. He fears that:

> increasingly 'sophisticated' – but ultimately self-defining and (arguably) self-serving – benchmarking and accreditation processes bring with them the further danger that regulators, seduced by an ostensibly objective 'audit-trail' approach to corporate performance and regulatory compliance, will retreat from their role of regulators and enforcers of social and environmental standards. Such an approach would lead to a situation in which only high-profile 'scandals,' evidencing the shortcomings of predominantly self-regulatory social protection mechanisms, would bring about effective intervention into an otherwise 'laissez-faire' environment more reminiscent of the developing markets of the 1890s than the globalized social economies of the early twenty-first century (Neal 2008, pp. 472–4).

However, from a reflexive labour law point of view, this view underestimates the limits of regulation which have to be taken seriously. Self-regulation is not just competing with state regulation. It is rarely a question of regulators 'retreating' from their duties when self-regulation is acknowledged. Linking into self-regulation is necessary for any external regulation to work at all and there are good reasons for an improvement of regulation when companies' capacities of self-regulation are put at the centre of regulatory strategies.

10.4   THE REGIME OF GLOBAL LABOUR LAW, HUMAN RIGHTS AND SOCIETAL CONSTITUTIONALISATION

The final section of the chapter looks at the field of global labour law at the societal level. Global labour law forms part of the legal system of the world society, which lacks unity and is essentially plural and fragmented (Teubner 1997; Koskenniemi 2007). The thesis put forward in the following is that at the societal level the field of global labour law operates as a regime within world law.

The notion of regime used here deviates from international relations theory, where it was originally introduced to describe close cooperation between states. The classical definition by Stephen D. Krasner views regimes as a set of 'principles, norms, rules, and decision-making procedures around which actor expectations converge in a given issue-area'

(Krasner 1982, p. 185; see also Krasner 1983). The advantage of this definition is that it puts law at the centre of regime formation, but it should be clear that regimes cannot be reduced to law. However, regimes can be distinguished according to the degree to which they are juridified. And in this respect the global labour law regime can be described as a regime that expresses increasing functional differentiation between law and politics and gains its autonomy through increased legalisation (Albert 2002, pp. 292–9; see also the special issue on 'Legalization and World Politics' of *International Organization* Vol. 54 (3), in summer 2000).

The formation of regimes is often the result of legal learning processes as well as conflicts between regimes. A good example of how international law regimes and the creation of new protective standards can emerge out of reflexive learning by state and non-state actors from previous failures of multilateral institutions and agreements is given by Gráinne de Burca in her analysis of negotiations that led to the UN Disability Convention. She could show that 'in this field of human rights . . . the presence of those most affected seems to have been crucial in advocating for, supporting and introducing many of these novel features into the Disability Convention' (De Burca 2010, p. 194). Jonathan Zeitlin has rightly interpreted this as a case of successful pragmatic transnational governance in the global economy (Zeitlin 2011). In a reflexive labour law perspective, the participation of those regulated by transnational regimes is crucial for their success.

The concept of regime captures the plural nature of a fragmented world law that is characterised by conflict. According to Paul Berman, we live in a world of overlapping legal authority that is best described as global legal pluralism characterised by hybridity and conflict. World law is governed by 'procedural mechanisms, institutions and practices that aim to manage, without eliminating, legal pluralism' (Berman 2012, p. 10). In Berman's world of global legal pluralism, regimes are hybrid cosmopolitan legal spaces that engage in normative dialogue and conceptual interactions with other regimes. However, more important than collaboration is conflict and the procedural mechanisms, institutions and practices used to manage pluralism are often resulting from 'regrettable compromises' (ibid., p. 188).

In a similar vein to Berman, Gunther Teubner and his colleagues emphasise the conflictual relations between transnational legal regimes in the world society (Teubner 2012, ch. 6; see also Fischer-Lescano and Teubner 2004). In a recent publication on conflicts resulting from global legal pluralism, the following five aspects of legal collision are highlighted:

(1) Legal collisions 'reflect the double fragmentation of world society and its law. The fragmentation is a double one because, firstly, the functional

differentiation of modern society causes collisions between different social functional systems and the legal norms coupled to them. Secondly, differences between social organisational principles cause clashes between the formal law of modern society and the socially embedded legal systems of indigenous societies'.

(2) Legal collisions 'are about the conflict of legal norms', either in the form that 'national legal orders collide with the transnational regime law' or that 'law collides with legal norms of indigenous cultures'.

(3) 'Neither public nor private international law offers an adequate solution for these new types of collisions. They have been constructed for coping with collisions of national legal orders and not for solving conflicts between national laws and transnational law or the law of indigenous cultures, respectively.'

(4) 'With regard to transnational regimes, collision rules have to be developed which take their character as "self-contained regimes" into account. Here, the substantive law approach which has been developed in private international law seems to be most suitable.'

(5) 'With regard to indigenous cultures, the collision rules to be developed must respect the social embeddedness of the legal norms. In this case, the model of the institutionalised and proceduralised protection of basic rights seems to be the most promising' (Teubner and Korth 2012, pp. 26–7).

This can be applied to global labour law. What is characteristic of global labour law is that there is fragmentation not only because of a multiplicity of sources of rules and norms at the level of the function systems law, economics and industrial relations as well as at the organisational level of multinational companies, but also fragmentation of the field of global labour law itself. Responsible for this is to some extent the social embeddedness of labour law in 'indigenous' industrial relations, which also applies to global labour law. National labour law norms, including those that govern collective bargaining, are in conflict with 'transnational regime law'. A good example of such regime collision has been the dispute over the *Viking* and *Laval* cases of the ECJ in which national strike law collided with EU law (see Deakin and Rogowski 2011).

It seems unlikely that the regime of global labour law is capable of achieving a similar degree of unity in comparison with national jurisdictions. However, it might be able to constitutionalise. The idea of societal constitutionalisation of world law that Gunther Teubner promotes (discussed in Chapter 1, section 1.4) can be tested in relation to global labour law. Following his suggestion we can ask if processes of constitutionalisation, albeit in fragmented form, can be found in the global labour law regime.

The lively debate over the constitutionalisation of international and global law in general has to a large extent focused on international organisations. A prominent example is the WTO and its role as regulator of international trade. In a survey of the literature on constitutionalisation of the WTO, Deborah Cass has introduced a useful distinction of approaches to theorising constitutionalisation. She calls them institutional managerialism, rights-based constitutionalisation and judicial norm-generation (Cass 2005). For global labour law, the rights-based approach is of particular interest since it includes a debate over social and human rights which, despite the rejection of a social clause referring to labour rights (see section 10.2.5.1 above), have been occasionally on the agenda of decision-making of the Dispute Settlement Body and the Appellate Body, the powerful quasi-court of the WTO (see Picciotto 2011, pp. 347–81 on the the Constitution of the WTO with reference to the well-known debate between Ernst Petersmann and Philip Alston).

A similar typology could be applied in discussing constitutionalisation processes in the ILO. The experience the ILO gained in defining labour rights and labour standards as human rights provides a good example of a rights-based constitutionalisation of the regime of global labour law. In fact, there is a lively debate about considering labour rights as human rights (see Alston 2005). However, it is by no means clear that promoting labour rights as human rights is beneficial for the regime of labour law.

Virginia Mantouvalou has provided a useful distinction of three approaches in the discussion of labour rights as human rights (Mantouvalou 2012). She calls them the positivist, the instrumental and the normative approach. The positivist approach is satisfied if human rights are grounded in legal documents and is sufficiently supported in law. The instrumental approach adopts, in contrast, a more contextual understanding of human rights and asks if either state or international institutions, such as courts, or civil society organisations, such as trade unions and NGOs, are actively promoting them. The third approach is taken in labour law scholarship and in human rights theory, which examines the issue as theoretical matter and occasionally in normative terms as a question of moral truth.

ILO policy in relation to labour rights as human rights largely belongs to the first approach. It is legalistic in nature and puts emphasis on formal statements that endorse labour standards. Although the ILO also promotes political campaigns, its main concern is legal support for labour rights and formal legal recognition is of considerable importance for the ILO.

An example of the third approach is Hugh Collins' interrogation into the capacity of human rights providing a normative basis for labour law. He has argued that a contrast exists between universal human rights and labour rights and that 'the latter are not a compelling candidate for presence in the pantheon of the former' (Collins 2006, p. 144). He questions whether human rights are capable of replacing the justification for labour law in terms of welfare or social justice.

The second approach is closest to a reflexive labour law understanding of labour rights. Harry Arthurs' enquiry about the usefulness of viewing labour rights as human rights is a good example of a critical assessment of the instrumental or functional aspect and the context of labour rights as human rights. He believes that this discourse disempowers workers by distracting them from political activities. In Arthurs' opinion, reform of labour law happens in political processes and not through human rights discourse or reliance on constitutionally protected rights. On the basis of his Canadian experience of campaigning for labour rights as human rights, he warns against relying too heavily on the judiciary or the ILO to accomplish labour law objectives that cannot be achieved through worker mobilisation (Arthurs 2006, pp. 61–6, 2009).

A more balanced view is taken by Kevin Kolben. He rejects Arthurs' downplaying of the human rights discourse. For him the campaigning for labour rights as human rights can legitimate the claims of workers to workplace rights and justice. A stronger constitutional protection for freedom of association helps to create a space for political mobilisation and campaigns for labour law and other social reforms. However, he also warns against drawbacks of over-reliance on the human rights discourse.

> While associating with the international human rights movement and adopting its discourse clearly has some potential benefits for labor advocates, both within and without the trade union movement, there are also some serious pitfalls. . . . the strategies and politics of the human rights movement, while perhaps highly effective in impacting state action on many issues, could be less effective, and in fact debilitating, for labor rights actors that work primarily in the private economic sphere. Labor movements do not necessarily benefit from the legalism, elitism, or the individualistic and philanthropic frames that often define human rights approaches to workers' rights (Kolben 2010, p. 484).

For reflexive labour law the emphasis shifts from a concern with political mobilisation to the societal level of interaction between the political, the economic and the legal systems. In his analysis of the role of human rights in the emerging law of the world society, Gunther Teubner adopts a rather optimistic view of the potential of combatting violations of human rights by 'private' transnational actors (Teubner 2006c). In his reflexive law perspective, human rights, including labour rights, should be understood as fundamental rights that have three dimensions: first, they constitute personal rights protecting the autonomy of 'the social artefacts called "persons"'; second, they protect the autonomy of social discourses such as art, science and religion against their subjugation to what Teubner calls 'the totalising tendencies of the communicative matrix'; and third, human rights limit societal communication, where the integrity of individuals' body and mind is endangered (Teubner 2006c).

For Teubner, fundamental rights have a 'horizontal' effect and impose obligations not only on governmental bodies but also directly on private actors. They play an important role in creating a corporate consciousness. The crucial new dimension is for Teubner that they become binding on 'social institutions' and not just on individuals.

> The problem of human rights in private law arises only where the endangerment of body/mind integrity comes from social 'institutions' (and not just from individual actors). In principle, institutions include private formal organisations and private regulatory systems. The most important examples here would be business firms, private associations, hospitals, schools, universities as formal organisations; and general terms of trade, private standardisation and similar rule-setting mechanisms as private regulatory systems. We must of course be clear that the term 'institution' represents only imperfectly the chains of communicative acts that endanger the integrity of mind and body, and does not completely grasp the expansive phenomenon that is really intended, that is the whole sense of the metaphor of the anonymous 'matrix'. But for lawyers, who are oriented toward rules and persons, 'institution' has the advantage of being defined as a bundle of norms and at the same time being able to be personified. The concept of the institution could accordingly respecify fundamental rights in social sectors (much as it can be employed for the State as institution and as person in the field of politics). The outcome would then be a formula of 'third-party effect' which could seem plausible also to a black-letter lawyer. It would not regard horizontal effect as a balancing between the fundamental rights of individual bearers of them, but instead as the protection of human rights and rights of discourses vis-à-vis expansive social institutions (Teubner 2006c, p. 344).

However, there is a further dimension to human rights for Teubner. And this is their contribution to constitutionalisation inside organisations. As mentioned previously in this chapter (see section 10.2.1), the ILO redefined core labour standards as human rights in the late 1970s. This has been an influential reflexive move in redirecting labour standard-setting and in constitutionalising the international organisation ILO. However, the debate of labour rights as human rights transcends the confines of international labour law. From a reflexive law perspective, we have to look beyond the realm of public international law. Gunther Teubner has proposed to think about societal constitutionalism and the constitutionalisation of private transnational regimes (Teubner 2010a, 2010b, 2012). In his approach, global private legal regimes make direct recourse to law and create their own substantive law.

> Today, the most prominent private legal regimes are the *lex mercatoria* of the international economy and the *lex digitalis* of the Internet. To these, however, we must add numerous private or private-public instances of regulation and conflict resolution which create autonomous law with a claim to global validity. These postnational formations are organised around principles of finance, recruitment, coordination, communication, and reproduction that are fundamentally postnational and not just multinational or international. Among them are multinational enterprises building their own internal legal order but also transnational regimes which regulate social issues worldwide. These private regimes clash frequently with the legal rules of nation states and other transnational regimes (Teubner 2010b, p. 332).

Following this line of analysis we can ask if, and to what extent, global labour law can be considered as a postnational legal regime. For this assessment the focus has to shift from public international law in the form of labour standard-setting by the ILO to private forms of regulation. The important arena for this type of constitutionalisation of the regime of global labour law is the adoption and operation of codes of conduct in companies.

Codes of conduct are an important mechanism of self-regulation in companies. They are important devices by which enterprises constitute their own legal orders (Muchlinski 1997). From a reflexive labour law perspective, their link to corporate social responsibility (CSR), labour rights and consultation with employees and their representatives is crucial. Noteworthy are developments in companies that produce trademark goods internationally. In the last two decades we have witnessed not only a rapid proliferation of codes concerned with CSR issues in these companies, but an expansion of their application from covering headquarters and foreign subsidiaries to the entire production chain. This was to a considerable extent the result of public pressure on enterprises, deriving from a range of factors including civil society, new technologies, trends in business, investors, consumers as well as scandals (McBarnet 2007) and last but not least trade unions (Preuss et al. 2006).

In particular these companies started adopting codes of conduct intended to apply to their subcontractors and suppliers. Codes have been designed in order to match the structure and operation of supply chains. In cases where the company has a long and complex supply chain, the design and implementation of the code require specific mechanisms. In analyses of these chains, the concept of network has been used and it has been argued that a successful transformation of the supply chain into a 'network mode of governance' requires 'the suppliers' proactive involvement in this process' (Fichter and Sydow 2002, p. 376).

It has also been observed that these processes provide fertile grounds for the development of reflexive governance structures in corporations

(Arthurs 2007a; Teubner 2010a; Kolben 2011). The demand for reflexive governance of corporations results from a range of external and internal demands. Among these have recently been the financial crisis (see Teubner 2011a, pp. 18–19) and environmental campaigns (Perez et al. 2009). However, in a system theoretical perspective, reflexive governance is the result of internal learning processes. Corporations perceive ILO labour rights or transnational corporate social responsibility schemes as regulatory contexts that generate normative proposals which must be translated into reflexive governance structures. Once 'rough consensus' is reached in internal processes, normative structures and bodies can emerge as 'running codes' (Calliess and Zumbansen 2010).

What distinguishes reflexive governance from other forms of corporate governance is a focus on procedural regulation. Aiming at procedures allows reflexive regulation to switch from command and control policies to developing strategies that facilitate development in companies based on dialogue and consensual decision-making. Reflexive legal mechanisms that aim at supporting reflexive governance structures are disclosure laws that require company policies to be transparent. They support the development of codes of conduct and of CSR schemes in general (Doorey 2005; Campbell and Vick 2007). Procedural regulation enables reflexive governance to support sustainable development (Voß and Kemp 2006).

In the European context we witness a number of encouraging legal and policy developments at the supranational level that support reflexive governance in companies. Legal measures that require the provision of information and consultation of employees in specific circumstances have been introduced in the EU since the 1970s (see Gospel and Willman 2002). They include areas such as collective redundancy or transfer of an undertaking and health and safety. Noteworthy is the 1994 Directive on European Works Councils (Directive 94/45/EC, updated by the recast Directive 2009/38/EC), which offers information and consultation in multinational companies and groups. European works councils are defined as standing bodies providing for the information and consultation of employees in companies with at least 1,000 employees within the member states and at least 150 employees in each of at least two member states of the EU. Despite considerable variation by sector and company structure, European works councils contribute to establishing 'Community collective autonomy' in European companies and in industrial relations systems at the European level (Marginson and Sisson 2006, pp. 238–45; Lo Faro 2000, p. 83).

Probably the most important European measure providing for information and consultation with employee representatives is Council Directive 2002/14. This directive establishes a general framework for informing and consulting employees in the European Union and applies to all undertakings employing at least 50 employees or EU establishments employing at least 20 employees. It defines information as the requirement on the part of the employer to transmit relevant data in order to enable employee representatives to engage in consultation, exchange of views and dialogue with the employer. This measure has been praised as the European social model of mandatory employee representation that not only establishes effective employee participation but acts as a productive factor (see the critical discussion in Gold 2010). However, implementation of the directive has been patchy and in the UK at least there is a need for reform of the implementing measure in order to promote 'active consultation' (Hall and Purcell 2012, pp. 172–9; see also Peccei et al. 2005).

From a reflexive labour law perspective, the European regulations on consultation provide the regulatory context for self-regulation in companies (Koukiadaki 2009). There is a special link between consultation with employees and efforts of companies to regulate their affairs by codes of conduct. Gunther Teubner has emphasised the special character of codes of conduct as mechanisms of governance of multinational corporations. They constitute a genuine instrument of self-regulation that neither directly aims at employee participation nor at shareholder interests.

> The corporate codes of multinationals are directed neither at the interests of their shareholders, nor at the participation of the trade unions. These codes are different instances of corporate social responsibility with a potential that is hard to gauge. The corporate codes of multinationals react to both new perils in the working environment and the disappearance of traditional actors due to the globalisation process: the worldwide inter-linking of markets, capital, and production facilitate a slackening of working conditions in developing countries and endanger the social achievements in developed industrial states, a situation in no way ameliorated by nation states policies. Hopes that traditional international organisations (particularly the International Labour Organization) would come to rescue, have been disappointed because, although binding, their founding inter-state treaties are unenforceable. Similarly, social clauses in international trade contracts promise little. A strategy in which the pressure amassed by worldwide social conflicts, protest movements, domestic courts, non-governmental and international organisations, coerces multinationals into adopting codes of conduct in which they assume an obligation to uphold social standards, is more likely to succeed (Teubner 2010a, pp. 203–4).

Teubner is interested in corporate codes as vehicles for the constitutionalisation of the private governance regimes of corporations (see also Anderson 2006). Constitutionalisation is for him the result of an intertwining of private and public corporate codes. 'Both types of corporate codes, taken together, represent the beginnings of specific transnational corporate constitutions conceived as constitutions in the strict sense' (Teubner 2011b, p. 620). These transnational corporate constitutions are constituted through double reflexivity of secondary legal norms and reflexive social structures.

> An autonomous, non-state, non-political, civic constitutionalisation of multi-nationals takes place if reflexive social processes, which concern the relation-ship of the multinational in its various environs, are interwoven with reflexive legal processes. Under these conditions, it makes sense to speak of elements of a genuine constitution in the corporate codes of multinationals.

Teubner identifies in corporate codes typical elements of a constitu-tion. He calls them 'norms of the upper level of the codes' which 'are neither substantive rules, such as the standards at the lower level, nor mere procedural norms such as those at the central level. Instead, they are explicit superior norms of the company constitution, which are for-mulated as general principles, and serve both as the departure point for internal norm-generation and as the yardsticks of the internal and external reviews' (Teubner 2010a, pp. 209–10).

Corporate constitutional norms include organisational and procedural rules regulating decision-making processes. Of particular concern for a reflexive labour law perspective is what Teubner calls 'codification of the boundaries of the organisation in relation to individual freedoms and civil liberties (basic rights)'. This aspect of codes regulates the fundamental relationship of the organisation to its employees, and he views these code provisions 'as genuine constitutional norms of the multinationals'. Thus codes of conduct are means of self-constitutionalisation of transnational corporations which to a significant extent are based on recognition of employee rights (Teubner 2011b).

Karl-Heinz Ladeur has voiced doubts about Teubner's concept of a self-constitutionalising global law. Ladeur argues that there are more similarities than differences when it comes to legal fragmentation at the national and the global level. He contends that Teubner's 'excessively complex' concept overlooks the importance of national law and its contri-bution in establishing new forms of societal global law.

> The postmodern 'national' law of the 'society of networks' is not fundamentally so very different from the fragmented global law that exists beyond the sphere of the state. Starting from this assumption, it seems easier to envisage that on the one hand, in a global law order which is entirely characterised by heterar-chy and asynchrony, new legal forms are being generated which are geared to operating with incompleteness and which are in particular procedural reflexive

and to some extent also strategically dimensioned, while at the same time the experimental transnational cooperation with national law (which is also changing), which is aimed at the stimulus of self-regulation, cannot be separated from global law (Ladeur 2012, pp. 253–5).

Ladeur's comment is based on arguments borrowed from his own concept of postmodern law (Ladeur 1995) and Nico Krisch's theory of a plural postnational global law (Krisch 2010). Ladeur's observation can be applied to the development of the regime of global labour law. The design and content of corporate codes of conduct of multinationals reflects not only international law but displays many examples of 'experimental transnational cooperation with national law'. National labour laws, including national constitutional provisions on labour rights, are important sources. This is particularly true for example in relation to so-called process rights of freedom of association guaranteed by national constitutions or codetermination law, which provide important backgrounds for corporate social responsibility schemes.

In a similar vein, constitutionalisation contributes to the development of global labour law into a regime by not only being instigated by transnational but also national law. Harry Arthurs defines constitutionalisation of employment in the global context as 'giving juridical, symbolic and practical effect to high labour standards across national boundaries' (Arthurs 2010, p. 410). In his account, there is not only interaction of global labour law and national labour law, but also cross-border interaction between national laws in the constitutionalisation process. Furthermore, on the basis of an assessment of national constitutionalisation in Canada, Arthurs argues that globalisation and the import of global labour undermined national constitution-based legal traditions and released a number of transformations, including privatisation of labour law and flexibilisation of employment leading to politicisation of labour issues (see also Arthurs 2006, 2009).

However, Arthurs underestimates the creative forces unleashed by globalisation and societal constitutionalisation. Charles Sabel and his colleagues have reminded us of the self-regulatory capacity of transnational corporations in actually producing labour regulations (Fung et al. 2001). Their concept of 'Ratcheting Labour Standards' sees a potential not only in strengthening international labour standards in the developing world. New governance techniques go beyond simply monitoring their implementation. They are important sources for the development and creation of new or revised labour standards. Thus labour standards do not derive in their view from external international law, but would rather be generated from the bottom up through deliberative institutions and processes (see also Flohr et al. 2010). This is congruent with a reflexive labour law perspective.

What we witness in global labour law is the overcoming of traditional boundaries of public and private law. In Teubner's account there is an important interaction between public and private codes of conduct and public codes serve as 'impulse-givers' for internal constitutionalisation of organisations through private codes of conduct (Teubner 2012, p. 46). In a similar perspective, Kevin Kolben detects in his analysis of the emergence of transnational private labour regulation not just a 'flow of norms' from public to private regimes but also parallel or complementary regulatory processes in the public and private spheres (Kolben 2011). In Kolben's view, transnational private labour regulation is not just the result of self-regulation by corporate actors, but crucially of pressure of transnational labour activist networks.

Kolben's transnational private labour regimes can be assessed in terms of reflexive labour law. His integrationist approach that wants to salvage a role for the nation state should be reminded that external regulation by public law needs to be supportive precisely in order to foster participation of collective actors in the operation of transnational private labour regulation (Kocher 2008). Furthermore, global labour law and global industrial relations are developing into multi-layered systems that due to their plural sources of norm production have capacities for generating their own legal structures. In addition, there are signs of secondary norm production and societal constitutionalisation that pose particular challenges for policy-making.

We can end our account of reflexive global labour law with the four conditions that David Trubek and his colleagues have proposed for the design of transnational multilevel labour regulation and industrial relations. They capture well the plural nature of the global labour law regime and the interplay of the global and the national, the private and the public level that reflexive policy-making for this regime has to take into account. In addition, they remind us of the importance of legal advocacy networks for the development of the global labour law regime.

> First, do not give up on national systems. National systems remain the foundation for industrial relations. But to be fully effective today, they should be buttressed both by the involvement of transnational actors in national arenas and by genuinely transnational norms that either affect or supersede domestic regulation. Second, do not rely exclusively on public action. We must remember that industrial relations systems should be – and always have been – created in part through various forms of private ordering. This includes exploring bottom-up forms of normative ordering arising out of private action such as external pressures on corporations to create codes of conduct covering labor

conditions. Third, don't look for one unitary source of normative order; a working transnational industrial relations regime can only be built by weaving together a variety of public and private normative sources at different levels. Finally, pay attention to transnational actors and advocacy networks. They are needed to mobilize norms from different systems to create a regulatory web that transcends the purely national (Trubek et al. 2000, p. 1193).

Bibliography

Aaron, B. (1985), 'The NLRB, Labor Courts, and Industrial Tribunals: A Selective Comparison', *Industrial and Labor Relations Review*, **39**(1), 35–45.

Adnett, N. (2001), 'Modernizing the European Social Model: Developing the Guidelines', *Journal of Common Market Studies*, **39**(2), 353–64.

Agamben, G. (1998), *Homo Sacer: Sovereign Power and Bare Life.* Stanford, CA: Stanford University Press.

Akyol, M., M. Neugart and S. Pichler (2012), 'Were the Hartz Reforms Worth Doing?' Available at http://www.vwl3.wi.tu-darmstadt.de/fachgebiete_10/forschung_3/forschung_30.de.jsp

Albert, M. (2002), *Zur Politik der Weltgesellschaft. Identität und Recht im Kontext internationaler Vergesellschaftung.* Weilerswist: Velbrück.

Albert, M. (2004a), 'Weltgesellschaft und Weltstaat', in M. Albert, B. Moltmann, and B. Schoch (eds), *Die Entgrenzung der Politik. Internationale Beziehungen und Friedensforschung.* Frankfurt am Main and New York: Campus Verlag, pp. 223–40.

Albert, M. (2004b), 'On the Modern Systems Theory of Society and IR. Contacts and Disjunctures between different Kinds of Theorizing', in M. Albert and L. Hilkermeier (eds), *Observing International Relations: Niklas Luhmann and World Politics.* London: Routledge, pp. 13–29.

Albert, M. (2005), 'Politik der Weltgesellschaft und Politik der Globalisierung: Überlegungnen zur Emergenz der Weltstaatlichkeit', in B. Heintz, R. Münch and H. Tyrell (eds), *Weltgesellschaft: Theoretische Zugänge und empirische Problemlagen.* Stuttgart: Lucius and Lucius, pp. 223–38.

Albert, M., L.-E. Cederman and A. Wendt (eds) (2010), *New Systems Theories of World Politics.* London: Palgrave.

Albert, M. and L. Hilkermeier (eds) (2004), *Observing International Relations: Niklas Luhmann and World Politics.* London and New York: Routledge.

Albert, M. and R. Schmalz-Bruns (2009), 'Antinomien der Weltgesellschaft. Mehr Weltstaatlichkeit, weniger Demokratie?' In H. Brunkhorst (ed), *Demokratie in der Weltgesellschaft.* Baden-Baden: Nomos, pp. 57–74.

Albrow, M. (1996), *The Global Age: State and Society beyond Modernity*. Cambridge, UK: Polity.

Alston, P. (ed) (2005), *Labour Rights as Human Rights*. Oxford: Oxford University Press.

Altvater, E. and B. Mahnkopf (1996), *Grenzen der Globalisierung. Ökonomie, Ökologie und Politik in der Weltgesellschaft*. Münster: Westfälisches Dampfboot.

Amstutz, M. (2001), *Evolutorisches Wirtschaftsrecht. Vorstudien zum Recht und seiner Methode in den Diskurskollisionen der Marktgesellschaft*. Baden-Baden: Nomos.

Anderman, S. (2004), 'Termination of Employment: Whose Property Rights?' In C. Barnard, S. Deakin and G.S. Morris (eds), *The Future of Labour Law: Liber Amicorum Bob Hepple QC*. Oxford and Portland, OR: Hart, pp. 101–28.

Anderson, G.W. (2005), *Constitutional Rights after Globalization*. Oxford and Portland, OR: Hart.

Anderson, G.W. (2006), 'Corporate Governance: A (Legal Pluralist) Constitutional Perspective', in S. Macleod (ed), *Global Governance and the Quest for Justice Vol II: Corporate Governance*. Oxford and Portland, OR: Hart, pp. 27–46.

Aoki, M. (1988), *Information, Incentives and Bargaining in the Japanese Economy*. Cambridge, UK: Cambridge University Press.

Appelbaum, E. and P. Berg (1994), *The New American Workplace: Transforming Work Systems in the United States*. Ithaca, NY: Cornell University ILR Press.

Archer, M. (2003), *Structure, Agency and the Internal Conversation*. Cambridge, UK: Cambridge University Press.

Archer, M.S. (2007), *Making Our Way through the World: Human Reflexivity and Social Mobility*. Cambridge, UK: Cambridge University Press.

Archer, M.S. (ed) (2010), *Conversations about Reflexivity*. London and New York: Routledge.

Archer, M.S. (2012), *The Reflexive Imperative in Late Modernity*. Cambridge, UK: Cambridge University Press.

Arendt, H. (1973), *The Origins of Totalitarianism*. New York: Harvest Books.

Armstrong, D., T. Farrell and H. Lambert (2012), *International Law and International Relations*. 2nd ed. Cambridge, UK: Cambridge University Press.

Armstrong, K.A. (2010), *Governing Social Inclusion: Europeanization through Policy Coordination*. Oxford: Oxford University Press.

Armstrong, K.A. (2012), 'The Lisbon Strategy and Europe 2020: From the Governance of Co-ordination to the Co-ordination of Governance', in P. Copeland and D. Papadimitriou (eds), *The EU's Lisbon Strategy: Evaluating Success, Understanding Failure*. Basingstoke: Palgrave Macmillan, pp. 208–28.

Armstrong, K.A., I. Begg and J. Zeitlin (2008b), 'The Open Method of Co-ordination and the Governance of the Lisbon Strategy', *Journal of Common Market Studies,* **46**(2), 436–50.

Arthurs, H. (1998), 'Landscape and Memory: Labour Law, Legal Pluralism and Globalization', in T. Wilthagen (ed), *Advancing Theory in Labour Law and Industrial Relations in a Global Context*. Amsterdam: North-Holland, pp. 21–4.

Arthurs, H. (2006), 'Who's Afraid of Globalization? Reflections on the Future of Labour Law', in J.D.R. Craig and S.M. Lynk (eds), *Globalization and the Future of Labour Law*. Cambridge, UK: Cambridge University Press, pp. 51–74.

Arthurs, H. (2007a), 'Corporate Self-Regulation: Political Economy, State Regulation and Reflexive Labour Law', in B. Bercusson and C. Estlund (eds), *Regulating Labour in the Wake of Globalisation: New Challenges, New Institutions*. Oxford and Portland, OR: Hart, pp. 19–35.

Arthurs, H. (2007b), 'Compared to What – The UCLA Comparative Labor Law Project and the Future of Comparative Labor Law', *Comparative Labor Law & Policy Journal*, **28**(3), pp. 591–612.

Arthurs, H. (2009), 'The Constitutionalization of Labour Rights', Lecture at the School of Law, University of Leicester, 24 November 2009. Available at http://papers.ssrn.com/sol3/papers.cfm?abstract_id=1531326.

Arthurs, H. (2010), 'The Constitutionalization of Employment Relations: Multiple Models, Pernicious Problems', *Social & Legal Studies*, **19**(4), 403–22.

Ashiagbor, D. (2001), 'EMU and the Shift in the European Labour Law Agenda: From "Social Policy" to "Employment Policy"', *European Law Journal*, **7**(3), 311–30.

Ashiagbor, D. (2005), *The European Employment Strategy: Labour Market Regulation and New Governance*. Oxford: Oxford University Press.

Atkinson T. (2002), 'Social Inclusion and the European Union', *Journal of Common Market Studies*, **40**(4), 625–43.

Atkinson, A.B., E. Marlier and B. Nolan (2004), 'Indicators and Targets for Social Inclusion in the European Union', *Journal of Common Market Studies*, **42**(1), 47–75.

Auer, P. (2001), 'Labour Market Policy: Flexibility and Security in Austria, Denmark, Ireland and the Netherlands', in G. Schmid and B. Gazier (eds), *The Dynamics of Full Employment: Social Integration*

Through Transitional Labour Markets. Cheltenham, UK: Edward Elgar, pp. 67–98.

Auer, P. (2006), 'Protected Mobility for Employment and Decent Work: Labour Market Security in a Globalized World', *Journal of Industrial Relations*, **48**(1), 21–40.

Auer, P. and B. Gazier (2011), 'Social and Labour Market Reforms: Four Agendas', in R. Rogowski, R. Salais and N. Whiteside (eds), *Transforming European Employment Policy, Labour Market Transitions and the Promotion of Capability*. Cheltenham, UK: Edward Elgar, pp. 27–45.

Ayres, I. and J. Braithwaite (1992), *Responsive Regulation: Transcending the Deregulation Debate*. New York and Oxford: Oxford University Press.

Backer, L.C. (2008), 'Multinational Corporations as Objects and Sources of Transnational Regulation', *ILSA Journal of International & Comparative Law*, **14**, 499–523.

Baecker, D. (1999), *Organisational System*. Frankfurt am Main: Suhrkamp.

Baldwin, R., M. Cave and M. Lodge (2010), *Understanding Regulation: Theory, Strategy, and Practice*. 2nd edition. Oxford: Oxford University Press.

Ball, S. (2001), 'The European Employment Strategy: The Will but not the Way?', *Industrial Law Journal*, **30**(4), 353–74.

Baltes, M. and K.U. Mayer (eds) (2001), *The Berlin Aging Study: Aging from 70 to 100*. Cambridge: Cambridge University Press.

Banakar, R. (1998), 'Reflexive Legitimacy in International Arbitration', in V. Gessner and A.C. Budak (eds), *Emerging Legal Certainties – Empirical Studies on the Globalisation of Law*. Dartmouth: Ashgate, pp. 347–98.

Barbash, J. (1979), *Collective Bargaining in a Changing World*. University of Wisconsin-Madison: Industrial Relations Research Institute.

Barbash, J. (1984), *The Elements of Industrial Relations*. Madison: The University of Wisconsin Press.

Barbier, C. (2005), 'Research on Open Methods of Coordination and National Social Policies. What Sociological Theories and Methods?' In T. Bredgaard and F. Larsen (eds), *Employment Policy from Different Angles*. Copenhagen: DJØF Publishing, pp. 47–74.

Barbier, C. (2008), *La Longue Marche vers l'Europe Sociale*. Paris: Presses Universitaires de France.

Barbier, C., R. Rogowski and F. Columb (eds) (forthcoming), *The Sustainability of the European Social Model. EU Governance, Social Protection and Social Rights in Europe*. Cheltenham, UK: Edward Elgar.

Barnard, C. (2000), 'Regulating Competitive Federalism in the European Union? The Case of EC Social Policy', in J. Shaw (ed), *Social Law and Policy in an Evolving European Union*. Oxford and Portland, OR: Hart, pp. 49–69.

Barnard, C. (2008), 'Viking and Laval: An Introduction', *Cambridge Yearbook of European Legal Studies*, 10, pp. 463–536.

Barnard, C. (2012), *EC Employment Law*. 4th ed. Oxford: Oxford University Press.

Barnard, C. and S. Deakin (2001), *Market Access and Regulatory Competition*, Jean Monnet Working Paper, No.9/01. New York: NYU Law School.

Barnard, C. and S. Deakin (2012), 'Social Policy and Labour Market Regulation', in A. Menon, E. Jones, and S. Weatherill (eds), *The Oxford Handbook of the European Union*. Oxford: Oxford University Press, pp. 542–55.

Barnard, C., S. Deakin and R. Hobbs (2005), 'Reflexive Law, Corporate Social Responsibility and the Evolution of Labour Standards: The Case of Working Time', in O. De Schutter and S. Deakin (eds), *Social Rights and Market Forces: Is the Open Method of Coordination of Employment and Social Policies the Future of Social Europe?* Brussels: Bruylant, pp. 205–44.

Bauman, Z. (1960), *Between Class and Elite: The Evolution of the British Labour Movement: A Sociological Study*. Manchester: Manchester University Press.

Bauman, Z. (2000), *The Individualized Society*. Cambridge: Polity.

Bauman, Z. (2004), *Europe*. Cambridge: Polity.

Bean, R. (1994), *Comparative Industrial Relations: An Introduction to Cross-National Perspectives*. 2nd ed. London: Routledge.

Beck, U. (1992), *Risk Society: Towards a New Modernity*. London: Sage.

Beck, U. (1999), *World Risk Society*. Cambridge: Polity.

Beck, U. and E. Beck-Gernsheim (2001), *Individualization: Institutionalized Individualism and its Social and Political Consequences*. London: Sage.

Beck, U. and B. Holzer (2004), 'Reflexivität und Reflexion', in U. Beck and C. Lau (eds), *Entgrenzung und Entscheidung: Was ist neu an der Theorie reflexiver Modernisierung?* Frankfurt am Main: Suhrkamp, pp. 165–92.

Beck, U., A. Giddens and S. Lash (1994), *Reflexive Modernization: Politics, Tradition and Aesthetics in the Modern Social Order*. Cambridge: Polity.

Beck, U., W. Bonss and C. Lau (2003), 'The Theory of Reflexive Modernization: Problematic, Hypotheses and Research Programme', *Theory, Culture & Society*, **20**(2), 1–33.

Becker, G.S. (1964), *Human Capital*. New York: Columbia University Press.

Behrens, M. (2007), 'Conflict, Arbitration, and Dispute Resolution in the German Workplace', *International Journal of Conflict Management*, **18**(2), 175–92.

Bekker, S. and T. Wilthagen (2008), 'Europe's Pathways to Flexicurity: Lessons Presented from and to the Netherlands', *Intereconomics: Review of European Economic Policy*, **43**(2), 68–73.

Bélanger, J., P.K. Edwards and L. Haiven (eds) (1994), *Workplace Industrial Relations and the Global*. Ithaca: ILR Press.

Bellamy, A.J. (ed) (2004), *International Society and its Critics*. Oxford: Oxford University Press.

Bender, G. (2006), 'Regulierte Selbstregulierung. Der Fall Tarifautonomie', in M. Vec, M.-T. Hütt and A.M. Freund (eds), *Selbstorganisation. Ein Denksystem für Natur und Gesellschaft*. Köln: Böhlau, pp. 355–71.

Bender, G. (2012), 'Tarifautonomie, Regulierte Selbstregulierung, Korporatismus', in P. Collin, G. Bender, S. Ruppert, M. Seckelmann and M. Stolleis (eds), *Regulierte Selbstregulierung im frühen Interventions- und Sozialstaat*. Frankfurt am Main: Klostermann, pp. 53–67.

Benhabib, S. (1992), *Situating the Self*. Cambridge: Polity.

Benjamin, P. (2002), 'Who needs Labour Law? Defining the Scope of Labour Protection', in J. Conaghan, R.M. Fischl and K. Klare (eds), *Labour Law in an Era of Globalization. Transformative Practice and Possibilities*. Oxford: Oxford University Press, pp. 75–93.

Bercusson, B. (1997), 'Globalizing Labour Law: Transnational Private Regulation and Countervailing Actors in European Labour Law', in G. Teubner (ed), *Global Law without a State*. Dartmouth: Aldershot, pp. 248–301.

Bercusson, B. (2006), 'Introduction', in B. Bercusson (ed), *European Labour Law and the EU Charter of Fundamental Rights*. Baden-Baden: Nomos.

Bercusson, B. (2009a), *European Labour Law*. 2nd edition. Cambridge: Cambridge University Press.

Bercusson, B. (2009b), *Labour Law and Social Europe. Selected Writings of Brian Bercusson*. Brussels: ETUI.

Bercusson, B. and C. Estlund (eds) (2007), *Regulating Labour in the Wake of Globalisation: New Challenges, New Institutions*. Oxford and Portland, OR: Hart.

Berg, a. van den and E. de Gier (2008), 'The European Employment Strategy and Transitional Labour Markets: Research in transitional labour markets: implications for the European employment strategy', in R. Rogowski (ed), *The European Social Model and Transitional Labour Markets – Law and Policy*. Aldershot: Ashgate, pp. 63–105.

Berman, P.S. (2012), *Global Legal Pluralism. A Jurisprudence of Law Beyond Borders*. Cambridge: Cambridge University Press.

Beveridge Report (1942), Social Insurance and Allied Services. Cmd 6404. London: HMSO.

Bieler, A. and I. Lindberg (eds) (2010), *Global Restructuring, Labour, and the Challenges for Transnational Solidarity*. Abingdon, Oxon and New York: Routledge.

Blanchard, O. and J. Tirole (2004), 'Redesigning the Employment Protection System', *De Economist*, 152 (1), pp. 1–20.

Blanke, T. (1994), 'Autonomisation of Labour Law through Judicial Interpretation', in R. Rogowski and T. Wilthagen (eds), *Reflexive Labour Law – Studies in Industrial Relations and Employment Regulation*. Deventer: Kluwer, pp. 207–47.

Blanke, T. (2006), 'Fair and Just Working Conditions', in B. Bercusson (ed), *European Labour Law and the EU Charter of Fundamental Rights*. Baden-Baden: Nomos, pp. 357–77.

Blankenburg, E. (1984), 'The Poverty of Evolutionism: A Critique of Teubner's Case for Reflexive Law', *Law and Society Review*, **18**(2), 273–89.

Blankenburg, E. and R. Rogowski (1986), 'German Labour Courts and the British Industrial Tribunal System. A Socio-legal Comparison of Degrees of Judicialisation', *Journal of Law and Society*, **13**(1), 67–92.

Blankenburg, E., S. Schönholz and R. Rogowski (1979), *Zur Soziologie des Arbeitsgerichtsverfahrens. Die Verrechtlichung von Arbeitskonflikten*. Darmstadt: Luchterhand.

Blankenburg, E., L. van den Heuvel and A. Houkema (eds) (1985), *Hoe goed werkt ontslagrecht?* Deventer: Kluwer.

Blanpain, R. (1979), *The OECD Guidelines for Multinational Enterprises and Labour Relations. Experience and Review*. Deventer: Kluwer.

Blanpain, R. (1983), *The OECD Guidelines for Multinational Enterprises and Labour Relations: Experience and Mid-term Report*. Deventer: Kluwer.

Blanpain, R. and R. Ben-Israel (eds) (1994), *Strikes and Lockouts in Industrialized Market Economies*. Deventer: Kluwer.

Blanpain, R. and B. Oversteyns (1993), 'Belgium', in R. Blanpain (ed), *Temporary Work and Labour Law*. Deventer: Kluwer.

Block, R.N., J. Beck and D.H. Kruger (1996), *Labor Law, Industrial Relations, and Employee Choice: The State of the Workplace in the 1990s*. Kalamzoo, MI: W.E. Upjohn Institute for Employment Research.

Borrás, S. and K. Jacobsson (2004), 'The Open Method of Co-ordination and New Governance Patterns in the EU', *Journal of European Public Policy*, **11**(2), 185–208.

Bosch, G. (1986), 'Hat das Normalarbeitsverhältnis eine Zukunft?', *WSI-Mitteilungen*, **39**(9), 163–76.

Bosch, G. (2004), 'Towards a New Standard Employment Relationship in Western Europe', *British Journal of Industrial Relations*, **42**(4), 617–36.

Boyer, R. (ed) (1988), *The Search for Labour Market Flexibility*. Oxford: Clarendon Press.

Boyer, R. (1990), *The Regulation School: A Critical Introduction*. New York: Columbia University Press.

Boyer, R. (1993), 'The Economics of Job Protection and Emerging New Capital-Labor Relations', in C.F. Buechtemann (ed), *Employment Security and Labor Market Behaviour. Interdisciplinary Approaches and International Evidence*. Ithaca: ILR Press, pp. 69–125.

Boyer, R. and D. Drache (1996), 'Introduction', in R. Boyer and D. Drache (eds), *States against Markets: The Limits of Globalization*. London: Routledge, pp. 1–27.

Boyer, R. and D. Drache (eds) (1996), *States against Markets: The Limits of Globalization*. London: Routledge, pp. 84–114.

Braithwaite, J. (2008), *Regulatory Capitalism: How it Works, Ideas for Making it Work Better*. Cheltenham: Edward Elgar.

Braithwaite, J. and P. Drahos (2001), *Global Business Regulation*. Cambridge: Cambridge University Press.

Bredgaard, T., F. Larsen and P.K. Madsen (2008), 'Transitional Labour Market and Flexicurity Arrangements in Denmark: What Can Europe Learn?' In R. Rogowski (ed), *The European Social Model and Transitional Labour Markets – Law and Policy*. Aldershot: Ashgate, pp. 189–208.

Breining-Kaufmann, C. (2007), *Globalisation and Labour Rights. The Conflict between Core Labour Rights and International Economic Law*. Oxford and Portland, OR: Hart.

Brodocz, A. (1996), 'Strukturelle Kopplung durch Verbände', *Soziale Systeme*, **2**(2), 361–87.

Bronstein, A. (2009), *International and Comparative Labour Law. Current Challenges*. Basingstoke: Palgrave and Geneva: International Labour Organization.

Brown, C. (2004) 'The "English School" and World Society', in M. Albert and L. Hilkermeier (eds), *Observing International Relations. Niklas Luhmann and World Politics*. London and New York: Routledge, pp. 59–71.

Büchs, M. (2007), *New Governance in European Social Policy. The Open Method of Coordination*. Basingstoke: Palgrave.

Budak, A.C. (1998), *Making Foreign People Pay – Law and Practice of Cross-Border Debt Collection*. Aldershot: Dartmouth.

Buechtemann, C.F. (1993a), 'Introduction: Employment Security and Labor Markets', in C.F. Buchtemann (ed), *Employment Security and Labor Market Behavior – Interdisciplinary Approaches and International Evidence*. Ithaca, NY: ILR Press, pp. 3–66.

Buechtemann, C.F. (1993b), 'Employment Security and Deregulation: The West German Experience', in C.F. Buchtemann (ed), *Employment Security and Labor Market Behavior – Interdisciplinary Approaches and International Evidence*. Ithaca, NY: ILR Press, pp. 272–96.

Buechtemann, C.F. and A. Höland (1989), Befristete Arbeitsverträge nach dem Beschäftigungsförderungsgesetz (BeschFG 1985) – Ergebnisse einer empirischen Untersuchung. Bonn: Bundesministerium für Arbeit und Sozialordnung.

Buechtemann, C.F. and U. Walwei (1996), 'Employment Security and Dismissal Protection', in G. Schmid, J. O'Reilly and K. Schömann (eds), *International Handbook of Labour Market Policy and Evaluation*. Cheltenham: Edward Elgar, pp. 62–81.

Buhmann, K. (2011), 'Integrating Human Rights in Emerging Regulation of Corporate Social Responsibility: the EU Case', *International Journal of Law in Context*, **7**(2), 139–79.

Bulmer, S. (2012), 'Governing the Lisbon Strategy: Uncertain Governance in Turbulent Economic Times', in P. Copeland and D. Papadimitriou (eds), *The EU's Lisbon Strategy: Evaluating Success, Understanding Failure*. Basingstoke: Palgrave Macmillan, pp. 29–49.

Bünger. D. and K. Moritz (1983), 'Schlichtung im Arbeitsverhältnis, Funktionsbedingungen paritätischer Kommissionen', in R. Voigt (ed), *Gegentendenzen zur Verrechtlichung. Jahrbuch für Rechtssoziologie und Rechtstheorie,* Bd. 9. Opladen: Westdeutscher Verlag, pp. 172–85.

Burgess, P., S. Corby and P. Latreille (2012), Labour Courts Abroad. Working paper ESRC project 'Lay Members as Judges in Employment Rights Cases'. University of Greenwich and ESRC.

Burton, J. (1972), *World Society*. Cambridge: Cambridge University Press.

Buzan, B. (2004), *From International to World Society? English School Theory and the Social Structure of Globalisation*. Cambridge: Cambridge University Press.

Calliess, G.P. (2002), 'Reflexive Transnational Law. The Privatisation of Civil Law and the Civilisation of Private Law', *Zeitschrift für Rechtssoziologie*, **23**(2), 185–216.

Calliess, G.P. and P.C. Zumbansen (2010), *Rough Consensus and Running Code. A Theory of Transnational Private Law*. Oxford and Portland, OR: Hart.

Campbell, K. and D. Vick (2007), 'Disclosure Law and the Market for Corporate Social Responsibility', in D. McBarnet, A. Voiculescu and T. Campbell (eds), *The New Corporate Accountability: Corporate Social Responsibility and the Law*. Cambridge: Cambridge University Press, pp. 242–78.

Casale, G. (2011), 'The Employment Relationship: A General Introduction', in G. Casale (ed), *The Employment Relationship, A Comparative Overview*. Oxford and Portland, OR: Hart, pp. 1–33.

Cass, D.Z. (2005), *The Constitutionalization of the World Trade Organization: Legitimacy, Democracy, and Community in the International Trading System*. New York: Oxford University Press.

Cassese, A. (2005), *International Law*. 2nd edition. Oxford: Oxford University Press.

Cassese, A. (ed) (2012), *Realizing Utopia – The Future of International Law*. Oxford: Oxford University Press.

Christodoulidis, E.A. (1998), *Law and Reflexive Politics*. Dordrecht: Kluwer.

Clam, J. (2000), 'Die Grundparadoxie des Rechts und ihre Ausfaltung. Beitrag zu einer Analytik des Paradoxen', *Zeitschrift für Rechtssoziologie*, **21**(1), 109–43.

Clancy, M. and R. Seifert (2000), *Fairness at Work? Disciplinary and Grievance Provisions of the 1999 Employment Rights Act*. London: Institute of Employment Rights.

Clark. I. (2007), *International Legitimacy and World Society*. Oxford: Oxford University Press.

Coase, R. (1988 [1937]), 'The Nature of the Firm', *Economica*, **4**, 386–405, reprinted in R. Coase, *The Firm, the Market and the Law*. Chicago: Chicago University Press, pp. 33–55.

Cohen, J. and C.F. Sabel (1997), 'Directly-Deliberative Polyarchy', *European Law Journal*, **3**(4), 313–42.

Collins, H. (1992), *Justice in Dismissal. The Law of Termination in Employment*. Oxford: Clarendon.

Collins, H. (1999), *Regulating Contracts*. Oxford: Oxford University Press.

Collins, H. (2000), 'Justifications and Techniques of Legal Regulation of the Employment Relation', in H. Collins, P. Davies and R. Rideout (eds), *Legal Regulation of the Employment Relation*. London, Cambridge, MA and Dordrecht: Kluwer, pp. 3–27.

Collins, H. (2006), 'Theories of Rights as Justifications for Labour Law', in G. Davidov and B. Langille (eds), *The Idea of Labour Law*. Oxford: Oxford University Press, pp. 137–55.

Collins, H. (2010), *Employment Law*. 2nd edition. Oxford: Clarendon.

Countouris, N. (2007), *The Changing Law of the Employment Relationship: Comparative Analyses in the European Context*. Aldershot: Ashgate.

Craig, J.D.R. and S.M. Lynk (eds) (2006), *Globalization and the Future of Labour Law*. Cambridge: Cambridge University Press.

Crevits, D. and B. van Buggenhout (2003), 'Globalisation, Worker Mobility and Social Protection', in D. Pieters (ed), *European Social*

Security and Global Politics. London and The Hague: Kluwer Law International, pp. 61–93.

Crouch, C. (1997), 'Skill-based Full-Employment, the Latest Philosopher's Stone', *British Journal of Industrial Relations*, **35**(3), 367–91.

Crouch, C. (2011), *The Strange Non-Death of Neo-Liberalism*. Cambridge: Polity.

Dahrendorf, R. (1959), *Class and Class Conflict in Industrial Society*. Stanford: Stanford University Press.

Dahrendorf, R. (2012 [2008]), *The Modern Social Conflict. The Politics of Liberty*. 2nd edition. New Brunswick, NJ: Transactions.

Dannin, E. (2006), *Taking Back the Workers' Law. How to Fight the Assault on Labor Rights*. Ithaca, NY and London: Cornell University Press.

Dashwood, H.S. (2012), *The Rise of Global Corporate Social Responsibility. Mining and the Spread of Global Norms*. Cambridge: Cambridge University Press.

Davidov, G. and B. Langille (eds) (2011), *The Idea of Labour Law*. Oxford: Oxford University Press.

Davies, A.C.L. (2008), 'One Step Forward and Two Steps Back: The Viking and Laval Cases in the ECJ', *Industrial Law Journal*, **37**(4), 126–48.

Davies, A.C.L. (2009), *Perspectives on Labour Law*. Cambridge: Cambridge University Press.

Davies, P. and M. Freedland (1993), *Labour Legislation and Public Policy: A Contemporary History*. Oxford: Clarendon Press.

Davies, P. and M. Freedland (2007), *Towards a Flexible Labour Market: Labour Legislation and Regulation since the 1990s*. Oxford: Oxford University Press.

Dawson, M. (2011), *New Governance and the Transformation of European Law. Coordinating EU Social Law and Policy*. Cambridge: Cambridge University Press.

De Burca, G. (2010), 'The European Union in the Negotiation of the UN Disability Convention', *European Law Review*, **35**(2), 174–96.

De la Porte, C. (2002), 'Is the Open Method of Coordination Appropriate for Organising Activities at European Level in Sensitive Policy Areas?', *European Law Journal*, **8**(1), 38–58.

De la Porte, C. (2003), 'The Soft Open Method of Co-Ordination in Social Protection', *European Trade Union Yearbook*, pp. 339–60.

De Schutter, O. and S. Deakin (2005), 'Reflexive Governance and the Dilemmas of Social Regulation. Introduction', in O. De Schutter and S. Deakin (eds), *Social Rights and Market Forces: Is the open method of coordination of employment and social policies the future of social Europe?* Brussels: Bruylant, pp. 1–17.

Deakin, S. (1996), 'Labour Law as Market Regulation, The Economic Foundations of European Social Policy', in P. Davies, A. Lyon-Caen, S. Sciarra and S. Simitis (eds), *Principles and Perspectives on EC Labour Law. Liber Amicorum for Lord Wedderburn*. Oxford: Oxford University Press, pp. 63–93.

Deakin, S. (1998), 'The Evolution of the Contract of Employment, 1900–1950: The Influence of the Welfare State', in N. Whiteside and R. Salais (eds), *Governance, Industry and Labour Markets in Britain and France: The Modernising State in the Mid-twentieth Century*. London: Routledge, pp. 213–30.

Deakin, S. (2002), 'The Many Futures of the Contract of Employment', in J. Conaghan, R.M. Fischl and K. Klare (eds), *Labour Law in an Era of Globalization. Transformative Practice and Possibilities*. Oxford: Oxford University Press, pp. 177–96.

Deakin, S. (2008), 'Regulatory Competition after Laval', *Cambridge Yearbook of European Legal Studies*, **10**(4), 581–609.

Deakin, S. (2009a), 'Capacitas: Contract Law, Capabilities, and the Legal Foundations of the Market', in S. Deakin and A. Supiot (eds), *Capacitas: Contract Law and the Institutional Preconditions of a Market Economy*. Oxford and Portland, OR: Hart, pp. 1–30.

Deakin, S. (2009b), 'Reflexive Harmonisation and European Company Law', *European Law Journal*, **15**(2), 224–45.

Deakin, S. (2010), 'Employment Laws', in P. Cane and H. Kritzer (eds), *The Oxford Handbook of Empirical Legal Research*. Oxford: Oxford University Press, pp. 331–52.

Deakin, S. (2012), 'The Law and Economics of Employment Protection Legislation', in C.L. Estlund and M.L.K. Wachter (eds), *Research Handbook on the Economics of Labor and Employment Law*. Cheltenham: Edward Elgar, pp. 330–56.

Deakin, S. and F. Carvalho (2010), 'System and Evolution in Corporate Governance', in P. Zumbansen and G.-P. Callies (eds), *Law, Economics and Evolutionary Theory*. Cheltenham: Edward Elgar, pp. 111–30.

Deakin, S. and G. Morris (2012), *Labour Law*, 6th edition. Oxford and Portland, OR: Hart.

Deakin, S. and U. Mückenberger (1989), 'From Deregulation to a European Floor of Rights: Labour Law, Flexibilisation and the European Single Market', *Zeitschrift für internationales Arbeits-und Sozialrecht*, **3**(2), 153–207.

Deakin, S. and H. Reed (2000a), 'River Crossing or Cold Bath? Deregulation and Employment in Britain in the 1980s', in G. Esping-Anderson and M. Regini (eds), *Why Deregulate Labour Markets?* Oxford: Oxford University Press, pp. 115–47.

Deakin, S. and H. Reed (2000b), 'The Contested Meaning of Labour Market Flexibility: Economic Theory and the Discourse of European Integration', in J. Shaw (ed), *Social Law and Policy in an Evolving European Union*. Oxford and Portland, OR: Hart, pp. 71–99.

Deakin, S. and R. Rogowski (2011), 'Reflexive Labour Law, Capabilities and the Future of Social Europe', in R. Rogowski, R. Salais and N. Whiteside (eds), *Transforming European Employment Policy – Labour Market Transitions and the Promotion of Capability*. Cheltenham: Edward Elgar, pp. 229–54.

Deakin, S. and F. Wilkinson (1994), 'Rights v. Efficiency? The Economic Case for Transnational Labour Standards', *Industrial Law Journal*, **23**(4), 289–310.

Deakin, S. and F. Wilkinson (2005), *The Law of the Labour Market. Industrialization, Employment and Legal Evolution*. Oxford: Oxford University Press.

Deakin, S., C. McLaughlin and D. Chai (2010), 'Gender Inequality and Reflexive law: The Potential of Different Regulatory Mechanisms', in L. Dickens (ed), *Making Employment Rights Effective: Issues of Enforcement and Compliance*. Oxford and Portland, OR: Hart, pp. 115–37.

Degryse, C. and P. Pochet (eds) (2003), *Social Developments in the European Union 2002: Fourth Annual Report*. Bruxelles: ETUI, OSE, SALTSA.

Department of Employment (1985), Building Businesses . . . Not Barriers. Government White Paper, Cmnd 9794. London: HMSO.

Department of Trade and Industry (1985), Burdens on Business: Report of a Scrutiny of Administrative and Legislative Requirements. London: HMSO.

Deregulierungskommission (1991), *Marktöffnung und Wettbewerb*. Stuttgart: C.E. Poeschel.

Dezalay, Y. and B. Garth (1998), *Dealing in Virtue – International Commercial Arbitration and the Construction of a Transnational Legal Order*. 2nd edition. Chicago: University of Chicago Press.

Dezalay, Y. and B. Garth (eds) (2012), *Lawyers and the Construction of Transnational Justice*. Abingdon and New York: Routledge.

Diamantopoulou, A. (2001), 'The European Social Model: Promoting Economic and Social Progress'. Address to the International Conference on Achieving Balanced Economic and Social Growth by the Commissioner responsible for Employment and Social Affairs at the European Commission. Tallinn, 19 March 2001.

Diamantopoulou, A. (2003), 'The European Social Model – Myth or Reality?' Speech of the Commissioner responsible for Employment and Social Affairs at the European Commission delivered at Labour Party Conference. Bournemouth, 29 September 2003.

Dickens, L. (1994), 'Deregulation of Employment Rights in Great Britain', in R. Rogowski and T. Wilthagen (eds), *Reflexive Labour Law – Studies in Industrial Relations and Employment Regulation*. Deventer: Kluwer, pp. 225–47.

Dickens, L. (2004), 'Problems of Fit: Changing Employment and Labour Regulation', *British Journal of Industrial Relations*, **42**(4), 595–616.

Dickens, L. (2012), 'Fairer Workplaces: Making Employment Rights Effective', in L. Dickens (ed), *Making Employment Rights Effective – Issues of Enforcement and Compliance*. Oxford and Portland, OR: Hart, pp. 205–28.

Dickens, L., M. Jones, B. Weekes and M. Hart (1985), *Dismissed. A Study of Unfair Dismissal and the Industrial Tribunal System*. Oxford: Blackwell.

Didry, C. (2011), 'Corporate Social Responsibility and Employment: A Plurality of Configurations', in R. Rogowski, R. Salais and N. Whiteside (eds), *Transforming European Employment Policy – Labour Market Transitions and the Promotion of Capability*. Cheltenham: Edward Elgar, pp. 208–28.

Dilling, O., M. Herberg and G. Winter (eds) (2008), *Responsible Business: Self-Governance and Law in Transnational Economic Transactions*. Oxford and Portland, OR: Hart.

Doeringer, P.B. and M.H. Piore (1971), *Internal Labor Markets and Manpower Analysis*. Lexington, MA: D.C. Heath, pp. 5–16.

Domergue, P. (1987), 'La convention de conversion', *Droit social* No. 3 (March 1987), 250–58.

Donovan Report (1968), Royal Commission on Trade Unions and Employers' Associations 1965–68. Report. Cmnd. 3623. London: HMSO.

Doorey, D.J. (2005), 'Who Made That? Influencing Foreign Labour Practices Through Reflexive Domestic Disclosure Regulation', *Osgoode Hall Law Journal*, **43**(4), 353–405.

Doorey, D.J. (2010), 'In Defense of Transnational Domestic Labor Regulation', *Vanderbilt Journal of Transnational Law*, **43**(3), 953–1010.

Dore, R. (1986), *Flexible Rigidities: Industrial Policy and Structural Adjustment in the Japanese Economy 1970–1980*. Stanford, CA: Stanford University Press.

DTI (2002), *Green Paper: High Performance Workplaces: The Role of Employee Involvement in a Modern Economy: A Discussion Paper*. London: Department of Trade and Industry.

DTI (2004), *DTI Guidance: The Information and Consultation of Employees Regulations*. London: Department of Trade and Industry.

Dukes, R. (2008), 'Constitutionalizing Employment Relations: Sinzheimer, Kahn-Freund, and the Role of Labour Law', *Journal of Law and Society*, **35**(3), 341–63.

Dunlop, J.T. (1958), *Industrial Relations Systems*. New York: Holt.

Dunlop, J.T. (1984), *Dispute Resolution. Negotiation and Consensus Building*. Denver: Auburn.

Dunlop, J.T. (1993 [1958]), *Industrial Relations Systems*. Revised edition with a new preface. Boston: Harvard Business School.

Dunning, J.H. (1992), *The Globalization of Business*. London: Routledge.

Dunning, J.H. (2001), *Global Capitalism at Bay*. London and New York: Routledge.

Ebbinghaus, B. (1999), 'Does a European Social Model Exist and Can It Survive?' In G. Huemer, M. Mesch and F. Traxler (eds), *The Role of Employer Associations and Labour Unions in the EMU. Institutional Requirements for European Economic Policies*. Aldershot: Ashgate, pp. 1–26.

Eder, K. (1986), 'Prozedurale Rationalität. Moderne Rechtsentwicklung jenseits von formaler Rationalität', *Zeitschrift für Rechtssoziologie*, **7**(1), 1–30.

Edwards, T., P. Marginson, P. Edwards, A. Ferner and O. Tregaskis (2007), *Corporate Social Responsibility in Multinational Companies: Management Initiatives or Negotiated Agreements*. ILO Discussion Paper Series. Geneva: International Labour Organization.

Ehrenberg, R.G. and G.H. Jakubson (1994), 'Why WARN? The Impact of Recent Plant-Closing and Lay-off Prenotification Legislation in the United States', in C.F. Buechtemann (ed), *Employment Security and Labor Market Behaviour. Interdisciplinary Approaches and International Evidence*. Ithaca: ILR Press, pp. 200–214.

Ehrlich, E. (2002 [1936]), *Fundamental Principles of the Sociology of Law*. New Brunswick, NJ: Transaction Publishers.

Ellis, E. and P. Watson (2012), *EU Anti-Discrimination Law*. 2nd edition. Oxford: Oxford University Press.

Elster, J. (1979), *Ulysses and the Sirens. Studies in Rationality and Irrationality*. Cambridge: Cambridge University Press.

Enclos, P. (1990), 'Le contentieux de l'insuffisance professionnelle dans les contrats de formation en alternance', *Droit social*, No 12, 896–903.

Esping-Anderson, G. (ed) (1996), *Welfare States in Transition. National Adaptations in Global Economies*. London: Sage, pp. 256–67.

Esping-Anderson, G. and M. Regini (eds) (2000), *Why Deregulate Labour Markets?* Oxford: Oxford University Press.

Estlund, C. (2003), *Working Together. How Workplace Bonds Strengthen a Diverse Democracy*. Oxford and New York: Oxford University Press.

Estlund, C. (2010), *Regoverning the Workplace. From Self-Regulation to Co-Regulation*. New Haven and London: Yale University Press.

ETUI (European Trade Union Institute) (2000), *Observatoire social européen (OSE), Social Developments in the European Union 2000*. Second annual report. Brussels: ETUI.

Eurofound (European Foundation for the Improvement of Living and Working Conditions) (2007), *Varieties of Flexicurity: Reflections on Key Elements of Flexibility and Security*. Background paper. Dublin: Eurofound.

Eurofound (European Foundation for the Improvement of Living and Working Conditions) (2009), *European and International Framework Agreements: Practical Experiences and Strategic Approaches*. Dublin: Eurofound.

Eurofound (European Foundation for the Improvement of Living and Working Conditions) (2010a), *Comparative Analysis of Working Time in the European Union*. Dublin: Eurofound.

Eurofound (European Foundation for the Improvement of Living and Working Conditions) (2010b), *Working Poor in Europe – Germany*. European Working Conditions Observatory (EWCO). Available at http://www.eurofound.europa.eu/ewco/studies/tn0910026s/de0910029q.htm.

European Commission (1992), 'The Regulation of Working Conditions in the Member States of the European Community', Vol. 1, *Social Europe*, Supplement 4/92, Brussels.

European Commission (1993), White Paper on Growth, Competitiveness and Employment, COM (1993) 700 final.

European Commission (1994), White Paper on European Social Policy – A Way Forward for the Union, COM (1994) 333 final.

European Commission (1995), The Future of Social Protection: A Framework for a European Debate, COM (1995) 466 final.

European Commission (1997), Communication from the Commission – Modernising and Improving Social Protection in the European Union, COM (1997) 102 final.

European Commission (1998a), Proposal for a Council Regulation on Coordination of Social Security Systems, COM (1998) 779 final.

European Commission (1998b), On the Organisation of Working Time in the Sectors and Activities Excluded from Directive 93/104/EC of 23 November 1993, Communication, COM (1998) 662 final.

European Commission (1998c), Communication on the Organisation of Working Time in the Sectors and Activities Excluded from Directive 93/104/EC of 23 November 1993, COM (1998) 662 final.

European Commission (1999), Communication on a Concerted Strategy for Modernising Social Protection, COM (1999) 347.

European Commission (2000), Communication from the Commission to the Council, the European Parliament, the Economic and Social Committee and the Committee of the Regions, Social Policy Agenda 2/26, COM (2000) 379 final.

European Commission (2001a), White Paper on European Governance, COM (2001) 428 final.

European Commission (2001b), Employment and Social Policies: Framework for Investing in Quality, COM (2001) 313.

European Commission (2001c), Communication on Promoting Core Labour Standards and Improving Social Governance in the Context of Globalization, COM (2001) 416 final.

European Commission (2002), Communication on Corporate Social Responsibility: A Business Contribution to Sustainable Development, COM (2002) 347 final.

European Commission (2003a), Communication on Strengthening the Social Dimension of the Lisbon Strategy: Streamlining Open Coordination in the Field of Social Protection, COM (2003) 261 final.

European Commission (2003b), Communication on the Future of the European Employment Strategy (EES), 'A strategy for full employment and better jobs for all', COM (2003) 6 final.

European Commission (2003c), Amended Proposal for a Regulation of the European Parliament and of the Council on Coordination of Social Security Systems, COM (2003) 596 final.

European Commission (2003d), Jobs, Jobs, Jobs. Creating More Employment in Europe, Report of the Employment Taskforce chaired by Wim Kok ('Kok I'), November 2003, Luxembourg: Office of the European Communities.

European Commission (2003e), Proposal for a Council Decision Establishing a Social Protection Committee, COM (2003) 305 final.

European Commission (2004a), Communication on Modernising Social Protection for the Development of High-Quality, Accessible and Sustainable Health Care and Long-Term Care; Support for the National Strategies using the 'Open Method of Coordination', COM (2004) 304 final.

European Commission (2004b), Facing the Challenge. The Lisbon Strategy for Growth and Employment, Report from the High Level Group chaired by Wim Kok ('Kok II'), November 2004, Luxembourg: Office of the European Communities.

European Commission (2004c), Proposal for a Directive amending Directive 2003/88/EC Concerning Certain Aspects of the Organisation of Working Time, COM (2004) 607 final.

European Commission (2004d), Report of the High Level Group on the Future of Social Policy in an Enlarged European Union. Directorate-General for Employment and Social Affairs.

European Commission (2006a), Modernising Labour Law to Meet the Challenges of the Twenty-First Century, Green Paper, COM (2006) 708 final.

European Commission (2006b), Communication on Implementing the Partnership for Growth and Jobs: Making Europe a Pole of Excellence on Corporate Social Responsibility, COM (2006) 0136 final.

European Commission (2007), Towards Common Principles of Flexicurity: More and Better Jobs through Flexibility and Security. Brussels: Directorate-General for Employment, Social Affairs and Equal Opportunities

European Commission (2010a), Communication EUROPE 2020 – A Strategy for Smart, Sustainable and Inclusive Growth, COM (2010) 2020 final.

European Commission (2010b), Lisbon Strategy Evaluation Document, SEC (2010), 114 final.

European Commission (2010c), Detailed Report on the Implementation by Member States of Directive 2003/88/EC Concerning Certain Aspects of the Organisation of Working Time ('The Working Time Directive'), Commission Staff Working Paper, SEC (2010) 1611 final.

European Commission (2010d), Communication Reviewing the Working Time Directive. COM (2010) 801 final.

European Commission (2012a), New Skills and Jobs in Europe: Pathways Towards Full Employment. Evaluation Report compiled by Günther Schmid. Luxembourg: Publications Office of the European Union.

European Commission (2012b), Transnational Company Agreements: Realising the Potential of Social Dialogue, Commission Staff Working Document, SWD (2012) 264 final.

European Convention on the Constitution (2003), Final Report of Working Group XI on Social Europe, CONV 516/03 20.

European Council (2000), Lisbon European Council, Presidency Conclusions, 23–24 March 2000, 100/1/00.

European Council (2002), Barcelona European Council, Presidency Conclusions, 15–16 March 2002, 100/1/02.

European Council (2006), Presidency Conclusions on the Social Dimension of the Revised Lisbon Strategy at the Informal EPSCO Council Meeting Villach, 20/1/2006.

European Economic and Social Committee (2004), Improving the Implementation of the Lisbon Strategy, ECO/153 – CESE 1438/2004.

Ewing, K.D. (ed) (1996), *Working Life: New Perspective on Labour Law.* London: Lawrence & Wishart.

Ewing, K. (2005), 'The Function of Trade Unions', *Industrial Law Journal*, **34**(1), 1–22.

Fairbrother P. and N. Hammer (2005), 'Global Unions: Past Efforts and Future Prospects', *Relations Industrielles/Industrial Relations*, **60**(3), 405–31.

Falke, J., A. Höland, B. Rohde and G. Zimmermann (1981), Kündigungspraxis und Kündigungsschutz in der Bundesrepublik Deutschland. Forschungsbericht des Bundesminmisters für Arbeit und Sozialordnung, Bd. 47.Bonn.

Falkner, G., E. Holzleithner and O. Treib (2008), *Compliance in the Enlarged European Union. Living Rights or Dead Letters?* Aldershot: Ashgate.

Falkner, G., O. Treib, M. Hartlapp and S. Leiber (2005), *Complying with Europe: EU Harmonisation and Soft Law in the Member States.* Cambridge: Cambridge University Press.

Feronas, A. (2004), The Europeanization of National Social Policies through the OMC, The Case of Greek Employment Policy. Paper for Contribution at the ESPAnet, Conference Oxford, 9–11 September.

Ferrera, M. (2004), 'Modernising the European Social Model: Sharpening Priorities, Stepping up Reforms', *Progressive Politics*, **3**(3), 70–77.

Fetzer, T. (2010), 'Industrial Democracy in the European Community: Trade Unions as a Defensive transnational Community', in M.-L. Djelic and S. Quack (eds), *Transnational Communities Shaping Global Economic Governance.* Cambridge: Cambridge University Press, pp. 282–304.

Fichter, M. and J. Sydow (2002), 'Using Networks Towards Global Labor Standards? Organizing Social Responsibility in Global Production Chains', *Industrielle Beziehungen*, **9**(4), 357–80.

Fischer-Lescano, A. and G. Teubner (2004), 'Regime-Collisions: The Vain Search for Legal Unity in the Fragmentation of Global Law', *Michigan Journal of International Law*, **25**(4), 999–1045.

Flanders, A. (1970), *Management and Trade Unions: The Theory and Reform of Industrial Relations.* London: Faber.

Flanders, A. (1974), 'The Tradition of Voluntarism', *British Journal of Industrial Relations*, **12**(3), 352–70.

Flohr, A., S. Schwindenhammer, K.D. Wolf and L. Rieth (2010), *The Role of Business in Global Governance: Corporations as Norm-Entrepreneurs.* Houndsmill, Basingstoke: Palgrave Macmillan.

Flood, J. (2008), 'Globalisation and Large Law Firms', in P. Cane and J. Conaghan (eds), *The New Oxford Companion to Law.* Oxford: Oxford University Press, pp. 501–2.

Forst, R. (2011), *The Right to Justification. Elements of a Constructivist Theory of Justice*. New York: Columbia University Press.

Forst, R. and K. Günther (eds) (2011), *Die Herausbildung normativer Ordnungen – Interdisziplinäre Perspektiven*. Frankfurt am Main and New York: Campus.

Foster, K. (2003), 'Is There a Global Sports Law?', *Entertainment Law*, **2**(1), 1–18.

Fraenkel, E. (1973 [1958]), 'Hugo Sinzheimer', in E. Fraenkel, *Reformismus und Pluralismus*, F. Esche and F. Grube (eds). Hamburg: Hofmann und Campe, pp. 11–26.

Freedland, M. (2003), *The Personal Employment Contract*. Oxford: Oxford University Press.

Freedland, M. and N. Kountouris (2011), *The Legal Construction of Personal Work Relations*. New York: Oxford University Press.

Freeman, R.B. and J. Medoff (1984), *What Do Unions Do?* New York: Basic Books.

Fuchs, M. (2002), 'Free Movement of Services and Social Security-Quo Vadis?', *European Law Journal*, **8**(4), 536–55.

Fuchs, S. and R. Schettkat (2000), 'Germany: A Regulated Flexibility', in G. Esping-Anderson and M. Regini (eds), *Why Deregulate Labour Markets?* Oxford: Oxford University Press, pp. 211–44.

Fuller, L.L. (1963), 'Collective Bargaining and the Arbitrator', *Wisconsin Law Review* **1963**(1), 3–46.

Fuller, L.L. (1978–79), 'The Forms and Limits of Adjudication', *Harvard Law Review*, **92**(2), 353–92.

Fung, A., D. O'Rourke and C. Sabel (2001), *Can We Put an End To Sweatshops?* Boston: Beacon Press.

Gash, V. and F. McGinnity (2007), 'Fixed-term Contracts – the New European Inequality? Comparing Men and Women in West Germany and France', *Socioeconomic Review*, **5**(3), 467–96.

Gazier, B. (2002), 'Transitional Labour Markets: From Positive Analysis to Policy Proposals', in G. Schmid and B. Gazier (eds), *The Dynamics of Full Employment: Social Integration Through Transitional Labour Markets*. Cheltenham: Edward Elgar, pp. 196–232.

Gazier, B. (2003), *Tous 'sublimes': vers un nouveau plein-emploi*. Paris: Flammarion.

Gazier, B. and. A. Lechevalier (2008), 'The European Employment Strategy and Transitional Labour Markets: Macroeconomic Policy and Institutional Regimes', in R. Rogowski (ed), *The European Social Model and Transitional Labour Markets – Law and Policy*. Aldershot: Ashgate, pp. 107–23.

Gerstenberg, O. (1997), 'Law's Polyarchy: A Comment on Cohen and Sabel', *European Law Journal,* **3**(4), 343–58.

Gerstenberg O. and C.F. Sabel (2002), 'Directly-Deliberative Polyarchy: An Institutional Idea for Europe', in C. Joerges and R. Dehousse (eds), *Good Governance in Europe's Integrated Market.* Oxford: Oxford University Press, pp. 289–341.

Gessner, V. (1998), 'Globalization and Legal Certainty', in V. Gessner and A.C. Budak (eds), *Emerging Legal Certainties – Empirical Studies on the Globalisation of Law.* Dartmouth: Ashgate, pp. 427–50.

Ghai, D. (2006), 'Decent Work: Universality and Diversity', in D. Ghai (ed), *Decent Work: Objectives and Strategies.* Geneva: International Labour Office, International Institute for Labour Studies, pp. 1–31.

Giddens, A. (1990), *The Consequences of Modernity.* Cambridge: Polity.

Gilbert, N. and A. Etzioni (2004), *Transformation of the Welfare State: The Silent Surrender of Public Responsibility.* Oxford and New York: Oxford University Press.

Gilbert, N. and B. Gilbert (1989), *The Enabling State: Modern Welfare Capitalism in America.* Oxford and New York: Oxford University Press.

Gladstone, A. (2010), 'Settlement of Disputes over Rights', in R. Blanpain (ed), *Comparative Labour Law and Industrial Relations in Industrialized Market Economies.* 10th edition. Deventer: Kluwer, pp. 720–50.

Glinski, C. (2008), 'Bridging the Gap: The Legal Potential of Private Regulation', in O. Dilling, M. Herberg and G. Winter (eds), *Responsible Business: Self-Governance and Law in Transnational Economic Transactions.* Oxford and Portland, OR: Hart, pp. 41–66.

Goetschy, J. (2003), 'The European Employment Strategy, Multi-level Governance, and Policy Coordination, Past, Present and Future', in J. Zeitlin and D. Trubek (eds), *Governing Work and Welfare in a New Economy – European and American Experiments.* Oxford: Oxford University Press, pp. 59–87.

Goetschy, J. (2012), 'The Lisbon Strategy, Industrial Relations and Social Europe: An Assessment of Theoretical Frameworks and Policy Developments', in S. Smismans (ed), *The European Union and Industrial Relations – New Procedures, New Context.* Manchester: Manchester University Press, pp. 190–205.

Gold, M. (1993), 'Overview of the Social Dimension', in M. Gold (ed), *The Social Dimension. Employment Policy in the European Community.* London: Macmillan, pp. 121–39.

Gold, M. (2010), 'Employee Participation in the EU. The Long and Winding Road to Legislation', *Economic and Industrial Democracy,* **31**(4S), 9–23.

Goldman, A. (2010), 'Settlement of Disputes over Interests', in R. Blanpain (ed), *Comparative Labour Law and Industrial Relations in Industrialized Market Economies*. 10th edition. Deventer: Kluwer, pp. 751–84.

Goll, U. (1980), *Arbeitskampfparität und Tariferfolg, Versuch einer rechtstatsächlichen Fundierung arbeitskampfrechtlicher Fragestellungen unter Berücksichtigung der 'collective bargaining'-Theorien*. Berlin: Duncker and Humblot.

Gollan, P. J. (2006), *Employee Representation in Non-Union Firms*. London: Sage.

Goodrich, P. (1999), 'Anti-Teubner: Autopoiesis, Paradox, and the Theory of Law', *Social Epistemology*, **13**(2), 197–214.

Gorter, C. (2000), 'The Dutch Miracle?' In G. Esping-Anderson and M. Regini (eds), *Why Deregulate Labour Markets?* Oxford: Oxford University Press, pp. 181–210.

Gospel, H. and P. Willman (2002), *The Right to Know: Disclosure of Information for Collective Bargaining and Joint Consultation in Germany, France, and Great Britain*. Discussion Paper No. 453, London, Centre for Economic Performance, London School of Economics.

Gould, W.B. (1993), 'Employment Protection and Job Security in the United States and Japan', in C.F. Buechtemann (ed), *Employment Security and Labor Market Behaviour. Interdisciplinary Approaches and International Evidence*. Ithaca: ILR Press, pp. 165–79.

Grant, C., K. Barysch and H. Brady (2009), *Cameron's Europe: Can the Conservatives Achieve their EU Objectives?* London: Centre for European Reform (CER).

Günther, K. (2004), 'Anwaltsimperien', in *Neue Rechtsordnungen. Kursbuch*, Heft 155, Berlin: Rowohlt, pp. 1–14.

Habermas, J. (1986), *Theory of Communicative Action. Vol. 2: Lifeworld and System*. Cambridge: Polity.

Habermas, J. (1987), *The Philosophical Discourse of Modernity*. Cambridge: Polity.

Habermas, J. (1996a), *Between Facts and Norms. Contributions to a Discourse Theory of Law and Democracy*. Cambridge: Polity.

Habermas, J. (1996b), 'Reply to Symposium Participants, Benjamin N. Cardozo School of Law', *Cardozo Law Review*, **17**(5), 1477–1558.

Habermas, J. (2006), 'Does the Constitutionalization of International Law Still Have a Chance?' In J. Habermas, *The Divided West*. Cambridge: Polity, pp. 115–93.

Habermas, J. (2008), 'A Political Constitution for the Pluralist World Society?' In J. Habermas, *Between Naturalism and Religion*. Cambridge: Polity, pp. 312–52.

Habermas, J. (2009), 'The Constitutionalization of International Law

and the Legitimation Problems of a Constitution for World Society',
in J. Habermas, *Europe: The Faltering Project*. Cambridge: Polity, pp.
165–201.

Habermas, J. (2012), 'The Crisis of the European Union in the Light
of a Constitutionalization of International Law – An Essay on the
Constitution of Europe', in J. Habermas, *The Crisis of the European
Union: A Response*. Cambridge: Polity, pp. 127–47.

Habermas, J. and N. Luhmann (1971), *Theorie der Gesellschaft oder
Sozialtechnologie*. Frankfurt am Main: Suhrkamp.

Hall, M. and J. Purcell (2012), *Consultation at Work – Regulation and
Practice*. Oxford: Oxford University Press.

Hamann, K. (2012), *The Politics of Industrial Relations: Labor Unions in
Spain*. New York and Abingdon: Routledge.

Hampton Report (2005), *Reducing Administrative Burdens: Effective
Inspection and Enforcement*. London: HM Treasury/ HMSO.

Harris, L., A. Tuckmana and J. Snooka (2012), 'Supporting Workplace
Dispute Resolution in Smaller Businesses: Policy Perspectives and
Operational Realities', *The International Journal of Human Resource
Management*, **23**(3), 607–623.

Hart, H.L.A. (1997), *The Concept of Law*. 2nd edition. Oxford: Clarendon
Press.

Hartlapp, M. (2005), *Die Kontrolle der nationalen Rechtsdurchsetzung
durch die Europäische Kommission*. Frankfurt am Main and New York:
Campus.

Hartmann, M. (1987), 'Reflexives Recht am Ende? Zum Eindringen
materiellen Rechts in die Tarifautonomie', *Zeitschrift für Soziologie*,
16(44), 16–32.

Hartwich, H.-H. (1996), 'Der Zerfall des Rechts der Arbeit', *Gwerkschaftliche
Monatshefte*, **11**(12), 742–7.

Hay, C., M. Watson and D. Wincott (1999), 'Globalisation, European
Integration and the Persistence of European Social Models', Working
Paper 3/99, POLSIS University of Birmingham.

Hayek, F.A. (1976). *Law, Legislation and Liberty. A New Statement of the
Liberal Principles of Justice and Political Economy, Vol.2: The Mirage of
Social Justice*. London: Routledge and Kegan Paul.

Heidenreich, M. and J. Zeitlin (eds) (2009), *Changing European Employment
and Welfare Regimes – The Influence of the Open Method of Coordination
on National Reforms*. London: Routledge.

Heijden, P.F. van der (1998), *Wege aus der Beschäftigungskrise: Das hol-
ländische Beispiel*. Cologne: Bund.

Hemerijck, A. (2002), 'The Self-Transformation of the European Social
Models', in G. Esping-Andersen, D. Gallie, A. Hemerijck and J. Myles

(eds), *Why We Need a New Welfare State*. Oxford: Oxford University Press, pp. 1–25.

Hemerijck, A. (2004), Recasting Europe's Semi-Sovereign Welfare States and the Role of the EU. Paper and talk delivered in the WZB seminar series 'The European Social Model' on 16 December 2004, Berlin. Available at http://www.europeanstudiesalliance.org/calendar/fall04 events/hemerijckPaper.pdf.

Henry, S. (1983), *Private Justice. Towards Integrated Theorising in the Sociology of Law*. London: RKP.

Hepple, B. (1981), 'A Right to Work?', *Industrial Law Journal*, **10**(1), 65–83.

Hepple, B. (1986), 'Restructuring Employment Rights', *Industrial Law Journal*, **15**(1), 69–83.

Hepple, B. (1993), 'United Kingdom', in R. Blanpain (ed), *Temporary Work and Labour Law*. Deventer: Kluwer, pp. 123–53.

Hepple, B. (2005), *Labour Laws and Global Trade*. Oxford and Portland, OR: Hart.

Hepple, B. (2006), 'Rights at Work', in D. Ghai (ed), *Decent Work: Objectives and Strategies*. Geneva: International Labour Office, International Institute for Labour Studies, pp. 33–75.

Hepple, B. (2010 [1986]), 'Welfare Legislation and Wage-Labour', in B. Hepple (ed), *The Making of Labour Law in Europe*. Portland and Portland, OR: Hart, pp. 114–53.

Hepple, B. (2011), 'Enforcing Equality Law: Two Steps Forward and Two Steps Backwards for Reflexive Regulation', *Industrial Law Journal*, **40**(4), 315–35.

Hepple, B. (2012), 'Agency Enforcement of Workplace Equality', in L. Dickens (ed), *Making Employment Rights Effective – Issues of Enforcement and Compliance*. Oxford and Portland, OR: Hart, pp. 49–66.

Herberg, M. (2007), *Globalisierung und private Selbstregulierung – Umweltschutz in multinationalen Unternehmen*. Frankfurt am Main and New York: Campus.

Herding, R. (1972), *Job Control and Union Structure: A study on Plant Level Industrial Conflict in the United States with a Comparative Perspective on West Germany*. Rotterdam: Rotterdam University Press.

Hervey, T. (1995), 'Migrant Workers and their Families in the European Union: the Pervasive Market Ideology of Community Law', in J. Shaw and G. More (eds), *New Legal Dynamics of European Union*. Oxford: Clarendon Press, pp. 91–110.

Hervey, T. (1998), *European Social Law and Policy*. London, New York: Longman.

Hervey, T. (2000), 'Social Solidarity: a Buttress Against Internal Market

Law?' In J. Shaw (ed), *Social Law and Policy in an Evolving European Union*. Oxford and Portland, OR: Hart, pp. 31–47.

Hervey, T. and J. Kenner (2003), *Economic and Social Rights under the EU Charter of Fundamental Rights: a Legal Perspective*. Oxford and Portland, OR: Hart.

Hirsch, J.M. (2012), 'A Comparative Perspective on Unjust Dismissal Laws'. UNC Legal Studies Research Paper No. 2095336. Available at http://papers.ssrn.com/sol3/papers.cfm?abstract_id=2095336.

Höcker, H. and B. Reissert (1995), *Beschäftigungsbrücken durch Stellenvertreterregelung in Dänemark und Schweden*. Berlin: Arbeitsmarktpolitische Schriftenreihe der Senatsverwaltung für Arbeit und Frauen.

Hodson, D. and I. Maher (2001), 'The Open Method as a New Mode of Governance – The Case of Soft Economic Policy Co-ordination', *Journal of Common Market Studies*, **39**(4), 719–46.

Hoffmann, E.A. (2012), *Co-operative Workplace Dispute Resolution. Organizational Structure, Ownership, and Ideology*. Farnham: Gower.

Höland, A. (1985), *Das Verhalten des Betriebsrats bei Kündigungen*. Frankfurt am Main and New York: Campus.

Holden, C. (2003), 'Decommodification and the Workfare State', *Political Studies Review*, **1**, 303–16.

Hyde, A. (1998), 'Silicon Valley's High-Velocity Labour Market', *Journal for Applied Corporate Finance*, **11**(2), 28–37.

Hyde, A. (2002), 'A Closer Look at the Emerging Employment Law of Silicon Valley's High-Velocity Labour Market', in J. Conaghan, R.M. Fischl and K. Klare (eds), *Labour Law in an Era of Globalization. Transformative Practices and Possibilities*. Oxford: Oxford University Press, pp. 233–51.

Hyde, A. (2003), *Working in Silicon Valley: Economic and Legal Analysis of a High-velocity Labor Market*. Armonk, NY and London: M.E. Sharpe.

Hyman, R. (1989), *The Political Economy of Industrial Relations. Theory and Practice in a Cold Climate*. London: Macmillan.

Hyman, R. (2010), 'Trade Unions, and Options for Solidarity', in A. Biele and I. Lindberg (eds), *Global Restructuring, Labour, and the Challenges for Transnational Solidarity*. Abingdon, Oxon and New York: Routledge.

ILO (1999), Report by the Director-General: 'Decent work'. 87th Session of the International Labour Conference. Geneva: International Labour Office.

ILO (2000), 'Your Voice at Work', *World of Work* 35. Geneva: International Labour Office, pp. 4–11.

ILO (2004), 'A Fair Globalization: Creating Opportunities for All'. Report of the World Commission on the Social Dimension of Globalization. Geneva: International Labour Office.

ILO (2008), 'The Decent Work Agenda – Looking Back, Looking Forward: A Growing Consensus', *World of Work* 64. Geneva: International Labour Office, pp. 6–9.

ILO (2012a), 'Social Justice for a Fair Globalization'. General Survey on the fundamental Conventions concerning rights at work in light of the ILO Declaration on Social Justice for a Fair Globalization 2008. Geneva: International Labour Office.

ILO (2012b), *Fundamental Principles and Rights at Work: From Commitment to Action*. Geneva: International Labour Office.

International Organisation of Employers (2006), 'The Evolving Debate on Trade & Labour Standards'. IOE Information Paper. Available at http://www.wto.org/english/forums_e/ngo_e/posp63_ioe_e.pdf.

Jacobs, A.T.J.M. (2004), *Labour Law in the Netherlands*. Deventer: Kluwer.

Jacobs, A.T.J.M. (2010), 'The Law of Strikes and Lock-outs', in R. Blanpain (ed), *Comparative Labour Law and Industrial Relations in Industrialized Market Economies*, 10th edition. Deventer: Kluwer, pp. 659–720.

Jenks, C.W. (1960), *Human Rights and International Labour Standards*. London: Stevens.

Jenks, C.W. (1969), *A New World of Law? A Study of the Creative Imagination in International Law*. Harlow: Longmans.

Jepsen, M. and A. Serrano Pasqual (2005), 'The European Social Model: an Exercise in Deconstruction', *Journal of European Social Policy*, **15**(3), 231–45.

Jepsen, M. and A. Serrano Pasqual (eds) (2006), *Unwrapping the European Social Model*. Bristol: Policy Press.

Jessop, B. (1993), 'Towards a Schumpeterian Workfare State? Preliminary Remarks on Post-Fordist Political Economy', *Studies in Political Economy*, **40**(7), 7–39.

Jessop, B. (2002), *The Future of the Capitalist State*. Cambridge: Polity.

Jimeno, J.F. and L. Toharia (1993), 'Spanish Labour Markets: Institutions and Outcomes', in J. Hartog and J. Theeuwes (eds), *Labour Market Contracts and Institutions. A Cross-National Comparison*. Amsterdam: North-Holland, pp. 299–322.

Joost, D. (2000), 'Deregulation and Labour Law in Germany', in R. Blanpain, R. Yamakawa and T. Araki (eds), *Deregulation and Labour Law – In Search of a Labour Concept for the 21st Century*. Bulletin of Comparative Labour Relations No. 38. The Hague: Kluwer, pp. 59–68.

Jørgensen, H. (2005), 'The European Employment Strategy up for Revision

– Effective Policy or European Cosmetics?' In T. Bredgaard and F. Larsen (eds), *Employment Policy from Different Angles*. Copenhagen: DJØF Publishing, pp. 23–46.

Kahn-Freund, O. (1978 [1954]), 'Intergroup Conflicts and their Settlement', in O. Kahn-Freund, *Selected Writings. Published under the Auspices of the Modern Law Review*. London: Stevens, pp. 41–78.

Kahn-Freund, O. (1983 [1972]), *Labour and the Law*. 3rd edition by P. Davies and M. Freedland. London: Stevens.

Kajtár, E. and R. Rogowski (2005), 'The Role of the European Employment Strategy in Activating Hungarian Labour Market Policies: Personalised Services, Educational Reform and Peer Review', in J. de Koning (ed), *Employment and Training Policies in Central and Eastern Europe*. Amsterdam: Dutch University Press, pp. 151–67.

Kaps, P. and H. Schütz (2011), 'Privatization of Placement Services in Light of the Transitional Labour Market Approach', in R. Rogowski, R. Salais and N. Whiteside (eds), *Transforming European Employment Policy, Labour Market Transitions and the Promotion of Capability*. Cheltenham: Edward Elgar, pp. 229–54.

Kaufman, B.E. (2004), *The Global Evolution of Industrial Relations: Events, Ideas and the IIRA: Ideas, People and the International Industrial Relations Association (IIRA)*. Geneva: International Labour Office.

Kearney, N. (1999), 'Corporate Codes of Conduct: the Privatized Application of Labour Standards', in S. Picciotto and R. Mayne (eds), *Regulating International Business: Beyond Liberalization*. Basingstoke: Macmillan, pp. 205–20.

Keller, B. and H. Seifert (1993), 'Regulierung atypischer Beschäftigungsverhältnisse', *WSI-Mitteilungen*, **46**(3), 538–45.

Keller, B. and H. Seifert (1997), 'Zwischenbilanz der Deregulierung', *WSI-Mitteilungen*, **50**(8), 478–89.

Kelsen, H. (1967), *Pure Theory of Law*. 2nd edition. Berkeley and Los Angeles, CA: University of California Press.

Keune, M. (2012), 'Flexicurity: a New Impulse for Social Dialogue in Europe?' In S. Smismans (ed), *The European Union and Industrial Relations – New Procedures, New Context*. Manchester: Manchester University Press, pp. 206–24.

Kilpatrick, C. (2001), 'Gender Equality, A Fundamental Dialogue', in S. Sciarra (ed), *Labour Law in the Courts, National Judges and the European Court of Justice*. Oxford and Portland, OR: Hart, pp. 31–130.

Kilpatrick, C. (2006), 'New EU Employment Governance and Constitutionalism', in G. de Burca and J. Scott (eds), *Law and New Governance in the EU and the US*. Oxford and Portland, OR: Hart, pp. 121–51.

King, J. (2012), *Judging Social Rights*. Cambridge: Cambridge University Press.

King, M. (2006), 'What's the Use of Luhmann's Theory?' In M. King and C. Thornhill (eds), *Luhmann on Law and Politics*. Oxford and Portland, OR: Hart, pp. 37–52.

King, M. and C. Thornhill (2003), *Niklas Luhmann's Theory of Politics and Law*. London: Palgrave.

Kingsbury, B., N. Krisch and R.B. Stewart (2005), 'The Emergence of Global Administrative Law', *Law and Contemporary Problems*, **68**(3), 15–62.

Kjaer, P.F. (2010), *Between Governing and Governance. On the Emergence, Function and Form of Europe's Post-National Condition*. Oxford and Portland, OR: Hart.

Kjaer, P.F. (2011), 'Legitimacy Through Constitutionalism', in P.F. Kjaer, G. Teubner and A. Febbrajo (eds), *The Financial Crisis in Constitutional Perspective. The Dark Side of Functional Differentiation*. Oxford and Portland, OR: Hart, pp. 395–430.

Kjaer, P.F. (2012), 'Law and Order Within and Beyond National Configurations', in A. Mascerano and K. Araujo (eds), *Legitimization in World Society*. Farnham: Ashgate, pp. 99–114.

Kjaer, P.F., G. Teubner and A. Febbrajo (eds) (2011), *The Financial Crisis in Constitutional Perspective. The Dark Side of Functional Differentiation*. Oxford and Portland, OR: Hart.

Klare, K. (1978), 'Judicial Deradicalization of the Wagner Act and the Origins of Modern Legal Consciousness, 1937–1941', *Minnesota Law Review*, **62**(3), 265–339.

Kleinman, M. (2002), 'A European Welfare State? European Union Social Policy in Context', *Journal of Social Policy*, **31**(4), 753–78.

Klosse, S. (2005), 'The European Employment Strategy: Which Way Forward?', *The International Journal of Comparative Labour Law and Industrial Relations*, **21**(1), 5–36.

Knodt, E.M. (1995), 'Foreword', in N. Luhmanned, *Social Systems*. Stanford: Stanford University Press, pp. IX–XXXVI.

Kocher, E. (2008), 'Codes of Conduct and Framework Agreements on Social Minimum Standards – Private Regulation?' In O. Dilling, M. Herberg and G. Winter (eds), *Responsible Business: Self-Governance and Law in Transnational Economic Transactions*. Oxford and Portland, OR: Hart, pp. 67–86.

Kolben, K. (2010), 'Labor Rights as Human Rights?', *Virginia Journal of International Law*, **50**(2), 449–84.

Kolben, K. (2011), 'Transnational Labor Regulation and the Limits of Governance', *Theoretical Inquiries in Law*, **12**(2), 403–37.

Koskenniemi, M. (2007), 'The Fate of Public International Law: Between Technique and Politics', *The Modern Law Review*, **70**(1), 1–30.

Kott, S. and J. Droux (eds) (2013), *Globalizing Social Rights. The International Labor Organization and Beyond*. Geneva and London: International Labour Office and Palgrave MacMillan.

Koukiadaki, A. (2009), 'Reflexive Law and the Reformulation of EC-Level Employee Consultation Norms in the British Systems of Labour Law and Industrial Relations', *International Journal of Law in Context*, **5**(4), 393–416.

Krasner, S.D. (ed) (1982), 'Structural Causes and Regime Consequences: Regimes as Intervening Variables', *International Organization*, **36**(2), 185–205.

Krasner, S.D. (ed) (1983), *International Regimes*. Ithaca, NY: Cornell University Press.

Krisch, N. (2010), *Beyond Constitutionalism. The Pluralist Structure of Postnational Law*. Oxford: Oxford University Press.

Kronke, H. (1990), *Regulierungen auf dem Arbeitsmarkt. Kernbereiche des Arbeitsrechts im internationalen Vergleich*. Baden-Baden: Nomos.

Krugman, P. (2009), *The Return of Depression Economics and the Crisis of 2008*. New York: W.W. Norton.

Krugman, P. (2012), *End this Depression Now!* New York: W.W. Norton.

Kubo, K. (1995), *Hugo Sinzheimer – Vater des deutschen Arbeitsrechts*. Cologne: Bund-Verlag.

Ladeur, K.-H. (1995), *Postmoderne Rechtstheorie. Selbstreferenz – Selbstorganisation – Prozeduralisierung*. 2nd edition. Berlin: Duncker & Humblot.

Ladeur, K.-H. (2012), 'The Evolution of the Law and the Possibility of a "Global Law" Extending beyond the Sphere of the State – Simultaneously, a Critique of the "Self-constitutionalisation" Thesis', *ANCILLA IURIS 2012*, 220–55.

Larrea Gayarre, J. (1992), 'Labour Market Flexibility and Work Organisation Activities in Spain', in OECD, *New Directions in Work Organisation. The Industrial Relations Response*. Paris: OECD, pp. 136–54.

Leighton, P. (2011), 'Classifying Employment Relationships – More Sliding Doors or a Better Regulatory Framework?', *Industrial Law Journal*, **40**(1), 5–44.

Lenoble, J. (2005), 'Open Method of Coordination and Theory of Reflexive Governance', in O. De Schutter and S. Deakin (eds), *Social Rights and Market Forces: Is the Open Method of Coordination of Employment and Social Policies the Future of Social Europe?* Brussels: Bruylant, pp. 19–38.

Lenoble, J. and M. Maesschalck (2010), *Democracy, Law and Governance*. Farnham: Ashgate.

Levin, H. (1980), 'Educational Vouchers and Social Policy', in R. Haskins and J.J. Gallagher (eds), *Care and Education of Young Children in America*. Norwood, NJ: Ablex Publishing Co, pp. 243–6.

Levin, H. (1983), 'Individual Entitlements', in H. Levin and H.G. Schutze (eds), *Financing Recurrent Education: Strategies for Increasing Employment, Job Opportunities and Productivity*. Beverly Hills, CA: Sage Publications, pp. 135–48.

Levin, H. (1991), 'The Economics of Educational Choice', *Economics of Education Review*, **10**(2), 137–58.

Levine, D.I. (1995), *Reinventing the Workplace: How Business and Employees Can Both Win*. Washington, D.C.: Brookings Institute.

Lewin, D. (1999), 'Theoretical and Empirical Research on the Grievance Procedure and Arbitration: A Critical Review', in A.E. Eaton and J.H. Keefe (eds), *Employment Dispute Resolution and Worker Rights in the Changing Workplace*. Champaign, IL: Industrial Relations Research Association, pp. 137–86.

Lewin, D. and R.B. Peterson (1988), *The Modern Grievance Procedure in the United States*. New York and London: Quorum.

Lewis, S. and J. Lewis (1996), *The Work-Family Challenge: Re-thinking Employment*. London: Sage.

Lieckweg, T. (2003), *Das Recht der Weltgesellschaft. Systemtheoretische Perspektiven auf die Globalisierung des Rechts*. Stuttgart: Lucius and Lucius.

Lindbeck, A. (1996), *Full Employment and the Welfare State*. IUI Working Paper No. 469. Stockholm.

Lipsky, D.B., R.L. Seeber and R. Fincher (2003), *Emerging Systems for Managing Workplace Conflict: Lessons from American Corporations for Managers and Dispute Resolution Professionals*. San Francisco: Jossey-Bass.

Lobel, O. (2004), 'The Renew Deal: The Fall of Regulation and the Rise of Governance in Contemporary Legal Thought', *Minnesota Law Review*, **89**(2), 342–470.

Locke, R.M., T. Kochan, M. Romis and F. Qin (2007a), 'Beyond Corporate Codes of Conduct: Work Organization and Labour Standards at Nike's Suppliers', *International Labour Review*, **146**(1–2), 21–37.

Locke, R.M., F. Qin and A. Brause (2007b), 'Does Monitoring Improve Labour Standards? Lessons from Nike', *Industrial and Labor Relations Review*, **61**(1), 1–25.

Locke R., B. Rissing and T. Pal (2012), *Complements or Substitutes? Private Codes, State Regulation and the Enforcement of Labour Standards in Global Supply Chains*. Massachusetts Institute of Technology Political Science Department Working Paper No. 2012-2. Cambridge, MA: MIT.

Lodovici, M.S. (2000), 'The Dynamics of Labour Market Reform in European Countries', in G. Esping-Anderson and M. Regini (eds), *Why Deregulate Labour Markets?* Oxford: Oxford University Press, pp. 30–65.

Lo Faro, A. (2000), *Regulating Social Europe. Reality and Myth of Collective Bargaining in the EC Legal Order.* Oxford and Portland, OR: Hart.

Luhmann, N. (1965), *Grundrechte als Institution: Ein Beitrag zur politischen Soziologie.* Berlin: Duncker & Humblot.

Luhmann, N. (1969), *Legitimation durch Verfahren.* Neuwied and Berlin: Luchterhand.

Luhmann, N. (1970), 'Reflexive Mechanismen', in N. Luhmann, *Soziologische Aufklärung*, Vol. 1. Opladen: Westdeutscher Verlag, pp. 92–112.

Luhmann, N. (1972), *Rechtssoziologie.* Two Vols. Reinbek: Rowohlt.

Luhmann, N. (1975 [1971]), 'Die Weltgesellschaft', in N. Luhmann, *Soziologische Aufklärung*, Vol. 2: *Aufsätze zur Theorie der Gesellschaft.* Opladen: Westdeutscher Verlag, pp. 63–88.

Luhmann, N. (1976), 'Generalized Media and the Problem of Contingency', in J.J. Loubser, R.C. Baum, A. Effrat and Victor M. Lidz (eds), *Explorations in General Theory in Social Science, Essays in Honor of Talcott Parsons*, Vol. 2. New York: The Free Press, pp. 507–32.

Luhmann, N. (1982), 'The Autonomy of the Legal System', in N. Luhmann, *The Differentiation of Society.* New York: Columbia University Press, pp. 122–37.

Luhmann, N. (1985a), *A Sociological Theory of Law.* London: Routledge and Kegan Paul.

Luhmann, N. (1985b), 'Zum Begriff der sozialen Klasse', in N. Luhmann (ed), *Soziale Differenzierung. Zur Geschichte einer Idee.* Opladen: Westdeutscher Verlag, pp. 5–20

Luhmann, N. (1987), 'Autopoiesis als soziologischer Begriff', in H. Haferkamp and M. Schmid (eds), *Sinn, Kommunikation und soziale Differenzierung. Beiträge zu Luhmanns Theorie sozialer Systeme.* Frankfurt am Main: Suhrkamp, pp. 90–134.

Luhmann, N. (1988a), *Die Wirtschaft der Gesellschaft.* Frankfurt am Main, Suhrkamp.

Luhmann, N. (1988b), 'The Unity of the Legal System', in G. Teubner (ed), *Autopoietic Law: A New Approach to Law and Society.* Berlin: De Gruyter, pp. 12–35.

Luhmann, N. (1989), *Ecological Communication.* Cambridge: Polity.

Luhmann, N. (1990a [1982]), 'The World Society as a Social System', in N. Luhmann, *Essays on Self-Reference.* New York: Columbia University

Press, pp. 175–90 (originally published in *International Journal of General Systems*, **8**(3), 131–8).

Luhmann, N. (1990b), 'The Self-reproduction of Law and its Limits', in N. Luhmann, *Essays on Self-Reference*, New York: Columbia University Press.

Luhmann, N. (1990c), *Die Wissenschaft der Gesellschaft*. Frankfurt am Main: Suhrkamp.

Luhmann, N. (1992), 'Some Problems with Reflexive Law', in G. Teubner and A. Febbrajo (eds), *State, Law and Economy as Autopoietic Systems. Regulation and Autonomy in a New Perspective. European Yearbook in the Sociology of Law*. Milan: Giuffrè, pp. 389–415.

Luhmann, N. (1993), *Das Recht der Gesellschaft*. Frankfurt am Main: Suhrkamp.

Luhmann, N. (1995a), *Social Systems*. Stanford: Stanford University Press.

Luhmann, N. (1995b), 'Why Does Society Describe Itself as Postmodern?', *Cultural Critique*, **30**, pp. 171–86.

Luhmann, N. (1996a), 'Quod Omnes Tangit. Remarks on Jürgen Habermas's Legal Theory', *Cardozo Law Review*, **17**(5), 883–900.

Luhmann, N. (1996b), *Protest. Systemtheorie und soziale Bewegungen*. Frankfurt am Main: Suhrkamp.

Luhmann, N. (1997a), *Die Gesellschaft der Gesellschaft*. Frankfurt am Main: Suhrkamp.

Luhmann, N. (1997b), 'Globalization or World Society? How to conceive of modern society'. *International Review of Sociology*, **7**(1), 67–79.

Luhmann, N. (1997c), 'Limits of Steering', *Theory, Culture & Society*, **14**(1), 41–57.

Luhmann, N. (2000a), *Die Politik der Gesellschaft*. Frankfurt am Main: Suhrkamp.

Luhmann, N. (2000b), *Organisation und Entscheidung*. Opladen: Westdeutscher Verlag.

Luhmann, N. (2004), *Law as a Social System*. Oxford: Oxford University Press.

Luhmann, N. (2012), *Theory of Society*, Vol. 1. Stanford: Stanford University Press.

Luhmann, N. (2013), *A Systems Theory of Religion*. Stanford: Stanford University Press.

Lynch-Fannon, I. (2006), 'The European Social Model of Corporate Governance: Prospects for Success in an Enlarged Europe', in P. Ali and G.N. Gregoriou (eds), *International Corporate Governance After Sarbanes-Oxley*. Hoboken, N.J. and Chichester: Wiley, pp. 423–44.

Lyon-Caen, A. (1993), 'Workers' Protection and the Regulation of Labor

Relations in France during the 1980s', in C.F. Buechtemann (ed), *Employment Security and Labor Market Behavior*. Ithaca: ILR Press, pp. 347–57.

Lyon-Caen, G. (1996), 'By Way of Conclusion: Labour Law and Employment Transitions', *International Labour Review*, **135**(6), 697–702.

Lyon-Caen, A. and A. Jeammaud (eds) (1986), *Droit du travail, democratie et crise*. Aries: Actes Sud.

Lyotard, J.-F. (1984 [1979]), *The Postmodern Condition: A Report on Knowledge*. Minneapolis: University of Minnesota Press.

Madsen, P.K. (1997), 'Lifelong Learning and Paid Leave Arrangements: Some General Arguments and an Illustration Using the Danish Experience in the 1990s', in OECD (ed), *Creativity, Innovation and Job Creation*. Paris: OECD, pp. 113–29.

Madsen, P.K. (1998a), 'Working Time Policy and Paid Leave Arrangements: the Danish Experience in the 1990s', *Transfer – European Review of Labour and Research*, **8**(4), 692–714.

Madsen, P.K. (1998b), 'A Transitional Labour Market: the Danish Paid Leave Arrangements', in H.U. Schwedler (ed), *New Institutional Arrangements in the Labour Market: Transitional Labour Markets as a New Full Employment Concept*. Berlin: European Academy of the Urban Environment/WZB, pp. 68–73.

Majone, G. (2005), *Dilemmas of European Integration*. Oxford: Oxford University Press.

Malo, A.A., L. Toharia and J. Gautié (2000), 'France: The Deregulation that Never Existed', in G. Esping-Anderson and M. Regini (eds), *Why Deregulate Labour Markets?* Oxford: Oxford University Press, pp. 245–70.

Mamic, I. (2004), *Implementing Codes of Conduct: How Businesses Manage Social Performance in Global Supply Chain*. Geneva: International Labor Office and Sheffield: Greenleaf Publishing.

Mantouvalou, V. (2012), 'Are Labour Rights Human Rights?', *European Labour Law Journal*, **3**(2), 151–72.

Marchington, M. and A. Wilkinson (2005), 'Direct Participation', in S. Bach (ed), *Managing Human Resources: A Comprehensive Guide to Theory and Practice*, 4th edition. Oxford: Blackwell.

Marginson, P. and K. Sisson (2006), *European Integration and Industrial Relation. Multi-level Governance in the Making*. Basingstoke and New York: Palgrave Macmillan.

Martin, A. and G. Ross (2004), 'Introduction: EMU and the European Social Model', in A. Martin and G. Ross (eds), *Euros and Europeans: Monetary Integration and the European Model of Society*. Cambridge: Cambridge University Press, pp. 1–19.

Mascerano, A. and K. Araujo (2012), 'On Legitimacy Once Again: New Challenges in World Society', in A. Mascerano and K. Araujo (eds), *Legitimization in World Society*. Farnham: Ashgate, pp. 1–21.

Matteraa, M., V. Baenab and J. Cerviñoa (2012), 'Analyzing Social Responsibility as a Driver of Firm's Brand Awareness', *Procedia – Social and Behavioral Sciences*, **58**, 1121–30.

Maus, I. (1986), 'Perspektiven "reflexiven Rechts" im Kontext gegenwärtiger Deregulierungstendenzen', *Kritsche Justiz* , **19**(4), 390–405.

Mayne, R. (1999), 'Regulating TNCs: The Role of Voluntary and Governmental Approaches', in S. Picciotto and R. Mayne (eds), *Regulating International Business: Beyond Liberalization*. Basingstoke: Macmillan, pp. 235–54.

McBarnet, D. (2007), 'Corporate Social Responsibility beyond Law, through Law, for Law: The New Corporate Accountability', in D. McBarnet, A. Voiculescu and T. Campbell (eds), *The New Corporate Accountability: Corporate Social Responsibility and the Law*. Cambridge: Cambridge University Press, pp. 9–56.

McCrudden, C. (2007a), *Buying Social Justice. Equality, Government Procurement and Legal Change*. Oxford: Oxford University Press.

McCrudden, C. (2007b), 'Equality Legislation and Reflexive Regulation: A Response to the Discrimination Law Review's Consultative Paper', *Industrial Law Journal*, **36**(3), 255–66.

Meardi, G. (2012), *Social Failures of EU Enlargement. A Case of Workers Voting with Their Feet*. New York and Abingdon, UK: Routledge.

Meer, M. van der (ed) (2000), *The Trade-off between Competitiveness and Employment in Collective Bargaining*. Amsterdam: Amsterdam Institute for Advanced Labour Studies.

Meltz, N.M. (1991), 'Dunlop's "Industrial Relations Systems" after Three Decades', in R.J. Adams (ed), *Comparative Industrial Relations. Contemporary Research and Theory*. London: Unwin Hyman, pp. 10–20.

Metzger, G.E. (2003), 'Privatization as Delegation', *Columbia Law Review*, **103**(6), 1367–1456.

Meyers, J.W. (2010), *World Society*. Ed. by G. Krücken and G.S. Drori. Oxford: Oxford University Press.

Mincer, J. (1974), *Schooling, Experience, and Earnings*. New York: Columbia University Press.

Minow, M. (1990), *Making all the Difference. Inclusion, Exclusion and American Law*. Ithaca: Cornell University Press.

Moreau, M.-A. (2000), 'Deregulation and Labour Law: French Report', in R. Blanpain, R. Yamakawa and T. Araki (eds), *Deregulation and Labour Law – In search of a Labour Concept for the 21st Century*. Bulletin of Comparative Labour Relations No. 38. The Hague: Kluwer, pp. 43–58.

Moreau, M.-A. (ed) (2011), *Before and After the Economic Crisis. What Implications for the European Social Model?* Cheltenham, UK: Edward Elgar.

Moreno, L. and B. Palier (2005), 'The Europeanization of Welfare. Paradigm Shifts and Social Policy Reforms', in P. Taylor-Gooby (ed), *Ideas and Welfare State Reform in Western Europe*. Basingstoke and New York: Palgrave Macmillan, pp. 145–75.

Morris, G.S. (2004), 'Britain's New Statutory Procedures: Routes to Resolution or Barriers to Justice?', *Comparative Labor Law Journal*, **25**(4), 477–86.

Mosher, J.S. and D.M. Trubek (2003), 'Alternative Approaches to Governance in the EU: EU Social Policy and the European Employment Strategy', *Journal of Common Market Studies*, **41**(1), 63–88.

Muchlinski, P.T. (1997), '"Global Bukowina" Examined: Viewing the Multinational Enterprise as a Transnational Law-making Community', in G. Teubner (ed), *Global Law without a State*. Dartmouth: Aldershot, pp. 79–108.

Muchlinski, P.T. (2007), *Multinational Enterprises and the Law*. 2nd edition. Oxford: Oxford University Press.

Mückenberger, U. (1985a), 'Der verfassungsrechtliche Schutz des Dauerarbeitsverhältnisses', *Neue Zeitschrift für Arbeitsrecht (NZA)*, Heft 16, pp. 518–26.

Mückenberger, U. (1985b), 'Die Krise des Normalarbeitsverhältnisses', *Zeitschrift für Sozialreform*, Heft 7 and 8, pp. 415–33 and pp. 457–74.

Mückenberger, U. (1989), 'Non-standard Forms of Employment in the Federal Republic of Germany: the Role and Effectiveness of the State', in G. Rodgers and J. Rodgers (eds), *Precarious Jobs in Labour Market Regulation. The Growth of Atypical Employment in Western Europe*. Geneva: International Institute for Labour Studies, pp. 267–85.

Mückenberger, U. (1990), 'Normalarbeitsverhältnis: Lohnarbeit als normativer Horizont sozialer Sicherheit?' In C. Sachsse and H.T. Engelhardt (eds), *Sicherheit und Freiheit. Zur Ethik des Wohlfahrtsstaats*. Frankfurt am Main: Suhrkamp, pp. 158–78.

Mückenberger, U. (2010), 'Krise des Normalarbeitsverhältnisses – nach 25 Jahren revisited', *Zeitschrift für Sozialreform*, **56**(4), 403–420.

Müller-Jentsch, W. (1983), 'Versuch über die Tarifautonomie. Entstehung und Funktionen kollektiver Verhandlungssysteme in Großbritannien und Deutschland', *Leviathan*, **11**(1), 118–49.

Müller-Jentsch, W. (1997), *Soziologie der industriellen Beziehungen*. 2nd edition. Frankfurt am Main and New York: Campus.

Müller-Jentsch, W. (2004), 'Theoretical Approaches to Industrial Relations', in B.E. Kaufman (ed), *Theoretical Approaches on Work and the Employment Relationship.* Champaign, Illinois: Industrial Relations Research Association, pp. 1–40.

Mundlak, G. (2007), 'The Right to Work – The Value of Work', in D. Barak-Erez and A.M. Gross (eds), *Exploring Social Rights: Between Theory and Practice.* Oxford and Portland, OR: Hart, pp. 341–66.

Mundlak, G. (2011), 'The Third Function of Labour Law: Distributing Labour Market Opportunities among Workers', in B. Langille and G. Davidov (eds), *The Idea of Labour Law.* Oxford: Oxford University Press, pp. 315–28.

Murray, J. (1999), 'Social Justice for Women? The ILO's Convention on Part-time Work', *International Journal of Comparative Labour Law and Industrial Relations*, **15**(1), 3–19.

Murray, J. (2001), *Transnational Labour Regulation: The ILO and EC Compared.* The Hague and London: Kluwer Law International.

Mutz, G., W. Ludwig-Mayerhofer, E.J. Koenen, K. Eder and W. Bonß (1995), *Diskontinuierliche Erwerbsverläufe. Analysen zur postindustriellen Arbeitslosigkeit.* Opladen: Leske and Budrich.

Myrdal, H.-G. (1994), 'The ILO in the Cross-fire: Would it Survive the Social Clause?' In W. Sengenberger and D. Campbell (eds), *International Labour Standards and Economic Interdependence.* Geneva: International Institute for Labour Studies.

Nagel, T. (2005), 'The Problem of Global Justice', *Philosophy and Public Affairs*, **33**(2), 113–47.

Neal, A.C. (2008), 'Corporate Social Responsibility: Governance Gain or Laissez Faire Figleaf?', *Comparative Labor Law and Policy Journal*, **29**(4), 459–74.

Neff, S.C. (1990), *Friends but no Allies. Economic Liberalism and the Law of Nations.* New York: Columbia University Press.

Nobles, R. and D. Schiff (2006), *A Sociology of Jurisprudence.* Oxford and Portland, OR: Hart.

Nonet, P. and P. Selznick (1978), *Law and Society in Transition: Toward Responsive Law.* New York: Harper.

Novitz, T. (2002), *Promoting Core Labour Standards and Improving Global Social Governance: An Assessment of EU Competence to Implement Commission Proposals.* EUI Working Paper RSC No. 2002/59. San Domenico di Fiesole: European University Institute, Robert Schuman Centre for Advanced Studies.

Novitz, T. (2005), 'The European Union and International Labour Standards: the Dynamics of Dialogue between the EU and the ILO', in P. Alston (ed), *Labour Rights as Human Rights.* Oxford: Oxford University Press, pp. 214–41.

Novitz, T. (2010), 'Core Labour Standards Conditionalities: a Means by which to Achieve Sustainable Development?' In J. Faundez and C. Tan (eds), *International Economic Law, Globalization and Developing Countries.* Cheltenham: Edward Elgar, pp. 234–51.

Nowack, T. (2008), 'The Working Time Directive and the European Court of Justice', *Maastricht Journal of European and Comparative Law*, **15**(4), 447–71.

Nussbaum, M. (2000), *Women and Human Development: The Capabilities Approach.* Cambridge: Cambridge University Press.

OECD (2004), *Employment Outlook.* Paris: OECD.

OECD (2011), *Divided We Stand: Why Inequality Keeps Rising.* Paris: OECD.

Offe, C. (2003), 'The European Model of "Social" Capitalism: Can it Survive European Integration?', *The Journal of Political Philosophy*, **11**(4), 437–69.

Ogus, A.I. (2004), *Regulation: Legal Form and Economic Theory.* Oxford and Portland, OR: Hart.

O'Higgins, P. (2002), 'The Interaction of the ILO, the Council of Europe and European Labour Standards', in B. Hepple (ed), *Social and Labour Rights in a Global Context. International and Comparative Perspectives.* Cambridge: Cambridge University Press, pp. 55–69.

Ohlin Report (1956), 'Social Aspects of European Economic Co-operation. Report by a Group of Experts', *International Labour Review*, **74**(2), 99–123.

Orbie, J. and L. Tortell (eds) (2009), *The European Union and the Social Dimension of Globalization. How the EU Influences the World.* Abingdon: Routledge.

O'Reilly, J. and C. Fagan (eds) (1998), *Part-time Prospects: An International Comparison of Part-time Work in Europe. North America and the Pacific Rim.* London: Routledge.

Osterman, P. (1994), 'Internal Labor Markets: Theory and Change', in C. Kerr and P.D. Staudohar (eds), *Labor Economics and Industrial Relations: Markets and Institutions.* Cambridge, MA: Harvard University Press, pp. 303–39.

Papadakis, K. (ed) (2008), *Cross-border Social Dialogue and Agreements: An Emerging Global Industrial Relations Framework?* Geneva: International Institute for Labour Studies, International Labour Organization.

Papadakis, K. (2011a), 'Globalizing Industrial Relations: What Role for International Framework Agreements?' In S. Hayter (ed), *The Role of Collective Bargaining in the Global Economy: Negotiating for Social Justice.* Cheltenham: Edward Elgar, pp. 277–304.

Papadakis, K. (ed) (2011b), *Shaping Global Industrial Relations. The Impact of International Framework Agreements.* Basingstoke: Palgrave Macmillan.

Parker, C. (2002), *The Open Corporation: Effective Self-regulation and Democracy*. Cambridge: Cambridge University Press.

Parker, C. (2007), 'Meta-Regulation: Legal Accountability for Corporate Social Responsibility', in D. McBarnet, A. Voiculescu and T. Campbell (eds), *The New Corporate Accountability: Corporate Social Responsibility and the Law*. Cambridge: Cambridge University Press, pp. 207–37.

Parsons, T. (1937), *The Structure of Social Action*. Glencoe: The Free Press.

Parsons, T. (1951), *The Social System*. London: Routledge and Kegan Paul.

Parsons, T. (1966), *Societies. Evolutionary and Comparative Perspectives*. Englewood Cliffs, NJ: Prentice-Hall.

Parsons, T. (1971), *The System of Modern Societies*. Englewood Cliffs, NJ: Prentice-Hall.

Parsons, T. and N.J. Smelser (1956), *Economy and Society. A Study in the Integration of Economic and Social Theory*. London: Routledge and Kegan Paul.

Paterson, J. (2000), *Behind the Mask: Regulating Health and Safety in Britain's Offshore Oil and Gas Industry*. Aldershot: Ashgate.

Paterson, J. (2006), 'Reflecting on Reflexive Law', in M. King and C. Thornhill (eds), *Luhmann on Law and Politics*. Oxford and Portland, OR: Hart, pp. 13–35.

Paterson, J. and G. Teubner (1998), 'Changing Maps: Empirical Legal Autopoiesis', *Social & Legal Studies*, **7**(1), 451–86.

Peccei, R., H. Bewley, H. Gospel and P. Willman (2005), 'Is it Good to Talk? Information Disclosure and Organizational Performance in the UK', *British Journal of Industrial Relations*, **43**(1), 11–39.

Peers, S. (2010), 'Non-regression Clauses: The Fig-Leaf Has Fallen', *Industrial Law Journal*, **39**(4), 436–443.

Pennings, F.J.L. (2010), *European Social Security Law*. 5th ed. Antwerp and Oxford: Intersentia.

Peoples, J. (ed) (1998), *Regulatory Reform and Labor Markets*. Boston and London: Kluwer Academic Publishers.

Perez, O. (2004), *Ecological Sensitivity and Global Legal Pluralism: Rethinking the Trade and Environment Conflict*. Oxford and Portland, OR: Hart.

Perez, O., Y. Hamburger and T. Shterental (2009), 'The Dynamic of Corporate Self-Regulation: ISO 14001, Environmental Commitment and Organizational Citizenship Behavior', *Law and Society Review*, **43**(3), 593–629.

Pernice, I., M. Müller and C. Peters (eds) (2012), *Konstituionalisierung jenseits des Staates*. Baden-Baden: Nomos.

Peterson, R.B. and D. Lewin (2000), 'Research on Unionized Grievance

Procedures: Management Issues and Recommendations', *Human Resource Management*, **39**(4), 395–406.

Pfau-Effinger, B. (1998), 'Culture or Structure as Explanation for Differences in Part-time Work in Germany, Finland and the Netherlands', in J. O'Reilly and C. Fagan (eds), *Part-time Prospects: an International Comparison of Part-time Work in Europe, North America and the Pacific Rim*. London and New York: Routledge, pp. 57–76.

Philippopoulos-Mihalopoulos, A. (2010), *Niklas Luhmann. Law, Justice, Society*. Abingdon, New York: Routledge.

Picciotto, S. (1999), 'Introduction: What Rules for the World Economy?' In S. Picciotto and R. Mayne (eds), *Regulating International Business: Beyond Liberalization*. Basingstoke: Macmillan, pp. 1–26.

Picciotto, S. (2011), *Regulating Global Corporate Capitalism*. Cambridge: Cambridge University Press.

Pinto, M. (1987), 'Portugal: Die Flexibilisierung des Arbeitsrechts – eine europäische Herausforderung?', *Zeitschrift für Internationales Arbeits- und Sozialrecht* (ZIAS), **1**(4), 564–87.

Pinto, M., P.F. Martins and A.E. de Carvalho (1993), 'Portugal', in R. Blanpain (ed), *Temporary Work and Labour Law*. Deventer: Kluwer, pp. 233–51.

Piquer, A.A. (2006), 'The North American Agreement on Labor Cooperation: An Effective Compromise between Harmonization of Labor Rights and Regulatory Competition?' In O. De Schutter (ed), *Transnational Corporations and Human Rights*. Oxford and Portland, OR: Hart, pp. 183–216.

Pochet, P. (2003), 'The European Employment Strategy at a Crossroad', in C. Degryse and P. Pochet (eds), *Social Developments in the European Union 2002*: *Fourth Annual Report*. Bruxelles: ETUI, OSE, SALTSA, pp. 61–95.

Pochet, P. (2005), 'The Open Method of Coordination and the Construction of Social Europe. A Historical Perspective', in J. Zeitlin and P. Pochet in collaboration with L. Magnusson (eds), *The Open Method of Co-ordination in Action: The European Employment and Social Inclusion Strategies*. Brussels: Peter Lang, pp. 37–82.

Pogge, T.W. (1989), *Realizing Rawls*. Ithaca, NY: Cornell University Press.

Pogge, T.W. (2007a), *John Rawls: His Life and Theory of Justice*. Oxford: Oxford University Press.

Pogge, T.W. (2007b), *World Poverty and Human Rights*. 2nd edition. Cambridge: Polity.

Pollert, A. (2005), 'The Unorganised Worker: The Decline in Collectivism and New Hurdles to Individual Employment Rights', *Industrial Law Journal*, **34**(3), 217–38.

Pound, R. (1908–09), 'Liberty of Contract', *Yale Law Journal*, **18**(7), 454–6.

Preuss, L., A. Haunschild and D. Matten (2006), 'Trade Unions and CSR: a European Research Agenda', *Journal of Public Affairs*, **6**(3–4), 256–68.

Priban, J. (2007), *Legal Symbolism. On Law, Time and Legal Identity*. Aldershot: Ashgate.

Prigge, W.-U. (1987), *Metallindustrielle Arbeitgeberverbände in Großbritannien und der Bundesrepublik Deutschland – eine system-theoretische Studie*. Opladen: Leske and Budrich (Forschungstexte Wirtschafts- und Sozialwissenschaften).

Raff, D.M.G. and L.M. Summers (1987), 'Did Henry Ford Pay Efficiency Wages?', *Journal of Labor Economics*, **5**(4), 57–86.

Rasche, A. and D.U. Gilbert (2012), 'Social Accountability 8000 and Socioeconomic Development', in P. Utting, D. Reed and A.M. Reed (eds), *Business Regulation and Non-State Actors: Whose Standards? Whose Development?* London: Routledge, pp. 68–80.

Rawls, J. (1972), *A Theory of Justice*. Oxford: Oxford University Press.

Rawls, J. (1999), *The Law of Peoples*. Cambridge, MA: Harvard University Press.

Regent, S. (2003), 'The Open Method of Coordination: a New Supranational Form of Governance?', *European Law Journal*, **9**(2), 190–214.

Reich, M., D.M. Gordon and R.C. Edwards (1973), 'Dual Labor Markets: A Theory of Labor Market Segmentation', *American Economic Review*, **63**(2), 359–65.

Reich, N. (2008), 'Free Movement versus Social Rights in an Enlarged Union: the Laval and Viking Cases before the European Court of Justice', *German Law Journal*, **9**(2), 125–60.

Rhode, D.L. (1989), *Justice and Gender*. Cambridge, MA: Harvard University Press.

Richard, J. and A. Pascal (2010), 'Pour le Renforcement de la Légitimité de l'Institution Prud'homale: Quelle Forme de Désignation des Conseillers Prud'hommes? Rapport'. Paris: Ministre du travail, de la solidarité et de la fonction publique.

Robertson, R. (1992), *Globalization. Social Theory and Global Culture*. London: Sage.

Rodgers, G. and J. Rodgers (eds) (1989), *Precarious Jobs in Labour Market Regulation. The Growth of Atypical Employment in Western Europe*. Geneva: International Institute for Labour Studies.

Rogowski, R. (1985), 'Meso-Corporatism and Labour Conflict Resolution', *International Journal of Comparative Labour Law and Industrial Relations*, **1**(3), 143–69.

Rogowski, R. (1994), 'Industrial Relations, Labour Conflict Resolution and Reflexive Labour Law', in R. Rogowski and T. Wilthagen (eds), *Reflexive Labour Law – Studies in Industrial Relations and Employment Regulation*. Deventer: Kluwer, pp. 53–93.

Rogowski, R. (1996), 'The Art of Mirroring. Comparative Law and Social Theory', in G. Wilson and R. Rogowski (eds), *Challenges to European Legal Scholarship, – Anglo-German Legal Essays*. London: Blackstone, pp. 213–32.

Rogowski, R. (1998), 'Autopoietic Industrial Relations and Reflexive Labour Law in the World Society', in T. Wilthagen (ed), *Advancing Theory in Labour Law and Industrial Relations in a Global Context*. Proceedings of the Royal Netherlands Academy of the Arts and Sciences. Amsterdam: North Holland, pp. 67–82.

Rogowski, R. (1999), 'Kollektives und individuelles Arbeitsrecht', in W. Müller–Jentsch (ed), *Konfliktpartnerschaft – Akteure und Institutionen der industriellen Beziehungen*. 3rd edition. München: Hampp, pp. 213–32.

Rogowski, R. (2000a), 'Industrial Relations as a Social System', *Industrielle Beziehungen – The German Journal of Industrial Relations*, **7**(2), 97–126.

Rogowski, R. (2000b), 'Recht und industrielle Beziehungen in Luhmanns Weltgesellschaft', *Zeitschrift für Rechtssoziologie*, **21**(2), 279–92.

Rogowski, R. (2001), 'The Concept of Reflexive Labour Law, Its Theoretical Background and Possible Applications', in D. Nelken and J. Priban (eds) *Law's New Boundaries. The Consequences of Legal Autopoiesis*. Aldershot: Ashgate, pp. 179–96.

Rogowski, R. (2006), 'Luhmann, Niklas', entry in *Blackwell Encyclopaedia of Sociology*. Ed. by G. Ritzer. Oxford: Blackwell, pp. 2675–8.

Rogowski, R. (2007), 'Flexicurity and Reflexive Coordination of European Social and Employment Policies', in H. Jørgensen and P.K. Madsen (eds), *Flexicurity and Beyond. Finding a New Agenda for the European Social Model*. Copenhagen: DJØF Publishing, pp. 131–53.

Rogowski, R. (ed) (2008), *The European Social Model and Transitional Labour Markets – Law and Policy*. Aldershot: Ashgate.

Rogowski, R. (2008a), 'The European Social Model and Law and Policy of Transitional Labour Markets in the European Union', in R. Rogowski (ed), *The European Social Model and Transitional Labour Markets–Law and Policy*. Aldershot: Ashgate, pp. 9–27.

Rogowski, R. (2008b), 'Governance of the European Social Model: The Case of Flexicurity', *Intereconomics: Review of European Economic Policy*, **43**(2), 82–91.

Rogowski, R. (forthcoming), 'Implementation of the EU Working Time Directive in the United Kingdom', in C. Barbier, R. Rogowski and F. Columb (eds), *The Sustainability of the European Social Model. EU*

Governance, Social Protection and Social Rights in Europe. Cheltenham: Edward Elgar.

Rogowski, R. and S. Deakin (2011), 'Labour Law, Capabilities and the Future of Social Europe', in R. Rogowski, R. Salais and N. Whiteside (eds), *Transforming European Employment Policy–Labour Market Transitions and the Promotion of Capability*. Cheltenham: Edward Elgar, pp. 229–54.

Rogowski, R. and G. Schmid (1998), 'Reflexive Deregulierung. Ein Ansatz zur Dynamisierung des Arbeitsmarkts', in B. Keller and H. Seifert (eds), *Deregulierung am Arbeitsmarkt. Eine empirische Zwischenbilanz*. Hamburg: VS Verlag, pp. 215–53.

Rogowski, R. and I. Schömann (2002), 'The Role and Impact of Social Partners on Training in the European Union', in S. Rouault, H. Oschmiansky and I. Schömann (eds), *Reacting in Time to Qualification Needs: Towards a Cooperative Implementation?* Discussion Paper, FS I 02–202. Berlin: Wissenschaftszentrum.

Rogowski, R. and K. Schömann (1996), 'Legal Regulation and Flexibility of Employment Contracts', in G. Schmid, J. O'Reilly and K. Schömann (eds), *International Handbook of Labour Market Policy and Evaluation*. Aldershot: Edward Elgar, pp. 623–51.

Rogowski, R. and A. Tooze (1992), 'Liberaler Korporatismus und Arbeitskonfliktlösung. Gewerbe- und Arbeitsgerichte in Frankreich, Großbritannien und Deutschland im historischen Vergleich', in H. Mohnhaupt and D. Simon (eds), *Vorträge zur Justizforschung*, Vol. 1. Frankfurt am Main: Vittorio Klostermann, pp. 317–86.

Rogowski, R. and T. Wilthagen (eds) (1994), *Reflexive Labour Law – Studies in Industrial Relations and Employment Regulation*. Deventer: Kluwer.

Rogowski, R. and T. Wilthagen (1994), 'Introduction', in R. Rogowski and T. Wilthagen (eds), *Reflexive Labour Law – Studies in Industrial Relations and Employment Regulation*. Deventer: Kluwer, pp. 1–19.

Rogowski, R. and T. Wilthagen (2001), 'The Legal Regulation of Transitional Labour Markets', in G. Schmid and B. Gazier (eds), *The Dynamics of Full Employment: Social Integration Through Transitional Labour Markets*. Cheltenham: Edward Elgar, pp. 233–73.

Rogowski, R., R. Salais and N. Whiteside (eds) (2011), *Transforming European Employment Policy–Labour Market Transitions and the Promotion of Capability*. Cheltenham: Edward Elgar.

Rosewitz, B. and U. Schimank (1988), 'Verselbständigung und politische Steuerbarkeit gesellschaftlicher Teilsysteme', in R. Mayntz, B. Rosewitz, U. Schimank and R. Stichweh (eds), *Differenzierung und Verselbständigung. Zur Entwicklung gesellschaftlicher Teilsysteme*. Frankfurt am Main, New York: Campus, pp. 295–329.

Rottleuthner, H. (1989), 'The Limits of Law–The Myth of a Regulatory Crisis', *International Journal of the Sociology of Law*, **17**(3), 273–85.

Rudolph, P.H. (2003), 'The History, Variations, Impact and Future of Self-regulation', in R. Mullerat (ed), *Corporate Social Responsibility: The Corporate Governance of the 21st Century*. The Hague: Kluwer, pp. 365–84.

Sabel, C.F. and J. Zeitlin (2008), 'Learning from Difference: The New Architecture of Experimentalist Governance in the European Union', *European Law Journal*, **14**(3), 278–80.

Santoro, M.A. (2003), 'Beyond Codes of Conduct and Monitoring: An Organizational Integrity Approach to Global Labour Practices', *Human Rights Quarterly*, **25**(2), 407–24.

Saxanian, A. (1994), *Regional Advantage. Culture and Competition in Silicon Valley and Route 128*. Cambridge, MA: Harvard University Press.

Schäfer, A. (2004), *A New Form of Governance? Comparing the Open Method of Coordination to Multilateral Surveillance by the IMF and the OECD*. MPIfG Working Paper 04/5. Cologne: Max Planck Institut für Gesellschaftsforschung.

Schäfer, A. (2006), 'Resolving Deadlock: Why International Organisations Introduce Soft Law', *European Law Journal*, **12**(2), 194–208.

Scharpf, F.W. (1999), *Governing in Europe: Effective and Democratic?* Oxford: Oxford University Press.

Scharpf, F.W. (2002), 'The European Social Model: Coping with the Challenges to Diversity', *Journal of Common Market Studies*, **40**(4), 645–70.

Schefer, K.N. (2010), *Social Regulation in the WTO. Trade Policy and International Legal Development*. Cheltenham: Edward Elgar.

Schepel, H. (2005), *The Constitution of Private Governance. Product Standards in the Regulation of Integrating Markets*. Oxford and Portland, OR: Hart.

Scherer, S. (2006), 'Non-standard Employment. Experiments in Regulation at the Local Level in Germany', in I. Regalia (ed), *Regulating New Forms of Employment in Europe – Local Experiments and Social Innovation in Europe*. London: Routledge, pp. 84–109.

Scheuerman, W.E. (2001), 'Reflexive Law and the Challenges of Globalization', *Journal of Political Philosophy*, **9**(1), 81–102.

Schienstock, G. (1982), *Industrielle Arbeitsbeziehungen. Eine vergleichende Analyse theoretischer Konzepte in der industrial relations Forschung*. Opladen: Leske and Budrich.

Schmid, G. (1992), 'Flexible Koordination. Instrumentarium erfolgreicher Beschäftigungspolitik aus internationaler Perspektive', *Mitteilungen aus der Arbeitsmarkt- und Berufsforschung*, **25**(3), 232–51.

Schmid, G. (1994), 'Flexibilisation of the Labour Market through Law? On Equity and Efficiency in the Regulation of Working Time', in R. Rogowski and T. Wilthagen (eds), *Reflexive Labour Law – Studies in Industrial Relations and Employment Regulation*. Deventer: Kluwer, pp. 178–92.

Schmid, G. (1997), 'Beschäftigungswunder Niederlände? Ein Vergleich der Beschäftigungssysteme in den Niederländen und in Deutschland', *Leviathan*, **25**(3), 302–37.

Schmid, G. (2001), 'Towards a Theory of Transitional Labour Markets', in G. Schmid and B. Gazier, (eds), *The Dynamics of Full Employment: Social Integration Through Transitional Labour Markets*. Cheltenham: Edward Elgar, pp. 151–95.

Schmid, G. (2002), *Wege in eine neue Vollbeschäftigung. Übergangsarbeitsmärkte und aktivierende Arbeitsmarktpolitik*. Frankfurt am Main und New York: Campus.

Schmid, G. (2006), 'Social Risk Management through Transitional Labour Markets', *Socioeconomic Revue*, **4**(1), 1–33.

Schmid, G. (2008a), *Full Employment in Europe. Managing Labour Market Transitions and Risks*. Cheltenham: Edward Elgar.

Schmid, G. (2008b), 'Sharing Risks – On Social Risk Management and the Governance of Labour Market Transitions', in R. Rogowski (ed), *The European Social Model and Transitional Labour Markets – Law and Policy*. Aldershot: Ashgate, pp. 29–60.

Schmid, G. (2011), 'Transitional Labour Markets and Flexicurity: Managing Social Risks over the Life Course', in R. Rogowski, R. Salais and N. Whiteside (eds), *Transforming European Employment Policy – Labour Market Transitions and the Promotion of Capability*. Cheltenham: Edward Elgar, pp. 46–70.

Schmid G. and P. Auer (1998), 'Transitional Labour Markets: Concepts and Examples in Europe', in European Academy of Urban Environment (ed), *New Institutional Arrangements in the Labour Market: Transitional Labour Markets as a New Full Employment Concept*. Berlin: European Academy of the Urban Environment, pp. 11–28.

Schmid, G. and B. Gazier (eds) (2001), *The Dynamics of Full Employment: Social Integration Through Transitional Labour Markets*. Cheltenham: Edward Elgar.

Schmid, G. and S. Kull (2004), 'Die Europäische Beschäftigungsstrategie. Perspektiven der Offenen Methode der Koordinierung', in H. Kaelble and G. Schmid (eds), *Das europäische Sozialmodell. Auf dem Weg zum transnationalen Sozialstaat*. WZB-Jahrbuch 2004, Berlin Sigma, pp. 317–43.

Schmid, G. and K. Schömann (1994), 'Institutional Choice and Flexible Coordination: A Socioeconomic Evaluation of Labor Market Policy in Europe', in G. Schmid (ed), *Labor Market Institutions in Europe. A Socioeconomic Evaluation of Performance.* Armonk, NY: M.E. Sharpe, pp. 9–57.

Schmid, G. and K. Schömann (2004), *Managing Social Risks Through Transitional Labour Markets: Towards a European Social Model.* Working Paper, No. 2004-01, Amsterdam: SISWO / Institute for the Social Sciences.

Schmid, G., J. O'Reilly and K. Schömann (eds) (1996), *International Handbook of Labour Market Policy and Evaluation.* Cheltenham: Edward Elgar, pp. 235–76.

Schmitter, P.C. (1974), 'Still the Century of Corporatism?', *The Review of Politics*, **36**(1), 85–131.

Schmitter, P.C. and W. Streeck (1985), 'Community, Market, State and Associations? The Prospective Contribution of Interest Governance to Social Order', in W. Streeck and P.C. Schmitter (eds), *Private Interest Government: Beyond Market and State.* Beverly Hills and London: Sage, pp. 1–29.

Scholte, J.A. (2005), *Globalization: A Critical Introduction.* 2nd edition. New York: St. Martin's.

Schömann, K., R. Rogowski and T. Kruppe (1998), *Labour Market Efficiency in the European Union, Employment Protection and Fixed-term Contracts.* London: Routledge, pp. 272–85.

Schulte, M. and R. Stichweh (eds) (2009), *Weltrecht.* Special issue of *Rechtstheorie*, **39**(2/3), 143–475.

Schuppert, G.F. (ed) (2005), *Der Gewährleistungsstaat – Ein Leitbild auf dem Prüfstand.* Baden-Baden: Nomos.

Schütz, A. (1997), 'The Twilight of Global Polis. On Losing Paradigms, Environing Systems and Observing World Society', in G. Teubner (ed), *Global Law without a State.* Aldershot: Dartmouth, pp. 257–93.

Sciarra, S. (1998), 'How "Global" is Labour Law? The Perspective of Social Rights in the European Union', in T. Wilthagen (ed), *Advancing Theory in Labour Law and Industrial Relations in a Global Context.* Proceedings of the Royal Netherlands Academy of the Arts and Sciences. Amsterdam: North Holland, pp. 67–82.

Sciarra, S. (2004), 'The Convergence of European Labour and Social Rights: Opening to the Open Method of Coordination', in G. Bermann and K. Pistor (eds), *Law and Governance in an Enlarged European Union.* Oxford and Portland, OR: Hart, pp. 155–76.

Sciulli, D. (1992), *Theory of Societal Constitutionalism.* Cambridge: Cambridge University Press.

Scott, C. (2008), 'Reflexive Governance, Meta-Regulation and Corporate Social Responsibility: The "Heineken Effect"', in N. Boeger, R. Murray and C. Villiers (eds), *Perspectives on Corporate Social Responsibility.* Cheltenham: Edward Elgar, pp. 170–85.

Scott. J. and D.M. Trubek (2002), 'Mind the Gap. Law and New Approaches to Governance in the European Union', *European Law Journal*, **8**(1), 1–18.

Seifert, H. (2011), 'Non-Regular Employment in the Germany', in *Non-regular Employment – Issues and Challenges Common to the Major Developed Countries.* JILPT REPORT No. 10. Tokyo: The Japan Institute for Labour Policy and Training, pp. 69–85.

Semlinger, K. (1995), *Arbeitsmarktpolitik für Existenzgründer. Plädoyer für eine arbeitsmarktpolitische Unterstützung des Existenzgründergeschehens.* WZB Discussion Paper FS I 95 – 204. Berlin: Wissenschaftszentrum Berlin.

Semlinger, K. and G. Schmid (1985), *Arbeitsmarktpolitik für Behinderte.* Basel, Boston, Stuttgart: Birkhäuser Verlag.

Sen, A. (1999), *Development as Freedom.* Oxford: Oxford University Press.

Sen, A. (2009), *The Idea of Justice.* London: Allen Lane.

Sengenberger, W. (2006), 'International Labour Standards in the Globalized Economy: Obstacles and Opportunities for Achieving Progress', in J.D.R. Craig and S.M. Lynk (eds), *Globalization and the Future of Labour Law.* Cambridge: Cambridge University Press, pp. 331–55.

Sennett, R. (1999), *The Corrosion of Character: Personal Consequences of Work in the New Capitalism.* New York and London: W.W. Norton.

Sennett, R. (2006), *The Culture of the New Capitalism.* New Haven: Yale University Press.

Serres, M. (1980), *Le Parasite.* Paris: Grasset.

Shalev, M. (1981), 'Theoretical Dilemmas and Value Analysis in Comparative Industrial Relations', in G. Dlugos, K. Weiermair and W. Dorow (eds), *Management under Differing Value Systems. Political, Social and Economic Perspectives in a Changing World.* Berlin and New York: De Gruyter, pp. 241–63.

Shannon, T.R. (1989), *An Introduction to the World-System Perspective.* Boulder: Westview.

Shapiro, C. and J.E. Stiglitz (1984), 'Equilibrium Unemployment as a Worker Discipline Device', *American Economic Review*, **74**(1), 433–44.

Shaw, M. (1994), *Global Society and International Relations: Sociological Concepts and Political Perspectives.* Cambridge: Polity.

Simitis, S. (1987), 'Juridification of Labor Relations', in G. Teubner (ed), *Juridification of Social Spheres: A Comparative Analysis in the Areas of*

Labour, Corporate, Antitrust and Social Welfare Law. Berlin and New York: De Gruyter, pp. 113–62.

Simitis, S. (1994a), 'Denationalizing Labor Law: The Case of Age Discrimination', *Comparative Labor Law Journal*, **15**(3), 321–39.

Simitis, S. (1994b), 'The Rediscovery of the Individual in Labour Law', in R. Rogowski and T. Wilthagen (eds), *Reflexive Labour Law – Studies in Industrial Relations and Employment Regulation*. Deventer: Kluwer, pp. 184–205.

Singh, R. (1976), 'Systems Theory in the Study of Industrial Relations: Time for a Re-appraisal', *Industrial Relations Journal*, **7**(3), 59–71.

Sinzheimer, H. (1976 [1916]), 'Ein Arbeitstarifgesetz. Die Idee der sozialen Selbstbestimmung im Recht', in H. Sinzheimer, *Arbeitsrecht und Rechtssoziologie, Gesammelte Aufsätze und Reden*, 1. Frankfurt am Main and Cologne: Europäische Verlagsanstalt, pp. 35–69.

Sinzheimer, H. (1977 [1907]), *Der korporative Arbeitsnormenvertrag*. Berlin: Duncker & Humblot.

Sirovátka, T. (forthcoming), 'Implementation of the EU Working Time Directive in the Czech Republic', in C. Barbier, R. Rogowski and F. Columb (eds), *The Sustainability of the European Social Model. EU Governance, Social Protection and Social Rights in Europe*. Cheltenham: Edward Elgar.

Sisson, K. (1987), *The Management of Collective Bargaining. An International Comparison*. Oxford: Blackwell.

Sisson, K. (1999), 'The "New" European Social Model: the End of the Search for an Orthodoxy or Another False Dawn?', *Employee Relations*, **21**(5), 445–62.

Skedinger, P. (2010), *Employment Protection Legislation – Evolution, Effects, Winners and Losers*. Cheltenham: Edward Elgar.

Sklair, L. (1995), *Sociology of the Global System*. 2nd edition. London: Prentice Hall/Harvester Wheatsheaf.

Sklair, L. (2002), *Globalization: Capitalism and its Alternatives*. 3rd edition. Oxford: Oxford University Press.

Slater, G. (2011), *Non-Regular Employment in the United Kingdom, in Non-regular Employment – Issues and Challenges Common to the Major Developed Countries*. JILPT REPORT No. 10. Tokyo: The Japan Institute for Labour Policy and Training, pp. 43–68.

Slaughter, A.-M. (2003), 'A Global Community of Courts', *Harvard International Law Journal*, **44**(1), 191–219.

Slaughter, A.-M. (2004), *A New World Order*. Princeton and Oxford: Princeton University Press.

Smismans, S. (2004), *Law, Legitimacy and European Governance. Functional Participation in Social Regulation*. Oxford: Oxford University Press.

Smismans, S. (2005), 'Reflexive Law in Support of Directly Deliberative Polyarchy: Reflexive-deliberative Polyarchy as a Normative Frame for the Open Method of Coordination', in O. De Schutter and S. Deakin (eds), *Social Rights and Market Forces: Is the Open Coordination of Employment and Social Policies the Future of Social Europe?* Brussels: Bruylant, pp. 99–144.

Smismans, S. (2008), 'New Modes of Governance and the Participatory Myth', *West European Politics*, **31**(5), 874–95.

Smismans, S. (2011), 'From Harmonization to Coordination? EU Law in the Lisbon Governance Architecture', *Journal of European Public Policy*, **18**(4), 502–22.

Smith, A. (1996 [1776]), *An Inquiry into the Nature and Causes of the Wealth of Nations.* Glasgow Edition of the Works and Correspondence of Adam Smith, Vol. I. Oxford: Oxford University Press.

Smith, G. and D. Feldman (2003), *Company Codes of Conduct and International Standards: An Analytical Comparison.* Washington, DC: The World Bank.

Sobczak, A. (2008), 'Legal Dimensions of International Framework Agreements in the Field of Corporate Social Responsibility', in K. Papadakis (ed), *Cross-border Social Dialogue and Agreements: An emerging global industrial relations framework*? Geneva: International Institute for Labour Studies, International Labour Organization, pp. 115–30.

Sol, E. and N. Ramos (forthcoming), 'Implementation of the EU Working Time Directive in the Netherlands', in C. Barbier, R. Rogowski and F. Columb (eds), *The Sustainability of the European Social Model. EU Governance, Social Protection and Social Rights in Europe.* Cheltenham: Edward Elgar.

Solow, R. (1990), *The Labour Market as a Social Institution.* Cambridge, MA: Basil Blackwell.

Sousa Santos, B. de (2002), *Toward a New Legal Common Sense: Law, Globalization, and Emancipation.* 2nd edition. London: Butterworths.

Standing, G. (1993), 'Labor Regulation in an Era of Fragmented Flexibility', in C.F. Büchtermann (ed), *Employment Security and Labor Market Behavior – Interdisciplinary Approaches and International Evidence.* Ithaca, NY: ILR Press, pp. 425–41.

Standing, G. (1999), *Global Labour Flexibility – Seeking Distributive Justice.* Basingstoke: Macmillan.

Standing, G. (2009), *Work after Globalization. Building Occupational Citizenship.* London: Bloomsbury Academic.

Standing, G. (2011), *The Precariat: The New Dangerous Class.* London: Bloomsbury Academic.

Stein (1995), *Lex Mercatoria. Realität und Theorie*. Frankfurt am Main: Klostermann.

Stevis, D. and T. Boswell (2007), 'International Framework Agreements: Opportunities and Challenges for Global Unionism', in K. Bronfenbrenner (ed), *Global Unions – Challenging Transnational Capital through Cross-border Campaigns*. Ithaca, NY: ILR Press, pp. 174–94.

Stichweh, R. (1995), 'Zur Theorie der Weltgesellschaft', *Soziale Systeme*, **1**(1), 29–45.

Stichweh, R. (2000a), *Die Weltgesellschaft – Soziologische Analysen*. Frankfurt am Main: Suhrkamp.

Stichweh, R. (2000b), 'On the Genesis of World Society: Innovations and Mechanisms', *Distinktion, Scandinavian Journal of Social Theory*, **1**(1), 27–38.

Stichweh, R. (2002), 'Politik und Weltgesellschaft', in K.-U. Hellmann and R. Schmalz-Bruns (eds), *Theorie der Politik. Niklas Luhmanns politische Soziologie*. Frankfurt am Main: Suhrkamp, pp. 287–96.

Stichweh, R. (2005), 'Zum Gesellschaftsbegriff der Systemtheorie: Parsons und Luhmann und die Hypothese der Weltgesellschaft', in B. Heintz, R. Münch and H. Tyrell (eds), *Weltgesellschaft: Theoretische Zugänge und empirische Problemlagen*. Stuttgart: Lucius and Lucius, pp. 174–85.

Stiglitz, J. (2003), *Globalization and Its Discontents*. Harmondsworth: Penguin.

Stiglitz, J. (2010), *Freefall. Free Markets and the Sinking of the Global Economy*. Harmondsworth: Penguin.

Stiglitz, J. (2012), *The Price of Inequality. The Avoidable Causes and Invisible Costs of Inequality*. London: Allen Lane.

Stone, K.V.W. (1981), 'The Post-war Paradigm in American Labor Law', *Yale Law Journal*, **90**(7), 1509–81.

Stone, K.V.W. (1994), 'The Prospects for Transnational Labor Regulation: Reconciling Globalization and Labor Rights in the EU and NAFTA', in T. Wilthagen (ed), *Advancing Theory in Labour Law and Industrial Relations in a Global Context*. Proceedings of the Royal Netherlands Academy of the Arts and Sciences. Amsterdam: North Holland, pp. 83–97.

Stone, K.V.W. (1999), 'Employment Arbitration under the Federal Arbitration Act', in A. Eaton and J. Keefe (eds), *Employment Dispute Resolution and Worker Rights in the Changing Workplace*. Madison, WI: Industrial Relations Research Association, pp. 27–65.

Streeck, W. (1982), 'Organisational Consequences of Corporatist Cooperation in West German Labor Unions', in G. Lehmbruch and P. Schmitter (eds), *Patterns of Corporatist Policy-making*. Beverly Hills and London: Sage, pp. 64–94.

Streeck, W. (1990), 'Status and Contract: Basic Categories of a Sociological Theory of Industrial Relations', in D. Sugarman and G. Teubner (eds), *Regulating Corporate Groups in Europe*. Baden-Baden: Nomos, pp. 105–45.

Streeck, W. (1991), 'On the Institutional Conditions of Diversified Quality Production', in E. Matzner and W. Streeck (eds), *Beyond Keynesianism: The Socio-Economics of Production and Employment*. London: Edward Elgar, pp. 21–61.

Streeck, W. (1992), 'Co-determination: After Four Decades', in W. Streeck, *Social Institutions and Economic Performance. Studies of Industrial Relations in Advanced Capitalist Economies*. London: Sage, pp. 64–94.

Streeck, W. (1996), 'Neo-Voluntarism: A New European Social Policy Regime', in G. Marks, F.W. Scharpf, P.C. Schmitter and W. Streeck (eds), *Governance in the European Union*. London: Sage, pp. 64–94.

Streeck, W. (1998), 'Bündnis für Arbeit: Bedingungen und Ziele', *Gewerkschaftliche Monatshefte*, **49**(8), 533–540.

Streeck, W. (1999), 'Competitive Solidarity: Rethinking the European Social Model', MPIfG Working Paper, 99/8. Cologne: Max-Planck-Institut für Gesellschaftsforschung.

Streeck, W. (2009), *Re-forming Capitalism. Institutional Change in the German Political Economy*. Oxford: Oxford University Press.

Supiot, A. (1999), 'The Transformation of Work and the Future of Labour Law in Europe: A Multidisciplinary Perspective', *International Labour Review*, **138**(1), pp. 31–46.

Supiot, A. (2010), *L'esprit de Philadelphie: la justice sociale face au marché total*. Paris: Seuil.

Supiot, A., M.E. Casas, J. De Munck, P. Hanau, A. Johansson, P. Meadows, E. Mingione, R. Salais and P. van der Heijden (1998), 'The Changing Nature of Work and the Future of Labour Law in Europe'. Final Report for the European Commission, Brussels.

Supiot, A., M.E. Casas, J. De Munck, P. Hanau, A. Johansson, P. Meadows, E. Mingione, R. Salais and P. van der Heijden (2001), *Beyond Employment, Changes in Work and the Future of Labour Law in Europe*. Oxford: Oxford University Press.

Sypris, P. (2000), 'The Integrationist Rationale for European Social Policy', in J. Shaw (ed), *Social Law and Policy in an Evolving European Union*. Oxford and Portland, OR: Hart, pp. 17–30.

Sypris, P. (2007), *EU Intervention in Domestic Labour Law*. Oxford: Oxford University Press.

Tabak, F. (1996), 'The World Labour Force', in T.K. Hopkins and I. Wallerstein (eds), *The Age of Transition. Trajectory of the World-System, 1945–2025*. London: Zed Books, pp. 87–116.

Tallberg, J. (2003), *European Governance and Supranational Institutions – Making States Comply*. London: Routledge.

Taylor-Gooby, P. (2003), 'Introduction: Open Markets versus Welfare Citizenship: Conflicting Approaches to Policy Convergence in Europe', *Social Policy & Administration*, **37**(6), 539–54.

Teubner, G. (1978), *Organisationsdemokratie und Verbandsverfassung. Rechtsmodelle für politisch relevante Verbände*. Tübingen: Mohr Siebeck.

Teubner, G. (1982), 'Reflexives Recht: Entwicklungsmodelle des Rechts in vergleichender Perspektive', *Archiv für Rechts- und Sozialphilosophie*, **68**(1), 13–59.

Teubner, G. (1983), 'Substantive and Reflexive Elements in Modern Law', *Law and Society Review*, **17**(2), 239–85.

Teubner, G. (1984), 'Autopoiesis in Law and Society: A Rejoinder to Blankenburg', *Law and Society Review*, **18**(2), 291–301.

Teubner, G. (1986), 'Industrial Democracy Through Law? Social Functions of Law in Institutional Innovations', in T.C. Daintith and G. Teubner (eds), *Contract and Organisation: Legal Analysis in the Light of Economic and Social Theory*. Berlin and New York: De Gruyter, pp. 261–73.

Teubner, G. (1987a), 'Unternehmenskorporatismus. New Industrial Policy und das Wesen der juristischen Person', *Kritische Vierteljahresschrift für Gesetzgebung und Rechtswissenschaft*, **2**(1), 61–85.

Teubner, G. (1987b), 'Episodenverknüpfung. Zur Steigerung von Selbstreferenz im Recht', in D. Baecker, J. Markowitz, R. Stichweh, H. Tyrell and H. Willke (eds), *Theorie als Passion. Niklas Luhmann zum 60. Geburtstag*. Frankfurt am Main: Suhrkamp, pp. 423–46.

Teubner, G. (1988), 'After Legal Instrumentalism: Strategic Models of Post-regulatory Law', in G. Teubner (ed), *Dilemmas of Law in the Welfare State*. Berlin and New York: De Gruyter, pp. 299–325.

Teubner, G. (ed) (1988), *Autopoietic Law: A New Approach to Law and Society*. Berlin: De Gruyter.

Teubner, G. (1989), 'How the Law Thinks: Toward a Constructivist Epistemology of Law', *Law and Society Review*, **23**(5), 727–57.

Teubner, G. (1990), 'Unitas Multiplex: Corporate Governance in Group Enterprises', in D. Sugarman and G. Teubner (eds), *Regulating Corporate Groups in Europe*. Baden-Baden: Nomos, pp. 87–92.

Teubner, G. (1991), 'Autopoiesis and Steering: How Politics Profits from the Normative Surplus of Capital', in R.J. in 't Veld, C.J.A.M. Termeer, L. Schaap and M.J.W. van Twist (eds), *Autopoiesis and Configuration Theory: New Approaches to Societal Steering*. Boston: Kluwer, pp. 127–41.

Teubner, G. (1993a), *Law as an Autopoietic System*. Oxford: Blackwell.

Teubner, G. (1993b), 'The Many-Headed Hydra: Networks as Higher-Order Collective Actors', in J. McCahery, J.S. Picciotto and C. Scott (eds), *Corporate Control and Accountability. Changing Structures and the Dynamics of Regulation*. Oxford: Clarendon Press, pp. 41–60.

Teubner, G. (1994), 'The Public Interest of the Company "in itself"', in R. Rogowski and T. Wilthagen (eds), *Reflexive Labour Law – Studies in Industrial Relations and Employment Regulation*. Deventer: Kluwer, pp. 21–52.

Teubner, G. (1997), 'Global Bukowina: Legal Pluralism in the World-Society', in G. Teubner (ed), *Global Law without a State*. Aldershot: Dartmouth, pp. 3–28.

Teubner, G. (ed) (1997), *Global Law without a State*. Aldershot: Dartmouth.

Teubner, G. (1998), 'Legal Irritants: Good Faith in British Law or How Unifying Law Ends Up in New Differences', *Modern Law Review*, **61**(1), 11–32.

Teubner, G. (2001), 'Economics of Gift – Positivity of Justice: The Mutual Paranoia of Jacques Derrida and Niklas Luhmann', *Theory, Culture & Society*, **18**(1), 29–47.

Teubner, G. (2002), 'Hybrid Laws: Constitutionalizing Private Governance Networks', in R. Kagan, M. Krygier and K. Winston (eds), *Legality and Community: On the Intellectual Legacy of Philip Selznick*. Lanham, Maryland: Rowman and Littlefield, pp. 311–31.

Teubner, G. (2004a), 'Global Private Regimes: Neo-spontaneous Law and Dual Constitution of Autonomous Sectors in World Society', in K.-H. Ladeur (ed), *Public Governance in the Age of Globalization*. Aldershot: Ashgate, pp. 71–87.

Teubner, G. (2004b), 'Societal Constitutionalism: Alternatives to State-centred Constitutional theory? ("Storrs Lectures 2003/04", Yale Law School)', in C. Joerges, I.-J. Sand and G. Teubner (eds), *Transnational Governance and Constitutionalism*. Oxford and Portland, OR: Hart, pp. 3–28.

Teubner, G. (2006a), 'Rights of Non-humans? Electronic Agents and Animals as New Actors in Politics and Law', *Journal of Law and Society*, **33**(4), 497–521.

Teubner, G. (2006b), 'Dealing with Paradoxes of Law: Derrida, Luhmann, Wiethölter. ("Storrs Lectures 2003/04", Yale Law School)', in O. Perez and G. Teubner (eds), *On Paradoxes and Inconsistencies in Law*. Oxford and Portland, OR: Hart, pp. 41–64.

Teubner, G. (2006c), 'The Anonymous Matrix: Human Rights Violations by "Private" Transnational Actors', *Modern Law Review*, **69**(3), 327–46.

Teubner, G. (2009), 'Self-subversive Justice: Contingency or Transcendence Formula of Law?', *Modern Law Review*, **72**(1), 1–23.

Teubner, G. (2010a), 'The Corporate Codes of Multinationals: Company Constitutions Beyond Corporate Governance and Co-Determination', in R. Nickel (ed), *Conflict of Laws and Laws of Conflict in Europe and Beyond: Patterns of Supranational and Transnational Juridification*. Oxford and Portland, OR: Hart, pp. 203–14.

Teubner, G. (2010b), 'Fragmented Foundations: Societal Constitutionalism Beyond the Nation State', in P. Dobner and M. Loughlin (eds), *The Twilight of Constitutionalism?* Oxford: Oxford University Press, pp. 327–41.

Teubner, G. (2011a), 'A Constitutional Moment? The Logics of "Hitting the Bottom"', in P. Kjaer, G. Teubner and A. Febbrajo (eds), *Financial Crisis in Constitutional Perspective: The Dark Side of Functional Differentiation*. Oxford and Portland, OR: Hart, pp. 3–42.

Teubner, G. (2011b), 'Self-constitutionalizing Transnational Corporations? On the Linkage of "Private" and "Public" Corporate Codes of Conduct', *Indiana Journal of Global Legal Studies*, **17**(2), 617–38.

Teubner, G. (2011c), 'Constitutionalizing Polycontexturality', *Social & Legal Studies*, **20**(2), 210–29.

Teubner, G. (2011d), *Networks as Connected Contracts*. Oxford and Portland, OR: Hart.

Teubner, G. (2012), *Constitutional Fragments. Societal Constitutionalism and Globalization*. Oxford: Oxford University Press.

Teubner, G. and A. Febbrajo (eds) (1990), *State, Law, Economy as Autopoietic Systems*. Milan: Giuffré.

Teubner, G. and P. Korth (2012), 'Two Kinds of Legal Pluralism: Collision of Transnational Regimes in the Double Fragmentation of World Society', in M. Young (ed), *Regime Interaction in International Law: Facing Fragmentation*. Cambridge: Cambridge University Press, pp. 23–54.

Teubner, G. and H. Willke (1984), 'Kontext und Autonomie. Gesellschaftliche Selbststeuerung durch reflexives Recht', *Zeitschrift für Rechtssoziologie*, **5**(1), 4–35.

Tharakanl, P.K.M. (2003), 'European Social Model under Pressure', *The World Economy*, **26**(10), 1417–24.

Tombs, S. and D. Whyte (2012), 'Reshaping Health and Safety Enforcement: Institutionalising Impunity', in L. Dickens (ed), *Making Employment Rights Effective: Issues of Enforcement and Compliance*. Oxford and Portland, OR: Hart, pp. 67–86.

Tomlins, C.L. (1985), 'New Deal, Collective Bargaining, and the Triumph of Industrial Pluralism', *Industrial and Labor Relations Review*, **39**(1), 19–34.

Treib, O. (2005), *Die Bedeutung der nationalen Parteipolitik für die Umsetzung europäischer Sozialrichtlinien*. Frankfurt am Main and New York: Campus.

Treiber, H. (1985), 'Crisis in Regulatory Policy? Remarks on a Topical Theme, or Reflexive Rationality in the Shadow of Codified Law', *Contemporary Crises*, **9**(3), 255–80.

Trubek, D.M. and J. Mosher (2003), 'New Governance, Employment Policy, and the European Social Model', in J. Zeitlin and D. Trubek (eds), *Governing Work and Welfare in a New Economy – European and American Experiments*. Oxford: Oxford University Press, pp. 33–58.

Trubek, D.M. and L.G. Trubek (2005), 'Hard and Soft Law in the Construction of Social Europe. The Role of the Open Method of Co-ordination', *European Law Journal*, **11**(3), 343–64.

Trubek, D.M. and L.G. Trubek (2010), 'The World Turned Upside Down: Reflections on New Governance and the Transformation of Law', *Wisconsin Law Review*, **2010**(2), 719–26.

Trubek, D.M., J. Mosher and J.S. Rothstein (2000), 'Transnationalism in the Regulation of Labor Relations: International Regimes and Transnational Advocacy Networks', *Law & Social Inquiry*, **25**(4), 1187–1211.

Trubek, D.M., P. Cottrell and M. Nance (2006), '"Soft Law", "Hard Law" and EU Integration', in G. de Burca and J. Scott (eds), *Law and New Governance in the EU and the US*. Oxford and Portland, OR: Hart, pp. 65–94.

Twining, W. (2000), *Globalisation and Legal Theory*. London: Butterworths.

Van Gendt, M.C.E. (1980), *The Voucher Concept and the Publicness of Basic Education*. Meppel: Krips Repro.

Verschraegen, G. (2002), 'Human Rights and Modern Society: A Sociological Analysis from the Perspective of Systems Theory', *Journal of Law and Society*, **29**(2), 258–81.

Verschraegen, G. (2006), 'Systems Theory and the Paradox of Human Rights', in M. King and C. Thornhill (eds), *Luhmann on Law and Politics*. Oxford and Portland, OR: Hart, pp. 101–25.

Visser, J. (2000), 'From Keynesianism to the Third Way: Labour Relations and Social Policy in Postwar Western Europe', *Economic and Industrial Democracy*, **21**(4), 421–56.

Visser, J. and A. Hemerijck (1997), *A Dutch Miracle. Job Growth, Welfare Reform and Corporatism in the Netherlands*. Amsterdam: Amsterdam University Press.

Vos, K., P. de Beer and E. de Gier (2004), 'Social Cohesion and the European Social Model', *Tijdschrift voor Arbeidsvraagstukken*, **20**(3), 336–43.

Vosko, L.F. (2002), '"Decent Work" – The Shifting Role of the ILO and the Struggle for Global Social Justice', *Global Social Policy*, **2**(1), 19–46.

Voß, J.-P. and R. Kemp (2006), 'Sustainability and Reflexive Governance: Introduction', in J. Voß, D. Bauknecht, and R. Kemp (eds), *Reflexive Governance for Sustainable Development*. Cheltenham: Edward Elgar, pp. 3–28.

Waddell, S. (2011), *The Global Compact: An Organizational Innovation to Realize UN Principles*. New York: United Nations.

Wallerstein, I. (1974–84), *The Modern World System. 3 Vols.* Cambridge: Cambridge University Press.

Wallerstein, I. (1991), *Unthinking Social Science. The Limits of Nineteenth Century Paradigms.* Cambridge: Polity.

Walwei, U. (1996), 'Flexibilisierung und Regulierung des Beschäftigungssystems: Optionen und Effekte', *Mitteilungen aus der Arbeitsmarkt- und Berufsforschung*, **29**(2), 219–27.

Waters, M. (2000), *Globalization*. 2nd edition. London: Routledge.

Watt, B. (2000), 'Regulating the Employment Relationship: From Rights to Relations', in H. Collins, P. Davies and R. Rideout (eds), *Legal Regulation of the Employment Relation*. London: Kluwer, pp. 373–401.

Webb, B. and S. Webb (1897), *Industrial Democracy*. London: Longmans.

Wedderburn, B. (1986), *The Worker and the Law*. 3rd edition. Harmondsworth: Penguin.

Wedderburn, B. (2002), 'Common Law, Labour Law, Global Law', in B. Hepple (ed), *Social and Labour Rights in a Global Context. International and Comparative Perspectives*. Cambridge: Cambridge University Press, pp. 19–54.

Wedderburn, B. et al. (1994), *Labour Law in the Post-Industrial Era*. Aldershot: Dartmouth, pp. 13–82.

Wedderburn, B., R. Lewis and J. Clark (eds) (1983), *Labour Law and Industrial Relations. Building on Kahn-Freund*. Oxford: Clarendon Press.

Weekes, B.C.M., M. Mellish, L. Dickens and J. Lloyd (1975), *Industrial Relations and the Limits of Law. The Industrial Effects of the Industrial Relations Act, 1971*. Oxford: Blackwell.

Weiler, P.C. (1990), *Governing the Workplace. The Future of Labor and Employment Law*. Cambridge, MA: Harvard University Press.

Weiss, M. (1996), *Fundamental Social Rights for the European Union*. Amsterdam: Hugo Sinzheimer Institute.

Weiss, M.S. (2003), 'Two Steps Forward, One Step Back – Or Vice Versa: Labor Rights under Free Trade Agreements from NAFTA', *University of San Francisco Law Review*, **37**, 689–754.

Weiss, M. (2004), 'The Institutional Conditions for Effective Labour Law in the New Member States. A Comment', in G. Bermann and K. Pistor (eds), *Law and Governance in an Enlarged European Union*. Oxford: Hart, pp. 97–141.

Weitbrecht, H. (1969), *Effektivität und Legitimität der Tarifautonomie. Eine soziologische Untersuchung am Beispiel der deutschen Metallindustrie*. Berlin: Duncker & Humblot.

White, L.J. (1981), *Reforming Regulation. Processes and Problems*. Englewood Cliffs, NJ: Prentice-Hall.

Wickham, J. (2002), *The End of the European Social Model: Before It Began?* Working Paper of the Irish TUC. Dublin.

Wiethölter, R. (1986), 'Materialization and Proceduralisation in Modern Law', in G. Teubner (ed), *Dilemmas of Law in the Welfare State*. Berlin: De Gruyter, pp. 221–49.

Williamson, O.E. (1994), 'Transaction Cost Economics and Organization Theory', in N.J. Smelser and R. Swedberg (eds), *The Handbook of Economic Sociology*. Princeton, NJ: Princeton University Press, pp. 77–107.

Willke, H. (1989), *Systemtheorie entwickelter Gesellschaften. Dynamik und Riskanz moderner gesellschaftlicher Selbstorganisation*. Weinheim and Munich: Juventa.

Willke, H. (1992), 'Societal Guidance through Law?' In G. Teubner and A. Febbrajo (eds), *State, Law and Economy as Autopoietic Systems. Regulation and Autonomy in a New Perspective. European Yearbook in the Sociology of Law*. Milan: Giuffrè, pp. 353–87.

Willke, H. (2001), *Atopia. Studien zur atopischen Gesellschaft*. Frankfurt am Main: Suhrkamp.

Wilthagen, T. (1994), 'Reflexive Rationality in the Regulation of Occupational Safety and Health', in R. Rogowski and T. Wilthagen (eds), *Reflexive Labour Law – Studies in Industrial Relations and Employment Regulation*. Deventer: Kluwer, pp. 345–76.

Wilthagen, T. (1998), 'Flexicurity: A New Paradigm for Labour Market Policy Reform?' WZB Discussion Paper, FS I 98-202, Berlin: Wissenschaftszentrum Berlin.

Wilthagen, T. (ed) (1998), *Advancing Theory in Labour Law and Industrial Relations in a Global Context*. Proceedings of the Royal Netherlands Academy of the Arts and Sciences. Amsterdam: North Holland.

Wilthagen, T. and R. Rogowski (2002), 'The Legal Regulation of Transitional Labour Markets', in G. Schmid and B. Gazier (eds), *The Dynamics of Full Employment. Social Integration through Transitional Labour Markets*. Cheltenham, UK and Brookfield, USA: Edward Elgar, pp. 233–73.

Wilthagen, T. and F. Tros (2004), 'The Concept of "Flexicurity": a New Approach to Regulating Employment and Labour Markets', *Transfer*, **10**(2), 166–86.

Wincott, D. (2003), 'Beyond Social Regulation? New Instruments and/or a New Agenda for Social Policy at Lisbon?', *Public Administration*, **81**(3), 533–53.

Wölfl, A. and J.S. Mora-Sanguinetti (2011), *Reforming the Labour Market in Spain*. Economics Department Working Paper No. 845. Paris: OECD.

Wood, J. (1992), 'Dispute Resolution: Conciliation. Mediation and Arbitration', in W. McCarthy (ed), *Legal Intervention in Industrial Relations*. Oxford: Blackwell, pp. 241–73.

Wood, S., A. Wagner, E. Armstrong, J. Goodman and J. Davis (1975), 'The Industrial Relations as a Basis for Theory in Industrial Relations', *British Journal of Industrial Relations*, **13**(3), 291–308.

World Bank (2012), *World Development Report 2012: Gender Equality and Development*. Washington, DC: World Bank.

Wotschack, P. (2011), 'Working-time Options over the Life Course: Challenges and Company Practices', in R. Rogowski, R. Salais and N. Whiteside (eds), *Transforming European Employment Policy – Labour Market Transitions and the Promotion of Capability*. Cheltenham: Edward Elgar, pp. 131–53.

Young, I.M. (1990), *Justice and the Politics of Difference*. Princeton: Princeton University Press.

Zeitlin, J. (2005), 'The Open Method of Coordination in Action. Theoretical Promise, Empirical Realities, Reform Strategy', in J. Zeitlin and P. Pochet in collaboration with L. Magnusson (eds), *The Open Method of Co-ordination in Action: The European Employment and Social Inclusion Strategies*. Brussels: Peter Lang, pp. 447–503.

Zeitlin, J. (2011), 'Pragmatic Transnationalism: Governance Across Borders in the Global Economy', *Socio-Economic Review*, **9**(1), 187–206.

Ziegert, K.A. (2000), 'Globalisierung des Rechts aus der Sicht der Rechtssoziologie', in R. Voigt (ed), *Globalisierung des Rechts*. Baden-Baden: Nomos, pp. 69–92.

Zumbansen, P. (2006), 'The Parallel Worlds of Corporate Governance and Labor Law', *Indiana Journal of Global Legal Studies*, **13**(1), 261–312.

Zumbansen, P. (2008), 'Law after the Welfare State: Formalism, Functionalism and the Ironic Turn of Reflexive Law', *American Journal of Comparative Law*, **56**(3), 769–805.

Zumbansen, P. (2011), 'The New Embeddedness of the Corporation', in C.A. Williams and P. Zumbansen (eds), *The Embedded Firm: Corporate Governance, Labor, and Finance Capitalism*. Cambridge: Cambridge University Press, pp. 119–48.

Index